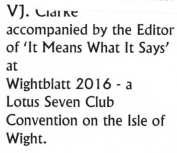

VJ. Clarke accompanied by the Editor of 'It Means What It Says' at Wightblatt 2016 - a Lotus Seven Club Convention on the Isle of Wight.

VJ has written an extremely extensive essay called 'Looking Out For Number One' : which examines the character of Number Six, his origins, past and future influences and nature as a fictional character. Thank you VJ for devoting so much time and detail to this piece.

The Editor seen here would like to thank R.Over for posing for this photograph taken by VJ Clarke. During the editing of this first of three volumes of 'It Means What It Says...' Ed Fordham says fending off weather balloons has been the least of his problems. He has previous experience of Royal Mail Payroll Work, A different type of Office/IT Work & Being a Customer Advisor in the Car Park which involved 8 years of pushing shopping trollies around while nearly being run over by 75% of the drivers.

"...for there is no joy on earth in my opinion so good as regaining one's liberty."
The Captive - Don Quixote, Part 1, Ch. XXXIX, p352, Cervantes,
trans. J.M Cohen, 1950, Penguin Books

It Means What It Says

Trying To Understand THE PRISONER

VOLUME 1

50th Anniversary Edition

To Ian for patience and understanding

© Unusual Number Publications 2017

Published exclusively by Amazon Kindle Direct Publishing 2017

UK Price : B & W: £9.99 (£1.96 to Ty Gobaith)

All profits from the sale of this book to go to:

Design by Warren Green see: www.warrengreenartist.co.uk

Introduction
By Ed Fordham -
Editor of 'It Means
What It Says'

When I first considered putting together a
selection of articles and essays about[1]
'The Prisoner' it was a seemingly
monumental task. Over the last 50
years a number of points of view about the series and the symbolism within it, its allegorical
elements and nature as a piece of art have emerged.

However I was happy to realise the support of so many fans of the show who were willing
to help with the project.

My friend Vickie Clarke has provided an excellent essay examining the question that should
be at the heart of understanding 'The Prisoner' — the question of 'Who Is Number Six?' in
'Looking Out For Number One' examining this question through a variety of lenses . I am
indebted to her for spending a great deal of her spare time examining this topic in particular. Vickie has supported the creation of this book from the beginning and without that it
may never have happened.

Stephen Matthews has worked tirelessly on an introduction to a return of his creation
'The Jailbird' in 'Out of Order' which will be continued in forthcoming Volumes of 'It
Means What It Says...' I'd also like to thank him for General (groan...) help and support
and for his two excellent articles which open out the discussion in radical directions.
Equally I would like to thank Arno Baumgärtel for help in establishing what impact the se
ries had in Germany and Rick Davy at the Unmutual Website for his help and support and
thought provoking foreword.

Thank you to Steven Ricks for allowing the use of his documentaries on 'The Prisoner' as
reference material.

While we are thanking those who have helped with this project a complete list of acknowledgements will follow this introduction but I'd like to particularly draw attention to

---

[1] The Editor being Menaced by Rover — Photo by Vickie Clarke 2016

everyone from the following Facebook Groups : 'The Prisoner', 'Patrick McGoohan Lives!' 'Free For All Archives', 'Everything McGoohan', 'Prisoner and Portmeirion Memories', 'Patrick McGoohan and The Prisoner Memorabilia'.

I'd especially like to say how grateful I am to my partner Ian and all my family for their support while I have tirelessly worked on this project.

From people who experienced the show on first broadcast, to potential answers to essential and unanswered questions. This book considers a variety of sometimes learned and serious, sometimes frivolous and humorous pieces. Together all the written items, essays and articles cover a great number (sic) of ideas and thoughtful avenues arising out of 'The Prisoner' and themes and ideas that arise from it.

Some of the pieces published here have appeared before on the Unmutual Website, Arno Baumgartel's German page for fans of 'The Prisoner' and in a magazine produced for Festival Number Six from which Mark Bennett's article was drawn. I'd like to say how much I appreciate everyone involved giving permission for their work to appear in this book.

As to the kind of debate you can find herein I'll use the trilogy of Anthony Skene's episodes 'A, B & C,' 'Many Happy Returns' and 'Dance of The Dead' as an example. All of these episodes have elements of distorted reality and references to dream states. In 'A, B & C' and 'Dance of the Dead' this essence of 'the unreal' for want of a better term is very clearly apparent. 'Dance of The Dead' has a dreamlike quality of its own — there is little conventional narrative with events following each other in an altered state of surrealism. 'A, B & C' takes these dreamlike elements to another extreme — by offering the Village control over Number Six's dreams. The surrealist touches are particularly clear in the final dream as Number Six attempts to control the dream from within its confines. However even the most conventional episode of the three — 'Many Happy Returns' has this feel to it; as a result of the deserted Village at the beginning of the episode. As Number Six explores 'the Village' in its empty state it seems increasingly unlikely to us as viewers after so many episodes with Villagers parading around in large numbers.

The question as to who is actually responsible for the development of the series is also one of vexed debate with McGoohan, George Markstein & David Tomblin all having input into its formative stages. Its probable that without Markstein and McGoohan to each state their case with the benefit of 50 years of hindsight it will never be possible to apportion this.[2]

There are of course as well a large number of original pieces looking at the series through various arenas and ideas that have never been published before. Huge topics like: 'Looking

---

[2] See Roger Goodman (ed.) 'George Markstein and The Prisoner' pandqmedia for further details; also Brian Gorman's 'Everyman' & Chapter 5 'The Prisoner Arrives' of Booth R, 'Not A Number' - Patrick McGoohan - A Life'

After Number One...'[3] and 'Democracy and Dictatorship in The Prisoner' the nature of 'The Butler Didn't Do It and Other Stories' the importance of 'Why Do We Forsake—Do Not Forsake Me...,' and a new work on the final episode — 'Not two, not One. The non-duality of Fall Out' and Chris Gran's 'Villager's — Strangely at Rhyme' — an epic poem about fictional characters and their views taking place during the series.

The Prisoner was of course about many themes there was a strong 'Orwellian' and 'Kafkaesque' Element with the seemingly constant surveillance and the paranoia but the series goes further than just taking the ideas of others and 'remixing them'. By the use of a fictional almost fairytale environment with 'the Village' McGoohan and the writers of the episodes were able to talk about a variety of intellectual themes. Medical Science, Psychiatry and Psychology, Inadequate Teaching Methods (learning by rote), issues regarding personal identity and freedom and the extent to which they could really be maintained, conformity within society and the ability to express views contrary to others both in our own and less democratic societies are all touched upon and developed in a variety of ways.

However at the heart of the show it retains a strong 'action-adventure' element — Number Six fights against enormous odds to retain the 'secret information' he is only too aware of. In 'The Chimes of Big Ben' Leo McKern's Number Two makes it only too clear that the 'resignation secret' is just a means of unravelling 'Number Six' and discovering other important confidential intelligence he has picked up:

"Just one small thing — and the rest will follow. Why did he resign?"
Leo McKern as Number Two in 'The Chimes of Big Ben' written by Vincent Tilsley 1966.

Theories on 'The Prisoner' are extensive and abundant including even the Postmodern concept that the images we see on our TV and increasingly computers, phones and tablet computers are 'hyperreal' in nature.

Certainly the mixture of ideas and concepts and even the architecture of Portmeirion alongside the sets designed by Jack Shampan are very postmodern and make 'The Prisoner' by extension maybe the first truly postmodern television series.

To clarify there is a surrealism or feeling of unreality in the substance that forms them, although usually they do not defy interpretation in different ways — they are a parade of imagery and ultimately we are forced to ever interpret them as reality or accept their 'allegorical nature'[4]. 'The Prisoner' is constructed — a narrative that has plot twists, the McGuffin of Number Six's resignation, at times it even seems the Village only exists for the sake of Number Six.

Baudrilliard uses the philosophical example of our assumption that 'The Gulf War' took place — which he addresses by stating that the images we see do not

---

[3]Vickie Clarke specially wrote this intelligent piece on this topic for this project.

[4] For allegorical content in the series see in particular the work of Peter Dunn in this book.

necessarily constitute reality and what we perceive as real is actually a stream of manipulated pictures and sound to match. [5] [6]This of course has particular relevance to our perceptions of 'The Prisoner' — for example in 'A, B and C' — a 'hyperreal'[7] French Party hosted by Madam Engadine is created but is being manipulated by Number Fourteen at the behest of Number Two by feeding pictures and sound into Number Six's Dream-state.

Ahead of you lies many attempts to provoke some understanding of 'The Prisoner' and more importantly to signpost both individual and different points of view.

Most importantly this book should continue the debate of what 'The Prisoner' is really about and hopefully an insight into those who toiled alongside Patrick McGoohan to create what many regard as the first work of art to spring from television.

I hope you gain new insights into the series as a whole through this work — there are included essays or commentary on a whole variety of relevant topics written by a large number of people who appreciate The Prisoner for being the most esteemed and best television series to emerge from the late 1960s. At the end of the day this was thinking person's television, not ephemeral drama, sitcoms or quiz shows that were here and then forgotten about. The Prisoner has left a lasting mark on our culture influenced many other writers, directors, artists, cartoons, graphic novels and lead to a raft of creative people realising that

"So much of TV seems to be chewing gum for the eyes".[8]

And as creative people they had a responsibility to ensure that programmes, films, books and other media were a cut above that of the norm.

It would be true to say that the 'onslaught of reality tv' has erased some of the impact of the creatives in television in particular but luckily there still remain programmes like 'Stranger Things', 'Lost','Dirk Gently's Holistic Detective Agency', 'Doctor Who' and we can hope the imminent revival of 'Twin Peaks' that require thought to follow and understand beyond that required for the quagmire of Reality TV Shows that saturate the tv stations schedules.

---

[5] Jean Baudriliard, The Gulf War Will Not Take Place "In this sense, the gravity of the non-event in the Gulf is even greater than the event of war: it corresponds to the highly toxic period which affects a rotting corpse" (p24)

[6] Jean Baudrilliard, The Gulf War Did Not Take Place : "At the desired place (the Gulf), nothing took place, non-war. At the desired place (TV, information), nothing took place, no images, nothing but filler." (p82)

[7] Baudrilliard's term for the unreal reality created by manipulated pictures and sound — which becomes part of the way human beings perceive all 'reality'

[8]A disputed quote attributed to John Mason Brown although an earlier version referring to movies and radio is attributed to Henri Peyre. Frank Lloyd Wright used the expression but this was 3 years after John Mason Brown in 1958.

Indeed increasingly quality tv and creative shows have moved to non-traditional distribution through sites like Netflix and Amazon Instant Video in the United Kingdom. In the US even the new Star Trek series 'Discovery' is set to premiere on a streaming site (CBS: All Access in the U.S./Netflix elsewhere)rather than on live TV.

Towards the end of this Volume we look briefly at Rafferty :— McGoohan's only other TV Series in a starring role to establish more about him as an actor and some of the choices he made following him leaving Britain in the wake of the negative feedback he received from those who did not appreciate 'Fall Out'.[9]

Finally a word about the money raised from the sale of this book – Ty Gobaith Children's Hospice in Conwy, Wales will receive 100% of the proceeds to help them continue their work working with children with life threatening illnesses. They provide high quality care for children, young people and their families and supply a playroom, multi-sensory area, computers, a lounge, a similar space for parents, a therapeutic room and importantly a kitchen and room for mealtimes. There is a garden for families who have been recently bereaved alongside an additional bedroom. There are also landscaped gardens and a playground which have full wheelchair access.[10]

Thank you for buying this book and being part of the 50th anniversary of 'The Prisoner'.

Be Seeing You! 🔥 Ed Fordham (born 9.30am 19th April 1976)

Photograph of Portmeirion Piazza looking towards Campanile and the Gothic Pavilion taken July 2016 (courtesy of Ed Fordham)

---

[9] This is a simplification of events as McGoohan had other plans for a series 'The Outsider' and a film version of 'Brand' which both fell through.

[10] http://www.hopehouse.org.uk/care/care-services/ty-gobaith-facilities.html

Acknowledgements:

Many Thanks To Dan Kreeger for Cover Design, Warren DSix Green for Inner Cover Designs, Steve Matthews for 'Out Of Order' — The Jailbird Returns... & Two Excellent and Thought Provoking Articles, Andy Worsfold for Village Livery Mini Moke Photograph, Vaughan Brunt for Reprints of Articles, Rick Davy for 'Help and Support' & for Providing A Foreword, Dave Stimpson for his Overarching Piece on the Prisoner at 50 & Photographs of Village Day, Jan Davis for Photos of the Portmeirion Camera Obscura and it's Internal Working and her short but incisive written item, Peter Dunn for his A-Z of Allegory Pieces Filed Under A, B & C, Mathew Lock whose Legacy of 4 Fan Films strove to innovate and take 'Prisoner Fan Films' in New Directions, Arno Baumgartel of the German Web Site http://www.match-cut.de; Ira Heffler , Vickie Clarke for 'Looking Out For Number One' — an analysis of 'The Prisoner' that searches for an understanding of who or what 'Number Six' represents, Vaughan Brunt on MEETING SIR CLOUGH at the first Portmeirion Convention, Mark Bennett for 'Return to Synchronicities, Manifestations & Revelations' and his 3D Images of Portmeirion/Prisoneresque Imagery, Leslie Glen for his analysis of 'The Big Seven' — which episodes best fit McGoohan's Golden 7 for the Prisoner Mini Series He Hoped To Create, Jeff Kuykendall for his essay on Allegory and 'The Prisoner', Chris Gray for the remote controlled Rover and Epic Poem, Steven Ricks for Documentary Material; Paul Weston & last but by no means least Tom Mayer for his articles and insight into 'Rafferty'.

Apologies to anyone accidentally left out this will be rectified in a second edition if you email: itmeanswhatitsays50@gmail.com. Please also let us know if you spot any errors or omissions so that they can be corrected in a second edition

SECTION A
SUBSECTION 6
PARAGRAPH 6

BACK TO THE BEGINNINGS...

Why 'The Prisoner' endures,
The Fabled Return of
'The Jailbird,' Who is Number Six?,
Germanisms and
Nummer 6/'The Prisoner', Peter Dunn's
A-Z of
Allegory and 'Looking Out
for Number One' with many, many
other stories!

"'It's our special training establishment,' said Ince. 'You'll get a full briefing when you get there.'

'Inverloch?' said Loach, as if repeating the name would explain a lot more.

'It's quite isolated,' said Ince. 'Has to be. We don't want anybody snooping around.'"

'The Cooler', George Markstein, 1974, Chapter 15

Foreword
By Rick Davy

When Patrick McGoohan was interviewed for The Observer in 1991, he was asked what The Prisoner was all about. He replied; "If I gave all the answers you would no longer have a role when watching it."

This statement from the show's enigmatic star, producer, co-creator, and driving force perfectly sums up the reason why, more than 50 years since the cameras first rolled on it, the series is respected, and discussed, in the measure that it is today.

The Prisoner is a unique television series. When I first saw it as an intrigued ten year old in 1983, as it began its long-awaited re-run on Channel 4, it was fair to say that not only was I hooked for the next 17 weeks, but that I was hooked for life. Growing up on standard fantasy shows such as 'Doctor Who', 'Blakes Seven', and 'Sapphire and Steel' (albeit very good ones, and also certainly off-beat with regard to the latter of those offerings), I had not seen anything like 'The Prisoner' previously, and I have not seen anything like it since.

It is a series continues to intrigue, and for many continues to baffle, and the interest in the series shows no signs of abating. Even as we reach the conclusion of the series' 50th anniversary year, there's a wealth of newly created books, events and celebrations, documentaries and HD box sets, and social media attention.

I receive emails via The Unmutual Website on a daily basis regarding the series, and all manner of related subjects, and am often asked why it is that we're still discussing the series so long after it was first screened. As with the questions the show itself asks the viewer, there is no definitive answer to that question.

It's not Kafkaesque, and it's not Orwellian, as writers and historian would want you to believe. It's far more than a homage to that which was previously created. Whilst certain things undoubtedly influenced some of the series creators and writers (Cocteau for Skene, for example), 'The Prisoner' is a unique cocktail. It is McGoohanesque, Marksteinesque, Tomblinesque, and Shampanesque all in equal measures (with perhaps a double measure of McGoohan as one reaches the end of the glass).

It's a show that can be watched on many levels. On the one level, it is an expertly filmed action adventure series, set in an exotic location with star actors of the time, and a different pretty female lead each week, with punch ups, gritty drama, and colourful scenes with vibrant music and fairytale-like storytelling depicting a man held captive. Typical ITC entertainment. But on another level it is an allegorical conundrum where every scene, every character, and every turn can be analysed and dissected for further meaning. A reflection of society, not only in the Cold War Britain of the mid 1960s, but today, 50 years on, in our increasingly Big Brother style state with CCTV monitoring and dehumanisation at its core. What the viewer gets from 'The Prisoner' is totally dependent on what the viewer puts into the experience. The viewer can shape the outcome of the series with his or her own involvement in its progression. I don't mean that viewers can change the outcome of the filmed scenes, like some sort of Steve Jackson Fighting Fantasy Adventure book from the 1980s where one can 'turn left by turning to page 85,' or 'turn right by turning to page 143,' but you get out what you put in. Action-adventure on one level, a unique thought experience on another. As Prisoner historian and Patrick McGoohan interviewer Roger Goodman so accurately stated in 1983s 'Six Into One: The Prisoner File' documentary; "The series threw down a huge gauntlet of 'follow that!"

34 years after that statement was made, that gauntlet still remains unclaimed. This is possibly because 'The Prisoner' could not have been made today. Not only is there not the appetite for series on such a fantastical level (with the possible exception of 'Twin Peaks' and 'Lost', no series since has attempted to push the boundaries of what the medium can provide the viewer above and beyond on-screen drama and action), but there is also no Lew Grade-type figure running things in 2017, willing to hand a primetime series over to a leading actor to spend millions on.

Imagine today if Tom Hiddlestone, or Benedict Cumberbatch or some other 'big thing' in the acting world, fresh from award winning successes such as 'The Night Manager' or 'Sherlock' respectively, approached the head of ITV with an idea for a new TV series which he'd like to make due to being bored by the formulaic plots of his biggest success. It simply wouldn't happen in 2017.

But yet that's exactly what happened in 1966 when Patrick McGoohan informed Lew Grade that he'd had enough of 'Danger Man' and, thus, 'The Prisoner' was born. It would have been easy for McGoohan to have created another great ITC adventure series, Drake Is a Prisoner or The Saint is Captive. Instead, in the 18 months or so that it took to create the series, he gave us a lifetime gift.

The production process, as has been well documented, was a mixture of unrivalled creativity, happy accidents, and tension. The last four episodes, it could be argued, were made 'on the hoof,' at a frantic pace, with a different crew to the previous 13, yet contain some of the most intriguing and thought-provoking sequences of the entire series.

So much has been discussed, perhaps over-analysed over the years, regarding the series. Script editor George Markstein stated on record that he felt much was analysed which was never meant to be. Go on any social media group for The Prisoner, or internet forum, and you'll see the same questions popping up every few months. Was Number Six John Drake? Was Rover signifying some greater essence of society? What did the Village represent? Did he really escape in the end? [n.b.: No, No, the World, No].

Even the creation of the series is as steeped in mystery and confusion as its climax, with both McGoohan and George Markstein claiming until their deaths that they thought it all up, and that the other had made exaggerated claims about themselves. Thank goodness they were both involved is my view, and music editor Eric Mival probably summed it up best in his memoirs of his time on the series, Cutting Edge: My Life in Film and Television (Quoit Media, 2016);

As George Markstein wanted a very straightforward thriller-type of show, I am sure that this would have been the way it would have gone had it been up to him. Whereas Pat had a more quixotic taste, and very much wanted to go down the more allegorical route. I think each of these concepts contributed to the creation of what we ended up seeing on screen, as it was a synthesis of the two main approaches.

If there is no definitive answer about even who created this masterpiece, then how can any of us hope to find an answer to the meanings and mysteries that we find woven into each of the 17 episodes? Well, that's the point. There are few, if any, concrete answers. Only answers personal to one's self. No theories are right or wrong, just those that lead to more questions, and more discussions. Even the ordering of the episodes has been the subject of books and never ending debate, with no definitive conclusion reached. About the only thing that can be agreed upon is that 'Arrival' must come first, and 'Once Upon a Time' and 'Fall Out' must be the last two episodes.

Or must it? My advice would be to watch 'Fall Out' first, and then watch 'Arrival'. It all then makes a lot more sense. 'The Prisoner'. It means what it says.
To each of us.

Rick Davy, June 2017

Steve Matt hard at work on 'Out of Order' with 'The Jailbird' watching over him.
Thanks to Candice Girouard from Massachusetts for the colour image of Pat Goon!

See also p42 /43

To Find Out What Winds Up Happening Next Go To Page 57...

Entering 'The Village' of Portmeirion: Courtesy of Mark Bennett

The Pri5Oner: As Good Today
As It's Always Been
by David A. Stimpson

What was it the President told the Prisoner-No.6? "Remember us, don't forget us, keep us in mind."[11] That could so easily be addressed to those who were watching, the television viewers themselves. Because 'The Prisoner' enjoyed the most powerful and dramatic opening sequence of its day, and the television viewer was captivated from that first clash of thunder as dark clouds gathered over a long and deserted runway. At least I was. 'The Prisoner' stays with you, fixed in the mind, and with the occasional screening is indelibly imprinted onto the cortex of the brain, rather like the Professor's lectures in the Speedlearn educational experiment in 'The General.'

The series has continued to withstand the test of time because at the time, it was ahead of its time. But now time has not only caught the series up, but has over taken it, not that that makes it less relevant today. And in that time much of what 'The Prisoner' predicted has come to fruition. The credit card, surveillance, Britain has the most surveillance cameras of all the countries in the world. Cordless telephones have become the norm in recent decades, and the reliance on technology has grown and grown, despite Patrick McGoohan's warning that man should slow down, and consolidate, rather than pursue greater technology. Hence the Penny Farthing bicycle seen in the series, and used as a symbol to indicate man is moving too quickly, and a warning which went unheeded.

'The Prisoner' has endured despite its flaws and imperfections. For example, what a pity that when the idea occurred to change the dark blazer worn by Curtis in 'The Schizoid Man' for a cream coloured one, they didn't bother to alter the script as well. Number 24 took several Polaroid pictures of Number 6. She was practicing for the photographic competition at The Village Festival in a month's time. It was such a Polaroid image which Number 6 {Curtis} produced from the breast pocket of his blazer in order to prove his identity as Number 6. Number 6 snatched the picture and studied it. I've never realised why Number 6 didn't pick up on the evidence of that Polaroid picture when it was in his hand, and right under his very nose. Instead of proving that Curtis was Number 6, it should actually have disproved his identity! Why? Because in the Polaroid picture Number 6 is wearing a dark piped blazer, while Number 6 {Curtis} is always seen to be wearing a cream blazer! Had they not decided to change the colour of one blazer, on the grounds that otherwise the television viewer at the time would find 'The Schizoid Man' too complicated, then there would not be the inaccuracy in the episode. I have always been of the opinion that Patrick McGoohan seriously misjudged the mentality of the television viewer of the 1960s. In fact had both Number 6's been wearing identical piped blazers, the identity of the real Number 6 would not have been revealed until the very end of the episode. "Susan died a year ago Number Six!"[12]

---

[11] Patrick McGoohan, 'Fall Out', 1967/8, Everyman Films

[12] Terence Feely, 'The Schizoid Man' , 1966/7, Everyman Films

A few months ago I encountered another fan of 'The Prisoner,' he was a complete stranger to me, and me to him, but we shared an affiliation and that made us instant friends. We still meet up occasionally and chat about 'The Prisoner.' I remember I asked him what his favourite episode was he said 'Fall Out.' My two favourite episodes are 'Arrival' and 'Checkmate.' I said. Then I asked him what his least favourite episode was? He said can you have a least favourite episode? I smiled, and said yes you can, and in my book that's 'Do Not Forsake Me, Oh My Darling.' There are more holes in that episode than there are in a wedge of Swiss cheese, from the need for a 'reversal process' of Doctor Seltzman's mind transference technique, to the moment when Number 6 wakes up and instantly knows who the Colonel is! And yet, for all its discrepancies, because a bad script was turned in to an incomprehensibly terrible script, then made even worse by Patrick McGoohan's editing of the episode, 'Do Not Forsake Me Oh My Darling' does have one redeeming quality, its unique incidental soundtrack music. The change in tempo as the Colonel arrives at The Village by helicopter. And the instrumental use of a traditional Scottish folk song, "My Bonnie lies over the ocean, my Bonnie lies over the sea, my Bonnie lies over the ocean, oh bring back my Bonnie to me"[13] which refers to "Bonnie Prince Charlie" – Charles Edward Stuart after the defeat of the Prince at the Battle of Culloden in 1746 and his subsequent exile. But in this instance, as far as 'Do Not Forsake Me Oh My Darling' is concerned, the word Bonnie can be exchanged for "body."

"My body lies over the ocean, my body lies over the sea, my body lies over the ocean, oh bring back my body to me" referring to the Colonel's body then occupied by Number 6's mind, somewhere across the sea! And the use of the theme music again as the Colonel drives off in the Lotus 7. It's dramatic, powerful, to say that the Prisoner, although his mind is wrongly housed in the Colonel's body, he's going to sort this situation out. "Get me Sir Charles............I said get me Sir Charles Portland at once!"[14]

And then there's the reluctance to use Number 6's name amongst friends and ex-colleagues, even between lovers. Schmitt, Duval, XO4, D6, ZM73, PR12, and XB4 but at least we know who XB4 is, Potter by name! And Jonathon Peregrine Danvers, born in Bootle, and apparently not at all important as he doesn't require a code name! And then there is the use of a different musical arrangement of the original theme music as the Colonel, having collected the photographic slides from the World Camera shop, drives through the streets of London to his home. The Lotus is Followed, not only by the undertakers in a

------

[13] A traditional folk song originating in Scotland possibly about 'Bonnie Prince Charlie' .

Infamously Tony Sheridan and the Beat Brothers recorded a cover version in 'rock and roll' style which got to #5 In West Germany in 1961. 'The Beat Brothers' were actually 'The Beatles' under a pseudonym as their moniker was likened to a particular German obscenity. This was given another commercial release when the 'Beatles Anthology 1' compilation was released in 1995.

[14] Vincent Tilsley 'Do Not Forsake Me, Oh My Darling' a.k.a. 'Face Unknown' 1967 * A series of rewrites were carried out on this script while McGoohan was filming 'Ice Station Zebra' - McGoohan was extremely unhappy with the episode and insisted on reediting and extra shots filmed with "Doubles" for Number Two and The Colonel. This was not overall successful — yet as examined later we may be too quick to dismiss this episode out of hand.

hearse, but also by ~~Potter~~ XB4, to Buckingham Place, but with Patrick McGoohan, and not Nigel Stock, seen behind the wheel of the Lotus 7. Its like watching the Prisoner returning home after having handed in his letter of resignation. Such is the use of, or reliance upon, film stock footage in certain later episodes. There seems to be an aversion throughout 'The Prisoner,' to use the Prisoner's name, to the point of going out of their way not to use it. Even in 'Many Happy Returns' the Colonel calls his ex-colleague Number 6! Perhaps because the Prisoner is supposed to be 'Everyman,' well he's certainly an extraordinary man. Number 2 in 'A, B and C' said he sometimes thinks Number 6 is not human! But to my mind, he will always be 'Danger Man' — John Drake, my boyhood hero.

'The Prisoner' has withstood the passage of time, and even after 50 years there still remains a mystique about it. There aren't many television series of which can be said the same. Devotees of 'The Prisoner' will say that we know hardly anything about Number 6. But we know even less about the diminutive Butler, who is an even more enigmatic character than Number 6.

Also a white meteorological balloon became intrinsic to the series, appearing in 8 of the seventeen episodes, as well as in the opening sequence and after the closing credits. Symbolically The Village Guardian has been described as representing ones own fears. When someone is confronted by the Guardian they are being confronted by their own fear. On a physical level some devotees think the Guardian is a "thing" from another World, if so, that would make it just as much a prisoner as anyone in The Village! Personally I like to think of the white membranic Guardian as having been genetically engineered. Possibly 'it' began life as membrane grown in a Petri dish by biologists and scientists in some laboratory somewhere in The Village. But I expect the smart money is on the Guardian simply being a meteorological weather balloon, which makes for a far superior Guardian than the original, which was to have been a Go-Kart with a fibreglass dome fitted with a blue light. One idea for 'Rover' as Number 6 once called it, was that it would have the capability of absorbing its victims, with the white membrane changing colour, taking on a reddish hue caused by the absorption of its' victims blood. But that effect was deemed to be too frightful for the television viewer of the '1960s'.

'The Prisoner' raised more questions than it answered. Making questions a burden to others, and answers a prison for oneself. The general idea being that you find the answers for yourself, answers that suit you, but which might not suit other fans. As Patrick McGoohan once said, one thousand people can each have a different answer and everyone would be right. What's more, questions still remain about 'The Prisoner,' questions which will now most likely never be answered. For example, in 'It's Your Funeral' Number 6 has retrieved the radio detonator for the bomb in the Great Seal of Office from Number 51-the Watchmaker. But standing in his way is Number 100 who is determined to retrieve the detonator from Number 6. There follows a brutal fist-fight between the two men, which ends in Number 6 knocking Number 100 out. So why did the Guardian attack Number 100? Obviously we do not see this in the finished episode, but in 'Arrival,' when the young man in a striped jersey and sunglasses is attacked by the Guardian, as he is being suffocated, the scene changes to a man wearing a pink blazer. It is obviously actor Mark Eden as Number 100 wearing the pink blazer. It's not so much the fact that a good action scene is spoilt by the insertion of a piece unnecessary stock footage film that concerns me, but the question as to why Number 100 would have been attacked by the Guardian in the first place. Especially when you recall how he was involved with 'Plan Division Q' and the radicalisation of the Watchmaker, which was carried out on the instructions of the interim Number 2.[15] [16]

Number 2 is another character whose background we know practically nothing about, except we do know the name of one, Mrs. Butterworth. And even if it isn't her real name, at least it is a name. And that another Number 2 holds a position in the House of Lords, within the Houses of Parliament.

As to the question of who is Number 1? It's only Number 6 who concerns himself with that question, perhaps because he's not an optimist! During 'The Chimes of Big Ben' Number 2 tells Number 6 that he's an optimist, that's why it doesn't matter who Number 1 is. But persistently during the opening sequence the Prisoner is heard to ask "Who is Number One?" to which Number 2 replies "You are Number 6." Of course its possible to make "You are Number 6" read and sound very differently depending on where you place the emphasis. But that only works after the advent of 'Fall Out,' because up until then we don't know who Number 1 is, even Patrick McGoohan hadn't decided, before he wrote the script for 'Fall Out.' So in Number 2's reply to who is Number 1, he's merely telling the Prisoner he's Number 6. I suppose it's all a question of interpretation, and much within 'The Prisoner' series is open to personal interpretation, or at times, misinterpretation. For example, when during the opening sequence of 'The Prisoner,' a man parks his Lotus Seven in an underground car park. Alighting from the car, he strides out and goes through a pair of doors marked 'Way Out.' This action has been interpreted by many fans of the Prisoner as demonstrating his rebellious nature by entering a building via the 'Way Out.' But the reality of the situation is, that the man is not entering a building, but is leaving the underground car park via the 'Way Out.' If it was otherwise, the words 'Way Out' would be on the opposite side of the doors.

'The Prisoner' is a remarkable television series which many enthusiasts describe as being a work of art. It is also a window through which one can observe Portmeirion as it was in the '1960s', because in more recent years the Italianate village has changed, it has lost that 'lived-in' look it once had. Also Patrick McGoohan said of 'The Prisoner' that it was never meant as a children's television series, and yet the author of this essay was twelve when he first watched it, and many of my contemporary fans were about that same age, possibly even younger. And yet for an adult series there is much childishness in it. So is it any wonder that 'The Prisoner' captivated the imagination of so many children, not only at the time, but also over the subsequent years and decades. That having been the case, Patrick McGoohan seems to have been the Pied Piper of his time. He called the tune, and we danced, not quite a "Dance of The Dead," but as children we followed. He may not have

---

[15] By this point Plan Division Q was deemed a failure or at least — not much of a success by the Observers in the Control Room. In order to destroy the evidence of Number 100 and his bungling a Rover was sent out

[16] You could say 'Dead on Schedule'

taken us body and soul, but he influenced our minds, The Village Administration would have been proud of him! However it could be said he gave us something in return, in showing what it is to be an individual. To question, and not simply accept things as they are, not simply in regard to 'The Prisoner,' but more importantly in life. But perhaps the series is better viewed through the eyes and mind of a child. I was once told by someone, that after watching 'The Prisoner' for the very first time and in the company of her son, and later meeting other people who had seen 'The Prisoner,' she couldn't understand what their problem was. Why they couldn't understand the series, why they were looking for explanations, not to mention those so termed "hidden meanings." She thought the reason why children get on so well with 'The Prisoner,' was that they do not expect to understand every detail, that they merely follow the story. She firmly believes that she was helped by watching 'The Prisoner' through her child's eyes. It would seem that as adults we tend to overcomplicate 'The Prisoner,' looking to give questions complicated answers, when a far simpler reasoning can be applied. But in time all good things must come to an end. And so it is 'Fall Out.'[17]

'Fall Out' not from nuclear blast, although a rocket is involved, but a falling out of former friends. Such as Number 48 who had been with them, but then he went and gone, put on trial for representing rebellious youth. Rebelling against nothing it can define. And a "late" Number 2, who apparently died, but who they couldn't even let rest in peace! And the former Number 6 is forced to witness these two trials. But at least they are allowed to state their case and address the Assembly, unlike Number 6. The delegates of the Assembly, each representative of different sections of society, are not prepared to listen to one single word Number 6 has to say. But they applaud his private war which is pure, for he has vindicated the right of the individual to be individual.

High praise indeed. Besides that, he's been given the key to his house, which has been prepared for him, as well as his car. A passport valid for anywhere, travellers cheques a million, and a leather string purse of petty cash. So now its come down to bribery has it? But in any case Number 6 has achieved the right to meet Number 1 who turns out to be himself. Number 6 has been his own worst enemy all the time, although I personally suspect this only came about when Patrick McGoohan made himself Number 1, when he wrote the script for 'Fall Out.' Up until then he had not decided who Number 1 would be. On the other hand, Number 1 might be the former Number 12 — Curtis who hadn't died that night in 'The Schizoid Man,' but had been kept "on ice" in the hospital. And now forced to impersonate Number 6 for a second time, well, it probably tilted his brain. No wonder he went berserk during that confrontation in the rocket! But that is a personal interpretation, everything in 'The Prisoner' is open to interpretation. However I disagree with what Patrick McGoohan said about 'Fall Out.' Yes, it might be an allegory as he said, but that only means it's a story or tale. He also said, he didn't want to give 'The Prisoner' a James Bond style of ending. But action-wise that's just what we did get. The finale to the series has all the qualities of a James Bond ending. Number 1 the villain in his lair, The Village,

---

[17] 'Fall Out' refers to nuclear material which will 'fall out' after nuclear warhead has been dispatched and detonated due to being toxic and dangerous. The use of this loaded term would no doubt have been deemed a concern in the wake of the 'Cuban Missile Crisis' in 1963 just 4-5 years earlier.

there's a vicious fire-fight in which even the Butler gets stuck in, and who at one point can be seen strangling a man to death! The villain despatched to his fate in the rocket. The lair evacuated, there's death, but no destruction, as The Village is not destroyed, and with the aid of four confederates the hero escapes to return to London. The End! But it's not the end, 'The Prisoner' has no ending, no proper ending or conclusion as such, only a beginning. For in the Prisoner's end is his beginning, as his future looks to continue the same as his immediate past.

Be seeing you 👌

David Stimpson with the Ex Admiral playing Chess on the Hotel Portmeirion Lawn During Production of 'Fan-Film' — 'Village Day'

The Jailbird by Steve Matt

The Balloon Is A Moon.
by Steven Matthews

Three writers are often overlooked when it comes to the subject of the creation of 'The Prisoner'. Too often than not, McGoohan is credited as the sole creator and with all due respect for the man, most if not all of his interviews on the subject support that notion.

But genuine fans of the show know better and are resolute in crediting writer and script editor George Markstein as co-creator of 'The Prisoner' but what of the other two?

I refer of course to Danger Man writers Donald Jonson and David Stone responsible respectively for the episodes 'Colony Three' (1964) and 'The Ubiquitous Mr Lovegrove' (1965).

Though not directly involved with creating 'The Prisoner' it cannot be denied that 'Colony Three' with its Village for spies behind the Iron Curtain and 'The Ubiquitous Mr Lovegrove.' with its surreal and psychological undertones had a significant role in inspiring what I believe to be the sequel (in my opinion) to 'Danger Man'. At least that's how it started out until George Markstein resigned once it was clear McGoohan was taking the show in an entirely different direction.

As much as it pains me to contradict Patrick McGoohan, no one is infallible and when one has access to facts certain inaccuracies come to light. Having spoken one to one with Frank Maher and several crew members on the show it's my understanding that McGoohan originally sold The Prisoner as a sequel to 'Danger Man'.

George Markstein supports this story during an interview in 'Six Into One'. Another detail that doesn't sit right with me is McGoohan's claim that he only intended to make 7 episodes when it's clear Lew Grade would never agree to such a low figure if he intended to sell the series overseas. I can only surmise that McGoohan invented this story as a result of sour grapes after Grade cancelled a second series and tried to save face. An understandable reaction (if my theory is true) by anyone who feels angry by bitter disappointment.

I think it would be fair to say that it's a 50/50 ratio amongst Prisoner enthusiasts concerning the identity of No. 6 and I've already made it clear that I believe No. 6 and Drake are one and the same but that wasn't always the case since I watched The Prisoner a considerable time before viewing Danger Man. Within that time it made perfect sense for the protagonist to be as mysterious as the surreal series as a whole –- an Everyman!

But then along came 'Danger Man' and I became emotionally invested in the character (due to McGoohan's usual hypnotic charisma and performance) just as original tv audiences must have when the series was originally broadcasted and suddenly the resignation sequence at the start of 'The Prisoner' took on a whole new meaning and had so much more impact. Surely (in my mind) this was the kind of emotion that McGoohan, Markstein and Grade originally wanted to evoke from their impressionable audience — complete surprise and shock! Here is a man "with a brilliant career, record impeccable"[18] for the last 7 years suddenly walking out! Surely this approach is far more dramatic and entertaining than just some anonymous guy resigning?!!!??

Then there's the inconvenient clues for those that believe No. 6 is not Drake. Why are they there if McGoohan was so adamant from the start that he didn't want both characters to be confused with each other? Our first clue is the publicity photo from 'Danger Man' and the second is the actress who is given the first speaking role, Patsy Smart. Is it just an incredible coincidence that 'Danger Man' creator Ralph Smart's sister was given this honour or can it be construed as a form of acknowledgement to make up for shrewdly avoiding royalty payments by emitting the name 'John Drake' from the script?

Another clue is Drake's (sorry) No. 6's resignation suit which Drake is also seen wearing in 2 or 3 episodes of Danger Man such as 'The Paper Chase'. One can argue that it's infact from McGoohan's own wardrobe but I don't recall the actor wearing the suit in any other roles!

---

[18] Tomblin D and Markstein G, 'Arrival', 1966, Everyman Films

Then there's John Drake's nervous habit and I'm not referring to nicotine. He's regularly seen clicking his fingers ('View From The Villa'), just as No. 6 demonstrates in 'The Schizoid Man'. Once again I don't recall seeing McGoohan adopt this quirk with any other role but I could be wrong. No one's infallible...

Of course then there is the fact that the door number of Drake's mews cottage at Groom Place in Belgravia was and still is NUMBER SIX! Its certainly possible that McGoohan picked up on this consciously or unconsciously when choosing a Number for his lead character. This would make another clear link between 'Danger Man' and 'The Prisoner'.

This brings me to what must be the most damning 'evidence' of all — the character of Potter in 'The Girl Who Was Death'. Ok so it's just a 'fairy story,' but one that exists in No 6's mind all the same and he apparently conjures up a name and image of an identical intelligence operative from the 'Danger Man' episode 'Koroshi' (1966). [19]

A well documented argument (2 in-fact) is that the story was originally planned for a 'Danger Man' episode though how this is an argument is anyone's guess. A stronger argument is a statement by the actor Christopher Benjamin who played the role in both 'Danger Man' and 'The Prisoner' claiming that he didn't play them as the same character. However I've always interpreted this as a comment from an actor who regards 2 roles as 'a couple of jobs' over a period of a year or so. He most likely accepted several other roles in between and forgot the characters shared the same surname the same way a shelf stacker forgets how much the price of cornflakes are from one week to the next.

Earlier this year Mr Benjamin unwittingly supported this argument by stating at the 2017 convention that:— "they could be the same character" after all. I imagine he'd been reminded that both characters had been called Potter and his common sense did the rest...

And what of 'The Prisoner' as a whole? What was it all about??? One of my interpretations leads us back to the Danger Man episode 'The Ubiquitous Mr Lovegrove'. The entire episode is played out in Drake's mind while he's unconscious after a road accident and this could be applied to all episodes of 'The Prisoner'! A road accident would certainly explain the clumsy cut from what resembles a test track or a runway to central London footage within the blink of an eye. Drake/No.6

---

[19] Despite the fact that Christopher Benjamin plays Potter differently doesn't mean he is a different person. We could assume that Potter (in No.6's story) is undercover — hence the seeming change of personality to avoid recognition.

then dreams of imprisonment of his own guilt and conscience, arguably envisioning the ghostlike victim of his reckless driving gazing down at him from the Bell Tower.

In the penultimate episode No. 2 and No. 6 play out a courtroom scenario in which No. 6 is on trial for reckless driving. Could this suggest that No. 2 somehow represents the Prisoner's conscience? The ubiquitous undertakers may be a clue as to whether this time Drake wasn't so fortunate in surviving the crash...

The fact that No. 6 sees the figure in the bell tower of all places may also be of significance as the location is a reference to time. Immediately after the figure apparently vanishes, the bell tower strikes the hour. We are all prisoners of time and unable to see the future or alter the past and this is where the ubiquitous Penny Farthing comes in. This suggests the victim of No 6's road accident was a cyclist and to a psychologist, the antiquated symbol could represent the desire to turn back the clock. And finally what of Rover? Could this be another reference to time? Before clocks Man used to go by the Moon's cycle to keep track of the months and the Earth's satellite was also worshipped amongst faiths including Hinduism and Witchcraft. This changes in size much in the same way the Moon appears to from an uneducated mind; the same way it appears to pursue us in the night sky while we're travelling long distances. Therefore its possible that as well as time, the orb also represents our fear of the unknown and as we all know, this can only be conquered through learning and understanding.

When one attaches this theory to Rover it makes perfect sense for the Village's guardian to finally be destroyed when No. 6 launches the rocket in 'Fall Out' for the rocket surely represents exploration and with exploration comes knowledge.

And as for the continuing debate on the identity of No. 6, I'm happy to compromise with those that still believe he was a different entity to John Drake. Though I still maintain that they are one and the same, by 'Fall Out' Drake/No. 6 became an 'Everyman'. Its the merger of the two that we see McGoohan banishing into the Rocket before we see him 'escaping' the persona for good — or at least that's what he'd hoped...

B.C.N.U.

'GERMANISMS IN NUMMER 6/THE PRISONER'
By Arno Baumgärtel[20]

There are a few instances in THE PRISONER where German expressions or phrases are spoken.

'Once Upon A Time'

In 'Once Upon A Time' some Germanisms surface which the German version chooses to ignore totally.

But that's not all to it. Some Führer snippets and cheering masses are heard from a tape-recorder and the Butler providing the special effects smoke from a can. These background sounds are almost inaudible in the German TV version.

Number Two and Number Six, turned 19 years old, with pilot caps and oxygen masks on, are seen sitting on a beam like on horseback acting out a bomb raid on Nazi Germany. The airplane is hit and they must get out of it. At the end of the episode Number Two's time is over, the patient and the therapist have changed their positions.
Number Two: Bail out, bail out!
Number Two now takes on the part of a German interrogation officer:
Number Two: You're are 19 years old. You are thirsty of glory. You kill without caring.
Number Six: I do not wish to kill.
Number Two: You kill without caring!
Number Six: The aircraft was hit. I had to...
Number Two: BAIL OUT...!
Number Six: ...over your territory. This is not my fault. There I cannot help bailing out.
Number Two: You drop many bombs!
Number Six: My arrival is a fact but I have to tell you nothing.
Number Two: Impertinent!
Number Six: Zero... go!
Number Two: How dare you...!
Number Six: Go, go, go, go...!
- Ha, ha, ha - zero... go! Ha, ha, ha!

With German Lines:
Nummer Zwei: Sie sind 19 jahre alt. Sie suchen ihren ruhm. Sie töten ohne gedacht.
Nummer Sechs: I do not wish to kill.
Nummer Zwei: Sie töten ohne gedacht!

---

[20] This article can be found in it's original form on the website: http://www.match-cut.de/spec/6of1.htm

Nummer Sechs: The aircraft was hit. I had to...
Nummer Zwei: BAIL OUT...!
Nummer Sechs: ...over your territory. This is not my fault. There I cannot help bailing out.
Nummer Zwei: Sie werfen viele bomben ab!
Nummer Sechs: My arrival is a fact but I have to tell you nothing.
Nummer Zwei: Unverschämt!
Nummer Sechs: Zero... go!
Nummer Zwei: How dare you...!
Nummer Sechs: Go, go, go, go...!
- Ha, ha, ha - zero... go! Ha, ha, ha!

'Hammer Into Anvil'
And in the 'Hammer Into Anvil' episode where in the confrontation between Number Six and Number Two Germany's first poet Johann Wolfgang Goethe is cited by the very *'arrogant and aggressive'*[21] Number Two, in German language, chiefly the last line for the title:

"Geh! Gehorche meinen Winken,
Nutze deine jungen Tage,
Lerne zeitig klüger sein:
Auf des Glückes großer Waage
Steht die Zunge selten ein;
Du musst steigen oder sinken,
Du musst herrschen und gewinnen,
Oder dienen und verlieren,
Leiden oder triumphieren,
Amboss oder Hammer sein."

My apology for giving only my own rather pedestrian translation. My knowledge of English, I'm afraid, isn't quite up to the height of poetry that is required here. On the web English renderings may easily be found on searching "Hammer into Anvil":

"Go! Obey my advice,
Use your days so young,
Early enough learn to be wiser:
On the big weigh of fortune
The needle ("tongue") seldom keeps the balance;
You must rise or fall (sink),
you must rule and win (prevail),
Or serve and lose,

---

[21] Added to original article the bold italic description of Number Two - possibly 'lost in translation' by the editor.

Suffer or triumph,
Be anvil or hammer."

'Arrival'
At the end of 'Arrival' Number Six's presumed dead colleague Cobb is seen off by Number Two in French saying "Au revoir!" and Cobb replies: "Auf wiedersehen!" No German viewer, of course, would have taken notice of the familiar salute. The German TV dubbing here opts for the usual "Wir sehen uns! — "Be seeing you!"

'Checkmate'
In the control room Number Two asks the Supervisor, "Can't you get the audio?" To which the Supervisor replies "The mic's kaputt, the electrics truck is on its way."

'Many Happy Returns'
Of the two gunrunners who are overpowered by Number Six on their boat at least one has a German name in the final English version: Gunter. The other one was supposed to be called Ernst. According to Anthony Skene's original script they were to speak more German than they eventually do. Only few expressions remained. Number Six causes smoke in the galley:

GERMAN TV VERSION
ORIGINAL ENGLISH DIALOGUE
Gunter: Los!* Da brennt was! Schnell, nimm das steuer!

Gunter: Da brennt was! Schnell, nimm das steuer!

Something's burning! Quick! Take the helm!

Ernst: Was ist denn? Was ist los?

What''s the matter? What's up?

Ernst: Gunter! Wo bist du?

Gunter! Where are you?

Not much of a difference here. But the word * "Los!" meaning "Go!" isn't 100 percent sure. Could also mean the name "Lou".

'Do Not Forsake Me, Oh My Darling'

There's only one small German word in 'Do Not Forsake Me, Oh My Darling'. Professor Seltzman is heavily urged to set up the reversal process he alone is capable of performing in order to transfer Number Six's mind back into his own body. At first he refuses to do so.

Number Two: Surely, you owe him some slight responsibility.
Prof. Seltzman: I will do it. On certain conditions.
Number Two: I'm sure they will be reasonable.
Prof. Seltzman: For once I'm dictating.

Number Two (raises his hand significantly): Heil!
Prof. Seltzman: I will do it. But alone. Under this condition only.
Number Two: I accept.

Professor Seltzman, the name itself is a German or Austrian and because of his first name being Jacob he could be a Jew. Apart from this, the character and actor Hugo Schuster's appearance in general don't do less than to insinuate the parallel Albert Einstein, something that would certainly be welcome by the script here.

Number Two intentionally uses the expression "Heil!" which was the common German salute to the "Führer" during the "Third Reich" and also his typical hand gesture. Why this? This little instance might hint to a darker past. We don't know. But Number Two certainly knows about Seltzman and his past. What if Seltzman had been suffering from Nazi terror? In reminding Seltzman of what had happened, actually threatening him, Number Two then would employ questionable but arguably cynical methods in order to make the professor work for him.

There may be a good chance Number Two's reply "Heil!" and his hand gesture would upset people. But it passes almost unheard in the German version. Not only is Seltzman's strong German accent lost in the dubbing, so is the one keyword of the original dialogue: "For once I'm dictating" in favour of the weaker "bestimmen" (= to determine, decide).

Village cynicism wins over the professor's scrupulous morality in order to gain control of Seltzman's invention. A proof of good script dialogue.

PETER DUNN'S A-Z OF ALLEGORY - A: ALLEGORY, ACTION, AND ADVENTURE.

This Article was previously published on the Unmutual Website and can be found at:

www.theunmutual.co.uk/articleatoza.htm

Many Prisoner fans hold the view that one of the things that makes "The Prisoner" stand out as a television series is its allegorical content. However, it often appears that no two individual fans appear to agree on what that allegorical content is or what philosophy (if any) it underpins. That being the case I should have little difficulty finding material for 26 columns exploring an A to Z of the various allegorical "explanations" of "The Prisoner" that have been thrown up over the last 26 years[22].

Where better then to start than with "A". A after all stands for Allegory - but also for Action and Adventure - and one cannot hope describe "The Prisoner" without recourse to all three of these words.

The Editor at 1 Buckingham Place in 2017 Photo By Ian Orchard

The world has seen many allegories from the parables of Jesus to the political satire of "Animal Farm"[23]. Mankind has also devised many tales of action and adventure from the tales of the 'Labours of Hercules'[24] to the small screen adventures of 'Danger Man'. However there are few works of fiction that have tried to combine allegory with action adventure and fewer still that have tried to do so in the format of a television series.

---

[22] Clearly this article was originally written in 1993.

[23] George Orwell's 'Animal Farm' restages the 'Russian Revolution' in a farmyard where "Two Legs Bad - Four Legs Good".

[24] Of course Hercules is in Portmeirion in the form of a statue and the Labours of Hercules are depicted on the relief plasterwork of the ceiling of Hercules Hall.

Before we go any further let us pause to consider what exactly we mean when we talk about allegory. An allegory is a narrative or visual description of one subject under the guise of another. People sometimes misunderstand the meaning of the word allegory thinking to mean a "hidden message" when in fact it is simply a "hidden description". An allegory hides a depiction of a particular state of affairs under the cover of the description of something completely different. The writer uses this device either because direct depiction of the allegorical subject could bring him or her

Hercules Hall
Portmeirion
Courtesy of Ed
Fordham

persecution or to draw attention to a subject that the author considers important that might not of itself be of sufficient interest to draw peoples' attention.

In the case of "The Prisoner," the popular medium of the action adventure is used to draw attention to the show's allegorical content to an audience which would not normally be attracted to considering such matters. It is quite literally a show designed to make one think.

Occasionally allegories will also contain a message or an answer to the questions and issues they raise — the best example of this being the parables of Jesus - but they need not do so. In fact it is more often the case that allegories do not deliver a handy answer to the problem situations they depict. The writer simply put alludes to the topic because he or she believes it is important that people think about that issue and possibly even debate it with others.

This in part explains why some allegories such as '1984,' 'Animal Farm' and 'The Prisoner' are so bleak — they point out not just an issue but a major problem for society without suggesting any form of solution.

This understanding of what an allegory is may help us to understand why "The Prisoner" often seems to explore a number of issues at a hidden level but yet, like Number 6, seems so loathe to provide us with any answers to the questions we may have about those issues. The reason for this is now quite clear. "The Prisoner" is an allegory of one or more things that its writers considered important at that time and which still may be just as important today. It offers no answers just the opportunity for us the viewers to perceive the problems and perhaps find our own solutions.

This allegorical content is what sets 'The Prisoner' apart from other TV shows. Of course I leave aside the TV dramatisations of the allegorical works of literature by authors such as George Orwell and CS Lewis ('1984', 'Animal Farm', 'The Lion the Witch and the Wardrobe' etc) but I hope that you would agree that it is 'The Prisoner' originality in being written for TV in the first place that sets it apart from these adaptations of great works of literary fiction.

Many modern TV shows have been cited as parallels to 'The Prisoner' but despite having strong elements of surrealism ,few — if any, really achieve its blend of allegory and adventure. That does not mean that these shows are in some way lesser than 'The Prisoner' it merely means that they are different.

Take for instance 'Twin Peaks' which has often been cited as 'The Prisoner' of the 1990s. Sadly such comparisons are made simply because of 'Twin Peaks' surreal nature. Yes, both shows were surreal and this element helped make them great viewing but 'Twin Peaks' lacked any allegorical meaning, either hidden or otherwise.[25] In fact the Director went out of his way to confuse, and infuriate any viewer attempting to extract any message or allegory from the show — and anyone who thought they were just being presented with a straight murder mystery was in for even rougher ride...

'Twin Peaks' works neither as an adventure story or as an allegory — nor was it intended to. Indeed the series is probably the most deserving recipient of the over used tongue in cheek accolade "a triumph of style over content". In fact much the same could be said about a number of other programmes including "Artemis 81" though the latter could be perhaps better described as a failure of both style and content.

There have been a number of other message laden action adventure programmes at least one of which, 'Edge of Darkness,' I have heard compared with "The Prisoner". All of these shows or episodes can be demonstrated to be bearers of unmistakable, unhidden messages rather than allegory.

In some the messages are often so thinly veiled or so bluntly delivered that they actually hinder the plot and action rather than hide in it — for instance the 'Star

---

[25] Even this is debatable — many fans of 'Twin Peaks' suggest that 'Bob' represents the hidden evil within us all in much the same way that 'Number One' does so in 'The Prisoner'.

Trek' original series episode 'Let This Be Your Last Battlefield' (the message being how destructive racial hate can be) and the running cold war theme in the 'Trek' episodes 'Omega Glory', 'A Taste of Armageddon' and 'Errand of Mercy'.

Others however have more delicately delivered messages but they are always clear messages on a single issue with a clear answer. For 'Edge of Darkness' and 'Doomwatch' the issue is the misuse or abuse of science. In 'Alien Nation' the poor treatment of the Newcomer aliens is a commentary on the racism and "alienation" felt by today's human minorities.

"The Prisoner" does not offer such clear advice but it does explore some options as solutions to the problems it presents. Typically these solutions; religion, politics, education etc are presented as being full of as many difficulties as the original problem.

What is "The Prisoner" offering as a central problem or allegorical theme? Does it have just one central theme? I mentioned earlier the great deal of disagreement between fans as to which allegorical avenues the series explores. One thing everyone can agree on is that the show examines the growing restrictions that society places on individual freedom. What people disagree on is which particular restrictions the show depicts and how those restrictions relate to our lives today (and has that changed if at all from the shows first airing several decades ago). Of course there may be somebody out there who disagrees with me on even that supposedly fundamental assertion — but if that's so you are just going to have to wait till I reach "F" in this A to Z.

BCNU
Peter Dunn

That was all 25 years ago
now rejoin our story already in progress on Page 57

Plan 6 and other films
The Legacy of Mathew Lock

Including an incredible joke before the opening titles begin[26] — Matthew Lock's 'Prisoner Fan Films' are a different kettle of fish altogether. 'Plan 6 from Out Of The Village' is a film I had a soft spot for ever since I first saw it in the mid 1990s - In fact for many years afterwards I had to convince myself if I had really seen it at all.

3 of the 4 films produce by Mathew Lock (who has sadly passed away) make no effort to create an addition to 'The Prisoner' itself — yet that is there very strength— and one of these is a spoof of B Movies that just happens to use the Village as its main location.

I will start by looking at 'Plan 6 From Out Of The Village' — a 17 minute homage to black and white sci-fi B Movies referencing in particular Ed Wood's 'Plan 9 From Outer Space'. Here of course Mathew's masterstroke was sending up a film genre where a limited budget is the very virtue of its creation. In its short running time — there are a number of clever jokes even at the expense of Dave Jones whose card trick to distract an alien invader involves him endlessly shuffling cards. Meanwhile Max Hora (former Prisoner Shopkeeper) is transmogrified into an alien villain masquerading as his character the keeper of Village Records 78 RPM. This seems to be a bit of a running gag for Mathew Lock as Max Hora appears in a villainous or semi-villainous role in 'Schrondinger's Cat' (albeit under control of the titular cat) and in 'The Paddy Fitz Affair' as well.

Having met Max Hora on a number of occasions — during the years when he was running the Prisoner shop I can very much assure you that Max was playing against type. He struck me as thoughtful, patient and generous with his time which is born out by the time he dedicated to various projects to do with 'The Prisoner' while he was running his 'Information Centre'.

The poor quality of the picture and occasional sound problems, the deliberate overacting and the 50's sci-fi B-Movie soundtrack all combine to create an accurate spoof of the genre of film it imitates. In addition the use of props such as a model train and model vehicles and a helicopter give the film the qualities of being made as a low budget B movie by actually being made as a low budget movie.

Hilariously a KORG Synthesiser stands in for the controls aboard the alien spaceship with their dastardly plan to turn everybody into numerals. A black board with white dots on it is used as a viewport showing a star-scape. A wobbly alien is even seen invading the Village with what seems to be a postcard of Portmeirion as the background commenting on the 'lovely views' and promising to send a 'postcard home'.

---

[26] 'Plan 6 from Out of The Village' opens with the Film Classification This Film Is Rated PMcG - Not Suitable For Irish Egomaniacs

A protracted laser gun fight leads to the Villagers seeking help from 78 RPM (who of course is an alien in disguise) and this leads to a potentially sticky end for the Villagers for those who haven't seen this film.

'Transference' (1995) Is a film that focuses on the Village being de-commissioned and is cleverly produced using sound and photographs rather than moving images. With a running time of approximately 12 minutes it is brave enough to recast Number Six — with the bulk of the film being a discussion between the Supervisor and the current Number Two. Number Two does his best to convince Number Six that he is free to go and it would be unfair of me to reveal anymore about this film. Despite no moving images it is a great short film achieving things that would be impossible on a budget otherwise.

'The Paddy Fitz Affair' (1989) with its tale of the murder of Max Hora at a Portmeirion Convention is a film about subterfuge and spies operating in Portmeirion. The music has been described as having a resemblance to Peter Davison era Doctor Who. It's a short film and its ultimate reveal will perhaps remind some of Fall Out in that you really have to pay attention to follow what is happening. 'The Paddy Fitz Affair' has a blink and you'll miss it plot twist, the film as a whole is rather well acted. The film proves that Mathew Lock could create an interesting film where all it's parts pull together even at this early stage.

'Schrondinger's Cat' (1994) begins with a body discovered in the West Country by the local police and a discussion with an officer about a 'youth training scheme' leading to a new constable being allocated to him. Max Hora is then seen talking to the cat's of Portmeirion as he makes his way to the Prisoner Shop (6 private) claiming cheerfully to his charmed audience that he will become an acclaimed actor or Hollywood Mogul. We become aware that he has a cat in a cardboard box which is exercising its powers of mind control over poor Max. Max is concerned that he will be fit to be "a politician or breakfast tv presenter" if Schrondinger damages his mind.

Meanwhile a Police Detective and his 'young' constable sidekick are sent on the trail of Schrondinger's Cat - it becomes clear that the younger of the two is prone to flights of fancy and has a form of psychosis and "possibly schizoid tendencies". After discussions with many locals they are directed to Max's shop.

Some of Max's scenes in the film are played in a slightly camp overacted manner as he uses the phrase 'if all the world were a cinema' and states theatrically that all the cats he looks after would be royalty. It is quite possible that Max is playing this deliberately over the top to reflect how Schrondinger is affecting him. Certainly the 'supposed psychosis' explains much of Hatstand's constable colleagues behaviour — until all is revealed. Once again I won't spoil the ending for those who haven't seen the film — suffice to say that it is another triumph for Mathew Lock's filmmaking.

Overall Mathew Lock's Four films are successful — three of them not occupying the same headspace as 'The Prisoner' (Plan 6 is clearly a spoof B-Movie in one very obvious sense but in another a very convoluted and inexplicable prequel for 'The Prisoner') If I were to be critical I would say that 'Schrondinger's Cat' either requires a few minutes pruned from it or that those viewing it need to understand the spirit behind it better. In essence it's a film that could be viewed in one of several ways and I believe we have not only Mathew Lock, his cast and crew to thank but McGoohan and Everyman Films as well.

Photo taken in Portmeirion - Summer 2014 courtesy of Ed Fordham/Ian Orchard

Horst Naumann – the German Number Six Voice
Interviewed by Uwe Huber; translated and transcribed by Arno Baumgärtel

Originally Available Online at:
http://www.match-cut.de/yrfile/Interview_Horst_Naumann-EN-long.pdf

"It is a virtue as well as a responsibility to do it as well as you possibly can, making it translate believably into German and so the character remains intact." - H.N.

Horst Naumann was born in Dresden, Germany, in 1925. His early film roles were in DEFA productions, the state-owned German Democratic Republic film company. In 1958 Naumann fled the GDR and went to the Federal Republic of Germany. His filming and television career took off in the early 1960s. He also did side jobs working as a dubbing artist.

Among others his voice was that of Lex Barker, Leslie Nielsen, Sean Connery and Pierre Brice ('Winnetou'). In the mid 1980s Naumann became a household name with a wider audience as a doctor in the TV series 'DIE SCHWARZWALDKLINIK'Winnetou ('The Black Forest Hospital') and also as the ship doctor on board the German variant of the series 'LOVE BOAT' known as 'DAS TRAUMSCHIFF,' both produced by the TV station ZDF that also broadcast NUMMER 6 in 1969.

Throughout the years Naumann would also continue playing on the theatre stage. In 2003, after 50 years of marriage, his wife Christa von Arvedi passed away. He has been married to Martina Linn-Naumann, the stage manager of the small Duisburg theatre "Säule" ("Column") since 2010.

At the time the interview was conducted Naumann had watched three of the 17 PRISONER episodes: 'Arrival,' 'The Chimes of Big Ben' and 'A. B. and C.'

WHEN THE DUBBING WORK STARTED

UH: Mr. Naumann, how did you get started with dubbing films?
HN: I did dubbing when I was still living in the East, in East Berlin. We did beautiful great Russian films, fairytale films, the titles of which I don't know any more. You'd have to learn entire book pages of text... Something which today is unimaginable! Today's only snippets, snippets..., one line, next line! Those lines running in front of you on a screen, all you do is read it. I have to say that I wouldn't want to do this today. Completely automated, it's awful. And it's nothing to do with human work. So, that's how I got started, learned how to do it and earned me my spurs. And when I was on the other side, in West Germany, this knowledge was very helpful. Everyone was enthusiastic. That's why I did so many dubbing jobs. I made money and in the beginning there was nothing else one could do.
UH: So then, it all started by the end of the 1950s in Munich, the dubbing studios of Munich. Which ones do you remember?

HN: There was the Aventin studio, the Arri studio, outside in Schwabing. There were a lot of others, smaller ones... Lots of them. They were popping up like anything because there really was a lot waiting to be dubbed. And the companies that were founded were all trying their best to prey on the situation. An awful lot to do.

We were a gang of people who'd meet out there day by day. We'd spend some quite enjoyable hours together and occasionally have one little schnapps or two. People also used to smoke a lot anyway, it was terrible, insane of course. Because the dubbing room would be filled with smoke so you could barely see the screen through the mist, all the smoke. That was later banned because it was simply unbearable.

A STRANGE, MORE THAN STRANGE SERIES

UH: Which one of the dubbing directors do you remember?

HN: Sachtleben, Brinkmann... Brinkmann also with NUMMER 6. A strange — more than strange — series we dubbed. One which — err — trying to understand it, it's still hard for me, even today. Even on watching it today. I think it's brilliantly made — the concept, the way it was done, all those crazy characters, the whimsical situation, including the Prisoner who, more or less, is trapped in himself. But even today I haven't reached a conclusion. Its great how it was made, fascinating. And I got hooked again although I must say I haven't watched all episodes. I wouldn't allow myself that much time for it. But it's an absolutely great thing.

THE END IS THE BEGINNING

UH: Now that you've been watching a number of episodes, after so many, many years, you mentioned recently that the end of it was like the beginning. At the end we're back where we got started.

HN: Basically yes, sure. Now then, finally he thinks he's overcome all his troubles, all those tricks and all that, he's stood the martyrdom and what they were trying to inflict on him, break him or coerce him into something he doesn't want. He thinks he's done with it. Does he really believe he'd gotten away into freedom? He went away with one lady who enticed him. There was that big wooden box in which they were lying, side by side separated by a wall. Then he opens a door, wants his freedom and winds up in the same garden* where they had taken him in the beginning and made him a prisoner. 'The Prisoner' — 'Number Six'[27]. It all starts again.

* HN refers to 'the Village' as such, apparently not knowing its name. When No. 6 walks out of the office, supposedly in London, the path leads him through a front garden of sorts (which was the MGM studio backlot).

A POLITICAL ISSUE BEHIND IT IN THE BROADEST SENSE

UH: What do you think people at the time were thinking as to what it was all about?

HN: I think there's a political issue behind it, in the broadest sense. The kidnapping, alienation, the changing of people's minds by the use of medical drugs or making them do

---

[27] I believe Horst is referring to the English and German titles of the series hence both are in inverted commas.

something else. I truly believe that there's quite something behind it. Brainwashing, as we'd call it today. I don't know whether it's this what's behind it but surely there must be at least some of it.

THE DESIGN OF 'NUMMER 6'

UH: What did you think of the visuals of the series that were totally different from everything people had seen, the visual aspect, the design?

HN: The whole plot involved people trying to force Number Six to conform, it was constructed for this purpose, let's put it that way. One can see it on the map of that - I don't have the name of it, there's a name, that whole area... Isolated by intention. They have parades in it... You can see it. Its crazy. They all must be crazy, actually.

REMEMBERING JOACHIM BRINKMANN DIALOGUE DIRECTOR OF THE GERMAN VERSION

UH: Do you remember Joachim Brinkmann? HN: Yes.

UH: What kind of personality was he? He wasn't only a dubbing director, I think he also did documentaries.

HN: Well, that's something I really cannot answer. I know him from the dubbing studio, in the first place. He used to do films that were not as easy to handle like most others, so to speak. He'd work with us. He was a specific personality, so you'd need to form your own picture of him in order to see what made him tick. But working with him was absolutely wonderful, the way he told us to do things. Of course, he'd try to explain things. But, taking the stories as they were, there wasn't much left to explain. All this remains peculiar and it remains strange as well. But I like it that way. [laughing]

What I don't know is how the director, main actor and the author, all in one, was able to get along with all this. I wouldn't be able to do it, actually, lacking in experience, perhaps not enough foresight of life.

You may say it's completely crazy and there's a serious background to it and, maybe, a political side angle too. However, I never endeavoured to try and get it all straight.

THAT'S HOW DUBBING WORKS

UH: What was it that you saw of the series while doing the dubbing? Was it only your own part you could see?

HN: Yes. That's because I, when I saw it, all those sequences — the processions they were doing, pomp and circumstance, costumes and things – I never got to see them back then. Only his [Patrick McGoohan's] reactions. But that's how dubbing works.

"VILLAGE" – THE TRANSLATION

UH: A while ago you mentioned, quite nicely and a little cryptically, that this 'area' did have a real name, yes. And there is one in English, it's just the Village – dorf [in German].
HN: Yes.
UH: Village, Dorf. Now, Brinkmann, he was a genius, he did not translate the word "Village", as one would have it, like "Dorf", because it isn't appropriate.
HN: ... yes...
UH: In English "Village" is different. And he [Number Six] in the prologue scene would always ask: "Where am I?"— "In the Village". — "Sie sind da." ["You are here."] He [Joachim Brinkmann] always used a circumscription for it. He never used the direct translation. Now, I'd like you to, please... [HN asked to repeat famous lines.]
HN: "You are here," - How could anyone explain what that means? All right, you've arrived. But, where did I come from? He was made unconscious, more or less. But again, that's something left obscured. We're not told as to who did something or not; the famous stream of gas through the keyhole and everything... Great thing. Oh yes, I'm able to relate to that. Now he's out cold — but: who did it...? [smiling, waving his arms: not the slightest notion].

PLEASE REPEAT! (46 YEARS AFTER)
[Naumannn reads the opening prologue.]
HN: Whenever I've got something like this, if it's a role, I read in the... [dialogue script] about how it is supposed to be. Now, if you tell me, well a bit more rigorously... Give it to me! [HN takes the paper from UH.] Does this appear anywhere?
UH: Yes. It's in the first episode. HN: Alright... Who's telling who? UH: Number Six to Number Two. HN: Oh yes.. Just wanted to know. UH: Mind you: aggressively.
HN: [reads the text, ponders] Yes, err... UH: He says it aggressively...
HN: Yes, yes, I know, I understand. I was just thinking about how to put it, the speed and so. Going to read again...
[HN speaks the German version of: "I will not be pushed, filed, stamped, indexed, briefed, debriefed or numbered. My life is my own."]
UH: Very good!
HN: Was it? Also the speed?
 UH: It was! HN: Good.
UH: Very good. That's exactly the speed. Exactly.
[HN once more repeats the text with a different accentuation. - Smiling.] UH: Wonderful!
[In 2010 Franco-German TV station ARTE for the first time dubbed the four missing PRISONER episodes „Free For All", „A Change of Mind", „The Schizoid Man" and „Living In Harmony". The question who would become the voice actor for Patrick McGoohan's Number Six was resolved by hiring German actor Bernd Rumpf for the job and not Horst Naumann. Naumann, however, had been invited to do a test. He confirms this in this interview. He also says that his voice was considered too old in order to adjust it to the dubbing of 1969.
He clearly denies, however, having been offered the role of Number Two in one of the four episodes. There had been some speculation about it.]

THE END OF THE DUBBING WORK
UH: At some point you quit dubbing. Why so?

HN: I was too busy. I said, now that I'm in the 'Black Forest' [German TV series: THE BLACK FOREST HOSPITAL] and with the 'LOVE BOAT' commencing [German TV series: DAS TRAUMSCHIFF] — why should I carry on running around, making money here and there? No, you've reached the point when its time to settle down, take more easy. It isn't that I wouldn't have loved to go on with it but — basically, it was a decision of rationality. Besides, many production managers would say, 'No need to call him, he isn't going to be available anyway.' That's how it came about.

HORST NAUMANN WATCHING NUMMER 6

[credit sequence: 'The Chimes of Big Ben']
UH: That car became a cult item, that Lotus 7.
HN: Yes... Now, here he's on the way to his boss, he resigns. That's as far as I understand everything [hand movement, laughing].
UH: The opening scenes, everything's so quick, many people didn't...
HN: [head shaking] ...realise.
UH: Did you immediately understand it or was it only from the second episode?
HN: [nodding] Yes, perhaps. Ah, well, here it is again, the famous stream of gas, yes... [Number Six losing consciousness]. Oops!
[prologue starting]
HN: Information. Information, of course! That's the Village.
 UH: That's Walter Reichelt's voice [dubbing for Leo McKern].
HN: Walter Reichelt. - I'm trying to get his picture but... Oh yes, now here's the famous airbag. And here is Number Two [on screen: Leo McKern]. 'The new Number Two, all right.' [end of the credit sequence; Radio-Village announcement: "Good morning, good morning...!"]
UH: Brainwashing, isn't it.
HN: Yes, I see. I say it.

IDENTIFICATION WITH HIS OWN DUBBING WORK

HN: It is a business. A commercial as well as an artistic process, to put it this way, in order to create the German version of a foreign product. You listen to it, don't you, you hear the mood which the foreign actor was in while he was acting and speaking. And one has to try to pick it up and trace it. That's it. It is a virtue as well as a responsibility to do it as well as you possibly can, seeing it translate believably into German and the character remains intact.

ONE PRISONERESQUE OCCURRENCE
IN THE "GERMAN DEMOCRATIC REPUBLIC"

[STASI = in the GDR the secret police, dreaded by people. HN wrote about it in his autobiography published as a book in 2005.]
UH: That's an impressive picture about your STASI experience, in your book... HN: I only wrote what I was going through, what happened. Nothing else.
UH: Thrilling.
HN: Yes, it was indeed thrilling. When those people arrived for the first time, then they returned... I was at the opening of a film in Dresden. We were accommodated in a hotel where they would also hold the press conference and so on. Suddenly some reception em-

ployee came to me and called me to the telephone. I went to the reception and here they were again, the STASI people. 'We wanted to ask you how you are doing today. We're here, too. Perhaps you can spare some time to talk to us...' So it went. I said, 'Now, leave me alone!' It continued until eventually I got loud and upset. [waving hands:] You've read this in my book...

UH: They knocked at your door, didn't they? And your wife Christa [HN's first wife, Christa von Arvedi]... — she was trembling with fear.

HN: Of course she was. Sure. Everybody else would have been scared. STASI was a strong keyword. But – eventually the point is reached when you tell yourself, no matter what's going to happen, I'm fed up with it [very decidedly]. "Now, you can hit the road and try somewhere else!"

[HN explains that he, and another actor, was probably privileged being under a permanent contract with DEFA which, at the time, was rather unusual. Almost every company run by the state was under surveillance by covert STASI agents.]

So, I went to the Central Committee [of the ruling GDR party "SED"] and I had a letter with me to Mr. Ulbricht [GDR party leader and head of state] as he was the supreme personality in the East. In the letter it read, 'My name is... and I feel threatened by our government body. I cannot stand all this psychological pressure, I can't work any more, can't tell anybody because there's no trust. I'm asking you... for a conversation.' I handed over my letter — and I even got a receipt for it, a curious thing, to be true. And they told me, 'We'll get back to you.' But there was nothing. Then the famous 20th [Communist] party congress took place in Moscow where Stalin was disempowered, and so on. About six weeks after this event a letter arrived, referring to my visit, saying, 'We ask you to visit us at the Central Committee office, room I- don't-know.'

Good Lord, I thought. But something had happened at last. So I went there, my passport was seized. There were two armed guards, one to the left, one to the right, leading me down through corridors and further corridors where the guards were replaced by two other guards. Because they, too, weren't supposed to know what was going on. The enemy never sleeps. They led me to a small room, there was a desk, a table, an armchair, a window — and a set of bookshelves. "Wait here!" Well, I waited.

Suddenly the bookshelves started rotating. Isn't it funny, all those associations coming to mind... like from a well-worn film. A little man appeared. The bookshelves rotated back to their closing position. He approached me and said, "Good afternoon, Herr Naumann..." I've never been a "comrade". "My name is Paul Herber. You've written something... You'll understand that, because of the events in Moscow, our Prime Minister currently isn't able to... It is my duty to hear what you have to say. What is it all about?"

I told him all that nonsense and our conversation got on quite well. Then he said, "Like you, we are quite concerned about the security forces becoming a state within the state. That's something we cannot tolerate and we don't want this to happen. Please... - what were the names of those gentlemen who came to see you?" As a matter of fact and according to their standard procedure they hadn't introduced themselves. He went on, "Now, go back home. Nobody's is going to bother you again, certainly. If someone does you should apply to me, Paul Herber. Here is my name card..." Like this.

I went home, got my passport back. Outside I thought, "Oh, oh... Take a deep breath!" [hand gesture] In fact, nobody ever came to me again. But half a year later my contract with DEFA was terminated. I didn't receive any role offers, neither film nor radio. Nothing. There was one programme, however, 'Der Schwarze Kanal' with Mr... [looking for the name] Karl-Eduard von Schnitzler.

[Karl-Eduard von Schnitzler was a presenter on GDR TV, known for his notorious programme 'Der Schwarze Kanal' — 'The Black Channel'. He commented on Cold War issues in general and the two Germanys in particular, always in a polemic and biased manner. As such he was chief propagandist of the GDR.]

But this I didn't accept, of course. I did not need that money. Then I said to myself, now they don't want you around anymore, so let's try something else. It took us two years until we made it to West Berlin in the end. And I'm convinced they kept me under surveillance all the time... [waving hands].
[By that time, in 1958, there was no Iron Curtain dividing the country nor the city of Berlin, just a rather ordinary border. There was still commuter traffic from the East to the West and back.]
My wife and I were in Adlershof which is the last suburban train station in East Berlin before you reach the borderline. As usual, I was carrying some stuff with me that I wanted to get to the West. On the train, next to the sliding doors, there was a glass wall behind which were the first seats of the train. I'd always keep standing there with my back to the glass wall, next to the exit, so I'd be able to get out quickly. One day, the train had already been given the "Go" signal, the police and the STASI people, they were everywhere, got on board where I was. They put themselves back to back to me, with that glass wall I mentioned between us facing the people on the train. They shouted, 'Everybody from this point get out of the train!' It was only me who was allowed to remain on the train [wiping brow gesture with his hand]. And that's it, that's 'THE PRISONER'! Yes,. That's basically something from 'THE PRISONER'.

SIGNING AUTOGRAPHS

[HN writing autographs.]

UH: Do you know what people in the Village say to each other as a salute? HN: Yes, one moment... What was it like? [looking up, hand gesture]

„Wir sehen uns!"

Interview conducted on April 8th, 2015

Interviewer: Uwe Huber (Koch-Media freelancer)

Camera: Jakob Legner

Length of edited video approx. 38 minutes; processing by Marc Christiansen www.nummer6-theprisoner.de

FREUNDE & FÖRDERER DER SERIE NUMMER 6

NUMMER 6 released in Germany on DVD/BD by Koch-Media

Castell Deudraeth a.k.a. 'The Hospital' from 'The Prisoner'
Ian Orchard/Ed Fordham 2014

Photo of Image
Generated By
The Portmeirion
Camera Obscura &
Interior of Camera
Obscura courtesy
Of Jan Davis

28 & 29

---

28 Foot of Steps to the Dome (Number 2's Residence) and Battery Square to Right — Location of General Stores/6 private

29 Palace Street as seen in 'Many Happy Returns' as Number Six awaits the return of 'Mrs Butterworth' — just around the corner from Buckingham Place — Photo by Rick Davy : Locations Guide on Unmutual Website

Can the Jailbird Foy-l Number Two's Dastardly Plan? Find Out On Page 117

'THE PRISONER' BY JASON KEITH PLATT.

My most vivid memory of 'The Prisoner' was my father explaining he was a man in a strange village and was chased by a big white balloon. I was always intrigued at what it was but I never saw it.

I was born in 1976 and to my recollection it was not shown on television. Or it was but I did not come across it. When I was a boy I grew up on 80s television such as 'Street Hawk,' 'The A Team' and my favourite show 'Magnum P.I.'

I actually finally came across 'The Prisoner' when I was in the Royal Air Force because I worked at JSU Northwood and lived in RAF Uxbridge in Middlesex there was not a lot to do apart from work, sleep and watch a bit of television until it was time to work again.

I saw the dvds for sale in MVC and said to myself 'That's that show!' I honestly think I said it out aloud when I saw them.

I purchased all five DVDs on the 6th March 2002. I know this as I still have the receipt safely inside the DVD cover. Little did I know how much the Number 6 meant.

I worked a 3 night, 3 day shift pattern and in between was known as a 'swing day' where I would finish at 7am and go to sleep until midday or so and get up and do whatever until going to sleep at a decent time and then back on shift 7am the following day for the day shifts.

My room was tiny. A bed, a wardrobe and a small table that housed my T.V, VHS player and DVD player. It was temporary accommodation until I was permanently living at JSU Northwood. This was my world for a short time and here was the start of my experience with 'The Prisoner.' I was at this point 26 years old and I remember at the end of 'Arrival,' once the shutters slammed closed and Patrick McGoohan's face was behind bars as the credits rolled I hit the menu button and started Episode 2 - 'The Chimes of Big Ben.'

I didn't even bother to see the end credits or even listen to the music. I was immediately hooked.

I did the first four episodes that evening before I was rudely interrupted by the need to go to sleep and work the next day. Over the course of the shift I finished the series and as I have stated above I worked a 3 night, 3 day rotation where I then had 6 days off. This included off duty time and 'Not required for work' duty. I was a Royal Air Force Senior Aircraftman working at a Joint Service Unit under Royal Navy regulations. I didn't argue. 6 on, 6 off. It worked for me. After my 6 on, 6 off shift ended I normally jumped on the tube to Paddington and headed home to Carmarthen, South Wales for my time off before I bought a car as this journey became tedious rather quickly.

After watching 'The Prisoner' I decided to stay on base for the 6 days off and rewatch all 17 episodes. The reason being I didn't get what I just saw. I understood mostly everything but the way 'Fall Out' ended I felt confusion, disappointment, anger and let down.

I stocked up on beer, snacks and food from the onsite Spar and watched them all again.

I loved the show. I grew up watching Patrick McGoohan in things like 'Silver Streak,' 'Escape from Alcatraz' and remembered him playing several killers in 'Columbo.'
This show was fast becoming my favourite show along with 'Magnum P.I.' I enjoyed everything about it. I enjoyed being baffled but I still had a problem with 'Fall Out.' Nothing major of course but I just wanted a resolution. My other favourite 60s television show was 'The Fugitive' and that ended with Dr. Richard Kimble being exonerated for the murder of his wife. That was an ending. That was closure.

'Fall Out' ended with Number 6 driving away through London and then on the lonely stretch of familiar tarmac and a familiar close up and.....hang on, that's the start of Episode 1.

The more I thought about it, I liked that it was a never-ending cycle that contained itself.
Yes,
From here on I was fan.

The 6 days I spent on base watching 'The Prisoner 'and other movies I felt like a Prisoner also. Yes I had the Spar, the mess hall that served hot food and the on base bar but it was a very long 6 days stuck in my room alone as my colleagues had all gone back to their homes. Thank God for snacks and my huge DVD collection. Incidentally I left the Royal Air Force officially on 6th October 2006.

A tradition of mine over the last several years has been to put on 'The Prisoner' over the Easter Bank Holiday weekend. To me this was 4 days off and this was time to relax with your feet up and watch DVDs. Seven years ago Lowri, my fiancee at the time and now my wife travelled North from her hometown in Aberystwyth over the Easter Weekend and visited castles and other places including an overnight stay in Porthmadog. Our journey ended in Caernarfon before we returned home but on our trip was my first visit to Portmeirion. Since discovering 'The Prisoner' was filmed there this was a dream destination.

There have been only a few places that I have wanted to visit in the world and Portmeirion was one of them. Walking around The Village for the fist time was a unique experience and I could picture in my head certain scenes from certain episodes just as if I was in 'The Prisoner'. I spent so much money in the Gift Shop I am sure my wife is still miffed seven years on.

After the visit and I got home, one of the first things I did was get 'The Prisoner' DVDs from my room and start off with 'Arrival.' Over the years I have come to interpret 'The Prisoner' in my own way. With every episode starting with the opening title sequence which in itself is the story how he got to The Village, I've come to see every episode as individual whereas every episode could be the first.

Number 2 has failed in extracting information from him so he's hit the 'reset button' and is letting him wake up for the first time. Obviously this theory doesn't hold any water as they keep introducing themselves as 'The New Number 2' meaning he HAS to have met the previous ones before.

As a collector of film and television merchandise, books and magazine spin offs I have sought out and own the novels related to 'The Prisoner' and the DC Comics 'Shattered Visage' graphic novel. This story was set 20 years later with an agent shipwrecked and washed up on the beach and discovering The Village abandoned with Number 6 living in the ruins of the Green Dome. This basically 'explained' Fall Out in one page by having the entire episode ruled as a drug fuelled hallucination.

The secrets were revealed by Leo McKern's Number 2 who wrote a 'tell all' book exposing The Village.

I do like material that expands on a property by telling more stories, incidentally Big Finish are now doing 'The Prisoner' audio dramas. I like expansion but over the years I have come to love 'Fall Out' as much as every other episode. I like the 'explanation' and possibility that 'Fall Out' was indeed a drug fuelled hallucination because the episode is outright bonkers. Some people need closure on things.

I originally needed the closure which I found on 'The Fugitive' but because it loops round to the start of 'Arrival,' it becomes an endless cycle. I'm happy with that. After 'Fall Out' I put on 'Arrival' again. Trapped in time. Trapped in The Village forever and whether he is John Drake or not (that's a totally different argument that deserves its own book) whoever Number 6 is or was, his fate is sealed within the 17 episodes.

Some fans are not kind to the episode 'Do Not Forsake Me Oh My Darling' because Patrick McGoohan was hardly in it. Personally I enjoy it. How many movies have we seen recently with someone waking up in another person's body and trying to convince friends who they really are.

Patrick McGoohan was tied up making 'Ice Station Zebra' and the writers came up with a simple yet creative way of having Number 6 in someone else's body. New actor. Sorted.

Out of the 17 episodes I can't say I have a 'least favourite' episode. I'll be honest in saying aside from watching all 17 in sequence, when I do watch select episodes every now and then I tend to leave out 'Living in Harmony', 'The Girl Who Was Death' and on occasion 'Do Not Forsake Me, Oh My Darling' among maybe one or two others.

Aside from 'Arrival' one of my favourite episodes is 'Hammer into Anvil'. A ruthless and sadistic Number 2 pushes a young woman to suicide and Number 6 swears revenge. His manipulation of Number 2's sensitive paranoia tips him to the point of madness. Each fan has his favourites, least favourites and personal bests.

My most recent visit to Portmeirion was the weekend of the 27th May 2017. My wife Lowri and I were visiting my mother in law in Aberystwyth and I planned on visiting Portmeirion on my own this time as my wife and mother in law had plans. After already watching 'The Prisoner' over the Easter Weekend — it is tradition after all— I was looking forward to returning after a few years to take some photographs and of course visit the Gift Shop. It would have been rude not to. This time my wife wasn't there to witness how much I spent there on Prisoner merchandise. I

Painting of the Pantheon and Battery Square, Portmeirion by Nigel Spencer Andrew

simply returned to Aberystwyth with a huge cheesy smile on my face and a Prisoner bag for life full of stuff.

August sees the Whitland carnival held and I once again hope to dress as Number 6 and this year I'm trying to persuade my wife to be Number 2.

In 'Do Not Forsake Me...' while on the way to the Ferry this location is seen the A41 Roundabout at Elstree, which stands in for part of the A1 During which Number Six's Lotus KAR 120C[30] is seen driving round the roundabout.

---

[30] Photo courtesy of Rick Davy - The Unmutual 'Prisoner' Locations Guide : - Almost certainly not the same KAR(!) as seen in 'Arrival' and possibly different to the one used in 'Fall Out' where Graham Nearn (later of Caterham Cars in seen) - the location seen in the photo is near the studios (sadly no more) at MGM Borehamwood

"The 'Play In Three Acts '
Or An Alphabetical Nightmare For Number Six"

A[31] (Played by Peter Bowles)

Number Two (Colin Gordon) manipulates the dreams of the Village's prize Prisoner using a wonder drug developed and tested rather too early on humans, with the reluctant assistance of Number Fourteen (Sheila Allen). 'A' is the pseudonym used for an agent of British powers that it is believed Number Six may have been selling out to — this forms part of a three act psychodrama in the episode 'A, B and C.'

They are brought together in Number Six's dreamscape — however the dreamer is increasingly reluctant to talk to A during Engadine's famous Paris party.

Using henchmen disguised as doormen employed by their hostess Engadine - 'A' resorts to force to try and obtain information and secrets that are invaluable to his new masters. There is even a supposed drive through the streets of Paris using backlots at MGM Borehamwood to create the illusion of travelling through the French capital. After Number Six fights off A's henchmen amidst some sparky dialogue it becomes eminently clear that Number Six and 'A' were never likely to make such a deal.

This forms merely part of 'A, B & C' — episode first televised in the UK: 3rd Episode in Broadcast order.

Conceived as utilising stock footage of the Village filmed in Portmeirion to link scenes in an episode largely shot at MGM's Borehamwood studios — writer Anthony Skene aimed for something better. Donning big boots (as referred to by Engadine in the script) he explored sets from recent productions that had not yet been struck from the studio backlot.

Finding a French Street, a suitably imposing doorway and other existing sets Skene built his script for manipulating the dreams of Number Six around this. Taking it's working title from the popular tv form (in a series that subverts it's conventions while also celebrating and rejoicing in certain action-adventure series tropes and archetypes) — the episode was known for some time as 'Play In 3 Acts' becoming known as 'A, B & C' at a much later stage.

The unsympathetic, yet debonair and disarmingly charming 'A' gives way to a close professional friend in the form of 'B' .

---

[31]   Why Number Six never names any of the characters represented by the Village Authorities given an alphabetical appellation is never satisfactorily explained. It seems even in his dreams he can't name 'A' or 'B' (perhaps just for once to borrow a phrase from MST3K* 'we should really just relax')

*'Mystery Science Theater 3000'

'B'

After some light conversation and even some dancing with 'B' — Number Two and Number Fourteen are put in a situation where they must force the issue. Unfortunately for them Number Fourteen's efforts to speak in the voice of 'B' lead to Number Six cleverly recognising she is a manipulated image of the real agent she pretends to be.

In many ways the Postmodern theory of the imagery we see on TV screens, Tablets, PCs, Laptops, MacBooks, iMacs and so on becoming 'Hyperreality' where we can no longer split the images and sound we see and hear from reality itself or find reality within it is nowhere more apparent than here. Without being aware of this Anthony Skene creates a primed situation — what we see is not how 'B' would have reacted given the situation. We see and hear Number Fourteen desperately trying to salvage her experiment on Number Six by distorting and manipulating the character of 'B'.

This is caused by Number Two (Colin Gordon) instructing Number Fourteen (Sheila Allen) to intervene in some manner. It becomes clear that Number Two has made a significant error of judgement as Number Fourteen puts words in 'B's mouth. Unfortunately her choice of words includes the phrase "We all make mistakes, sometimes we have too" and reveals to our fateful hero that all is not as it seems.[32] Following a bridging sequence in which Number Fourteen is tailed to her secret laboratory somewhere on the Village outskirts, we see Number Six turn the tables. There follows a sequence that questions the value of Village surveillance as important secret medical experiments are not routinely monitored. Number Six gains access and pieces together the plot against him that has been constructed by Anthony Skene and Number Two and Number Fourteen within the fiction. In order for the conclusion to allow Number Six some sort of positive outcome, defeating the purpose of the experiment he waters down the drug. This is particularly odd as we see during the episode a point where the Village drugs Number Six's water.[33]

The search for the unknown quantity known as 'C' is an exercise in misdirection and subterfuge on both the part of the episode's author Anthony Skene and in the narrative by Number Six.

In fact the method by which Number Six regains control of his own dreams is very enigmatic using symbolism in straightening the mirror, referring to the party as being 'Dreamy' a word associated with the "turn on, tune in, drop out" Generation of the late 1960s. The games being played by Number Six in his dream are literally pointing to Engadine as a potential character to sell out to and this is highlighted by her key phrase:

"Even I have to work for someone..."

---

[32] A similar wording is used by Number Fourteen earlier in the episode when speaking to Number Six outside the Old People's Home. The deviation from the phrase was a fluffed line that was kept in the final version, in an unusual move.

[33] This actually fed into paranoia that existed about the authorities adding substances such as fluoride to water supplies in the real world.

Engadine, 'A,B & C', Anthony Skene

In context she means a higher authority, but plot-wise Engadine is a pawn in Skene's Human Chess game albeit played here with a handful of key pieces. Number Six/Skene manipulates the character of Engadine (in the same manner that Number Fourteen did earlier). Lucid Dreaming is the term now commonly used for what Number Six is achieving in the final segment of 'A, B and C.' Through this method both the character in control of the narrative and Anthony Skene construct a plot device to create suspense and mystery regarding the identity of 'D'.

When the mysterious character (using Robert Rietty's voice to cover his true form) becomes apparent as an image of Number Two (Colin Gordon) his mirror image in the 'reality' of the Village refers to him/himself as a fool for not opening the proffered papers fast enough. The conclusion — the reveal that the papers were holiday brochures as flagged up in a much earlier scene with Engadine shows how in control Number Six has become. Perhaps after all his apparent collapse was part of a subterfuge or an attempt by Number Fourteen to discredit her wonder drug so that it may never be used again.

Number Two's expression as he fails is made almost terminal by the shrill bleeping of the red 'ear trumpet sculpture' hotline to Number One. It is suggested he will pay dearly for his personal failure at extracting information from Number Six.[34]

---

[34] This is a running theme in 'A, B & C' with Colin Gordon's Number Two repeatedly responding to the threat of Number One's calls in an alarmed manner. It raises questions as to why the Village utilise him again in 'The General'. There are a variety of problems which ever way these two episodes are placed in a 'running order'.

Some Essential Notes on 'The Prisoner'

The Writers Guide to 'The Prisoner' states that Number Six 'is a man who held a highly confidential job'. In effect we are not told that he is a secret agent, this is an assumption based on several points.

1) That McGoohan had until recently played a secret agent named John Drake in 'Danger Man'. Many viewers see 'The Prisoner' as a direct follow on from 'Danger Man' despite the facts.[35] He is never referred to as Drake or John Drake in the series and he never meets his superiors from the Danger Man series in 'The Prisoner'.

2) The nature of Number Six's former job is 'confidential' and 'secret' but this could equally mean that he is a scientist or an engineer on a secret project. Whatever it is pays handsomely as he is able to afford a Lotus 7 car (note however that in 'Many Happy Returns' he insists he built it himself ie: it was not custom built for him and was therefore slightly cheaper) and a home in a wealthy district of London. Recent quotes for 1 Buckingham Place have been around a cool million pounds.

3) The manner of his abduction, the references to him having 'gone over' or returning from 'the other side of the Iron Curtain,' the manner in which the Village authorities seem desperate to get our hero to disclose his secrets all point to a secret agent being involved. However thinking laterally we can see that these facts could be equally valid if Number Six had been working on another secret project in some capacity, he could be a physicist, an engineer, someone working on a secret space programme (note how he handles the controls in 'Fall Out'). Perhaps he was a biologist who was being coerced into working on some form of 'biological warfare' and wanted out because he couldn't stand being involved.

4) The closest we get to an answer is that, 'it was a matter of conscience' which doesn't necessarily mean he was a secret agent at all. From circumstantial evidence in the series we have built a vision of who Number Six really is. Unfortunately the truth is all of the evidence that is provided in the seventeen episodes doesn't really add up to a hill of beans. Perhaps McGoohan's production company name 'Everyman Films' wasn't so far from the truth anyway; as we can see it's very difficult to pin an occupation on a man who refuses to be a number.

Have you ever signed a contract with the company that you work for not to publicly reveal any private information about your work or customers. Does this make your job 'top secret' and 'confidential' too?

---

[35] Even these facts can be disputed — like much in 'The Prisoner' all is up to the individual's interpretation.

If this is the case be careful about handing in a letter marked 'private and confidential — by hand' to your boss or Human Resources department. After all do you really want to return home to the odour of anaesthetic gas coming through your keyhole!

36   Photograph courtesy of the Editor — *Village Square/Portmeirion Piazza 2006* prior to the permanent chessboards 'Arrival'.

Background on Portmeirion Shoot : September 1966.

The First Portmeirion Shoot needed a very experienced director so that a very distinctive look and feel was created in the initial episodes. McGoohan along with David Tomblin (who had incidentally cowritten the initial script for 'Arrival' with George Markstein) chose Don Chaffey to direct. They had been suitably impressed with his work on a number of episodes of 'Danger Man'. In many ways anyone who could comfortably direct the strong will of McGoohan would prove to be a bonus at this early stage.

The crew was largely drawn from the existing crew for 'Danger Man' as they had considerable experience both technically and working with the foibles of McGoohan. While speaking of these so called 'difficult qualities' that Patrick had it is important to note that Patrick wanted the absolute best he could get from everyone.[37] He could be uncompromising in this regard and indeed a number of directors would suffer the fate of being replaced by McGoohan as the series developed. However there are many tales of McGoohan accepting he had behaved wrongly towards cast and crew in pursuit of his creation of a startling end product. It was not out of character for Patrick to apologise to someone he had upset the very next day as an act of remorse.

Sidney Palmer as Property Buyer knew from the start that the Village required an emblem of some kind to tie the various aspects together. Jack Shampan had drawn various ideas to show to McGoohan and while they were acceptable they were not quite up to scratch. Patrick was looking for something iconic and memorable and happened to spot a penny farthing while away from the studio. He decided that this was exactly what he was looking for.[38]

The addition of the canopy to the emblem led to the mini-mokes, the signposts outside residences and even public address speakers in the Village having this added aspect attached.[39]

Gerald Kelsey, Vincent Tilsley and Anthony Skene were all asked by George Markstein to come up with ideas and scripts for the series at a very early stage. Unfortunately this meant that all of these scripts and McGoohan's own script that dealt with

---

[37] Kenneth Griffith in 'The Prisoner Investigated' and 'The Prisoner In Depth 6' by Steven Ricks, TR 7 Productions

[38] 'The Prisoner Investigated' TR7 Productions 1990

[39] Ibid

the concept of free elections all had the feel of being the second episode of the series. [40]

The solution ultimately made in this regard was to split these episodes across the first 9 episodes of the series. Many enthusiasts of the series still see this as illogical to this day, in particular dialogue of the type that Number Six uses in 'Dance of the Dead' such as 'I'm new here' and being unaware that he cannot enter the Town Hall without permission.

Angelo Muscat's role as the Butler is particularly interesting as his character is described as being tall and not out of place in an E type Jag in the original 'Arrival' script. [41] The 4ft 9in Actor from Malta brought a very different quality to his scenes. In particular he brought an enigmatic nature to the Butler never speaking and acting as a close assistant to the various Number Two authority figures who graced the Village. At the time of first broadcast there was even a suggestion that he might turn out to be the mysterious Number One character who was ultimately behind the operation of the Village. [42]

We see in 'Fall Out' the visceral image of a Number Six seemingly driven insane by the integrity of the communities efforts to break his mirror image. Is this an image of the dark heart of every human being — the part of us that is afraid to change things and seek out freedom for ourselves in whatever form we require? Is Number One the part of us imprisoned by financial circumstances, miserable soul-destroying jobs, loveless marriages, fear of losing control, addiction to alcohol or drugs or ill health amongst other circumstances?

In other words are we both a prisoner of ourselves and our own circumstances. Sometimes as in the Village escape is impossible; while sometimes it is not only within our grasp but achievable. With dedication and the help of others combined with the required willpower it may be possible to break free and be ourselves. [43]

---

[40] Ibid

[41] 'The Prisoner' Original Scripts Volume 1 Edited and Annotated by Robert Fairclough

[42] Carraze A & Oswald H 'The Prisoner' A Televisionary Masterpiece 1990, p233, W H Allen & Co plc

[43] Steven Ricks 'The Prisoner Investigated' and 'The Prisoner In Depth 1-6" were invaluable in writing this item

Reflections from an Original Fan...
by Ira Heffler

An older, "original" fan who watched the show during its initial broadcast...

I've been a member of this Facebook page[44] for a number of years, however — posting only an occasionally "like" and an even more rare comment or two — mostly as an observer.

But not anymore...

I'm probably one of the very few on this page who — at the age of 20 – watched 'The Prisoner' when it first aired in the United States as a summer replacement for the 'Jackie Gleason Show' in early June of 1968.[45]

It affected me profoundly.

And I needed to see it again. But this was well before DVDs and Blu-rays, let alone VCRs.

Finally – a few years later in the early 1970s — our local PBS (Public Broadcasting System) re-aired the episodes. I remember a psychologist sitting in a comfy armchair and — with his dog beside him wearing a red scarf — discussing each episode and offering his insights and interpretations.[46]

One of the best things about the show being repeated was that I was prepared; I had my camera ready (on a tripod) and took photos (slides) off the TV. Snapping away, I got many shots of the iconic opening.

In the 1970s, I joined the original 'Six of One Appreciation Society'. In the mail I received a packet including many one off sheets, a badge, a record album (45 rpm), and a penny farthing sticker. They also included a half-dozen glossy, black and white photographs which I mounted in a handsome frame. And they included a map of where much of the opening sequence was filmed.

I projected my slides of 'The Prisoner' opening sequence on my Kodak Carousel Slide Projector and coordinated it with the opening sequence music from the record I received

---

[44]   This was originally written for 'The Prisoner' Facebook page and is reproduced in full here.

[45]   'The Jackie Gleason Show' - Mr. Gleason's final variety series, which sometimes comprised of normal variety shows with top quality guest stars and on every other episode featured remakes of old "Honeymooners" sketches with a 'musical' twist. Ran for 83 episodes between 1966-1970.*

[46]   PBS stations often bought in British shows and repackaged them for US broadcast in this way.

* The Jackie Gleason Show had run in a previous form from 1952-1966

from the fan club. Not bad![47]

In the early 1980s I went on a vacation to England, Scotland, and Wales. The tour included Betwsy-y-Coed. The guide knew of 'The Prisoner.' I was told I was quite close to Portmeirion! But no one wanted to go with me. The guide, the bus driver, and some people on the tour bus, knowing of my passion for the series, urged me to go on my solo pilgrimage. I didn't go. To this day, it haunts me I didn't listen them... or to myself.

But my trip across the pond was not a total loss. When in London I set out to #1 Buckingham Place. My camera in one hand, my Six of One map in another, I headed out to find the home of Number 6.

I still remember rounding a corner... and suddenly there it was! I stood and stared at the building. I took a photo of the building, doing my best to mirror it from a snap shot I took off the TV, using the red mailbox to line it up. I still have the two photographs side-by-side in one frame.

I then walked up and opened the door. It was an office with women at typewriters. I stared at them; they stared at me. When I started to explain why I was there, one woman smiled and said she knew. I had the feeling they got this a lot.[48]

I went back outside and took more pictures. A chauffeur was watching me. He came up to me and was pleased to see me there. He told me when the show first aired in London, there was little traffic in the streets because people were home watching. And he told me how frustrated people were with the ending, calling the TV station and even tossing things at Patrick's home.

So why the visceral appeal of the show?

First, the unique look of the show. The sets, the Penny farthing, the chess game on the lawn, the unique letter font, the mini-mokes, the 'Tally Ho!' newspaper, the striped shirts, the flowing capes, the colourful umbrellas, the lava lights[49], the spherical chairs, the food in the refrigerator, the surveillance cameras, the phones, the badges with numbers, the blazers with the piping, the Lotus 7 with its KAR 120C license plate, Rover (I'm so glad the first, mechanical version was replaced), and of course Portmeirion itself.

Truly a costume designer's, art director's, and set decorator's dream. A different world was created... with an extremely impressive attention to detail.

---

[47]   Pre-video and the advent of the internet/downloads and streaming services this would be the closest you could get to watching the series.

[48]   1 Buckingham Place is still accessible, the front door has changed colour but you can still have your photo taken outside — just keep a lookout for an Austin Princess hearse!

[49]   Mathmos - the official manufacturer are still in existence today and you can buy a replica Prisoner lava lamp online.

But the look of the show is dependent on solid, effective cinematography.

The opening sequence is beautifully filmed and particularly impressive: the clap of thunder; the Lotus darting through traffic, then veering off; POV shots behind the steering wheel; and, as he purposefully walks down the corridor, ceiling beams casting shadows on his face. The sequence was shot with the production values of a major feature film. The opening set-up of this series is arguably the best TV opening ever done. It is truly iconic.

One more comment about the show's cinematography: with truly beautiful shots too numerous to mention here, I won't go into a review of each episode; however, that is a stunning shot of Mary Morris as the new Number 6/Peter Pan standing along the estuary.

And, of course, the strong, stirring music in the opening sequence. (I'm so glad Patrick nixed the first two themes.)

Plus the brilliant selection of other miscellaneous music: the ragtime march and the anthem. Yes, they're my ringtones!

But none of this really matters without the ambitious content and theme of the show.

I've always been fascinated with the question of what we do with people in our own government who know too much when they resign or retire. Either we kill them or we change their identity and put them in a relocation centre, maybe a farm in the middle of the country.

With the parting of George Markstein, I now understand the conflict of vision and the different direction the show took.

McGoohan wanted a metaphor, an allegory. The show was not about the village; it was about us. How cerebral and ambitious!

And ambiguous.

But on this we can all agree: the show is more relevant now than when it originated, 50 years ago. Especially given our digital age.

It's been a half a century, yet I vividly remember watching the final episode when it first aired in the States in September of 1968. At the ripe old age of 21, I remember feeling frustrated. But I was in conflict because it was so damn compelling. And I was at a huge disadvantage: no Internet to allow for discussion.

Was the last episode flawed? Perhaps. But given the circumstances and time pressure to get it done, it turned out amazingly daring, raw, and bold.

I still get a chill watching The Kid as he sticks out his thumb hoping to get a ride.

And hearing the beautiful, stirring music.

And that quick shot of Patrick's profile in London as we see his breath exhaled in the chilly air.

Watching Number 6 doing a jig in front of the bobby.

Watching Number 6 and the butler, holding hands, running along Whitehall. Honestly, is there a more exhilarating shot in the history of television? I think not.

Watching Leo McKern walking into London's Parliament building.

He and The Kid... a metaphor for the Establishment and Youth, rebellious and questioning authority.

Spoiler alert: Watching Number 6's apartment door opening on its own... and hearing the same motorised sound. It still gives me chills.

Brilliant.

Was there a numeral '1' on his front door? Was that actually planned? Brilliant.

The end credits listing Patrick McGoohan as 'Prisoner' (with no "The") is a smart implication that we all are prisoners. Brilliant.

And that final tight shot of Patrick's face as he speeds in his Lotus. The circle is complete. Snap to black.

Brilliant.

And now we have digital media with its DVDs and Blu-rays.

The BluRay is in such brilliant, pristine condition. Whoever is responsible for it obviously was in love with the series and must be applauded.

And we have the Internet, with it's sharing of 'information'... your ideas, theories, and photos.

Your comments are smart and articulate (i.e., one comment mentioned that the scenes shot on a soundstage with an obvious backdrop painting actually enhance the feel of the show, giving it a more surreal look. Agree or disagree, it's a compelling argument.)

And other comments are more witty and playful.

I particularly love the creative shot-for-shot parodies of the iconic opening. (I hope you all saw the young girl driving a lawnmower?) Imitation, of course, is the sincerest form of flattery.

And now it has been 50 years. I have little doubt that in another 50 years the show will continue to be revered by a new generation of intelligent, passionate fans same as yourselves.

Thank you...
and
Be seeing you...

Dictatorship and Democracy and its relation to 'The Prisoner' Or 'Everyone Votes for a Dictator' By Ed Fordham (BA.Hons. Politics)

Various key episodes and scenes in 'The Prisoner' bring out the nature of the conflict between the ideas and ideals of Dictatorship and Democracy. In 'Free for All' this conflict reaches its earliest extended study and Number Six states that, "Everybody votes for a Dictator" despite Eric Portman's 'Number Two' protestations of a 'democratic society'.

Examining the question of what democracy is has become difficult, particularly when we take into account the ever-changing almost 'polymorphic' nature of the term. We can trace a definition back as far as such luminaries as Plato, though perhaps given the nature of his ideas Pliny* should be factored out of any following discussion.

This will confine itself to major references to 'Free For All,' 'Dance of the Dead,' 'A Change of Mind' and the relevant sections of 'Once Upon A Time' & 'Fall Out' in order to be a more cohesive and coherent discussion. While other episodes can be perceived as being relevant to this discourse, these episodes will — as will become apparent — be key to what follows.

In any literal sense taking the Greek root word 'Demos' - from which we gain the word Democracy is a system of government by everyman (or 'the people' if you prefer) in society. It is a convoluted term — loaded with problems in definition :- ranging from the question of 'who' is considered to be the people to understanding when the government acts directly for 'the people' and when a dominant group or classes needs are emphasised. In 'Free for All' we are supposed to be convinced initially that the Village operates to protect the interests of 'the Villager's' however if they support anyone or anything that tries to govern them blindly can this be true? Certainly there is a fine line between this blind unthinking lumpen majority in a Democratic system and a society ruled by fear, scapegoating and iron will. While it is argued that one person's will cannot influence a Democracy significantly we need only look to the 1979-1992 period to see that this is not so in the United Kingdom. Can the infamous milk snatcher also be equated with the alcohol free Cat & Mouse Nightclub in 'Free for All'?

The Truth Test that Number Six is sent on leaves him spouting empty rhetoric : '(I'll) Do my best to give him [Number Two] a run for his money...'. In many ways he has been brainwashed to tow 'the party line'. He refers to freedom for Villagers as being the freedom to 'partake in other perhaps more hazardous sports' in return for providing the Village with the details they require from them. In effect Number Six is being turned into just another Village Administrator, or to put it in our 'real world' Party Leader. Increasingly the different parties and individuals within them squabble over details, although our experience suggests that no matter what happens the reality of our own lives will barely change.

'Fall Out' shows that chaos reigns when they try to run under democratic principles 'the Kid' & Leo McKern's 'Ex-Number Two' bite the Village's hand. When Number Six or 'Sir' takes the stand he is shouted down for his individualism 'I' reflecting his ego and the 'Aye' chant — like the voices of politicians in the Houses of Parliament. They agree tacitly but will not give him the opportunity to speak out.

So how by contrast do we define the term 'dictatorship' — could one group or one party or organisation largely getting their own way muddy the waters between a 'democracy' and a 'dictatorship'. What if rather than representing the people, the government represent their own self-interests — is the country still a liberal democracy just because the President or Prime Minister or Government Minister's say it is?

Dictatorship is rife in the Village as well — the physical slapping of Number Six by Number Fifty-Eight in 'Free for All' coupled with her menacing words and values metaphorically and physically indicate the return to an extremely centralised and unquestioned power-base. We get the impression that democracy is a bit of flimflam a facade as real as some off the facades built by Sir Clough Williams Ellis in Portmeirion.

The Green Dome is usually occupied by Number Two & The Butler only with the very occasional appearance of an aide or two for Number Two and on very rare occasions a Supervisor. The Butler serves Number Two (largely unthinkingly) until 'Once Upon A Times' final moments when he apparently becomes Number Six's closest ally.

The CCTV system is designed to prevent free-thinking individuals being able to pursue their myriad goals, against the authorities express wishes; regardless of their nature. Making your own decisions is treated as 'anti-social' in the Village — you do as you are told —as indicated in the experiment on the Rook inspired by Pavlov.

Postmodern theorists such as Baudrilliard argue that the central conflict between these two competing schools of thought and practice did not end with the collapse of the Berlin Wall and the so-called dismantling of Communism. Instead it is cogently asserted that we now witness 'The Illusion of The End' and that far from this proving Democracy to be winning out as the norm-the situation is as unreal as any fictional film or television programme. We witness instead a travesty of Democratic principles — a "grand parade of lifeless packaging" — to borrow a Peter Gabriel reference.[50] Democracy is systematically deboned and debunked by itself as it's so-called adherents support the rich and penalise and scapegoat those living below the breadline. In fact notably people in these circumstances often end up doing numerous good works for their local community as volunteers, expecting little in return. The idea that Government is "Of the people, By the people, For the people" is driven into the ground — like a boot stomping on a face forever.

"...we took the events in Eastern Europe at face value, with their good solid coin of freedom and 'democratic values', and the Gulf War, with its Human Rights and New World Order! These events were auctioned off well above their value. The historical scene today is like the art market."

51

Key to understanding the nature of Village society comes in the episode 'A Change of Mind' — as far back as the script for 'Arrival' there is a reference to PMCs or Public Minded Citizens. In this particular episode we discover the mirror image of PMCs - 'Unmutuals'
Yet the governmental system we might most identify with 'the Village' is that of a dictatorship. Al-

though the origins of this term in the Roman Republic gave an appointed person 'extraordinary powers' this was something that could only take place in military or civil crisis. The period was usually restricted to 6 months — the appointee had to have been recommended by the senate, nominated by a consul and have their position confirmed by the Comitia Curiata.[52]

[50] Jean Baudrillard, Trans. by Chris Turner, 'The Illusion of the End', Stanford University Press, California, 1994 p1-16

[51] Ibid p16-17

[52] Scruton R, (1983) 'A Dictionary of Political Thought' (p127)

In modern societies however the term dictatorship is applied somewhat differently as any society where a single individual, political party, group or organisation seizes power and wields it in an absolute fashion. By extension this leads to absolute rule with no legal restrictions no need for a formal or informal constitution, and the absence of other social or political groups interfering in the power of the state. [53] A dictator has become an increasingly important aspect of totalitarian regimes during the twentieth century therefore three key examples are Hitler's Germany, Stalin's Russia and Mussolini's Italy. They are governed in such a way as to not allow either opposition of any kind and to reduce personal freedom to virtually nill. In Marxist terms the Soviet system was given it's legitimate status by the concept of the 'dictatorship of the proletariat' which Marx saw to be of paramount necessity in historical terms following the revolution and destroying the bourgeoisie and the strength of their grip on power.

Unfortunately totalitarian regimes however seemingly cosy — the Village clearly teeters on the verge of this (often falling straight into the quagmire) while insisting it is a 'pocket democracy' — treat the general population with contempt.

 To take the Village example there is the mode of being relentlessly cheerful out of fear for most of the Villagers — note phrases such as "I've said too much...", "I've found out its wisest not to ask questions", "A Still Tongue Makes A Happy Life", "Questions Are A Burden For Others, Answers A Prison For Oneself" and so on. There's the constant surveillance and paranoia that this creates for everyone in the Village — suspicion and mistrust abound. The way the Village wants you to deal with all this is to be good and do exactly what they ask. Quite possibly it's only the value of Number Six that keeps him alive, the repeated mantra "We mustn't damage the (brain) tissue".

Those that stand firm against the Village frequently fail — Number Six's escape by helicopter in 'Arrival', the Speedboat chase in 'Free For All', even the recruitment drive in 'Checkmate' falls to pieces because those chosen think Number Six is a warder and not a Prisoner.

Note that except in 'Free for All' we never see any kind of evidence that the democratic process exists in the Village. Democracy is a pretence in 'The Prisoner' a piece of flimflam to keep the Villager's marching happily around the environs, to keep the brass bands playing and the umbrellas twirling. If they think they have some sort of choice it will stop the population rebelling. Usually this works well for this society but 'It's Your Funeral' muddies the waters... did the watchmaker's anger

[53] Oxford Reference : http://www.oxfordreference.com/view/10.1093/oi/authority. 20110803095716950?rskey=dCHZMk&result=10

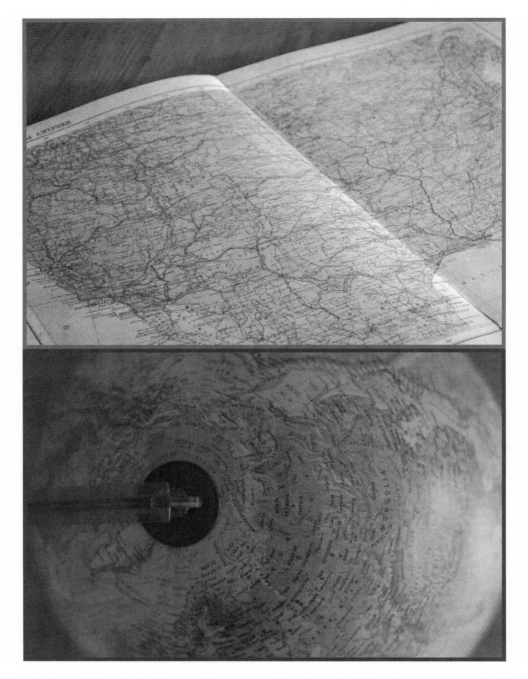

about the Village system lead to his co-option by Plan Division Q or did Number 1 Double Zero stir things up at the behest of his boss Number Two (Derren Nesbitt)?

All bets are off — why do they particularly want to strike back at Andre Van Gyseghem's Number Two : is it because of his age and length of service and he therefore has extensive knowledge about the Village which needs protecting or some other sinister reason. Also was the Watchmaker coerced into his plan by fair means or fowl — the Village Authorities drugged his daughter without her knowledge : perhaps they brainwashed her father into carrying out the assassination of Number Two? Shades of the 'Manchurian Candidate' or the NKVD's activities in this area.[54]

We only see the glimmer of 'Democracy' as we know it in 'Free For All' and it is as false and hollow as the democratic process can ever seem. Number Six wins because he toes the Village party line. He offers a 'limited freedom' — new sporting activities that are requested for example but only in exchange for the information the Village authorities. It is very much as if Number Six has absorbed the ideals of Village politics having undergone the truth test. Interesting the two shapes that move towards the silhouette of McGoohan's head represent truth and lies and the test ends when both shapes merge into his cranium. Metaphorically he accepts the Village truth — even if realistically it is made up of the Village's outpouring of lies that they are 'democratic...in some ways...'.

Yet is the truth regarding 'the Village' that it exists on the fringes of democracy and dictatorships — in many ways the vision of society we see is no less democratic than our own at times. A vote in the House of Commons on Article 50 and Brexit leading to key members of the Labour Party being sacked because they voted against 'Party Policy'. You see a democracy can be a democracy on its own terms :- 'Burn Beatles Memorabilia', 'Close Down The Coal Mines', 'Snatch Free School Milk Away From Our Nations Children', 'Start A War For Shady Reasons', 'Form a Government As A Minority Party - By Providing A £1.5 billion Sweetener To Get Another Party To Vote With You.' In reality you can choose to publicly protest and then the authorities will eventually arrest you - sounds like a dictatorship by proxy to me.

All photographs from https://stocksnap.io/ Free stock images with no copyright restrictions

---

[54] See page 221 for more on the possibilities of Brainwashing and Mind Control and the relevance they have to the series as a whole.

PETER DUNN'S A-Z OF ALLEGORY
B: BE SEEING YOU.
THIS ARTICLE WAS PREVIOUSLY PUBLISHED ON THE UNMUTUAL WEBSITE AND CAN BE FOUND AT:

www.theunmutual.co.uk/articleatozb.htm

Troyer: This is kind of a banal question, I guess, but if you could leave one sentence or paragraph in the head of everyone who watched The Prisoner series, the whole series, one thing for them to carry around for a while, when it was over, what would it be?

McGoohan: Be seeing you.

Troyer: Just that?.....Enigmatic to the end.

McGoohan: Be seeing you. That means quite a lot.

Troyer: It does indeed.

McGoohan: Be seeing you. Yeah.

The above extract from McGoohan's March 1977 interview with Warner Troyer for the Ontario Educational Communications Authority clearly gives us the ideal subject to explore in chapter B of our alphabetical odyssey through the allegories of 'The Prisoner' — "Be Seeing You"

Of course one has to take everything McGoohan says with a large pinch of salt. If we did not then at least one of his interviews would oblige us to look at the allegorical importance of coat hangers in "The Prisoner" in my next column! However lets us give him the benefit of the doubt on this occasion and explore the importance of a phrase which normally adorns the end of articles on "The Prisoner" but on this occasion begins one.

I know what many of you who know me well are thinking (and everything you think here is in the strictest confidence of course) — you believe I am about to use the "Be seeing you" salute as a sneaky way of discussing links between 'The Prisoner' and Christianity. Well, I am not going to — much rubbish has been talked about the "Be seeing you" salute as being a version of the ancient Christian "icthous" or fish sign that early persecuted Christians used to secretly identify each other and which in more modern times often appears on the rear end of cars owned by Christians. To suggest the salute is based on that symbol is clearly nonsense as the salute looks nothing like the icthous. I shall of course cover the issue of religion in a future column (those of you who know your alphabet and my religious leanings can probably work out exactly how soon......).

OK so the salute is not an ancient Christian symbol —what is it then? Well, like much in the show it is what it says it is — a clear visual and verbal reference to visual observation. The words "Be seeing you" are accompanied by an action in which the thumb and finger encircle the eye — the organ of visual observation. Is it that simple then? Just a reference to the fact that each Villager is being watched? Does this mean that, 'The Prisoner' is simply '1984' packaged as a TV action adventure?

There are some clear parallels '1984s' Big Brother and the Village both make use of paranoia as a means of social control. Both societies use their own citizens to spy on each other. No one knows who are the warders/thought police and who are the prisoners/ thought criminals. Betrayal to authority by one's friends and lovers is a theme of both the book/film and the show. For instance Number Six is kept under observation by the Queen in 'Checkmate' who is encouraged by the Village's mind control techniques to fall in love with Number Six and then unwittingly allows the Village to use her to keep tabs on its most difficult Prisoner. Similarly in '1984' the thought police allow and encourage Winston Smith's "sex crimes" with Julia until it reaches the point where they can reel them both in for reindoctrination.

Again in 'Checkmate'" Number Six finds himself betrayed by the paranoia of a friend (the Rook) in a similar way to how friends and relations betray each other in '1984'. 'Checkmate' and 'Arrival' are perhaps the two most Orwellian episodes of "The Prisoner" with their focus on paranoia, betrayal, and high tech observation and control. However it has always amused me how the Village authorities seem to have missed a key trick explored by Orwell. In '1984' the authorities make great use of televisions with a two way visual function which let the thought police see into every home and which can never be turned off. In the Village, either because of a misreading of '1984' or budget cuts at the town hall, it is the radios — not the televisions — that refuse to be switched off! It will not surprise you to learn that aside from that somewhat facetious example I believe that 'The Prisoner' is much more than a televisual recycling of Orwell's exploration of dictatorship.

Let us look more closely at the "Be seeing you" salute. We have already seen that it contains a double emphasis on visual observation. The eye is in every way the centre of the salute and this is not the only time that the eye and sight take on metaphysical dimensions in the show.

There are other references to the eye throughout the show ie the close up on the Professor's eye during the speed learn process in 'The General, and the movement of the square and circle towards Number Six's silhouetted eye during the civil servant's interrogation in 'Free for All'. But out of 17 episodes there is one which stands out as the metaphysical motherlode of the series. If you want to find allegory and double meaning, go to 'Fall Out'. This episode positively brims with half rendered meanings, allegorical asides and attempts at explanation. It is no surprise that eye symbols and semi mystical discussions of sight and seeing abound here. Some of these could perhaps be packaged in Orwellian terms — such as Number One being rendered for the first half of the episode as a giant opening and closing eye on the rocket. But even here we begin to see that this may mean a little more than a crude reference to surveillance. Let us examine the many references to sight in Leo McKern's dialogue during his confrontation with the eye. The underlining that follows is mine not the scripts:

No2: This is the nearest I've ever been. Watch. He gets annoyed if you look at him for too long. Shall I give him a stare?
President: You transgress!
No2: I'll give him a stare. Look me in the eye. Whoever you are. Whatever you are.
President: You'll die!

No2: Let me die. I'll die with my own mind you evil smelling demon. You'll hypnotise me no longer! <u>Look me in the eye.</u> (...HE LEANS FORWARD AND SPITS <u>INTO THE HEART OF THE EYE)</u>[55]

Obviously there is something more than mere observation and control going on here but it is unclear as to what. It also goes on a little to long simply to be an amusing reference to Leo McKern's artificial glass left eye — and besides that has already been done once with the suggestion that his character "wink a blind surveillance eye" In 'Chimes'. It does begin to get a little clearer later in the episode when Number Six gets his chance to wax metaphysical about the question of sight as the next section of dialogue shows (again the underlining that follows is mine not the scripts):

P: Why?
President: You are pure. You know the way. Show us.
P: Why?
President: Your revolt is good and honest. You are the only individual and we need you.
P: <u>I see.</u>
President: You do. You see all.
P: I'm an individual?
President: You're on your own.
P: <u>I fail to see.</u>
President: All about you is yours. We concede. We offer. We plead for you to lead us.[56]

At last it becomes clear the observation and detention of the Prisoner within the Village has not been to control him, in the way suffered by the citizens of Air Strip 1 in '1984,' but to test him and watch him in the hope that will get that illusive "information" they have sought since his capture.

That 'information' is not a collection of facts and data but is his direction, his leadership, and his vision. They lack and covet his single-minded sense of purpose and his clear individuality. They seek answers which they hope that his vision will supply. However he sees his vision as personal to him and is loathe to share it and therefore dilute it.

The Village has thus doubly lost. It failed to disprove or undermine his individuality or his strength and vision and they fail to share in those strengths of character as he rejects them ("I fail to see"). This may help to explain the chants of the delegates as he makes his final speech. I often thought what they were chanting was "I, I, I, I,...". However the script makes clear that what in fact they are chanting is "Aye, Aye, Aye,..." Is it too much to point out the visual and audible resemblance of this word to "eye"?? Perhaps it was meant to convey all three - I, Aye, Eye.

At the very last the metaphor of sight and vision is used again when Number Six confronts Number One - is this a version of Number Six who did dilute and corrupt his vision? Does the foresight of the crashing bars in the crystal ball held by Number One give Number Six a future vision of the prison he will make for himself if he does share his individuality with the

---

[55] Leo McKern as No.2 and Kenneth Griffith as President from 'Fall Out' - P.McGoohan c.End 1967/ early 1968

[56] Quote from 'Fall Out' written by Patrick McGoohan c.late1967/early 1968

Village?

What then is McGoohan trying to say? I think he is saying "find your own vision" — and when you have found it cherish it and do not dilute it by sharing it with others. I am not very comfortable with this message. Those of you who know me well know I subscribe to a vision that cries out be shared. If you want to know more about that vision read my next column. If not I will be seeing you at column D - perhaps in more ways than we can currently imagine.......

BCNU
Peter Dunn

'The Jailbird' © Steve Matt Reproduced With Permission

Looking Out For
Number One
A New Look at Themes and Tropes in
'The Prisoner'
By VJ Clarke BA (Hons), FVCM

Everyman for Himself!

One of the great questions poised to viewers of The Prisoner is the great question, "Who is Number One?" But the question which gets rarely raised is a much more fundamental one. Who is Number Six?

We are primed from the opening titles of Arrival to view this mystery man as an Everyman. This of course was McGoohan's intention, and the reason he gave his production company this enigmatic moniker. The Everyman character is one of the oldest in literature, and dates back to a medieval morality play of the same name. The medieval Everyman was an individual, who like our main protagonist is stripped of individuality and defining features. He gives us as the viewer a character who we can freely identify with, an ordinary individual in extraordinary circumstances, so that we can imagine how we would act or react in their situation. Because of this, the Everyman has no special

---

[57] VJ Clarke is the New Number Two — courtesy VJ Clarke

skills, magical powers or superior intellect or knowledge which the everyday man would not possess. This allows the Everyman character to occupy the role of protagonist without being a "hero". One of the most famous Everyman characters in English literature appears in John Bunyan's Pilgrim's Progress, a "morality" story with many similarities to The Prisoner. Other well known Everyman characters from English literature, movies and theatre are Shakespeare's Bottom, from a Midsummer Night's Dream, Bilbo Baggins from the Lord of the Rings, Arthur Dent from The Hitchhiker's Guide to the Galaxy, Emmett from The Lego Movie, Walter Mitty and in a slight variation on the theme, the majority of the Doctor's companions in Doctor Who. Sometimes the Everyman is an Everywoman, such as in the cases of Dorothy in Frank L Baum's Oz stories, Lewis Carroll's Alice, and Margaret Attwood's Offred in The Handmaid's Tale. (We will look closer at these in a later chapter) All these represent the "accidental hero", an ordinary person finding themselves in an extraordinary situation, rather than someone who's job as a lawman, spy or soldier leads them to seek out adventure and drama, and save the day. Very often too, the Everyman's journey is a personal one in which they learn deep truths about themselves and in the end are able to "rise to the occasion" and out do themselves.

The 1973 concept album by Genesis, 'The Lamb Lies Down on Broadway' is a great example of the modern day 'morality play'. It is, in essence, a retelling of Henrik Ibsen's classic fairy story 'Peer Gynt'. In Peer Gynt, the titular hero is a deeply flawed and irresponsible character who is betrothed to be married to the ever patient maiden Solvieg. However, Peer is led astray into hedonism in the world of the trolls, and finds himself guilty of raping the daughter of the Mountain King, his punishment, - to be made into a troll himself. The rest of Peer's journey is of self redemption, whist all along back in his homeland Solvieg is growing old, she remains faithful to him until the time that he returns to her as a reformed man. He is finally found and reformed by the Button Maker, who considers him a button which was not cast correctly and has to be melted down and recast, so he can be reunited with his patient, ageing and self depreciating lover, Solvieg. In Peter Gabriel's "Lamb" story, a similar fate befalls his hero, Rael. Rael is a New York Puerto Rican character based on the characters in the then extremely popular opera, West Side Story, although his name is deliberately spelled Rael instead of Raul, which would be correct, but Rael has several meanings, firstly it's an anagram of Real, and shows his struggle to tell fantasy from reality, secondly it allows the phrase Is Rael or Israel, which underlines the recurring messianic motif of the piece. There is a third and maybe now arcane meaning, Raelians are a fringe religious cult who believe the human race were descended from aliens, and that the aliens will return to save us.

Like Peer, Rael is led into the underworld in order to rescue his twin brother John, who has been imprisoned there. He sees his brother herded into a processing plant with many other people from his old gang, where he is stamped on the forehead with a number, Number 9. After a series of bizarre and surreal events, he is tempted into an underground limpid pool, where he is seduced, this time, not by a troll maiden but by the Lamia, who are snake like creatures with the faces and torsos of attractive women. After he eats of their flesh, he is transformed into the deformed monstrosity with gigantic testicles, the Slipperman, and the only way he can be saved from this fate worse than death is to be castrated by Doktor Diaper. In a very Prisoner like twist, Rael finally catches sight of his brother and pursues him into the rapids. John falls into a river and is drowning, but Rael throws himself in to save him, and dragged his body back to the shore. When he finally turns the drowned man over onto his back, the face he sees is not his brother at all, but himself. There are many similarities in this story to The Pilgrim's Progress and the aforementioned Peer Gynt, both are stories of Everyman characters led into temptation, broken, treated and eventually redeemed, just as Number 6 is in The Prisoner.

However, despite McGoohan's allusions to Number 6 as an Everyman, he fails the remit for several reasons. Firstly, Number 6 is what is called in literature a "dynamic character". This means that his character undergoes development during the course of the story. He is not in anyway a two dimensional character either, instead a highly complex and mercurial individual with hidden motives and inner conflicts. It too is open to debate whether he is even a sympathetic character. Sympathetic characters in fiction can be either heroes or villains, but are essentially characters who we choose to side with emotionally. There is always some form of emotional manipulation going on in order to elicit this response. Heroines are often described as gentle, graceful and beautiful, the same applies to heroes being handsome, noble and altruistic. Characters who show emotion, humility, shed tears, and act selflessly, out of love of a significant other, or the sheer kindness of their hearts. You as the reader, identify with their situation and root for them, which makes underdogs and outcasts such popular dramatic fare. Although physically imposing, Number 6 (McGoohan) is not what you might call conventionally handsome. A Disney Prince he is not. We are never emotionally manipulated into sympathizing with him. He rarely shows any emotion above a simmering, righteous anger. After all, Number 6 is a man with a strong moral principles. He never shows any sign of weakness, even when subjected to mind control and torture. Although put into a situation beyond his control, an underdog he is not, and as for humility and selflessness, well, you get the picture. Ironically, the much maligned and "unloved" 2009 AMC miniseries creates a "6" played by Jim Cavaizel (Jesus from Passion of the Christ) who much better fits the remit for an "Everyman", although it's actually his lack of charisma which makes the series so uninteresting. (As a side note, Ian McKellan is great in his Number 2 role).

"O Superman!" Laurie Anderson 1981

Secondly, Number 6 is a Hero. I write this in capitals because it is so important to understand this in the context of the series as a whole. There is a recurring trope which defines the action movie genre, which is sometimes called either the Jason Bourne effect, or the Jason Statham effect. The Jason Statham trope exists because Statham himself is a stereotype of himself. It is difficult to see Statham in any role except the stereotypical badass, he has not as yet made a kiddy movie like Schwarzenegger's Jingle All The Way, or Vin Diesel's Pacifier. (although he does play a pastiche of himself in Melissa McCarthy's movie Spy) Statham, in a similar way to McGoohan plays all of his characters as himself, never conceding to show a softer nature, or a warm smile. He has become the trope. Likewise, in the Bourne series, Matt Damon portrays a "bullet proof hero", who's both physically and mentally superior despite suffering amnesia, and numerous failed attempts to kill him. In the action genre, it is not only common, but a requisite to exaggerate the Hero's abilities beyond what is humanly possible. That is what makes cinema so exciting. It lets the Lone Ranger ride a horse on top of a locomotive, Indiana Jones to survive a nuclear bomb blast by hiding inside a fridge, and the Fonz from Happy Days to "Jump the Shark" (it's this scene the trope gets its name from) because more often than not, the effect is ridiculous and incredulous and designed as "ratings bait". (The Scotsman critic, Stephen McGinty would save this judgment for Living In Harmony)

Instead of being given an Everyman we can relate to, we are given a Superman to admire and aspire to. For this reason, it is difficult to see Number 6 as anything but the second, a hero with exaggerated superhuman abilities, who can out-fox anybody with his towering intellect, win at a sport which doesn't exist, destroy a supercomputer with an existential crisis, correct his mind control by deliberately electrocuting himself, perform gymnastics and water skiing before breakfast, be a great horseman and fastest gun in the West, last eighteen days at sea living on a single can of corned beef and take three men in a fight!!! Now, I'm sure that Pat was a very fit man when he made the series, but not superhuman. It's hard to see how the action hero stereotype fits with the idea of the theatrical Everyman, although these constraints would have been purely commercial, super heroes sell, and action gets better ratings pound for pound than talky intellectual stuff. It is less common to see the combination of brains and brawn we see in Number 6. Superman can fire lasers out of his eyes, lift trucks into the air with one hand, create hurricanes with his breath and fly, but rarely do Superman's endeavors require any mental exertion.

From the outset, Number 6, all bulging forehead and icy blue eyes is portrayed as a mental force to be reckoned with, which puts him more in the "mastermind" league of the super villain, the Lex Luthors, Blofelds and the Hannibals than the muscle bound action hero. It's quite funny to see the brilliant Prisoner pastiche "Brainwashed" from Steven Spielberg's classic cartoon, Pinky and the

Brain, how well Brain slots into McGoohan's role, to comic effect. (Except it's the Land of Hats, instead of the Village) Patrick's earlier role, that of John Drake was also a man who used his wits before resorting to violence, and unlike his compatriot, James Bond, very rarely carried a gun and never appeared in gratuitous sexual scenes. This of course was contrary to the studio's wishes, but Patrick was a moral (and some would argue deeply religious) man who stood by his principles, this is why it is so easy to read aspects of Pat into the characters he portrayed, rather than allowing them to become transparent. You can more or less boil down all the actors in Hollywood into two groups. There are the highly skilled, chameleon type "method actors", able to slip into the skin of any character and become another person, (try Daniel Day-Lewis) and then there are the actors who have so strong and willful a presence that they only ever appear to play characters who are basically exaggerations of themselves. (Like Nicolas Cage) Patrick was definitely of the second variety, almost laughably so. He even managed to take characters written by somebody else and negotiate script rewrite after script rewrite until he was happy with it sitting both morally and intellectually within his principles. Whilst the studio was writing an "kiss, kiss, bang, bang" action hero, a la Bond, to Pat, Drake was a more cerebral character, with a much less hedonistic bent and a sturdier moral compass. Bond needs his Q to kit him out with the tools he needs to win. Drake's technology isn't "magic" like Bonds, it's based on real world technology which a real secret agent would have access to in the sixties. Drake needed his wits about him and was always really to use his brain before his fists. Pat was clearly profoundly erudite, proud of his mental capacities, and brought this characteristic to his screen roles. But would our Everyman hero really read Goethe in the original German (Faust, presumably) or quote Shakespeare, as Number 6 did?

The genius as hero is most commonly associated detective characters such as Sherlock Holmes, but finds later expression in characters such as Lisbeth Salander of Stiig Larsson's Millennium Trilogy and Harry Potter's Hermione Granger. (Ironically, this trope, as late, has been applied to female characters who buck the trend for brainiac nerds, and provide positive role models as a contrast from the eye candy, damsels in distress or sexual conquests common in the 1960's/70's action genre, and still common now) Marvel's Tony Stark, aka Iron Man is a great example, no great physical threat without his eponymous Iron Man suit, likewise Bruce Banner is no circus strong man unless you get him really angry!

The stereotypical "clever" character is very often portrayed as having poor social skills, (Big Bang Theory's Sheldon Cooper) or appearing "dorky" bespectacled or unfit, (Leonard Hofstadter, also from the Big Bang Theory, or corduroy clad liberal Graham Garden from the Goodies) so it is rare to see a character both brainy and muscular, charming and debonair. In other words, Drake and Number 6 are perfect. They are perfect examples of mankind, in both mind and body, the paragon of Nietzsche's Übermensch. This imaginary Superman, taken to extremes by the Nazi master race eugenics breeding programs and the resulting evil, "ethnic cleansing", and euthanasia or forced sterilization of human beings who do not make the grade, is the aspirational model represented, and culturally enforced by the action hero of popular fiction. Not an Everyman, but Beyond Man, an "Over Man".

Opposite Numbers

So when is the Everyman an Everywoman? This is a fair question and one worth exploring. In most literature, there is something of a Smurfette Principle. This idea comes from the popular kids comic The Smurfs, whereby all the Smurfs are male and are defined by their occupations or interests, except for poor Smurfette, who is only defined by her femaleness. (also the fact she was created by the evil wizard Gargamelle in order to lead the male Smurfs astray) The default is male, and the "other" is female. When you consider the invisibility of women in many of the great classics, it is really rather shocking. Women in these writings take secondary roles, that of wives, mothers, secretaries and disposable sex objects, but are never the hero. The Bechdel Test is a test of sexism in fiction, and asks whether a work contains at least two named female characters, who converse with each other about something other than a man. Even Number 2 and Bo Peep, thought emancipated characters in Dance of the Dead fail, as they are discussing the fate of a man, Number 6. The Prisoner is not alone, almost all of its contemporaries from the 1960s and earlier, miserably fail this simple test. The Everyman character ordinarily is a generic template that both male and female readers or viewers are intended to relate to, in essence a cookie cutter character we can project our own values on. There is an assumption that writings by men represent the human experience, when in fact, they only represent half of it. That is not to say that Everywoman characters do not exist. Here are several examples from literature and TV, which have been created by female authors.

In Margaret Attwood's dystopia 'The Handmaid's Tale', the USA has after a bitter civil war, fallen to a fundamentalist Christian religious cult called 'The Republic of Gilead' which has removed all women's rights. Years of radioactive fallout, chemical weaponry and pollution has rendered most women infertile, so the powerful men have adopted the practice of imprisoning fertile young women as breeding stock. June, renamed "Offred", or "Of Fred" to show which commander she belongs to, has the bad luck of being fertile and suitable handmaid material, so is given to Commander Waterford, where she is forced into unconsential sex so she can bear his child. Taking her name and her identity is a form of dehumanization similar to the numbers in The Village, as is the mode of dress the handmaids wear. It brings to mind the Taliban and the fundamentalist Islamic cultures in the Middle East and the way women are robbed of their identity, bodily autonomy and rights, be being denied freedom, dignity, education, property and self-expression. Some fundamentalist Christian sects, especially those in the USA, such as Quiverfull, Mormonism and the Amish are surprisingly close to The Republic of Gilead in real life.

Katniss Everdeen is the hero of Suzanne Collins' Hunger Games trilogy. This is another dystopian drama set in the futuristic North American nation of Panem. The country has been divided into poor ghettos, where the residents are used for cheap labour or slavery, while the elites rule from the prosperous and decadent Capitol. Katniss is from the impoverished District 12 area, takes her sister's place in the yearly battle known as "the Hunger Games" where two "tributes", young men and women aged between 12 and 16 are forced to fight to the death in an elaborately staged TV reality show. The reward is food, clothing and medical supplies for the destitute citizens of their District. Katniss starts out as a naive young woman, but soon discovers the conspiracy of power behind the Hunger Games, and becomes a revolutionary leader, leading the denizens of the Districts against the corrupt political hierarchy of the Capitol. This story is similar to several other dystopias depicted on-screen, from Soylent Green, Logan's Run to the Schwarzenegger vehicle "The Running Man", which is based on a similar premise, in which convicted criminals are forced to fight to the death on a prime time TV reality show. Oddly, this idea was very prescient, reality TV in that form, the neo gladatorial combat, didn't exist back in the eighties. The Japanese film, Battle Royale was a big influence on the Hunger Games, in that story too, children are forced to fight to the death for sadistic entertainment purposes.

The series which I feel has the most in common with The Prisoner is the Divergent series by Veronica Roth, as it questions identity, intelligence and personality traits, and what it means to conform. Chicago, of the post apocalyptic future, has been divided into five factions based on the attributes and temperament traits of its denizens. Abnegation (selfless), Amity (peaceful), Candour (honest), Dauntless (brave) and Erudite (intellectual). Each child is undergoes a psychological aptitude test at the age of 16, where, like a twisted version of Harry Potter's Sorting Hat ceremony, they are sorted into the faction which best suits their personality type. However, some people do not fit into any one group, and therefore cannot join any faction, these people have no civil rights and are made to live as pariahs from society with the rest of the "factionless". Our Number 6 style character is Tris Prior, a young woman who is born into the Abnegation faction. When she is tested, she shows the rare quality of equal traits of several factions, so she is branded "Divergent". Divergent people are regarded as very dangerous as they can think independently, and are therefore harder for the government to control. In a society where we value psychometric testing, IQ tests, and personality profiling and are willing to gamble children's futures on the eleven plus and grammar school selection, we can see a foreshadowing of this dystopia in our modern age, and that truly is frightening. Tris, like Katniss, becomes something of a revolutionary, and sets out with the mysterious fellow Divergent "Four", (so named because he shares traits of four different factions) to discover what secrets the government are hiding from them, and what really exists outside the city walls.

"Why, sometimes I've believed as many as six impossible things before breakfast" - Alice through the Looking Glass

When I first started writing this essay, there had been a recent discussion on one of the Facebook Prisoner fan groups regarding Ridley Scott directing a remake of the Prisoner. After the failure of the 2009 AMC series, this was not a popular suggestion. After choosing and suggesting male actors to play Number 6, from encumbent Bond, Daniel Craig, to Homeland's Damien Lewis, all of which received unfair comparison to Patrick McGoohan, I suggested, thinking outside the box, Tilda Swinton. I was surprised that so many people were aghast at casting a female Number 6, as it had worked up to a point with the Alice Drake character in the DC Shattered Visage comic book series, Broken Sea's audio drama adaptation and it's audio sequel Torchbearer.

As it is the current fashion to "remake" old dystopian dramas with young female protagonists, remaking The Prisoner based on this model makes some sense. If it were not for Soylent Green, Logan's Run, The Running Man and 1984, there would be no Divergent or The Hunger Games. The Lawnmower Man, in which a man with learning disabilitiesis made superhuman by the use of technology, even resurfaced in the Scarlett Johansson movie Lucy. While I was thinking about this trope, it occurred to me that casting a woman as the lead in The Prisoner was not as odd as it sounds, because the odd surreal setting of The Village is unlike these post apocalyptic dystopias, and much more like Wonderland and Oz. So our male protagonist is already subverting this trope, which is usually reserved for young female heroes, from Alice to Dorothy on to more recent characters like Neil Gaiman's Coraline, and the little girls Susan and Lucy who along with their brothers are transported to Narnia through C.S. Lewis's magic wardrobe into a land ruled by a cruel witch. Number 6's arrival in The Village has more than a touch of Alice in Wonderland about it. (Number 6 plays the same part in the Checkmate chess game as Alice, in a nod to this, White Queen's Pawn) The Village appears to be benign, but just like Wonderland and Oz there is something nasty bubbling under the surface. Instead of finding witches and flying monkeys, he has to take on a series of Number 2's, each hell bent on destroying his sanity. His departure is just as odd as his arrival, was it all a dream? Is he still a Prisoner? Will he ever wake up?

There is a also beautifully animated 2013 movie, written and directed by Israeli filmmaker Ari Folman, called "The Congress", which is loosely based on the book "The Futuralogical Congress" by Stanisław Lem, the Cold War satirist who also wrote Solaris. In this we have an Alice in Wonderland, everywoman character, Robin Wright, played by the real life actress Robin Wright. In a metaphysical twist, she is essentially playing herself, although the details of her on-screen personal life are fictional. In the movie, Robin is reaching the end of her acting career, but her agent offers her the chance to be digitised, so that Miramount studios can use a digital facsimile of her in future movies. Struggling to bring up a disabled son, Aaron, who is fast becoming blind and deaf, she accepts the offer. Fast forward twenty years, Robin, now in her mid sixties, is summoned to Abrahama City, to speak at Miramount Studio's Futuralogical Congress. Abrahama City is an animated zone, accessed by taking an ampule of a hallucinogenic drug, in order to become a cartoon avatar of one's self. Robin's digital likeness has become a lucrative product in the future, and Miramount have even patented a new technology to enable anyone to transform themselves into her, by eating or drinking her digital code. Robin is horrified at this prospect, and speaks out about it, and soon the Congress is attacked by violent protesters opposed to the technology. Robin, assisted by her lead animator Dylan, go on the run, and they fall in love, but Robin dearly wishes to return to the real world to be reunited with her son, instead of living in a world where you can be anyone, or do anything.   The real world is in a state of misery and disrepair, as most people are choosing to live in the brightly colored magical delusion of the animated world. Robin is told that Aaron, now blind and deaf, had chosen to cross over, but she wouldn't be able to find him as he had created a new cartoon identity for himself. Unable to return to Dylan, as that world was simply a product of her subconscious, Robin chooses to relive her son's early years, by taking an ampule, and choosing to take his animated form.

Like The Prisoner, the film explores the concepts of identity and personal agency, and takes place in a idyllic utopia, visually inspired by Heironymus Bosch's famous triptych, The Garden of Earthly Delights.

"Call me prissy Pat, I see TV as the third parent. Every week a different girl? Served up piping hot for tea? With the children and grannies watching?" - Patrick McGoohan

It's interesting to consider sexuality when discussing Number 6 as the universal everyman. I think there has been a tenancy to avoid this topic, as most know about Patrick McGoohan's Catholicism, and the reason he avoided contact with members of the opposite sex whilst filming, even getting his teenage daughter to stand in for sexy Russian spy Nadia in The Chimes of Big Ben. From the episode Do Not Forsake Me, Oh My Darling, we can assume Number 6 is engaged to by married to his boss's daughter, Janet Portman. However, he does not seem to have any family ties, or any significant others, and if he does, did he act like he misses them? Not one bit. There is no longing, only anger. He is angry because he is imprisoned and manipulated, not because he is being kept from his loved ones. I would personally consider Number 6 to be aromatic and asexual. He keeps his distance from all female characters, (and their cats) often being aggressive and obnoxious around them, especially the maids and poor Number 8 in Checkmate who had been brainwashed into falling in love with him. (Nadia in The Chimes of Big Ben is also a Number 8, he also meets her during a chess game, go figure) Even the flirty Mrs Butterfield fails to break through his armor, even though she gave him tea and cakes. Despite this, I think it is his asexuality which makes him relatable by people of all genders and sexual orientations. He does not view women as disposable conquests like so many heroes on the TV and in movies. In fact, most female characters fare pretty well on The Prisoner, compared to the everyday sexism you find in most TV shows of the era, women can be scientists, super spies, supervisors, even Number 2, or Death herself.

The character I would say who has the deepest emotional connection with Number 6 is Leo Mc Kern's version of Number 2. This relationship of mutual respect, and dare I say, fear, is first encountered in The Chimes of Big Ben, then taken to it's natural conclusion in Once Upon A Time. Psychologists talk about a phenomena called "transference", where the patient redirects their feelings for a another person such as a significant other or family member onto their therapist. This is what happens during Degree Absolute, where Number 2 takes Number 6 through Shakespeare's "Seven Ages of Man", by first becoming his teacher, then his commander and finally his judge. Whether anything homoerotic can be read into this is a matter of opinion, but there is an interesting S&M interplay whereby Number 2's enters the Embryo Room as the dominant party, but ends up being the submissive. As Number 2 quotes the marriage ceremony, the sacred vow "Till Death do us Part", he's talking about his own death, as he and Number 6 are bonded together till the bitter end. There is an old adage that if you kill someone, you have married them, as they will stay with you for life. In the case of Number 6 and Number 2, this is certainly true.

Who is Number Six?

So now we have explored Number 6's role as a hero or an Everyman, it's time to take a look at the clues we are given in the series regarding his backstory. The Prisoner appeared on television during an era of deep seated paranoia about Communism, the nuclear bomb and "moral decline" brought about by feminism and the Civil Rights movement. McCarthyism inspired the witch hunt allegory The Crucible, and thousands of Americans were being falsely accused of being communist sympathizers and interrogated by private committees in "kangaroo courts", particularly union members, academics, musicians, actors, screenwriters, directors and other entertainment industry professions, leading to many people losing their jobs and livelihoods unfairly, and be put on the Hollywood Blacklist. If you look back to early Bond movies, and other examples from the era such as The Man From UNCLE, The Saint, the Avengers etc, they appear very dated to the modern viewer, but for the most part, The Prisoner has aged very well. Maybe this is because it was "ahead of its time", and now modernity is finally catching up with McGoohan's vision. The reason that The Prisoner has aged so well is that despite its allusions to the contrary, it is not a spy drama or a Cold War piece. The Prisoner's predecessor, Danger Man was conceived by Ralph Smart, and in a wonderfully circular irony, begins in the Village. Brian Clements, who later created The Avengers penned the pilot episode, 'View from the Villa', which although set in Roma, Italy, due to budget constraints was filmed in the beautiful Italianate village of Portmeirion, North Wales. Something must have resonated deep within McGoohan, as it was this very location he would choose for his Prisoner's gilded cage. It was Danger Man, known as Secret Agent in the USA, which made a star of McGoohan, and led him to be twice offered the role of James Bond, which he declined on moral grounds. Patrick was the biggest paid TV actor in the United Kingdom, but had had unhappy experiences with the movie industry, under contract with Rank, who had signed him for his looks and boxing skills, but hadn't challenged him as an actor, casting him as stereotypical bad boys. His favorite theatrical role was as Brand, who he personally empathised with, a tormented Priest, at odds with the world and dedicated to doing God's will, sacrificing his family and material bonds for the sake of his his parishioners eternal souls. He got to play this role once again for the BBC as part of their World Theatre series. McGoohan won the Best Actor BAFTA TV Award in 1960, surprisingly for an actor of his calibre, the only major award he won, other than two Primetime Emmys, both for roles on Colombo.

So what do we know about our hero? Throughout the series, we can piece together a backstory, but even then, we are fed false and conflicting information. The show begins with the man we come to know of as Number 6 speeding past the Houses of Parliament in his Lotus Super 7, eye-catching and eccentric in it's 1960's green and gold, actually Golden Virginia's racing colours from the days when smoking was cool and motor sport was sponsored by the tobacco companies. His face is set in determination, the wind blowing the hair back from his proud forehead, he is the embodiment of the "man on a mission". It's at once awesome and iconic. The car is tiny and somewhat impractical for this imposing character, like a glorified go cart, a feisty little buggy revving it's little heart out like a roaring tiger disguised as a pussy cat. The Lotus Seven, and the later Caterham models were banned from racing in the USA, in the sixties, then later in the UK for "being too fast". This unorthodox choice of car at one sets our hero apart as a maverick, an anarchist from the very start. The car first offered to McGoohan by Lotus was an Elan, but these had already seen heavy rotation in the Avengers and so forth, and had become boring. Choosing the Elan would have been little more than more product placement by Lotus. As the story goes, Patrick saw the Seven in the yard and told them emphatically, "that's the car I want". A first act as an auteur, with a distinct vision always two steps ahead, confusing and frustrating to those who wanted to put him in a neat little box labeled "Prime Time TV".

It was Patrick who produced the fifty page 'show-bible' for the writers and producers to work from. In it, he outlined everything significant about Village life, from the food they ate to the clothes they wore, what music the listened to, what they did for fun. McGoohan even concocted the rules for the bizarre martial art of "Kosho", the Village's equivalent to Quiddich in the Harry Potter universe, played on two trampolines straddling a pool of water, the winner is the one who manages to make the other player fall in. It has been hotly debated amidst fans and academics who it was who created the original concept for The Prisoner. George Markstein had a background in espionage thriller, and had earlier introduced McGoohan to a place called Inverlair Lodge. There were several known "retirement homes" for secret service agents dotted around the United Kingdom and the USA, where ex CIA and MI6 operatives were sent so that top secret information would not be leaked when they fell to mental illnesses or dementia. To Markstein, who had claimed to be an ex special services operative himself, it appears that the Village was a physical place, just like these retirement homes for spys. He was to write about Inverlair Lodge again in his wartime secret agent novel, The Cooler. McGoohan, tho had a very different idea of the Village, and the series in general, which is why he and Markstein were destined to Fall Out. (See what I did there!)

"Good afternoon, good evening and good night" - Truman Burbank 1998

There are many clues that the Village is not what it at first appears to be. The weather is constantly good, it appears to have a mild, Mediterranean climate. For the length of Number 6's captivity, which was around two years, we never see rain or snow. People wear light clothes, t-shirts and sun hats, rarely outside coats other than the colourful carnival like capes. It appears to be artificially climate controlled. The Village seems to be ageless, it's quaint edifices echoing architectures from the world over, from Italy to India, China to Latin America. It's full of blind alleys and set dressing, elegant Potemkin villas hiding the horrors and disarray behind their colorful facades from the public eye. Everyone seems to be happy and peaceable, those who are not are quickly removed for "therapy" so they well better fit into society. There are surveillance cameras everywhere, to monitor the Villagers' behaviour, and quickly send security to intervene, or the ominous Rover, if anyone is dumb enough to attempt escape. For all the claims that it's an international community, there are few people of colour, it's majority of citizens are white, and English speaking. There are no children. (except for the ones seen in The Girl Who Was Death, and a little boy briefly seen in Living In Harmony) It is patrolled by what can only be described as a supernatural, alien presence, which appears to be a living thing rather than any form of terrestrial technology. In the events where Number 6 actually manages to "escape" the Village, all his attempts to pinpoint it's location are wrong, as if the laws of physics no longer apply to it. (And judging by Number 2's "resurrection" in Fall Out, it's even possible for time to run backwards!) Nothing seems to be natural. The Village can be compared directly with the sunny coastal resort from the Jim Carrey movie, The Truman Show, directed by Peter Weir and written by Andrew Nichol. (Which was itself inspired by a J Michael Straczynski penned Twilight Zone episode, Special Service) In this story, our Everyman hero is content living his everyday existence in the mild and beautiful, white picket fenced, village of Seahaven, but in truth, he is the unsuspecting star of a syndicated reality show, and every event in his life, from his school, his work, and his relationships, from his birth and for the last thirty years, have been engineered and televised around the world, and his home town, nothing but an enormous film set.

In the first Prisoner episode, Arrival, it is suggested that Number 6 has lived a similar existence. He has certainly been observed enough to anticipate his breakfast choices. But, even going further back than that, it appears that Number 6 was observed even as a child and a youth. It's never reveled what Number 2's dossier on Number 6 contains, but there are clues in the episode Once Upon A Time. We are told that, even as a child there was something in his brain that made him different, a puzzlement. In other words, he has always been singled out as "special", a gifted child perhaps? Number 2 regresses Number 6 back to childhood, in the Embryo Room, in an attempt to break him so he gives up his secrets. It's reasonable to believe that the episodes are events taken from Number 6's dossier and culled from his past. So Number 6 is Truman Burbank, and the Village his Seahaven? If this is the case, than yes, the whole world does revolve around him. The Village only exists for him, and he is it's only Prisoner, and his inmates simply the "extras" he suspects them to be in Checkmate. Like Truman, he has been singled out, for whatever reason, and the convenient McGuffin of his "resignation" is not it. The startling thing about this is, the covert observation of the person who was to become Number 6 began long before his captivity in the Village. The 1960's had their own bogeymen, the constant fear of the "Reds under the bed", stories of fictional Russian spy satellites and double agents, working to subvert western civilian through their corruption of the spheres of media and academia, but as a viewer in the post cold war era, the 2000's onwards, this serves as an uneasy harbinger, one we should have noticed.

Since the advent of Social Media, and Facebook in particular, we are all under constant surveillance. People post everything from their date of birth, address, political affiliations, religion, employment status and relationship status for everybody to see. This would have been unthinkable during the post war era, and during the Cold War, when people were bombarded with maxims like "be like dad, keep mum", and "loose lips sink ships". Now nobody's business means everybody's business, and where there used to be friendly neighborhood bobbies to keep their eyes out for ne-erdowells, now we are under constant surveillance and there is nowhere to hide from CCTV cameras, Google Maps and other technological intrusions on our, once valued, privacy. This is the mentality that Number 6 fought against. The threat was never the Russians, but our own stupidity. In the fifty years since the first screening of The Prisoner, the world has changed immensely, and whilst a great many of these changes have been for the better, society has enslaved itself by allowing technology to take over, and dominate rather than being a useful tool for learning and labour saving. The TV has become the cheap babysitter, and it's sad to see children being brainwashed so young, and exposed to so much fakery and propaganda, advertising and consumerism. Like in the episode The General, where television is used to program the Villagers, the TV is used to manipulate and hypnotize us into buying things we don't want, shaping society's political viewpoints and believing things which are untrue, by inducing alpha brainwaves, the lowest and most susceptible state. There is an excellent documentary by Adam Curtis worth watching called The Century of the Self, which goes into deeper detail about how Freudian psychology was adapted by Eduard Bernaise and the ad men at Madison Avenue for that very purpose. A more recent documentary, also by Curtis, "Hypernormalisation" examines how the media has created a fake world for the benefit of financiers, corporations and politicians, as seen in the recent "fake news" scandals surrounding the Trump presidency. One of the highest grossing TV shows in the world is Big Brother, which takes its name and concept from the George Orwell novel 1984. The difference these days is that people have chosen to live their lives on camera, to be part of the "selfie generation", and inhabit the "Global Village", (a term first coined in 1964 by media and communication theorist Marshall McLuhan, which implies the world has been "shrunk" by improved telecommunications technology) the very world Number 2 spoke of in The Chimes of Big Ben, ".....the whole Earth as The Village". The Village as an allegory, as claimed by McGoohan is a much better fit than it simply being Markstein's post war "cooler" for ex spies.

Degree Absolute.

What is reveled about Number 6? We can piece together a backstory, but there are contradictions. Number 6 confirms his birthday as 19th March 1928. This is actually McGoohan's own birthday. Many of the other skills attributed to Number 6 are also McGoohan's, his proficiency at mathematics and his boxing prowess. We are shown in the episode A Change of Mind that he had remarkable hypnotic powers, where did he learn this? Was he a mind control handler or "mesmerist" in a former life?. He demonstrates in both The Chimes of Big Ben and The General that he is an accomplished and talented artist and sculptor, as well as being a resourceful craftsman and seaman. He was top of his class at woodwork at age 15. In Once Upon A Time, we are told that he was involved in a near fatal motor accident as a young man, that he was privately educated, he worked for an established British bank, (high up of course, in management, not a simple teller, was he a billionaire "bankster"?) it was there where he was recruited for a top secret assignment, and that he served in WW2 as a bomber, who was shot down and taken prisoner by the Germans, where he was subjected to interrogation and torture. We are told nothing about his parents or family, but we can guess their social status would be highly privileged and well off. Given his date of birth, he would have been a very precocious youth, did he have special "Joe 90" like skills which saw him serve in the military as a young teenager? He seems to have been singled out from a very young age for a "higher calling".

The recent Wikileaks furore might be another clue why Number 6 was incarcerated. It would be easy to imagine the likes of Edward Snowdon and Julian Assange as docile villagers dressed in striped t-shirts and colourful capes playing chess ad infinitum beside the stone boat, and periodically being dragged away to the hospital for "reprogramming". Like Number 6, they have heads full of dangerous and incriminating information and threats to national security. Could he have been a whistle-blower? Did he, like Chelsea Manning, commit treason for releasing confidential military information on human rights abuses or civilian deaths at the hands of the U.S. or British armed forces? Did he witness something so terrible he was unable to live with it on his conscience? Did he come across information which challenged his allegiances and made it impossible for him to be able to tell good from evil? We find out in the weird mind swap episode Do Not Forsake Me Oh My Darling, not only his code names, Schmidt, Duvall and ZM-73, that Number 6 is engaged to a woman, Janet Portland, the daughter of his boss, Sir Charles Portland, thought this is problematic for several reasons. Firstly, his fiancee, Janet is never mentioned before this idiosyncratic episode. There is no suggestion that Number 6 has been separated from a significant other, he appears to have no emotional ties at all to the outside world, other than his desire for freedom. He doesn't seem to miss anybody. Would an engaged and very much in love man behave this way? I think if Janet were real, it would have been much more of a plot point. In McGoohan's earlier role as Drake, romantic attachments would have been shunned due to his dangerous job, and wish to not put others at risk. It makes more sense to regard the whole plot of DNFMOMD and the two episodes which follow it as elaborate delusions.

The Old Boy Network.

In keeping with the trope I discussed earlier, the Public School background of Number 6 is rather insidious. Number 6 stands out, rather jarringly to the modern viewer as a stereotypical Public School boy. He is highly cultured, well versed in languages and literature, plays chess, and is skilled in boxing and fencing. He has sophisticated tastes, from the oriental decor of his plush Number 1 Buckingham Place residence, (£1000 p/w rent at 2016 prices) to his cigars and how he takes his tea. He is well mannered, well spoken and has the air of aristocracy. He is invited to the most fashionable parties, well dressed and debonair, he rubs shoulders with high society hosts like Madame Engadine, and her well connected guests. He fits into the TV trope of "Cultured Badass". However, the British public schools, much like the well known US Ivy League fraternities, the Skull and Bones and the Lock and Key, are known for their elitism and arcane rituals, and are recruiting grounds for the secret society networks (rather like the Murder Brotherhood in the two final Danger Man episodes, "Koroshi" and "Shinda Shima"). It's not too much of a stretch of the imagination to see Number 6 as a Bonesman or a Bullington Boy, a member of a secret brotherhood where he would have rubbed shoulders with the high rollers, the heads of state, captains of industry, political puppet masters and the banking giants, Rothschilds, Rockefellers and such like. Could he have worshipped the fifty foot owl, Moloch, draped in a red velvet robe at Bohemia Grove, where according to legend the Manhattan Project was conceived? Is this where Number 6, ZM-73, Schmitt, Duvall, his real identify undisclosed was made privy to secret information, so dangerous that the contents of his head were considered a threat to national security? Did he know about a secret technology, a new weapon or even how to transfer one person's soul, or persona, into another man's body? According to Number 2, Number 6 is "valuable", a man like him would be "worth a fortune on the open market". Really? Is this a market in individuals we are speaking of? If so he means slavery, not employment. Somebody owns him. If he really were a high level secret society member, he would have sworn under oath to remain true to his brethren, to the bitter end. Their are many stories, with differing levels of credibility, which would suggest that a member of the higher level secret societies, (not your local overgrown boy scouts Blue Lodge chapter, mind), is not allowed to leave under any circumstances, on pain of death. The 2000 movie The Skulls, starring Paul Walker depicts an Ivy League fraternity where members are bonded to a "soulmate" who they have to defend even to the point of murder. Number 2 gives the air of an Old Etonian, part of the "old boy network" with his college scarf, shooting stick and clipped English tone.

There are other secret society and Masonic symbols scattered throughout The Prisoner, from the Eye on the Pyramid, Nimrod, presiding over the council chamber, a suggestion of the "hidden hand" of the secret societies making the real decisions, the myth of Democracy, the one eyed salute, "Be Seeing You", as a reminder that the All Seeing Eye is never far away, to the black and white chess board symbolising the duality of good and evil. (In Margaret Attwood's dystopian novel and subsequent television series 'The Handmaid's Tale' they use the similar and even more ominous greeting, "Under His Eye") One of the rituals associated with Freemasonry is the initiate lying in a coffin and being declared "dead", this happens to Number 6 as he is drugged and transported to the Village in a hearse, and in Dance Of The Dress, a macabre masked ball, where he is informed that the dead body in the morgue is really his. In the finale, Fall Out, a court of hooded figures wearing masks are evocative not only of Albert Pike's KKK, the chorus line from Jerry Springer, the Opera, also Stanley Kubrick's final movie, Eyes Wide Shut. It suggests that there is something much nastier going on before the surface, below the sunny, friendly hotel resort of The Village than could have ever been imagined, debauchery, bestiality and even human sacrifice. Another famous TV village, loaded with Masonic symbolism and secrecy, David Lynch's eponymous Twin Peaks appears at first to be a benign logging town, with quaint diners and parochial 1950's values, despite the incest, murder and demonic influences of the Black Lodge and it's bizarre inhabitants. Did Number 6 betray his brethren and leave a secret society? Was he asked to cover up an act with went against his strong moral, Christian, principles? Was he a risk to them, a loose cannon they feared would revel their secrets? The various forms of torture and mind control used on Number 6 in order to get him to reveal his secrets have a real life origin, the secret CIA Scientific Intelligence Division operation MK Ultra, which utilised the experience of ex Nazi engineers, doctors and scientists taken to the USA as part of Operation Paperclip, to prevent their knowledge falling into the hands of, not only the Soviets, but the British, and to prevent Germany from rebuilding its military research facilities. Although these operations were illegal, thousands of experiments were carried out on civilian human subjects, including children and the disabled, against their will, where they were subjected to electro shock, LSD and other "truth drugs", hypnosis, sexual and emotional abuse, torture, isolation and sensory derivation all under the auspices of "science". The operation was financed by CIA "front organisations" and endorsed by the U.S. military, who planned to use these methods for interrogating enemy agents and prisoners of war, to force confessions, and to create "mind controlled assassins", like in the movie the Manchurian Candidate. So sometimes the truth really is as strange and terrifying as fiction.

The Beast and His Image.

It's a startling image, and one of the most iconic in television, McGoohan standing silhouetted in the doorway of his former employer, his arms stretched out, crucifix like. Is he our saviour or redeemer? Is he a sacrifice? Many have noted that he is dressed in a black suit like that of John Drake, and use this to reinforce the "Number 6 is Drake" theory, but I would like to point out another, more powerful and symbolic resemblance. He is wearing a old fashioned black collarless button down shirt, that of a defiant priest. The man who strikes this imposing figure is the image of McGoohan's former stage role, Brand. Number 6 definitely has a good dose of Brand's intensity, compared to the generally mild and courteous John Drake. It is very apt that Brand in Norwegian, Swedish and Danish means "fire", as this is one of McGoohan's most intense and harrowing screen roles. In Henrik Ibsen's play, Brand is a man torn between the Will of Man and the Will of God. He is driven by his dedication to do God's Will, and to cut himself off from carnal, materialistic bondage, even to the expense of losing his family, his sanity and in the end, his earthly life, for the redemption of his immortal soul and the souls of his flock. He is at odds with the strangely Number 2 like Provost, who rather than sharing Brand's vision sees the church, and "organised religion" as a control system, a way of keeping the villagers in check, after all he says, "good Christians are good citizens". Whereas Brand treats his parishioners as individuals, with individual spiritual problems and needs, the Provost sees them as simply a herd to be manipulated, even lied to, just as they are led astray by the Mayor's claims of a miracle draft of fishes in the final act. Just like the Provost, Number 2 appears to act as a pope-like intermediary between man and "God", ie Number One. Number 6 is prevented at all costs from contacting Number One himself, until he has proven his worth by the fatal defeat of Number 2. Like Number 6 also, Brand exhibits an unshakable pride of will. His devotion to Jehovah is resolute, he is not a disciple of the "gentle" Jesus, the Prince of Peace, tolerance and kindness, quite the reverse, he sees weakness in this approach; choosing instead dedication to the wrathful, unforgiving and cruel God of the Old Testament. There is no saving grace from Brand's God, just personal responsibility, and judgment. It has to be"All or Nothing", uncompromising and final. Brand tortures, constantly judges and convicts himself, knowing he will never succeed in reaching the high standard of godliness he has set for himself. Instead of being a "sinner saved by grace", Brand's goal is to empty himself of his own selfishness, and become like Jehovah himself, an impossible feat for a mere mortal of flesh and blood.

Much has been made of McGoohan's own "Catholic guilt", so I think that for McGoohan, he greatly identified with the role of Brand. Being both a believer and a highly intelligent man, he was a person who asked questions and was conflicted between gnosis and blind faith, forever trying to find reconciliation of the two, between spirit and science, the seen and the unseen. For all of Brand's idealism and religious fanaticism, he is a man who believes in agency, personal responsibility for ones actions, rather than the action of the State. It is this struggle between individualism and herd mentality which makes Brand as good candidate as any for "Number 6" as any other McGoohan role. Like Number 6, he too is devoid of love, until he realises God's love at the moment of his death. There is little love, or even compassion in Number 6, and he rarely shows anymore than brief demonstrations of affection for the crying "damsels in distress" or Number 2's black cat. He appears self controlled, unsentimental. Just like Brand's austere and cold reaction to the death of his child, Number 6 never shows a human side and concedes to his emotions, instead staying true to his calling. This is one of his virtues, but as well, his bitterest foe. The President in the final episode, "Fall Out" tells Number 6 that he "is pure, you know the way, show us". As their leader, he would be their shepherd and their messiah. Number 6 does not fit the stereotype of a spiritual man, but he is the most spiritual of the Village's denizens, being a man with a higher calling, a greater purpose than to be an anonymous member of the rabble. His spiritual gift is his strength of character and his ability to inspire others, just as he demonstrates in the final episode. This has another religious subtext, when Jesus was tempted in the wilderness by Satan, he was offered power over all he surveyed if he were to bow down and worship him. But this dominion over all corners of the earth in reality was already his, as it belonged to God the Father. And, like Christ, this dominion was already Number 6's. Number 6 is given a similar choice to make by the President, representing Lucifer. He is offered not only his freedom, but materialistic rewards, money, the keys to his London abode and his car, if only he will concede to lead them. He is expected to make a "Faustian pact", to gain the world at the expense of his own soul. His soul is pure and his anger righteous, like Brand's. But by leading them, he would be robbing them of their agency and making them his disciples, his herd. A row of brainwashed cabbages. No longer individuals. The irony of this is the scene in Fall Out where Number 6, now The Man, no longer a number, betrays his principles and along with Number 2, Number 48 "the Kid" and the silent Butler, go crazy with assault rifles to the strains of the Beatles "All You Need Is Love". All you need is love, indeed. If God is Love, who then, is God? Is Number 1 God? Or is Number 1 something more malevolent, The Beast of Revelation? Or was Nietzsche right, is God dead? Or does God, "Number 1" even exist?

Let's take a look at the other religious symbols presented in the Prisoner. The chanting of "6,6,6!" of course is an easy one. The Book of Revelation tells of 666, (sometimes translated as 616) being the number of a man. A common explanation for the enigmatic 666 cipher was that Roman citizens used code numbers when they criticised their rulers, because criticising a Roman emperor was punishable by death. Some think 666 was the code number for Nero. Citizens of the Village are all assigned a number instead of using their name, just like we as citizens are reduced and dehumanized by such things as National Insurance or Social Security numbers. Like McGoohan said in Warner Troyer's 1977 interview, The Prisoner Puzzle, we are all becoming ciphers. There are many conspiracy theories and stories of doom from End Time preachers regarding the nature of the "Mark of the Beast". Some people associate it with the common or garden bar code, others see a future in which people are prevented from trading, or even buying necessities, food and water, without submitting to being chipped with the RFID chip, similar to the chips commonly inserted into your pets, or otherwise marked or tattooed like branded farm animals. Number Six is issued with Village ration cards, "work units" (how these are earned is anyone's guess) but from the outset, refuses to be known by his number. Whilst the other Villagers wear their number badges with no protest. Number 6, as a good Christian, and a "righteous rebel" refuses to take the Mark of the Beast. (Interestingly, the song "The Prisoner" by British new wave metal band Iron Maiden appears on their classic 1982 album, "Number of the Beast" and features audio samples from the series)

The curious one eyed salute, usually accompanied with the phrase "Be Seeing You", is considered to represent the "sign of the fish" as used by early Christians to identify each other. This claim is made in the American A&E documentary, The Prisoner Video Companion and also Matthew White and Jarrar Ali's book, The Official Prisoner Companion, who claim that actress Norma West (Little Bo Peep from the episode The Dance of the Dead) was told this in person by McGoohan. The fish is a Christian sign because in Greek, the same letters that make up Ichthus, which means fish, are the acronym for " Jesus Christ, Son of God, Saviour". This is also depicted by the fish shaped "Jesus Fish" sign you see on Christian bumper stickers, which in turn is based on the earlier Pagan symbol the Vesica Pisces, or womb, used in Christian art to represent the Virgin Mary, and used by Pagans to represent Atergatis or Aphrodite, also known as Delphine, or "Dolphin", the Sea Goddess. Being born on the 18th March, McGoohan, and Number 6 of course, had the star sign Pisces. The hand signal, with a circle made by the index finger and thumb and the other three fingers spread out, seen in The Prisoner, also resembles the sign for "O.K.", which some interpret as a satanic sign. When the sign is formed with the right hand, it resembles the number 666! The "O.K" sign is acceptable to is the the UK and the US, but in some countries such as Brazil, Germany and Russia out is considered very rude, and represents an obscene body part. To Hindus, this is a sacred mudra which means perfection or infinity. In Egyptian mythology, it signifies the Wadjet eye, or "Eye of Horus". In Arab countries, making this sign whist shaking the hand means you are giving somebody "the Evil Eye".

The Second Commandment

"You shall have no other gods before me.

You shall not make for yourself a graven image

or any likeness of anything that is in heaven above,

or that is in the earth beneath,

or that is in the water under the earth;

you shall not bow down to them or serve them;

for I the LORD your God am a jealous God,

visiting the iniquity of the fathers

upon the children to the third and the fourth

generation of those who hate me,

but showing steadfast love to thousands of those

who love me and keep my commandments."

The second episode, (based on original transmission order) The Chimes of Big Ben is loaded with religious symbolism. The arts and crafts exhibition in the Village Hall is very interesting. Other than Number 6's "abstract sculpture", all the other denizens have produced artwork which glorifies Leo McKern's Number 2. This act is evocative of the "personality cult", often associated with despotic leaders such as Joseph Stalin, or other idolized figures such as Elvis or Marilyn Monroe (used to effect in Ken Russell's movie version of the Who's Tommy, in the healing scene) The Second Commandment given to Moses expressly forbids the making of idols to be worshipped, but it really does seem that the Village folk worship Number 2 as a "god". In keeping with his staunchly Christian morals, Number 6 does not. Despite him not kowtowing to popularity, he is awarded First Prize, and 30 Work Units for his efforts. There are two more notable examples of "graven images" (not counting the spooky statues with camera eyes dotted around the Village) - The Professor's wife's busts of various Village personalities, including an ultra lifelike effigy of her husband, and the creepy statue of Number 6, which shows up again in the final episode, wearing his (Brand's or Drake's) black mourning suit. (In a blink and you'll miss it moment in Arrival, we see the suit being worn by the babbling bald headed man with electrodes stuck to his head, he appears to be participating in some kind of Psy experiment, and his vocalizations on the soundtrack are dubbed in by McGoohan himself!)

There is a section of dialog snipped from Vincent Tilsley's original "Chimes" script at McGoohan's behest. It's investing to read in ours original format. The reason this was cut by McGoohan is probably it's criticism of religion.

Woman: What puzzled me, No.6 was the fact you'd given the group a title. `Escape'. We don't quite see...

Prisoner: This piece. What does it suggest to you

Man Two: A church door?

Prisoner: Right first time. A barrier. The barrier to human truth and progress.

Man Two: Oh, I see. Don't know that I agree though.

Woman: I certainly don't

Man One: Is that official policy?

Prisoner: Now this piece - exactly the same shape, you'll notice. But hollow. You can walk through it. [HE DOES SO] The barrier has gone. The door is open. we can escape to... this - THE POLE WITH THE CROSS PIECE.

Man One: What is it?

Prisoner: A symbol of human aspiration. Up. Straight up. To knowledge; freedom; escape.

Man One: I see. But why the cross piece?

Prisoner: The very word. A cross. Because our escape leads us back to - discipline. Faith. Organisation. In fact - religion.

Instead, Number 6 identifies the "church door" as a road to freedom.

Despite McGoohan's claims to the contrary, the final episode "Fall Out" is loaded with messianic symbolism. I have already talked about Brand, and Christ's temptation in the wilderness, but let's shift our focus onto the other two characters present in this scene, namely Leo Mc Kern's Number 2, and Alexis Kanner's Number 48. When Christ was tried by the Romans in the gospels, and sentenced to death, there were two "rebels" crucified with him. Both of the rebels recognised Christ as The True Son of God, and accepted him as their saviour. Likewise, both Number 2 and Number 48 accept Number 6 "the Man" as their saviour, and exit to London (or not!) with him. Both Number 48 and Number 2 have another important thing in common, both have been "resurrected" from the dead - Number 2 dies of a heart attack or exhaustion at the end of "Once Upon A Time" whilst the deranged Number 6 chants "die, die, die", and Number 48, also known as "The Kid" (Number 8) in "Living In Harmony". "The Kid" is actually killed twice, first by Number 6 in the quick draw duel, then again when he tries to confront Number 6 from a balcony, he slips and falls to his death. Number 6 also, is a "resurrection". The last time in the series we see him given his black mourning suit to wear was in the uncanny masquerade party in "Dance Of The Dead", where he is told in no uncertain terms by Mary Morris's Peter Pan that to the outside world he is "dead". Being allowed to be "himself" is giving him his life back.

It's often said that the Village has no church, so therefore it is a secular society, maybe even militant atheist, like the early Soviet Union, where religion might actually be illegal, or at least dissuaded by the authorities. Although we see funerals and the Village graveyard in several episodes, we never see a priest or member of the clergy. Or do we? There is a strange scene towards the end of the episode "Free for All" which suggests otherwise. As Number 6 is taken into the catacombs below the Village, we briefly see four men wearing sunglasses sitting around an incumbent Rover, as if worshipping it. This mysterious "Cult of Rover" is presided over by another graven image, a priestly figure in a white hood and robe just like the one we see Number 1, and the jury members wearing in the final episode "Fall Out". Who is this? It resembles one of the statues with the camera eyes we see in the woods. Is this hooded figure an effigy of Number One? If so, it's shocking how close Number 6 gets to him without revealing who he is. And what of Rover? We know that Rover is a source of deep psychological terror among the villagers, and the reverent way they all freeze before him. In "A Change of Mind" we see videos of Rover being played over and over to terrorised victims in the mental hospital's "aversion therapy" suites. Rover is always there, all seeing and omnipotent, as a silent threat to punish sins, such as being "unmutual", disharmonious, or running away and escaping. His very existence is enough to prevent docile villages from even the thought of it. You could even say that Rover instills the "fear of God" into them. Rover represents an amorphous, white, suffocating form of "divine retribution". Is Rover Number One's avatar? Is Rover the will of God Himself, or an inescapable, irredeemable nebula of perpetual guilt in the mind of the tormented sinner?

An Electric Banana

There is a great similarity between Alexis Kanner's "Kid" character, and that of Alex DeLarge, the central character in Anthony Burgess's "A Clockwork Orange", especially the way he is portrayed by the great British actor Malcolm McDowell (geeks will note, his character Doctor Tolian Soran killed Captain Kirk in the 1994 Star Trek movie, Generations) in Stanley Kubrick's 1971 controversial cult movie adaptation. It is almost like the Prisoner foreshadowed Kubrick's movie, which is a great example of quirky British psychedelia, with its colorful sets, highly stylised costumes, flawlessly choreographed action scenes and surreal electronic soundtrack by Wendy Carlos. The book, which was published in 1962 is universally regarded as one of the 100 greatest works of English literature. Alex DeLarge is a youth obsessed with both Beethoven and ultra-violence, regularly drinking drug-infused milk at the Korova milk bar amongst grotesque sexualized female mannequins, before going on the rampage with his gang, beating up tramps, joyriding, breaking and entering, and raping women. (ironically, even though the film was banned in the UK for explicitly depicting rape until 2001, the TV comedy series The Goodies parodied the scene in a 1973 episode "Invasion of the Moon Creatures". As The Goodies was widely regarded as a "kids show", this has to be seen to be believed!) After he accidentally kills a victim, and is abandoned by his so-called friends, he is imprisoned, but there is a way out, a way for him to be redeemed and rehabilitated into polite society. His redemption is the new experimental therapy for ultra violent criminals, the Ludovico Technique.

Alex undergoes grueling "aversion therapy" where he is forced to watch (his eyes are clamped open with what looks like a medieval torture devise) scenes of sex and violence, whilst being injected with nausea inducing drugs. Eventually he is conditioned to become physically sick at the mere thought of violence, and the sound of Beethoven's Fifth. However, after he is driven insane by his programming and attempts suicide by throwing himself out of a window, (similarities again with Number 8's death in LIH) the Ludovico Technique comes under criticism for being unethical.

This was a common theme in the sixties, the youth revolution, breaking down the old traditions and railing against the establishment. Vietnam had given youth an excuse to rebel, choosing not to go abroad to fight in a foreign, unjust war. (Some consider the reason Living in Harmony was omitted from the original run on US television is the fact that Number 6's "Man with no No Name" refused to carry a gun, seeing it as a commentary on the Vietnam war, although this view has been contested. It appears that the writer, Ian Rakoff was inspired by his experiences of being a member of a left wing movement in South Africa during the Apartheid regime, where he has been encouraged to become a pacifist, rather than participating in sectarian violence) People such as Timothy Leary promoted the use of LSD for the expansion of the mind, and the philosophy "turn on, tune in, and drop out". Aldous Huxley encouraged people to explore higher states of consciousness through meditation and medication in his groundbreaking book "The Doors of Perception". People were exploring eastern religions and the occult through the writings of Alistair Crowley, and L.Ron Hubbard, the father of Scientology, was promoting his Dianetics doctrine as a cure all, and road to self-fulfillment. Psychologists such as RD Laing, the author of "The Divided Self", and Thomas Szasz author of "The Myth of Mental Illness" were even questioning the very nature of mental illness, considering the schizophrenic mind to be a mind operating on a higher plane. This became known as the Anti Psychiatry movement, and argued that the inhuman cures for psychiatric conditions were far worse than the psychiatric conditions themselves, because the patient is robbed of his essence, his individuality, and his passion. This philosophy is explored in Peter Shaffer's 1973 play Equus, in which a psychologist is sent to treat a young man with a religious and sexual fixation with horses, but eventually becomes envious of the boy's passion and free spirit. A Clockwork Orange deals with a similar theme, as does The Prisoner, especially in the episode "A Change of Mind", which calls this process "social conversion".

The Prisoner's The Kid character is another example of the disobedient child, the youth out of control, the delinquent, just like Alex and his Droogs. The Kid too, when we first meet him in the episode Living In Harmony, as Number 8, is an eccentricly dressed mute, who looks like he might have run away from the circus and would not be out of place amongst Alex's Droogs. He also has a proclivity for violence against women, first sexually assaulting and then strangling saloon hostess Kathy. Number 8 dies twice in this episode, firstly in the duel with Number 6, where he is shot dead, then back in the "reality" of the Village, where he commits suicide by throwing himself off of a balcony. The next time we meet Kanner's "Kid" character, he is known as Number 48. Again, he's an oddly dressed dandy, this time in a top hat and ruffled jacket, but far from being a mute. On his presentation to the court, he refuses to cooperate, instead breaking into a hearty rendition of the spiritual "Dem Bones".

The song "Dem Bones" is based on a bible story found in the Book of Isaiah.

37 The hand of the Lord was on me, and he brought me out by the Spirit of the Lord and set me in the middle of a valley; it was full of bones.

2 He led me back and forth among them, and I saw a great many bones on the floor of the valley, bones that were very dry.

3 He asked me, "Son of man, can these bones live?"I said, "Sovereign Lord, you alone know."

4 Then he said to me, "Prophesy to these bones and say to them, 'Dry bones, hear the word of the Lord!

5 This is what the Sovereign Lord says to these bones: I will make breath enter you, and you will come to life.

6 I will attach tendons to you and make flesh come upon you and cover you with skin; I will put breath in you, and you will come to life. Then you will know that I am the Lord.'"

7 So I prophesied as I was commanded. And as I was prophesying, there was a noise, a rattling sound, and the bones came together, bone to bone.

8 I looked, and tendons and flesh appeared on them and skin covered them, but there was no breath in them.

9 Then he said to me, "Prophesy to the breath; prophesy, son of man, and say to it, 'This is what the Sovereign Lord says: Come, breath, from the four winds and breathe into these slain, that they may live.'" 10 So I prophesied as he commanded me, and breath entered them; they came to life and stood up on their feet—a vast army.

11 Then he said to me: "Son of man, these bones are the people of Israel. They say, 'Our bones are dried up and our hope is gone; we are cut off.'

12 Therefore prophesy and say to them: 'This is what the Sovereign Lord says: My people, I am going to open your graves and bring you up from them; I will bring you back to the land of Israel.

13 Then you, my people, will know that I am the Lord, when I open your graves and bring you up from them.

14 I will put my Spirit in you and you will live, and I will settle you in your own land. Then you will know that I the Lord have spoken, and I have done it, declares the Lord.'"

Like the "people of Israel", referred to in the scripture, the compliant, brainwashed citizens of the Village have become "dry bones", awaiting their Lord to breathe new life into them and give flesh to their bones.

C.S.Lewis called these people "men without chests", unable to grasp objective reality and objective truth without the intermediary between their intellect and animalistic nature. This serves as a very apt description of the denizens of the Village.

Number 48 addresses the Judge as "Daddy", and says that the bones came from him. Is he referring to Yahweh, the God of Abraham here? Will Number 6, as the new messiah, the Son of Man or Christ figure bring about a new covenant, and restore the Village captives to a new life of freedom? We have already explored Number 6's Faustian pact, but what is more ominous is that the moment he is offered the Throne, he BECOMES Number 1. This is his ascension from Man to God. He is the absolute ruler and author of the Village, the King of all he surveys. Coming face to face with himself, he sees his own frailty and insanity. The white robe and black and white mask he wears is exactly the same as the ones we see the members of the assembly wearing, the only distinction being a large (1) in case we haven't realised who he is. Black and white, remember, signifies duality, good vs evil, sacred vs profane, just like the checkerboard floor of the Masonic temple. As Number 6 rips the mask from his face, he is first confronted with a gibbering monkey's face. Is this a reminder of evolution, that we have all come from apes? Or is it a symbol of the first man, Adam, of the earth, earthly? Or is it the Beast himself, the old 666, to take us full circle from Genesis to Revelation? There is an eerily similar scene in David Lynch's Twin Peaks prequel, Fire Walk With Me, where Mrs Tremond's enigmatic grandson removes a white plaster death mask to reveal a fleeting glimpse of a grinning cappuchin monkey. I assume this short scene was a nod by Lynch, master of the surreal, to The Prisoner as a fellow fan. Number 6 rips off the monkey mask to then reveal the face of madness, himself, deranged and eyes boggling with insanity. Has humanity evolved at all, or are we all, underneath, just animals? Freud talked about the Id, which is the impulsive, animalistic part of ourselves, the inner chimp which has no conscience and no impulses control, only existing to be instantly gratified, like a screaming newborn baby. Then there is our conscience selves, the Ego, and above that, our Super Ego, our Higher Self. Number 6, it can be said, has a strong Ego, represented in his tenacity and willfullness to fight the powers that be in the never ending struggle to defend his own sense of self, of his individualism, and to not back down into the herd and resign himself to the fact that he's nothing but another statistic. His Super Ego can be seen his his moral judgments, his religiosity, righteous anger and his strong sense of right and wrong. Are we being shown a metaphor for the ascent of Man, from a primordial ape to a God? Has the fictional Number 6 just caught a glimpse of his wild eyed altar ego, the Great Architect?

Our second "rebel" is our good friend, Leo Mc Kern's Number 2. Again, he is resurrected, made over and transformed. Instead of representing youthful rebellion, Number 2's rebellion is of a jaded older man, who had given the best years of his life to the establishment and the figures of authority, tradition and the conservative way of life. He is well educated, probably a parliamentarian, MP or at least someone closely connected with Westminster and the British Crown. Number 6 fits between the youth of Number 48 and the age of Number 2, and since we have explored the very deep emotional bond between Numbers 2 and 6, it is very fitting that he is one of the companions Number 6 takes with him back to London. Number 48 is fittingly something of a protege to Number 6, who sees something of himself in 48's refusal to be put in a box. Alexis Kanner, likewise was something of a protege to McGoohan, who worked with him several times in movies after the Prisoner has ended. Number 6's third companion who leaves the Village with him is our other dear friend, the diminutive and silent Butler.

The Butler, played by Angelo Muscatt was always something of a fan favorite, and during the course of the show a common fan theory was that, of course in the age of Bond villains, such as Odd Job, he would turn out to be Number 1. Looking back, that would have been a ridiculous and trite ending, but even after all these years the Butler remains something of an enigma. For starters, he doesn't have a number. He equally serves Number 2 and Number 6, with no thought of rank. He could be like a little Jiminy Cricket, an embodiment of "conscience". Dwarves and small people, pixies and fairies etc, in folk lore have always been seen as magical beings and guardians of secret knowledge. I'm pretty sure the Butler always knew the identity of Number 1, but his silence meant this remained a secret. The character I feel parallels the Prisoner's Butler character is Twin Peak's "Man From Another Place", as played by Michael J Anderson. While not silent, he does speak backwards, in riddles and enigmas, and he is the custodian of deep spiritual knowledge and inhabits the Red Room, a waiting room for the Final Judgement between the good White Lodge and the evil Black Lodge. Other fictional dwarves include Shakespeare's character Puck, from a Midsummer Night's Dream. S/he (The character is agender) embodies the archetype of the trickster or the wise knave. As well as being a gender, Puck is amoral, neither good nor bad, a bit like our Butler and our "Man From Another Place". The Grimm Brothers' character Rumplestiltskin represents another kind of dwarf or imp character, this time not so benign, a blackmailer with unpleasant designs on young girls. Not all fictional dwarves are magical, George R.R. Martin's character Tyrion Lannister, as played by Peter Dinklage in "Game of Thrones" is thoroughly profane, cynical and self-indulgent, but has learned to get by on his wits and high intelligence. The "Austin Powers" spy comedy series has the hilarious Mini Me played by Verne Troyer, Doctor Evil's pint size clone he practically keeps as a pet. Like the Butler, Mini Me is silent too, probably so he doesn't give away any of his master's evil secrets!

"Numerology...we're all becoming ciphers..." McGoohan, 1977

It's interesting to note that date of birth given by Number 6, which was actually McGoohan's own bithdate, 18th of March 1928, when reduced to a numerology number gives him Life Path 6. People on Life Path 6 are seen as a feminine, harmony seeking and represent balance. The meaning is somewhat different in Christianity, where 6 represents Man and incompletion. This is because mankind was created on the sixth day, and on the seventh, God rested. So the number 7 is the Number of completion, the Number of God and "perfection". (Fans of the Pixies will know the song "Monkey Gone To Heaven" from their 1989 album Doolittle, it seems very fitting!) And of course, $6 + 1 = 7$, which has special significance when you realise the identity of Number 1 and how the story ends (or indeed, begins). Stranger still, the Number 7 is a number often omitted or ignored in the Prisoner, the are very few Villagers who have this number, even the buttons on the Public Information display in the first episode, Arrival, have other numbers substituted for the missing sevens. The famous Lotus 7 car is only ever seen in London, never in the Village. It could be that McGoohan was simply superstitious, as in Judeo Christian mythology it's considered it a sacred number. It could also be that the Village, was simply a godless world, (it doesn't have a church or temple, despite having a cemetery) and he chose to depict this by omitting the number 7. McGoohan had originally only planned the series to have seven episodes, which are generally considered to be Arrival, Free For All, Dance of the Dead, Checkmate, The Chimes of Big Ben, Once Upon A Time and Fall Out, although McGoohan has never confirmed this. In the episode Hammer into Anvil, we see a Number 73, a young woman in hospital, although she is not wearing a badge. When Number 6 intervenes to prevent her abuse, she throws herself from the hospital window and kills herself. It's odd that in ham radio parlance, 73, is used for "goodbye", although it actually means "best regards" or "my love to you". One of Number 6's given code names is also ZM-73. 73 is the 21st prime number, a star number and a permutable prime with 37, and the number of books in the Catholic Bible. Type 6 on the Enneagram is known as "The Loyalist", and are seen as reliable, hard working, responsible and trustworthy. (It is very unlikely that Number 6 is a Type 6, as his temperament is a better fit for Type 4, the Individualist)

A study into Number 6's, (and by extension Patrick McGoohan's) personality type would require whole book by itself. There is a lot that can be gathered from anecdotal evidence and the few spare interviews he gave that build up a pretty detailed, if sometimes conflicting image of the man. He is a pretty good fit for the Myers Briggs Type Indicator (MBTI) "Mastermind", or INTJ (Introverted, iNtuitive, Thinking, Judging). This is a Type he shares with a good many villains, including Lex Luthor, Stewie Griffin and Hannibal Lector!!

There is no doubt that McGoohan was a genuine polymath, one of those unusual and special people able to turn their hand with success to very many diverse fields, a bit like the talented dog professor from Mr Peabody and Sherman. He was extremely talented, and his interests and accomplishments went way beyond his acting prowess. For the movie "All Night Long" where he played an arrogant and disgruntled jazz drummer, he threw himself body and soul into the role, driving his neighbors bananas with his obsessive practicing. When you view the film, despite him miming to a pre recorded drum track, his rhythm is faultless. There are more clues to his musical abilities when you consider the origins of Ron Grainer's theme tune. The had been two failed attempts by composers Robert Farnon and Wilfred Josephs to score the opening titles to the Prisoner, but neither found favour with the hard to please, perfectionist McGoohan. Finally he asked for Ron Grainer, famous for his Doctor Who theme, to produce a piece of music for the opening titles, but on hearing it, McGoohan wasn't happy with the "rather weedy" score, so he took to the control room of the studio and had it out with Grainer, insisting he "beef it up". And the rest is history...

"To Infinity, and Beyond!!" Buzz Lightyear, 1996

The big McGuffin of the series is Number 6's Resignation. We assume that he was a highly paid secret service agent, who one day without warning, stormed into his boss's, presumably Sir Portland's office, slams down his fist on the desk, smashing the startled bosses tea cup, and delivers, a hand written notice saying I QUIT. Obviously, this letter contained nothing in the way of an explanation for his leaving, otherwise there would be no reason for the series. So if Number 6 is a secret agent, is he John Drake? Patrick McGoohan answered this question quite aptly himself. "He was never called John Drake, he just happened to look like him" - well of course he would, wouldn't he?

If you do know know about film "lore" you might be confused as to what I mean by McGuffin. It's a common plot device in thrillers which seeks to give the protagonist a motive. When there isn't a clear motivation for the protagonist to do what they do, it's simple to just make one up. The first of two major McGuffins presented in the series is the "why did you resign?" question. It gives Number 6's incarceration in the Village a purpose, and a purpose for the unending mind games of the succession of Number 2's and their minions, who try to break him and brainwash his into telling them this, obviously very important information. As the Prisoner was seen by both Markstein and Lew Grade, who financed the series, as a sequel or continuation of Danger Man, the first McGuffin, the question of the Prisoner's resignation can be easily answered. McGoohan had become frustrated with the Danger Man franchise, and soon after making the first two hour-long episodes in colour, quit his role as John Drake. So the person who resigned, in a very meta twist was in fact McGoohan himself. He actually delivers his hand written letter of resignation, (McGoohan's own handwriting), in the dramatic Prisoner opening titles to a balding bespectacled man behind a desk who is in fact, meta fiction alert! George Markstein! So how does this work in the Danger Man fictional universe? If we are to believe the information we are fed, in universe, about the man who is to become the Prisoner, he was at least on a first inspection, an agent, if not Drake, then somebody very much like him. We see this dramatic storming into the office scene. We see him packing his cases, there appears to be a travel brochure of some kind, pictures of palm trees, perhaps somewhere exotic like Barbados, somewhere in the Caribbean? Cuba perhaps? So he's just going on holiday right? One of the running gags in the first series of Danger Man was he could never get the holiday he deserved! Or, is he off on another secret mission, for his real masters? Is he a double agent? If Number 6, as a "fictional character" is "self aware", then he truly believes his "in universe" back story. But consider this. Is anything we think we know about him correct? There are many levels of interpretation which mix meta narratives and McGoohan's real life story together into a post modern soup. Maybe Number 6 is a lot like Toy Story's Buzz Lightyear character.

When we are first introduced to Buzz Lightyear, in the 1996 Disney/Pixar movie, he believes that he is a genuine "Space Ranger", a heroic galactic explorer who has been awakened from hyper sleep only to find himself in a bizarre world of talking dinosaurs, piggy banks and cowboys, which unbeknownst to him, is actually a small child's bedroom. It is well into the film before Buzz finally realises the awful truth, that he isn't a super hero at all, but just a child's play thing, an "action figure". Likewise, the Number 6 who comes to from drug induced sleep, in a room which looks very much like his own, or an elaborately designed sound stage, clearly believes his own back story. He is not aware that he is a non-person, a fictional character, with no true will of his own, and no agency, at the mercy of McGoohan and his writing team, just like Will Ferrell's character in the 2006 fantasy drama, Stranger than Fiction. Number 6's background is a hotch potch of details from Patrick McGoohan's playbook, some fiction, some reality, some John Drake some Brand, some Dr Syn (some the Scarecrow), the rest Pat himself. Disney played a similar trick to the one seen in Toy Story in the 2008 animated action adventure "Bolt". Bolt is a dog who has been brought up on a movie set since he was a puppy, and really believes himself to be a "super dog" with super human magical powers. Like Truman Burbank, who we discussed in an earlier chapter, the studio who owns him put considerable effort into maintaining the illusion and creating a synthetic environment for him, where he can beat the "bad guys" with his ultrasonic bark and can shoot lasers out of his eyes, but this is all achieved with special effects. Like Buzz, he had a very rude wakeup call when he realises that in the real world, he's just an ordinary dog, with no super powers, so ordinary in fact, that he really doesn't matter and the studio can replace him at any time with any other ordinary dog, who vaguely resembles him.

Another movie which plays with meta fiction, and the role of the auteur is Charlie Kaufman's "Synedoche New York". In this movie, a film director called Caden Cottard (played by the incredible late Philip Seymour Hoffman) builds a huge movie set in which to stage a production based on his own life. As the movie gets bigger and bigger, lines are blurred between fiction and reality, with players playing players playing real people, and an inception like set within a set within a set. The production eventually consumes everything, including Caden himself, who's death becomes a part of the act. The title Synecdoche, which means a part of something which represents the whole, or vice versa, is a play on Schenectady, a real life New York borough. The auteurship of Patrick McGoohan can be compared to Caden's endeavor as it integrated numerous real world and fictional events into one whole drama, and McGoohan's health, both mentally and physically suffered as a result.

Deadpool, the "Merc with the Mouth", is a popular wise cracking Marvel Comics character, who got his own movie in 2016, after first appearing in The New Mutants #98 in 1991. Deadpool is a unique character in the Marvel Comics Universe, as unlike most of the other "superheroes", he is fully aware that he is a fictional character from a comic book. This is played for laughs in the movie when he refers to the actors playing the characters, the writers and other real world cultural references. In both the movie and the comics, he frequently breaks "the fourth wall" by directly addressing the reader and acknowledging that his adventures are fiction being watched on a cinema screen, or read in a comic book. Deadpool's backstory or biography is likewise patchy and inconsistent, subject to writers whims and random revisions. There are hints in the final few episodes that maybe Number 6 is a little like Deadpool, fully aware of the fictional nature of his situation and the story he has been written in. Suddenly his resignation and the other McGuffins have no further relevance, because nothing can prepare us for the insanity to come. When Number 6 turns to the camera in The Girl Who Was Death, and slyly mimics BBC Radio storyteller Uncle Mac's catchphrase, "Goodnight Children, everywhere", I somehow think that was meant for us, the viewer!

Suckerpunched!!

As is well known to fans, McGoohan had only intended to make seven episodes. This was padded out to thirteen at the request of Lew Grade, who wanted a show he could syndicate internationally. It's usually stated that Grade wanted 26, but McGoohan compromised with 17, in Roger Langley's book, it is claimed that 30 were planned all along, with Grade only pulling the plug at episode 16 as they were behind schedule and way over budget. I find this unlikely, because McGoohan had already planned his modem morality play to have a distinct beginning, middle and end, even if a lot of the details changed and evolved from day to day of script edits and filming, it was never intended to continue, soap opera like, indefinitely like so many other syndicated dramas.

There is a distinct change of pace towards the end of the series, dividing the show into two parts, pre "a Change of Mind", and post "a Change of Mind". Why should the show pivot on the outcome of one, not particularly important episode? The True Order of episodes even now, fifty years later is still disputed by fans, but I believe the original broadcast order is the order which makes the most sense, as it places the whacked out final episodes after 'A Change of Mind'. My theory, and it is just a theory, is that in this pivotal episode, Number 6's pre frontal lobotomy was successful. There are several movies which use similar devices, from the 1990 cult movie starring Tim Robbins, Jacob's Ladder. In this mind bending movie, a Vietnam veteran is tormented by visions of his dead child and appears to shift between realities and parallel dimensions before it is finally revealed that he was a guinea pig in an experiment where soldiers were given LSD, and the hallucinations and shifting realities throughout the movie all took place in his final dying moments. Martin Scorsese's brilliant psychological drama from 2010 Shutter Island, starring Leonardo DiCaprio, is another good example, where we are led to believe that we are following an investigation into a woman's disappearance but instead it is revealed that the investigator is actually an amnesiac inmate. The small detail of DiCaprio's band aid on his temple reminds me of McGoohan's in 'A Change of Mind'.

But the one movie which I consider to have a similar structure to The Prisoner is Zac Snyder's 2011 movie Suckerpunch, which received mixed reviews on its release and performed poorly in the cinema but has proved a cult classic. Suckerpunch is the story of a teenage girl played by Emily Browning, who we know only as Babydoll, who has been committed to a mental asylum by her abusive stepfather, who blamed her for the death of her sister. The wicked stepfather bribes the psychiatrist into lobotomising her so she cannot recall the true cause of the her sister's death. Babydoll creates an elaborate fantasy where the mental hospital becomes a brothel, and she enlists the help of several fellow show girls to help her collect a series of items she can use to escape. All the young female characters are dehumanized and infantalised by being given childish porn star nicknames, such as the aforementioned Babydoll, Sweet Pea, Rocket, Amber and Blondie. We are never told their real names. Each section takes the form of an erotic dance, a music video, where Babydoll and her companions collect the items she needs to escape the brothel. They are guided by a wise man, who gives them instructions and guidance on how to do this. This is something of a dream within a dream, because, of course she isn't in a brothel, she is a patient in a mental institution, and she is about to be lobotomised. In an echoing of The Prisoner's ending, we are led to believe that Babydoll surrendered herself to allow for Sweet Pea's escape. However, the bus driver who arrives to take her away is the same wise man we have met in the fantasy segments. Did this whole story take place in the few seconds it took for Babydoll to be lobotomised, just like the LSD dream in Jacob's Ladder?

Once you get used to viewing A Change of Mind as the turning point, the fever dreams which follow make perfect sense. There was no body swap, no Janet Portman, no fish and chips western, no Girl Who Was Death. Perhaps, even the two colour Danger Man episodes, Koroshi and Shinda Shima, screened during the Prisoner's hiatus, are also Number 6's delusions? (There are certainly continuity points, look at Drake's red suitcase, blue with white soled deck shoes, and the presence of Potter) These were illusions, just like the dance music videos in Suckerpunch, just like the switching realities in Jacob's Ladder. And like Sweet Pea, Number 6 does not escape either, he just falls through into another dream, where he has escaped to London with his betrothed, Number 2, and his "Man From Another Place", the ever present silent Butler.

What is all this driving the Jailbird to(o)?? — Seek Out Page 160

Reds Under the Bed

In very nearly fifty years of analysis and academic thought, although the central message of the Prisoner has been used to support various forms of Libertarian thought, and other anti authoritarian belief systems, it has always been unfashionable to see Number 6 as a socialist. This of course is due to the political climate of the Cold War era, the Communist bogeyman looming large over popular media, from James Bond to the Avengers, and the spirit of Stalin and Mao Zedong's authoritarian dictatorships. Many people were led to believe that the Village was a mock British town somewhere behind the Iron Curtain, although this was debunked in the series very early on in The Chimes of Big Ben, where it becomes very obvious that Number 6 is being held captive at "Her Majesty's pleasure", and it is the British establishment, the masters he one served, who are retaining him. It would be wrong to ascribe political views to McGoohan, as, as far as I have read he spoke little of politics in his interviews, and was never an activist. What we do know from his 1977 interview with Canadian TV presenter Warner Troyer he did not appear to be a big fan of consumer culture, criticising the advertising industry, television and Madison Avenue, and as he did not capitalise on his popularity to be a big Hollywood star, did not appear to be motivated by the acquisition of vast wealth.

The mock British town behind the Iron Curtain has it's roots in a 1962 anti-communist propaganda film titled "Freedom and You", which was made by Warner Bros for the Department of Defense. It is sometimes shown in an edited form as an "educational film" to school children as "Red Nightmare", and both versions are freely available to watch on YouTube, if you are interested in seeing them. In the movie, narrator Jack Webb shows the viewer a mock mid American town, built as a training centre in the Soviet Union for espionage agents spies and moles infiltrating US society, to acclimatise them to American culture. In a very Prisoneresque scene, the hero of the piece wakes up and crawls from his bed to the window, to find he has been spirited away from his cosy middle class white American home to a Soviet Bizzarro world, where everything is the same but different, his children are Young Pioneers, the church is now a museum and his factory has switched to a quota system. Whether these towns existed or not, or were simply scaremongering tactics is unknown, but this movie inspired the infamous Danger Man season 2 episode "Colony 3", itself said to be an early inspiration for The Prisoner. In this episode, Drake, in the guise of a civil servant, is sent behind the Iron Curtain to a typical British town, complete with red phone boxes and black cabs. In typical Drake style, he saves the day with his home made spy camera, and returns to his bosses with convicting photographs identifying the Russian moles. The idea of a fake, film set town being used to train or "re-educate" spies resonates with the Prisoner, though Number 6's reasons for being sent there are very different. He is not being trained to take on an espionage mission, he's there to have the information in his head extracted. He isn't there to infiltrate the Village and identify miscreants on orders from above. If Number 6 was indeed an agent, it seems likely he would have been a double agent on the payroll of both sides of the Cold War. There might be a clue to this in the infamous press conference McGoohan staged before the Prisoner was screened, where he answered questions in a deliberately oblique manner from behind the bars of the cage seen in Once Upon A Time. Instead of appearing in a nice dinner suit, McGoohan played to the crowd dressed in his red oriental style Kosho dress, and a Russian astrakhan hat, famously worn by members of the Politbuto. Was this a intentional depiction of the USSR and China, or just a happy coincidence?

The 1960's fear of nuclear holocaust is played with throughout the series, from The Girl Who Was Death, the Pop! scene in Once Upon A Time, the alternative end credits on The Chimes of Big Ben, to the missile seen in Fall Out. Fall Out is itself, a play on the idea of nuclear fallout, the radioactive dust which will kill us all, even if we survive the initial blast. It's not surprising that The Prisoner comes just five years after the Cuban Missile Crisis, which many people were convinced would bring about the end of the world. In the 1977 interview with Canadian TV, McGoohan comments on this, that the world is is danger due to progress, we are constantly creating bigger and better weapons, and there has never been a weapon created which hasn't been used. In the 1980's, CND activists, The Greenham Common women among others in the UK, protested against cruise missiles, and now, even in 2017, this is a contentious issue, with current political debates over the renewing of Trident. At the end of Fall Out, we see the launch of a missile, and people running in terror from the Village, but what we don't know is, was the Village evacuated? Was it destroyed? Did it ever really exist in the first place?

The idea of people being "reprogrammed" in mental facilities was definitely inspired by what was happening within the Stalinist USSR and Mao's China. People were sent to the Gulag, or forced labor camps, for disobeying their masters, as Aleksandr Solzhenitsyn testifies in his horrifying 1973 expose, The Gulag Archipelago. Even into the 1980's, there were horrific mental institutions in countries such as Romania, where even very young children were kept naked, shaved and chained to the bed. There were even, as Margaret Attwood illustrates in her book The Handmaid's Tale, intensive breeding programs to create the next generation of loyal workers.

There are several different approaches to mind control in The Prisoner, from the use of advanced medication, classical conditioning in the style of John Watson and Ivan Pavlov, (famous for his dog experiment) to operant conditioning, in the style of B.F Skinner (famous for his rat experiments) and there is also an element of the famous Milgram experiment, and Zimbardo's Stanford Prison experiment.

The famous Milgram experiment proved that people do as they are told, especially if they are told by someone they consider to be their superior. The trial of Nazi war criminal Adolph Eichmann took place in 1961, and his claim that he "was just following orders" inspired Milgram to investigate this phenomenon, and see if generally kind, reasonable individuals could commit acts which went against their moral values if told to do them by an authority figure. Milgram recruited 40 men who he told would participating in a learning experiment, these men would be expected to administer an electric shock to a person they believed to be a fellow volunteer, "Mr Wallace", but was in fact a stooge, every time he got a question wrong. The more questions the stooge got wrong, an authoritarian figure in a lab coat would urge the volunteer to increase the intensity of the shocks, and heard "Mr Wallace" crying out in pain and shouting, "get me out of here!" but they were told to ignore his discomfort as it would ruin the experiment. Even when "Mr Wallace" stopped responding, the participant was urged by the man in the lab coat to continue. Of course, the shocks were fake, but the participant didn't know this, many of the volunteers suffered emotional breakdowns and even seizures, but astonishingly, all 40 of the participants choose to carry on torturing "Mr Wallace" at the command of the man in the white lab coat.

Zimbardo's Prison Experiment took place in a basement at Stanford University in 1971. Zimbardo chose 24 emotionally healthy middle class male students to take part in the experiment, who were divided into prisoners and guards at the flip of a coin. To make the experience as realistic as possible, the prisoners were arrested at their homes, strip searched, deloused, given prison uniforms and were further dehumanized by having to wear a chain around their ankle, and were only referred to by their number, not their name. The guards were kitted out with military uniforms, dark glasses to prevent eye contact, and carried whistles, clubs and handcuffs. The guards were on duty 24 hours a day, and were given complete control over the prisoners, to maintain order by any means necessary. Zimbardo was horrified at how quickly the guards became abusive authoritarians, getting the prisoners to do demeaning things like clean toilet bowls with their bare hands, or play degrading games. One of the prisoners had to be released after just 36 hours because of his severe depression and fits of rage. After Zimbardo realised the situation had become dangerous, he had to bring the experiment to an early close. However, the experiment was successful in proving that good, reasonable, rational people can be induced into behaving in evil ways by immersion in "total situations" and ideologies that allow and legitimise the abuse of power.

In The Prisoner, it's easy to see that both Number 6, and the myriad of Number 2s are prisoners, but Number 2 has been given authority, even if he has not been given his freedom. In Checkmate, part of the game is figuring out who is a "prisoner" and who is one of "them", a stooge working for the Village authorities as a "guardian". The Rook, Number 58, undergoes social conversion therapy, so appears to Number 6 to be a fellow prisoner, so he seeks an alliance with him to make an escape plan. Unfortunately, Number 6's confident, authoritarian demeanor makes him appear to be one of the villages guardians! In the episode Hammer Into Anvil, Number 6 uses a mind game known as "Gaslighting" to drive Number 2 to have a nervous breakdown. Gaslighting gets its name from a 1938 play "Gas Light", (known also as Angel Street) whereby a husband tries to convince his wife that she is going insane by manipulating small details of her environment, then insists that she is delusional when she notices the changes. Another film which shows this technique in action is the quirky 2001 French comedy "Amelie", where she gets her revenge on the bullying green grocer, Collignon, by breaking into his house and fiddling with his possessions.

The various forms of torture and mind control used on Number 6 in order to get him to reveal his secrets have a real life origin, the secret CIA Scientific Intelligence Division operation MK Ultra, which utilised the experience of ex Nazi engineers, doctors and scientists taken to the USA as part of Operation Paperclip, to prevent their knowledge falling into the hands of, not only the Soviets, but the British, and to prevent Germany from rebuilding its military research facilities. Although these operations were illegal, thousands of experiments were carried out on civilian human subjects, including children and the disabled, against their will, where they were subjected to electro shock, LSD and other "truth drugs", hypnosis, sexual and emotional abuse, torture, isolation and sensory derivation all under the auspices of "science". The operation was financed by CIA "front organisations" and endorsed by the U.S. military, who planned to use these methods for interrogating enemy agents and prisoners of war, to force confessions, and to create "mind controlled assassins", like in the movie the Manchurian Candidate. So sometimes the truth really is as strange and terrifying as fiction. (Continued on Page 304).

VJ Clarke in the driving seat of a Caterham Seven (the company that now owns the Lotus marque) in Battery Square, Portmeirion

58 Buckingham Place Street Sign, Abingdon Street Car Park Entrance, Park Lane Car Park Entrance Barrier seen in 'Arrival' and view of Buckingham Place showing postbox next to No 1 ; from The Unmutual Prisoner Locations Guide used with the permission of Rick Davy.

59 In general all photos by Rick Davy come from the source mentioned in footnote 58.

<u>MEETING SIR CLOUGH</u>
VAUGHAN BRUNT RECALLS THE FIRST PRISONER CONVENTION IN 1977...
This can also be found on
The Unmutual Website at:
http://theunmutual.co.uk/sirclough.htm

Have you ever wondered what the ideal circumstances might be for watching an episode of 'The Prisoner'? It's impossible that we will ever be able to watch 'Fall Out' alongside McGoohan himself but back in the '1970s', some of us were lucky enough to be a part of something almost as unique. It was the culmination of the very first fan convention on a typically drizzly Sunday afternoon. The date was 17th April 1977...

Castell Deudraeth aka 'The Hospital' from 'The Prisoner' : courtesy Ian Orchard

There were no fancy dress homages in those days, no Max's shop, not even a noisy evening disco. The hippies in charge of the society back then would never have condoned such common vulgarity. ITC, it turned out, had brought down a 16 mm black and white print of 'Arrival' which was shown in the Hercules Hall. What made that screening unique was that in the crowded audience was none other than the creator of Portmeirion himself, Sir Clough Williams-Ellis. I must admit at this point that my own ignorance of Portmeirion's architectural history was degree absolute. Phil Kendrick, on the other hand, had been to the village before and knew something of its development.

So there Phil and I stood, next to the side door by the bar, chatting to the great man himself. He certainly looked the part of the eccentric genius with his legendary plus-fours, dapper waistcoat and buttonhole flower in his jacket. Sir Clough had quite clearly been intrigued by all this new activity. In '77 we did not take control of the place as we did in later years. He said he had enjoyed watching the episode on our medium-size screen and thought his "brain child looked impressive". A fine tribute to McGoohan's efforts.

Sir Clough told us that McGoohan and he had become friends prior to filming and he felt he could therefore trust him enough to allow Paddy to shoot his magnum opus in the village. This trust, it appears, was not to prove misplaced. It was then that he mentioned to us for the first time, as far as 'Six of One' was concerned anyway, what was to become known over the years as the 'original' Rover. Sir Clough said that it had failed to work and if memory had served him correctly how it had sunk in the sea. His comments about this surprised us both as information on the production, even in Six of One, was virtually nil in 1977. We later mentioned what Sir Clough had told us to others and several people wondered whether this was a very old man's failing memory but I can tell you for nothing that Sir Clough's mind was sharper than anyone else's in the village that day. He also said how the young people (well this was 25 years ago) in attendance had pleased him as he liked to see "all that colour and life" wandering around his creation.
Thanks to Steven Ricks' video[60], many of us have now had the chance to see the go-kart Rover although its ultimate fate is still uncertain.

Since Sir Clough Williams-Ellis' death in 1978, the village has become more commercially successful. It is debatable whether in the interim it has lost a part of its original dignity and some could well say its survival depends upon an economic compromise of Sir Clough's '1920s' ideals.

(Adapted and edited from a feature by Vaughan Brunt, with his kind permission, from CAMERA OBSCURA No.15)

---

[60] 'The Prisoner In Production' - Steven Ricks - TR7 Productions, 1993

"The Butler (Didn't) Do It and other stories" [61]By Ed Fordham, (BA Hons.) Politics

The little man in society — so often Angelo Muscat's role within The Prisoner is sidelined. We see him providing refreshment for Number Two and Number Six repeatedly, providing massage treatment to a couple of (presumably tense and stressed) Number Two's and sadly being threatened by Number Two during Patrick Cargill's tour de force performance in Hammer Into Anvil.

Yet it is surprising what our Butler friend turns his hand to, no matter whether Number Six can fly an Allouette II helicopter with an Electropass - the Butler is seen flying it with two passengers. He can play various pieces on an organ to suit Leo McKern's Number Two's mood in 'Once Upon A Time'. He is seen watching over the chess game in Checkmate and copying the moves on his own chessboard so we can assume he has a very good knowledge of the game.

In Dance of the Dead towards the end of the episode — Angelo plays a significant symbolic role. Although the verdict is passed by a small group of Villagers the Butler 'kills' Number Six's pre-Village persona in passing the black hat to symbolically destroy his past self.

Notably in the original screening order — from this point on — Number Six works within the Village aiming to dismantle it from inside. There is a problem, an anomaly, known as 'Checkmate' this follows 'Dance of The Dead' and Number Six is back on the path of seeking escape. The way to resolve this will be acknowledged in a discussion on the screening order yet to come.

For the moment we could simply swap the two episodes around but place 'Many Happy Returns' in between them. The references to Number Six being new here become logical if you account for the absence of over a month from the Village, spending significant time at sea, encountering and outwitting and escaping from Gunrunners, obtaining nourishment from a group of Romanies, jumping into a NETCO Lorry, finding himself in London, returning home and being dismissed by Mrs Butterworth's maid Martha, meeting the extremely smitten Mrs Butterworth who struggles to conceal her attraction to Number Six, snaffling a whole plate of sandwiches and a fruitcake provided for him, borrowing 'Dear Arthur's' clothes, Meeting the man he presented his resignation too, having his story torn to shreds by the Colonel and Thorpe until he persuades them to check his story, arranging to fly over an area considered to be the most likely location for the Villager and being ejected with a parachute onto the Village's beach.

After all those events it would make complete sense for Number Six to feel he is new here 'again' in 'Dance of the Dead'

This is largely coincidental but suggests that the Butler's appearance at the end of 'Dance of the

---

[61] The Hotel Portmeirion/The Old People's Home : courtesy Ed Fordham

Dead' is highly significant. Number Six has wandered into the labyrinth of the underworld of the Village – an area normally out of bounds to the other Villagers. The metaphor is made physical by the sinister suggestion by Mary Morris's Number Two that the body found on the beach will be (surgically) altered[62] to look like Number Six, cutting himself off from the outside world permanently. In the episodes that follow Number Six's objective is not to escape the Village any longer, even in 'The General' he agrees to transmit the Professor's message about Speadlearn being slavery because Number Twelve assures him it will enable his escape.

So a part of Number Six has died and he focuses on what changes he can make within the structures, environment, administration, bureaucracy and community of the Village. In 'Hammer Into Anvil' this is made immediately clear as Number Six enters a battle of wills and wits with Number Two which ultimately leads to the Butler packing his bags to leave the Green Dome.

In the past a lot has been made about the Butler never speaking and some have suggested that he is incapable of speech or even has poor hearing, when Leo's Number Two repeats orders to him in 'Once Upon A Time' about removing the breakfast and leaving the coffee. However the suggestion is made in the way the scene is filmed with the Butler's use of a handbell to summon Number Two and the Arrival of Rover in the Black spherical chair in which Number Two normally sits that the Butler is temporarily in charge and the feeling is that Number Two should not be respected.

After all Leo's Number Two was involved in an elaborate scheme to convince Number Six that he had escaped involving a Village agent and some of Number Six's former colleagues. The detail about the watch set to the wrong time zone which unravelled the plan showed that this Number Two will have to fight to regain the Butler's respect.

The Butler is the closest we get to a major recurring character in The Prisoner indeed there are merely a handful of episodes in which he makes no appearance. He is always smartly dressed, takes his position seriously and even when his patience could be stretched by Number Two's demands he is methodical and never becomes confrontational. Yet he remains the enigma, the only character who appears in nearly as many episodes as Number Six yet unlike the combative barbs of Number Two and Number Six he remains stoic and just carries out his duties meticulously.

During the initial screening the obvious question arose — applying the literary trope and also that of films and television that, 'The Butler Did It' and maybe he would be revealed as Number One. We could apply the same backwards looking way of understanding films like 'Fight Club' & 'The Sixth Sense' in this regard.

The Butler answers the door to Number Two's residence and invites him into Number Two's inner sanctum in Arrival &(it is the Butler who actually) provides breakfast and tea preferences for Number Six which are kept on file. We can safely assume that the Butler has access to personal files about the Villagers in order to carry out this process. Who would ultimately have access to those files and be in regular contact with each Number Two? Would it not be Number One and where better to place Number One than hidden in plain sight, watching over Number Two and indeed whenever possible Number Six?

We could even theorise that the automatically opening door to NUMBER 1 Buckingham Place,

---

62   We assume surgical but given other duplicated characters in the series perhaps the Village has cloning technology.

which allows the Butler to enter is a massive clue or another red herring deliberately calculated by McGoohan. But that would mean ignoring the masked manic McGoohan in his white hooded robe laughing in hysteria at Number Six and that would be downright nutty.[63]

Perhaps the point I'm trying to make once again is there a case for not putting too much analysis into The Prisoner.

Though will we may be searching for a perceptive understanding are we over-thinking and therefore creating a situation where we can no longer watch and enjoy the episodes as an excellent example of late 1960s television.

Or perhaps we just haven't found the right angle on understanding 'The Prisoner' yet — all our energy expended to finding answers with a tv series that left us with more questions than answers. We keep trying to tie loose ends together and find that the episodes contradict each other on a basic level — perhaps that's why we have spent 50 years 'trying' to understand 'this incredible classy, classic television show.' The human mind is designed to want to make sense of things, to understand our surroundings and McGoohan left us with loose ends dangling absolutely deliberately. That is why this book exists as we try to grapple with ideas like 'individual freedom,' the purpose of government and the state, cold war politics, the existence of camps like Inverlair Lodge in Scotland for ex-spys or spys who had failed training but couldn't be left to have their freedom. We even have questions about how much control McGoohan exercised over individual episodes and parts of the series development.

The Butler is therefore the little person in society — the unimportant day to day people we see in the street, in shops, who work in offices — in essence all of us — 'unimportant' only to those who laud authority — by sweetening the deal. No wonder Number Six didn't take sugar![64]

Photo Courtesy of Rick Davy

Yet the Butler intrigues us — he attends to his duties silently and usually with little fuss — the main exceptions being in 'Once Upon A Time' and 'Fall Out'.

He seems to watch over the activity in the Village even attending to the Committee meetings regarding 'Unmutuals' and we might question why is he silent.

---

[63] OK allow me one Troy McClure reference in a book about 'The Prisoner' — from 'The Simpsons' — 'The 138th Episode Spectacular'.

[64] I make no apologies for expressing my views about the deal between Theresa May's Government and the DUP - After all if you are a nurse in the NHS there is no magic money tree to pay you a respectable salary but Theresa May can produce £1.5 billion for the DUP to keep her job.

Is this a coded message — that if Number Six can hold his tongue he will be rewarded? Or are we looking too deeply into the role of a man who provides tea, coffee, breakfast and lunch for Number Two and their guests.

The Butler is an accomplished masseuse ensuring that Anton Rodgers and Peter Wyngarde's Number Two character are relieved of any tension caused by the work of Chief Administrator.

In addition we often see the Butler patrolling the Village beneath his black and white umbrella. Is this symbolic does the Butler and by extension the Village authorities see things in win or lose terms. Perhaps they need to be reminded by the Villagers multicoloured parasols that things are not quite so clear cut. However let us note well that 'Number Six' wears what appears to be a black blazer with white piping (although the supposed black material is actually a very dark brown shade) is the Butler in some way linked to Number Six representing part of his psyche? Is the Butler the part of Number Six that really believes 'a still tongue makes a happy life' or does he represent a potential future for the Villagers' unable to fight back only able to do the Villages' bidding— without the ability to speak out and decry what the Village represents?

Or is he just a subservient little man who occasionally helps out with (sorry) the little things in life?

The Butler remains a mystery — he has no number like Number Six yet he's clearly either heavily conditioned to assist or has finally accepted his lot and tows the line (sorry) for a quiet life? Could he really have been the man behind the big door, as No 1 Buckingham Place's front entrance humms open we ask perhaps it was the Butler who did it. Silently all along.

PETER DUNN'S A-Z OF PRISONER ALLEGORY
C - Cross Pieces, Christ and Crucifix Positions.

This article was originally published on the Unmutual Website and can be found at:
https://www.theunmutual.co.uk/articleatozc.htm

So what were you expecting then? A column on cats? OK, so I am biased. Yes, I am a Christian which gives the content a certain inevitability... or does it? First let me detail two surprises:

SURPRISE NUMBER ONE

'The Prisoner' is not, and was not intended to be, an allegory of Christianity. What's this? Has Peter Dunn become an atheist? Is he retracting his long held views because McGoohan has issued a Fatwa against him? No - I am simply stating the obvious. 'The Prisoner' was born out of the adventure series 'Danger Man,' it was conceptualised by George Markstein as a pure adventure story and by McGoohan as vague vehicle for exploring the concepts of freedom and individuality. I could also argue that it is unlikely that Jewish born Lew Grade would finance a televisual Christian allegory but I would then find it kind of hard to explain his backing of 'Jesus of Nazareth.'

So why even bother with an article on Christianity? My answer? Christianity is of vital importance to my life, it was also central to McGoohan's life. As 'The Prisoner' progressed it became more and more a reflection of McGoohan's will and McGoohan's angst and less and less the adventure series intended by Markstein. McGoohan's own personal agenda spilled into 'The Prisoner' both in script and on screen. His view of women, politics, education, personal freedom, the cold war, youth rebellion increasingly came to the fore and, at the very end, out in front of the cameras, came that which he held most dear yet perhaps questioned most — his faith.

'Fall Out,' I believe, is the only episode to carry direct allegorical references to Christianity sanctioned by McGoohan. This episode is clearly the most allegorical. This was his last chance to explore the issues that were dear to him — and he took that chance. 'Fall Out's' script has no space for tidy boring plot resolution, instead Patrick McGoohan pours into the text his thoughts on politics, the cold war, youth rebellion, the collapse of authority and many other issues that concerned everyone living in the late 60s — he also throws into that crazy melting pot a much more personal and timeless concern — faith and religion.

SURPRISE NUMBER TWO

Hold on a minute. What about all that guff we Christians have always said about strong Christian elements appearing in other episodes such as the 'icthous' "Be Seeing You" salute and the cross piece in 'The Chimes Of Big Ben'? All nonsense, I am afraid. I have never argued that the 'Be Seeing You' salute related to the ancient Christian 'icthous' symbol — the secret fish-shaped sign that Christians used to identify each other under Roman persecution. I know some of my fellow Christians have claimed this but they are really deluding themselves. The salute looks nothing like a fish (unless you do your fishing near Chernobyl) and if it is meant to be an allegory of a secret symbol how come it is the official Village salute used by everyone from Number 2 to the waiters in the old folk's home. Now if it were a symbol used by the Jammers then I might think differently... If you want to know what that salute really signifies then read part B of these articles.

Ok, what about the cross piece in 'The Chimes Of Big Ben' then? Yes, I must admit that even I have argued in the past that this scene, in which Number 6 explains his carved exhibit `Escape' to the awards committee, is a clear reference to Christianity and there is no doubt that the script writer intended it to be. Hold on a minute, am I not contradicting what I said under 'Surprise Number One'? Yes... and no! Lets look at script writer Vincent Tilsley's original dialogue for that scene:

Woman: What puzzled me, No.6 was the fact you'd given the group a title. `Escape'. We don't quite see...
Prisoner: This piece. What does it suggest to you
Man Two: A church door?
Prisoner: Right first time. A barrier. The barrier to human truth and progress.
Man Two: Oh, I see. Don't know that I agree though.
Woman: I certainly don't
Man One: Is that official policy?
Prisoner: Now this piece — exactly the same shape, you'll notice. But hollow. You can walk through it. [HE DOES SO] The barrier has gone. The door is open. We can escape to... this - THE POLE WITH THE CROSS PIECE.
Man One: What is it?
Prisoner: A symbol of human aspiration. Up. Straight up. To knowledge; freedom; escape.
Man One: I see. But why the cross piece?
Prisoner: The very word. A cross. Because our escape leads us back to — discipline. Faith. Organisation. In fact — religion.[65]

Mmmm... not quite how that scene was actually broadcast, eh? You will note that much of the original dialogue recorded above was dropped from the scene or replaced with much less precise phraseology. Most noticeably the detailed answer by Number 6 to the question "Why the cross piece?" is replaced by the rather trite (but somehow more appropriate) line "Why not?". It is clear then that Tilsley intended a clear and negative statement about religion to be made at this point but that McGoohan dropped it in favour of more an ambiguous statement on the nature of escape. Any remaining traces of Christian symbolism (i.e., the references to a church door and a cross piece are turned into humorous remarks by Number 6 to play along with the awards committee). It is also important to note that an extra element (a piece of wood with large circle-shaped holes cut into it) is added to the

---

[65] Vincent Tilsley, 'The Chimes of Big Ben' Everyman Films 1966

sculpture not mentioned in the script which physically prevents Number 6 from walking through the `church door' as intended in the original script. Clearly McGoohan went a long way to excise much of the religious content of this scene. Why did he do so if he was later to make so much of Christianity in 'Fall Out'?

I believe there are three reasons for this. Firstly the allegorical content of this piece was, in truth, not very allegorical — it was too specific, blunt and direct and not in keeping with the rest of the show. For the same reason cuts are also made to Tilsley's script when Number 6 and Leo McKern's Number 2 are discussing politics during Nadia's swim. Here a number of direct references to nationalism are cut:-

Number 2: What do you think of Nationalism? As such?
Prisoner: Depends whose side you're on.
Number 2: No, I'm an optimist myself. Nationalism's a disease but it breeds its own antibodies. That's why it doesn't matter who Number 1 is. It doesn't matter which side   runs the Village.

These religious references by Tilsley are also cut because they are entirely negative and anti Christianity. While Patrick McGoohan may have had questions about his faith, as most Christians do, he did not, at this point at least, completely reject it in the way Tilsley's original script does.

NO MORE SURPRISES
OK, so we are left with 'Fall Out'. Why can't the religious references here be argued away as easily as the way we have dealt with 'The Chimes Of Big Ben'? Sorry, but the evidence is too strong and overlapping. Do not get me wrong, 'Fall Out' is not just an allegory of Christianity. It is the last stop clearing house for all McGoohan's thoughts on life, the universe and everything, and his thoughts on faith are just one element of that episode. It is however a very strong element and it is clearly centred around the theme of Christian resurrection.

Few people would argue against the fact that at least one character is actually resurrected in 'Fall Out'. Leo McKern's Number 2 clearly dies in 'Once Upon A Time' and is resurrected in 'Fall Out. He is described as being `DEAD' twice in the script, is referred to as a 'late Number 2,' and the character also declares that he at least 'apparently died. I think he could not be deader even if Doctor McCoy from 'Star Trek' was to wander on set and declare "He's dead Jim". Yet up he pops, back to life, saying things like "I feel a new man," (adopting a crucifix style stance as he says that line) and later singing along to Dem

[66]Bones - a song based directly on the biblical story (in Ezekiel 37) when God resurrects a living army from dead dry bones. Three clear signifiers that this is Christian resurrection we are presented with. But is it just coincidence? Oh no, for we have a second resurrection depicted just to drive the point home.

Number 48 is, I believe, the resurrected Kid/Number 8 from 'Living In Harmony.' Why so? — after all it would not be the first time an actor has played two different roles in 'The Prisoner'. I could argue that 6 times 8 equals 48 but that would not mean much. However, I do think what is significant is the character's costume. The character wears a top hat just as the Kid did in 'Harmony'. "So what?" I hear you say. Well, not only that but the original 'Fall Out' script also specifies that he should be wearing a red shirt — just like a certain mute gunslinger character. What more do you want him to do? Wear a six shooter and mutely tap out the tune to Dem Bones rather than sing it? Yes, the red shirt was dropped from the script but it is important to note that this was an original idea in a script by Patrick McGoohan himself and thus gives us insights to his thinking on the show that we would not get from dropped scenes or dialogue from commissioned writers such as Vincent Tilsley. In other words I can have my cake and eat it in this debate!

While on the subject of script changes, it is also interesting to note this passage of dialogue written by McGoohan dropped into the final version of 'Fall Out':

Young Man: Got the word?
President: Ah yes. Yes, Indeed.
Young Man: The bright light, Dad. Got the sign.
President: The sign?
Young Man: The light.
President: Light.
Young Man: The message.
President: Then you went and gone?

Clearly there are lots of Christian references here, the bright light of conversion on the Damascus Road, the word, the sign, the message, the light. But a bit too direct, however, so McGoohan drops them (just as he did Tilsley's in "The Chimes Of Big Ben"), preferring to use more subtle clues to the Christian perspective of Number 48's resurrection. He, like Number 2, adopts a crucifix position. He refers to himself as being "born all over" and of course leads several rousing choruses of Dem Bones. I could, at this juncture, point out that Dem Bones is directly specified in the script and that Patrick McGoohan considered it so important that he sent Eric Mival out to scour the shops to collect up all the versions of the song that he could. Eric Mival has said time and again when questioned that he believed that McGoohan wished to use that specific song to make some sort of spiritual reference — but then Eric is also an evangelical Christian and equally as biased as me......However, that does not preclude the possibility that we may actually be right!

---

[66] Photo of Dome and Hercules Statue on previous page (p131) - courtesy Ian Orchard

I could go on to list more Christian parallels in 'Fall Out' such as the strapping in of Number 2 and Number 48 in orbit tubes beside an empty one intended perhaps for Number 6 in a way representative of the position of the two thieves crucified beside Christ, but I think that would probably be going too far....So where are we going? We have established that there is lots of Christian imagery but what, if anything, is Patrick McGoohan saying by its use?

I believe these various Christian references climax in the unmasking of Number 1. Here Number 6 reveals that the identity of his own jailer is in fact a manic version of himself who delights in wearing an animal mask. "Oh dear," says the great viewing public, "it's not the Russians, it's not the British, it's not even `Dr. No' running the Village - instead it is an Allegorical representation of an aspect of Number 6/Patrick McGoohan." (Or alternatively you could say its 'Prisoner' extra Roy Beck in a big white cloak but only sad boring pedantic fans would reduce it to that level!). OK, so what aspect of Patrick McGoohan/Number 6 is Number 1? Well, if we follow the Christian theme through, I believe we see that Number 6 is imprisoned by himself, by its own evil side (n.b.. The animal mask and the manic features of his alter-ego) by his own sinful fallen nature. One cannot escape oneself. As Patrick McGoohan himself put it:

"It was about the most evil human being — human essence — and that is ourselves. It is within each of us, that is, the most dangerous thing on earth is what is within us. And so, therefore, that's what I made Number 1 - one's self, an image of himself which he was trying to beat."

Number 6 could not escape the big I, I, I, I. He could not escape himself and indeed he does not. When he returns to London the door to his own house has adopted an opening hum peculiar to the Village - the end credits still depict him as 'Prisoner,' and the series ends exactly as it begins with him driving down the runway. Is there then any hope given in the show? Is there any escape? Yes, there is and it can be summed up in one word — resurrection. Of course it could also be summed up with words from a particular text. Here is Paul's letter to the Romans, chapter 6 verses 4-7: "...just as Christ was raised from the dead through the glory of the Father, we too may live a new life. For we know that our old self was crucified with him so that the body of sin might be rendered powerless, that we should no longer be slaves to sin because anyone who has died has been freed from sin."

Or as Psalm 146 verse 7 puts it:-"The Lord Sets Prisoners Free". So there is a way out for Number 6, for Patrick McGoohan, for you, and for me....Yet it is clear that Number 6 does take that way out and it might even be the case that McGoohan himself has not taken this path... What do I mean? Well, I think I should end this article on that enigmatic note thus reflecting the show itself, i.e., by provoking thought but not necessarily answering all the questions. If you want me to elaborate on this last sentence I'd be glad to — stop me at an event or write something to an online Prisoner forum but remember once you start a dialogue on religion or politics with Ulster folk like me it is quite difficult to shut us up!

George Orwell – 'Nineteen Eighty-Four'

Orwell's 'Nineteen Eighty-Four' and 'The Prisoner' – Thoughtcrime and the Unmutual

Image from https://stocksnap.io

The strength of Orwell's Nineteen Eighty-Four lies not just in the dystopian London in which Winston Smith and Julia's relationship develops and the back story of Oceania's war with Eurasia that acts as a backdrop to this.

The concepts that Orwell devises to underpin the story—the notion of 'Thoughtcrime' where the very idea of being anti-party in 'Own-life' is criminal and the idea of Big Brother watching constantly over the citizens yet never seen are intelligent ideas. However if this were the limit of Orwell's creation then Nineteen Eighty-Four would simply be a very clever and thoughtful novel.

What Orwell depicts is a shaken up and somewhat distorted Post World War II landscape in which the world is divided into three political boundaries. The tele-screens and their two way function predict quite clearly the incorporation of CCTV into the modern world. The idea of Newspeak and its role in foreseeing the way we text, tweet and talk online in abbreviated ways and acronyms is only a short step from truncating spoken language. Comedian's over the last few years such as Bill Bailey have got much material out of hearing the acronym lol being used out loud.[67]

It's clear that there is much Orwellian in nature to be seen in "The Prisoner" what McGoohan and his writers did was take the grim London of Oceania and replace it with a candy striped and architectural home for fallen buildings.

The Village is often depicted as a place of suspicion, mistrust and paranoia where individuals are marked out as against the authorities that govern the Village. Villagers are either

---

[67] Comedian Bill Bailey has got a stream of material out of hearing a young girl using LOL (laugh out loud) instead of actually laughing at something she found amusing.

sheep who unconditionally follow the rules or part of the administration governing the Village watching over 'the sheep' not to be trusted by those who try to break down the system.

In Orwell's 1984 'Thoughtcrime' is considered to be any internal ideas that are anti-party and we can clearly associate this with two concepts introduced in The Prisoner.
In 'A Change of Mind' the concept of being 'Unmutual' seems to be akin to 'Thoughtcrime' except that it extends to 'unsocial incidents'. The factor here is what is considered 'unsocial' - Number Six's use of his private woodland gymnasium is grounds for him being 'antisocial' but he is clearly provoked by two [68] interlopers before he faces the committee. Another less well defined concept is the idea of the PMC or Public Minded Citizen (this appears in the original script for 'Arrival') but is neatly removed due to a sequence being reshot featuring a replacement for Rover.

The PMC is a member of Village society that not only follows but helps to uphold the rules of the Village and would presumably be provoked to act if there was any activity that they considered 'Unmutual'. In many ways they act in the same way that Party members do if they are suspicious of others activity in the Oceania settlement of 1984 depicted in Orwell's novel.

Where McGoohan steps beyond the confines of pure Orwell is in the use of the Village, he uses Portmeirion as a cypher, symbolic of all society and yet visually appearing to be no where definable. Throughout the series physical locations are given that are contradictory in Many Happy Returns - the coast of Morocco, south west of Spain and Portugal, near Lithuania on the Baltic in The Chimes of Big Ben and just down the A1 from London in Fall Out.

The Village is therefore given a sense of unreality from a simple lack of continuity between episodes but perhaps we can cogently argue for a reason for this. Number Six's experiences in the Village often appear to be unreal. Events occur in such a way that would not be possible if what we saw was truly real. While 1984 strives for realism in its construction of a possible future society (albeit one that cleverly and clearly reflects on the present), The Prisoner increasingly strives to be more offbeat, even downright surreal in its depiction of society.

However the surrealism of The Prisoner is used to enable it to warp its own reality, never more so than in the Anthony Skene episode 'Dance of The Dead' — the imagery draws on such sources as Jean Cocteau's version of Orpheus in the Underworld, while sets draw on those used in elements of German Expressionism such as 'Fritz Lang's Metropolis and M'. The episode follows dreamlike logic with events segueing into each other rather than following a clearly defined path. Roland Walton Dutton representing a link to Number Six's past which is destroyed in effect by both the metaphorical death of Number Six and the seemingly brainwashed state in which Dutton appears as a character witness.

---

[68] Photo of the replaced 'Green' Dome and Hercules Statue: Portmeirion 2014 by Ian Orchard

The Orwellian conceit of being spied upon by concealed cameras is incorporated into the design of the Village environment, statues or seemingly static stone busts are rotated to follow wandering Villagers who stray outside the main Village boundaries. The design of Portmeirion thus suggests the manner in which these cameras are concealed since similar structures are dotted around the resort, the master stroke being to duplicate them at MGM Borehamwood and turn them into another way of observing others. The obsession with what is seen, who is seen doing what and by whom is carried a stage further as the miniature cameras appear in the statues eyes to enable this.

This notion of being seen is particularly relevant in 'Hammer Into Anvil' — after the new Number Two (Patrick Cargill) attempts to interrogate Number Seventy-Three about her supposedly philandering husband, a scream is heard and Number Six rushes to the rescue. Just too late to save her, she jumps from the Hospital window and we see a shot of her wearing red splayed on the ground. The red clothing is used to represent the death of Number Seventy-Three, presumably in line with McGoohan's attempts to make the show suitable for all the family. The battle of wits that follows as Number Six realises that Number Two has a character flaw (being afraid of his masters) is one of the most entertaining, if somewhat more straightforward to follow episodes. In successive events Number Six behaves in an increasingly suspicious way — he studies all the copies of Le Arlessiane in the General Stores in a Record Booth (unsurprisingly there are six copies) he returns them claiming he isn't satisfied with the recording and then accidentally leaves the Tally Ho newspaper behind with the word Security circled in the headline Security of the Community followed by a question mark. The shopkeeper passes this information onto Number Two.

Various events in Hammer Into Anvil reflect on Number Six's understanding of how the Village is run, the general atmosphere of paranoia and the fact that Number Six is certain by this point that Number Two is keeping a close eye on him. Gradually Number Two is lead to believe the Number Six is an internal spy checking on Village security. He uses the surveillance operations which he knows are in place to help carry out his plan progressively driving Number Two to believe that the Supervisor, the Head of the Department of Psychiatry, his assistant, the Butler, the Laboratory Scientists and others are all conspiring against him to help Number Six to discredit him.

Patrick Cargill's Number Two in 'Hammer Into Anvil' shows that the Village's techniques can be used against those who are supposedly in control of the Village themselves. He becomes increasingly unhinged and when finally confronted with the fact that he destroyed himself is left to report his own breakdown in control and request he be replaced.

What the creators of 'The Prisoner' did was take the grim London landscape of Oceania and replace it with a Village with candy-striped signs and an architectural home for fallen buildings.

The Village (like Oceania) is often depicted as a place of suspicion, mistrust and paranoia where individuals are marked out as against the authorities that govern the Village. Villager's can either be sheep who unconditionally follow the rules or part of the administration governing the Village watching over the 'sheep' and not to be trusted by anyone trying to break down the system.

However there are two other groups to consider – Villager's like 'Number Six' who are still individuals and those members of the Administration of The Village who choose to assist those who remain individuals.[69]

It's interesting that the 'White Queen' in 'Checkmate' is conditioned to fall in love with Number Six to allow 'Control' to keep an eye on him. In Orwell's novel Winston Smith's 'own-life' is un-done by having a relationship with Julia - what is not clear however is the extent to which Winston's downfall is connected with this, whether he was betrayed at some point by the shopkeeper or Julia. In Checkmate this subplot Peters out when the 'White Queen' asks Number Six if he is coming for a swim and also why if he is not in love with her— she has a locket with his photograph. The reaction transmitter that is found inside then feeds into the main 'Escape Plot' involving Number Six, the Rook and their 'reliable men'.[70] [71]

Even working with insiders within the Village system is fraught with danger as Number Six discovers in 'The General'. Number Twelve offers him a potential ticket out of the Village — knowing that the Professor harbours 'anti-Speedlearn' leanings. However it soon becomes clear that a simple escape is not on the cards — instead there is the possibility of utilising Speedlearn to decry it. This would have worked out okay if Number Twelve had not clumsily given security passes to Number Six : since Number Two realises he would have issued them through Administration. The ugly truth is had Number Six not asked an insoluble question — W.H.Y? then both the Professor and Number Twelve could have survived. Ironically 'The General' is destroyed by existentialism — a concept discussed in philosophy — and we were told there was no question on educational grounds it couldn't answer.

It's intriguing that the themes that are most prominent in Orwell's 'Nineteen-Eighty Four' are 'role-playing and deception'. Winston Smith deceives the Party, the Party deceives everybody, O'Brien & Charrington deceive Winston and Winston deceives himself.[72] Indeed the very nature of Truth and meaning are constantly in a state of flux in both the book and 'The Prisoner'.[73] The Village controls 'truth' and even 'reality' — today it is democratic and we have an Election — tomorrow it's a smokescreen. Interesting what it all boils down to in both Orwell's book and 'The Prisoner' is who or what you can trust. A clever segue into our next article.

---

[69] Number 9 (Virginia Maskell) in 'Arrival' and Number Twelve (J.Castle) in 'The General' seem to fit this category but as always in 'The Prisoner' it is hard to be sure.

[70] Does this suggest a bias on the part of Number Six, his misogynist leanings conditioned by prior experience with female characters or does it suggest at this point when homosexuality was about to be legalised that he 'prefers the company of men'.

[71] The suggestion at the end of footnote 70 was initially provided by Steve Matt - although I also invite you to watch the scene at the beginning of 'The General' where Number Twelve spots Number Six and the scenes with A in 'A.B and C' with this in mind.

[72] Bowker G 2003 'George Orwell', Little Brown, p388

[73] Ibid pp388-389

BETRAYAL OF TRUST by JANE ROWE

Adapted from an article written by Jane Rowe in 1999, with her kind permission.
Also found at :
http://theunmutual.co.uk/article21.htm

FOR:
Mary Morris: Dance Of The Dead, Leo McKern: Once Upon A Time, debatable in Fall Out.

INDIFFERENT:
Leo McKern: The Chimes Of Big Ben, Eric Portman: Free For All, Kenneth Griffiths: The Girl Who Was Death, Kenneth Bauer: Living In Harmony, Clifford Evans: Do Not Forsake Me Oh My Darling.

AGAINST:
Guy Doleman/George Baker: Arrival, Anton Rodgers: The Schizoid Man - Cunning, Patrick Cargill: Hammer Into Anvil -Sadistic, Colin Gordon: A, B & C, The General, Georgina Cookson: Many Happy Returns - Heartless and calculating, Rachel Herbert: Free For All - Malicious, Peter Wyngarde: Checkmate, Derren Nesbitt: It's Your Funeral, John Sharpe: A Change Of Mind, Nadia, Fotheringay, Colonel J: The Chimes Of Big Ben, Cobb: Arrival.

When viewing "The Prisoner" a number of themes strike me as important, the most noticeable one being betrayal and linked to this are the secondary themes of loneliness and paranoia. As a background I have given a list of Number 2's and some notable characters and how I think their sympathies lay for Number 6.

From the list above I think that the vast majority of Number 2's were against Number 6 or impassive towards his plight. However, I feel that a couple of them actually regarded him with sympathy and regretted the situation he was in and their role in trying to break him. Leo McKern's Number 2 seemed to grow more sympathetic as time went on. Mary Morris's character was rather ambiguous, but I feel that she respected Number 6 and felt sorry for him.

It is no wonder that, with this balance of the Village authority for and against him, Number 6 was paranoid, but on top of this he had to contend with villagers and supposed friends and work colleagues from the past betraying him. There were various levels of betrayal from the villagers, there were those who callously and knowingly betrayed him such as Nadia, others who were forced into it i.e. Alison and Virginia Maskell and a final group who did it unwittingly, like the Rook and Queen in Checkmate.

It is perhaps not surprising that Number 6 couldn't trust other villagers, but he might, reasonably, have been expected to trust his former `friends' and work colleagues. Why did these people betray his trust? What had Number 6 done to Cobb or Fotheringay for instance? Or was it their own untrustworthiness? I think the people from Number 6's past betrayed him of their own free will and that there could have been various motives. They themselves could have been traitors, which to me seems highly probable in the case of Cobb - who was seen at the end of "Arrival" going off "to meet his new masters". Some of them may have been envious of Number 6 and wished to discredit him and in that way gain recognition for them-selves. A third possibility and one which may give some honour and integrity to Number 6's colleagues, is that they may have been misled into thinking that Number 6 had done something despicable or treacherous and hence was deserving of their betrayal.

As well as being betrayed by individuals, on occasions Number 6 was isolated and betrayed by the whole village. Two examples of this spring to mind, the first is in "Many Happy Returns" when the village is deserted, the villagers must have co-operated in this, and the second is "A Change Of Mind" when Number 6 is declared unmutual. These two episodes also put Number 6 in isolation. In "Many Happy Returns" we see a determined Number 6 with a purpose and he seems unaffected by loneliness. However, in "A Change of Mind" when he is ostracised by the people around him and has no immediate purpose he seems lonely and homesick. Incidentally, these feelings strike me as coming across strongly in "Dance Of The Dead" in conversations with Mary Morris - first on the lookout, then on the beach.

I mentioned at the beginning that there is a sense of paranoia in a number of episodes, however Number 6 may have just cause to be paranoid. Not only is he stabbed in the back while he is in the village, he has little joy in the outside world. Take Janet for instance — she is supposed to be his fiancee, but she hardly seems perturbed by the fact that Number 6 has been missing for a year and she quite easily accepts a total stranger as him — but that's a different story! Janet seems to have done absolutely nothing in the way of finding out what had happened to her fiancé, one would have expected her to have kicked up a fuss. The real life plight of journalist John McCarthy illustrates this, with his girlfriend Jill Morrell doing everything possible to bring attention to his predicament. Also what of Number 6's parents, or are we to assume that they are dead?

It seems to me that even before Number 6 was abducted he had few (if any) friends he could really trust or rely upon. This situation begs Number 6's favourite question - Why? Was it because it made him less vulnerable as a secret agent if there were few people who could be threatened to make him do something. Or perhaps as a scientist he may have been too tied up in his research to socialise. Whatever the reason in the series, is it indicative of Patrick McGoohan's own life? As has been pointed out elsewhere he moved about a lot when young and thus lacked a stable environment, it is also likely that any friends he made would be lost in subsequent moves. Is this instability responsible for the subconscious feelings of betrayal, loneliness and paranoia which surfaced in "The Prisoner"?

"Where Am I and What Do You Want?" — Unanswered Questions, The Prisoner, Psychological Warfare and Why? By Ed Fordham BA (Hons.)

Photo from https://stocksnap.io

There are many questions left unanswered at the end of 'The Prisoner' : this is entirely appropriate I will argue... Because 'The Prisoner' was about Questions being "a burden to others, answers a prison for oneself" (Anthony Skene, 'Dance of the Dead,' 1966). In other words as early as the first 5 episodes being filmed in part in Portmeirion in September 1966, the concept of unanswered questions was a recurring theme.

If — for a moment — we assume Number Six is a real person then who is he and what job exactly did he resign from? George Markstein strongly believed that Number Six was a secret agent called Drake who quit and to be sure there is a group of people in 'Prisoner fandom' who would agree. Except there is no real evidence to support this — you can argue that he looks like Drake but then we are charged with the argument that Dr Sid Rafferty is John Drake or Number Six! Number Six whoever he is, this being something of a quagmire as addressed in Vickie Clarke's excellent essay, is certainly not Drake just because he is played by the same actor. Taken to its logical conclusion this would mean that John Drake is also Edward Longshanks having discovered time travel and disguised himself as an English King.

So and to unpick this a bit more is he a secret agent? Again we have problems answering this question because we never have it definitely confirmed, even Anthony Skene's 'A,B and C' doesn't scupper this as we only know he knew members of the spy community. He could easily have a top secret, confidential job of another nature an engineer, a rocket scientist (given his actions in 'Fall Out'), a biologist working for some governmental department.

Or he doesn't exist! Could Number Six be McGoohan's construct of himself as auteur— a cypher of the actor: a self created clone who is capable of flying helicopters, driving speedboats and in 'Many Happy Returns' creating an axe out of nowhere unless the rules have been relaxed somewhat since 'The Chimes of Big Ben'...

So where is the Village? Is it in Lithuania on the Baltic or an island southwest of Spain and Portugal? Is it just a short drive away from London as suggested in 'Fall Out'? Or to take us out of the narrative is it partially Portmeirion and partially MGM Borehamwood. Is the Village part or Number Six's subconscious, is it just imagery created by his own fears of the aftermath of his resignation?

At the end of the series is Number Six driving alone down a 'long and lonesome road'[74] or is he on his way to deliver his resignation?

---

[74] Quote from Tenacious D song 'Tribute'

What Did The Village Want? You may answer that this is simple that they wanted to know the reason for his resignation but I draw your attention to Guy Doleman's line in 'Arrival'

"One Likes To Know Everything"
(George Markstein and David Tomblin, 'Arrival,' 1966)

This is supplemented by the discussion between Leo McKern's Number Two and his Assistant in 'The Chimes of Big Ben': (my underscored words)

"it only takes one small thing and the rest will follow, why did he resign?"
(Vincent Tilsley, 'The Chimes of Big Ben,' 1966)

On the whole this suggests that they are hoping to unravel a great deal more than just the secret of his why he resigned — there is the hope that having teased out from him this piece of information that other confidential material will be revealed by Number Six. In other words discovering the reason for Number Six's resignation is actually merely the tip of the iceberg.

Psychologically 'The Prisoner' is all about the determination of one man not to concede or give anything of himself away. Even with Alison in 'The Schizoid Man' we discover that they 'share little things' due to being 'in simpatico' they cannot literally see into each others minds. This is probably fortunate for Number Six as they would likely have used Alison against him rather than create or obtain Curtis to break him.

Another thought that occurs concerns memory — between resigning and awakening in the Village Number Six is gassed to knock him unconscious so that he can be taken to the Village. What if the gas used affected Number Six's memory in some unexpected way? Notice his reactions when Guy Doleman's Number Two goes through his file in 'Arrival' — could it be that vast chunks of his past are missing from his memory and that is part of the reason he never reveals anything. Over the (lets say) 18 months to 2 years he spends in the Village he gradually remembers certain memories but the reason for his resignation remains clouded and unavailable to him. No wonder Number Six is aggressive to anyone who asks him to reveal the reason for his resignation, he can't remember himself.

Effectively his short-term memory and long-term memories remain fine, he can hold his own in any conversation about the present or people he knew prior to his resignation.It is a combination of the traumatic event of his resignation (he certainly seemed furious about something) and the effect of the gas on Number Six's brain that caused this situation. Well its a theory and in the end with 'The Prisoner' isn't that all we have?[75]

Or to further this perhaps if we follow the path of Number Six we can understand his plight better. If we begin with 'Fall Out' & follow up with 'Arrival' the cyclic nature of the series deepens. If we assume that Number Six is forever caught in a cyclical trap of resigning and being abducted to the Village each time certain things make more sense.[76] The end of Fall Out is actually before each resignation loop as it were, Number Two's desperation in 'A, B and C' makes even more sense if the

---

[75] Kandell Eric R. 'In Search Of Memory : The Emergence Of A New Science of Mind' W.W. Norton, New York & London pp125-pp129

[76] Obviously a lot of things don't make sense unless you accept my theory that the gas pumped into his home affects his 'memory' as well.

Village is trapped in the cycle with Number Six. Beyond this is the possibility that something happened after his resignation and before he returned home — perhaps Number Six experiences the Village because he is in a coma following some near tragic accident. We could assume that in Number Six's warped mind the event of his resignation and the accident become linked — in effect he sees it as the trigger. However the accident becomes the triggering event for the resignation — perhaps the indistinct figure in the bellower in 'Arrival' is Seltzman or to take a trip through some sliding doors perhaps he accidentally kills someone on the way home after resigning that he was assigned to kill which is why he resigned.

The Village is Purgatory for Number Six whatever your beliefs he continually punishes himself by trying desperately to confront what happened. Each Number Two becomes not someone out to trip Number Six up — rather to free him from his own self blame. Number Six is so desperate not to acknowledge what has actually happened that he throws himself round and round the cycle. It warps the Village inside out, the laughter at him saying he is a free man is because he has forged the eternal bars of his internal prison in his head. The Number Two's are not trying to break him at all. "I don't want him broken," "We mustn't damage the tissue." "Don't worry there will be no remembrances..." "He must be won over", "You can't talk it out of this man", "Sometimes in my dreams I resign my job...", "We could lose Number Six — Do you hear that lose him..."

The trouble with Number Six is that he is resilient — like Rover he can't be shot full of holes so that the information will spill out. Number Six experiences Social Distance from the Villagers' he is 'prejudiced' in a way because he sees them as sheep.[77] He doesn't realise that his freedom is locked away because he won't open up and share his fears — I've made you think then haven't I. The Village is the reverse to what it seems it is trying to allow its inhabitants the only freedom they can have to live a full life unfettered by their fears — but it's being filtered through a man who becomes increasingly delusional. He might not have a Napoleon Complex but he has some psychological problems which cause him to perceive his helpers through a filter as those trying to prevent him from leaving — maybe they were doing it for his own safety after all.[78]

[77] Abercrombie N, Hill S & Turner Bryan S. (1988) 'The Penguin Dictionary Of Sociology' Penguin Books p226

[78] I think this is just one of many explanations for the series and I'd like to acknowledge Steve Matt for sparking some of my thoughts on the subject.

Return to Synchronicities, Manifestations & Revelations

Originally Published in British Ideas
Corporation Magazine
Issue 0.6 Festival Number 6 Issue
- Edited by Lee Gale © 2014

STILL DEBATED BY FANS AND SUBJECT TO ACADEMIC SCRUTINY, 'THE PRISONER' IS A MULTI-LAYERED SPY/SCI-FI SERIES WITH CLUES AND SECRETS EMBEDDED WITHIN. FORTEAN TIMES WRITER MARK BENNETT IS OUR GUIDE

3D Photograph taken at Portmeirion courtesy of Mark Bennett

I was first exposed to the unusual and paranormal at an early age. In my teens, my favourite book was 'Phenomena: A Book Of Wonders' by John Michell and Robert JM Rickard. The latter was the founder and editor of 'Fortean Times;' little did I know that I would go on to write for his magazine. My best friend when growing up was Tim Solar, who lived across the back parking lot of the library from me in Hudson, Canada. I discovered that his grandmother, Margaret Hamilton Bach, had written several books about her father Thomas Glendenning Hamilton. A respected doctor in Winnipeg in the Twenties, TG Hamilton was also a paranormal investigator. He was visited by Sir Arthur Conan Doyle to review his research and sit in on his live experiments.

While TG Hamilton's book 'Intention And Survival' was pretty dull, it did have weird photos of his séances and at one point, Margaret's brother found a shoebox of old glass negatives from the sessions and I was more than happy to print up the stereo photos on Holmes cards (the old-fashioned stereoscope photographs, where two images are printed side by side). Sadly, I never kept a set for myself but my first foray into journalism was an interview with Margaret.

Photography saved me through high school. You know those American teen dramas about clique warfare? It's really like that. The camera provided a shield and weapon, while expanding my education from abstract numbers and writing into hands-on science. I would work weekends at Finnegan's Market, a sprawling Saturday car-boot sale in Hudson, keeping my eyes peeled for Fifties science and pulp sci-fi magazines like 'Galaxy Science Fiction.'

It was during one summer working at the market that I discovered 'The Prisoner.' I'd race home at 4.30pm, after the market had been cleared of trash, to watch it. I'd sit down, having arrived just in time, hungry to watch a show that was unlike anything ever presented or available on television. It was a transmission from a different world.

The plotline, you all know. Patrick McGoohan, the lead actor and series creator, resigns from a possible spy job (although there's no real proof) and gets taken to a surreal, remote village where "they" proceed to attempt to extract why he resigned and any vital secrets. Something resonated about McGoohan's struggle against his situation and his captors. Maybe it was teenage rebellion against a creepy, underlying "something's not right". I could never put my finger on it, but I drank in each of the 17 episodes eagerly. Was it a spy show? Was it science fiction? Social commentary? Philosophy? Six of one and half a dozen of the other? The author and agnostic mystic Robert Anton Wilson was once reported to have said, "Find the Others." Perhaps 'The Prisoner' is an encrypted message? A secret handshake for those initiated to see?

Synchronicity:

While working at the market, it turns out that David Cronenberg was filming 'Scanners' down the road, starring Patrick McGoohan, in the Hoffman-LaRoche pharmaceutical building and factory complex six miles away.

When I was in college at 17 and padding out my incompletes in social science with extra courses in fine art, each year we would take a five-day road trip to New York City to absorb culture, visit museums and buy art supplies from Pearl Paint on Canal Street. Our cheap, tourist hotel was off Times Square on 47th Street. While passing by the discount-ticket office, I spotted that Patrick McGoohan was starring in 'A Pack Of Lies' off Broadway and decided immediately to dump my art group and go see it alone. The thought never crossed my mind to explain The Prisoner to them. They would have needed to have seen it, been a fan and an initiate. They'd never understand the secret handshake the series provided, no matter how many times you demonstrated it to them.

'A Pack Of Lies' is based on a real-life story about an American couple in England, masquerading as Canadians and in fact spying for the Russians — selling nuclear secrets. After the play, I decided I must at least meet McGoohan and went backstage. There was a small group of people waiting for him.

I attached myself to them and followed them in when security cleared us. I discovered that they were not fans, but old friends. McGoohan was polite and sorry he couldn't talk to me. I improvised a story that I worked on my college newspaper and would love to interview him. He said he was booked for dinner with his friends and had to go — but how about in the morning? My hotel or his? I was packed like a sardine on the floor at my hotel (which I didn't mention), so I suggested his would be better. I left in shock. This was my first meeting with a childhood idol –- a man who was almost James Bond. I scoured the electronic shops of 42nd Street for blank audiotapes to record the interview.

The hotel was just off Central Park. Not the Ritz, but one of the bijou versions with the same level of decor and service. Our art-class tour of galleries, I just ditched. I arrived and I remember how bloody tall he was. He made tea and said, "No recording." My shorthand didn't exist, so note taking was impossible, besides some keywords and the imitation of do-ing something. I was nervous, really nervous. I asked utterly stupid questions like, "Was The Prisoner political?" As if I had any depth of understanding of world politics. He replied, pointing at the teacup made in China, "Is the teacup political?" I was plainly out of my depth.

I told McGoohan the story of a friend, a phone phreak and computer hacker who went by the name of 'The Prisoner'. My friend had been arrested using an Apple IIe that he used to phone phreak. I explained phone phreaking to McGoohan, pointing out that Steve Jobs and Steve Wozniak both started off as phone phreaks before setting up Apple. In fact, one of Apple's first employees was the famed Captain Crunch. I wanted to use 'The Prisoner' as my own "alias" or handle, but my friend used it first and was pretty well-known in the sub-culture, so I opted for 'John Drake' (McGoohan's character on 'Danger Man'). 'The Pris-oner' hacker was a keen fan and had all 'The Prisoner' episodes on VHS when they were $80 each. I was able to revisit the tapes again when in college.

McGoohan told me the story about wanting to sleep in Al Capone's cell during the filming of 'Escape From Alcatraz,' while my queries ran along the lines of the film-making process, which continues to fascinate me today. I had done some documentary 8mm footage, inevitable Plas-ticine time lapse, but the drama of it always escaped me. "So how, as a director and lead actor, does one direct oneself?" McGoohan's answers barely registered, such were my nerves. Having no experience in directing or acting, I wouldn't have any context for the response anyway.

In alchemy and mythology, the "language of the birds" is a secret, perfect tongue that is seen as the key to pure knowledge. The power to understand bird language was regarded as a sign of wisdom. It could be a clue to 'The Prisoner.' My first trip to Portmeirion was in the late Eighties, accompanied by hacker and phone phreak Russell Davies (not that one). I had joined 'Six of One,' the official Prisoner appreciation society, and timed our visit with the annual convention.

Stepping onto a television or movie set is a surreal experience. You transcend space and time. There were the memories of seeing 'The Prisoner' on a small, black-and-white TV set when I was ten, then in colour on VHS, to meeting the man himself seven years later, and now, actually stepping into the Prisoner world. It was vertiginous. The hard-core fans and conventioneers were dressed as residents of the show, parading around, driving Mini Mokes and recreating scenes in ritualistic devotion. This was before the idea of LARPing (live-action role-play) was a common term.

Alchemical brother

I found Portmeirion beautiful and unique. A singular vision of its creator Sir Clough Williams-Ellis (one of the first naturalists), it brings to mind the quote which has been attributed to several sources: "The secret of change is to focus all your energy not into fighting the old but on building the new." He wanted a village that fits into the surroundings naturally and to be harmonious with the landscape. Interestingly, the key foundation to understanding alchemy is "to follow in nature's footsteps".

Over 20 years would pass before I set foot in Portmeirion again. From handprinting black-and-white photos of parapsychology stereocards dating from the Twenties to now using a Sony DEV-3 Binocular Stereo HD Videocamera, I could now film the 'Six of One' convention in 3-D. My tentative plan was to capture the events, the recreated scenes and interviews (including legend Max Hora, who ran the Prisoner shop for years), along with sufficient B-roll, to edit a teaser for a much longer 3-D documentary.

Having been involved with multiple published research articles about lost science – including how Leonardo da Vinci faked the Turin Shroud using an early form of photography, re-engineering the Ark of the Covenant, and the ongoing Orgonite experiments (for more on these, go to forteantimes.com) – I became increasingly versed on decoding visuals and seeing how cargo cults evolved. I've most recently p***ed off a fundraising Tibetan monk in Brighton's North Laines who was spinning his prayer wheel: I asked him if he had one that actually worked. The prayer wheel is, after all, a dynamo, akin to what you use on your bicycle to power your lights. It's all very good that the Knights Templar in Scotland claim to have three Ark of the Covenants, but have they been able to turn them on? They might as well be monkeys with car keys.

With a new set of comparative toolsets to use, I started to notice unusual elements at Portmeirion. The religious iconography is obvious and well documented. But what of the scallop shells scattered around buildings in the village? They are fundamentally known as a Christian symbol of baptism but they were also used like hobo signs to mark houses where alchemists were at work. The other blatant in-your-face symbolism is the iron fencing and gates used around Portmeirion that, like so many other architectural features, make the place utterly unique. Had the Starbucks founders visited Portmeirion?

I've researched the Cathars (inspired by Ken Campbell, a comedian who was almost 'Dr Who') and the legends of Mary Magdalene fleeing to France, then up to Cornwall, up through Wales and beyond. At the home of No.2 in the series, leading up to the Green Dome, you will see a mermaid with two tails. This indicates two bloodlines from male sources; the tridents/staffs are offspring.

These elements are, for most people, just decorations but what were their original purpose? What layers of information and stories do they tell when you dig deeper? How many Parisians and tourists, for example, know that the front of Notre-Dame Cathedral is, in fact, an encoded alchemical cookbook for creating the Great Work. Portmeirion is thick with these clues, icons and coded messages. It makes 'The Da Vinci Code' look like an issue of The Beano.

In last year's visit to Portmeirion, when my 3-D footage was shown to conventioneers, I heard rumours of a French woman present who had found a book on Portmeirion that revealed its hermetic secrets. I left my card with various members in the hope of tracking her down. Finally, on the last day, we met and she told me of an author who had decoded that there was a life-sized tarot deck built into the architecture. My first memories of the tarot was in the James Bond film 'Live And Let Die.' Prior to that, I'd never heard of it. Nowadays, it's a common thing in new-age shops. There are multiple versions and even Amanda Palmer of 'The Dresden Dolls' – married to comic-book legend Neil Gaiman – now has a set based on her. So for an architect in the Twenties to build a new world and encode a full tarot deck into its landscape shows he was way ahead of his time, to say the least (see mysteryarts.com/portmeirion/tarot/)

Original tweets

I ran various observations on the shells, the alchemical connections and symbolism past several senior members of the appreciation society and none had noticed it, but thought it would make a good article for their magazine.

In spring, I returned with my friend, the one who had loaned me the VHS cassettes in college. It was his first trip to Portmeirion. He was equally impressed — and hit by vertigo — when driving into something that had only previously existed on a TV screen from childhood (although it's now on Blu-ray in restored high-definition). We stayed in the quayside hotel and one thing I immediately noticed was that in the upstairs hallway, there were paintings of volcanoes both active and inactive. Nearby Snowdon is an old volcano, which is a curious coincidence, as the black sands of the Nile, which keep that region fertile, originate from a volcano. It is suggested that Nile sand is the first "matter" for alchemy.

Earlier this year, I rediscovered an alchemical fact that I had forgotten about — Stanley Kubrick's use of the alchemical language of birds in '2001: A Space Odyssey'. Coincidentally, '2001' was filmed in the same studio as 'The Prisoner' and at the same time. In fact, the starfield background was loaned to the producers of 'The Prisoner' to use in their series.[79] [80] The use of '2001's language of birds is easy to demonstrate. How many black obelisks are in the film? There's one more than you think, as the film ratio of 2001 in its native cinema format is the same ratio — 2.21:1 — as the mysterious obelisk. You are staring into the hidden one when watching the film.

The alchemical language of birds compares form and function of an object/space to another, regardless of what it is called. This way you can break free of the "spell-branding" that saturates the world we live in.

These are some of the tools I'm using to look both at the self-contained world that Sir Clough Williams-Ellis created in Portmeirion and the enigma of Patrick McGoohan's cult TV series that still has resonance in today's world. I've only been able to share a fraction of my research here. As you walk around Portmeirion, study the symbolism — it could be the start of your own personal journey.

Mark Bennett is a writer and documentary maker. alchemicalshadows.com; youtube.com/black-icemagazine

---

[79] See 'The Alternative Chimes of Big Ben' — Ironically this is actually a preview edit of the episode which has been broadcast by accident in the past. The Triquetrum scene includes the borrowed star-field cut from the final broadcast edit.

[80] The scene was presumably cut because the device would have given away the true location of the Village to Number Six and perhaps make him question the new Number 8's — sorry Nadia Rakovsky's story.

The Willing Suspension of Disbelief and 'The Prisoner' or "Why is there a giant balloon chasing him?!"

The Village and by extension 'The Prisoner' calls upon us to suspend our disbelief numerous times across 17 50 minute episodes of television. The question is should we take the oath laid down by the MYSTies [81] that 'we should really just relax' or should we hop on to the inter- web and register our wrath. Taking an example is it rational to jump up and down and suggest that 'The Girl Who Was Death' doesn't follow any logical path with relation to the rest of the series.

A list:-

1) Your phone table and your statuette of a figure on a horse shouldn't swap places while you look out the window.

2) The letter 'h' should not on any typewriter cover a photograph with streams of letter x.

3) In 'The Chimes of Big Ben' and 'Free For All' - Rover suddenly gives birth to two smaller Rovers for no apparent reason (which proves she is female I suppose) other than to help 'float' Nadia [82] and Number Six back onto the Village's beach. Picture from https://stocksnap.io

4) How do they justify treating Nadia in this way:- attacking her with a vengeful set of white spheres which are 'a nasty experience' and then shutting her in a room with a floor that would electrocute her if she takes longer than 3 seconds to get to the door while Peter Swanwick interrogates her repeatedly about why she went for a swim. Probably at least gives her an opportunity to get away from this crazy scheme to convince Number Six to sail with her to a fishing village in 'Poland' for a while...

5) The sudden appearance of a group of children in 'The Village' for Number Six to read a story too through the handy device of the Village Story Book. Funny that it wasn't even on the book shelf last week.

6) Instead of eating your food when at sea just eat the corn-beef — we wouldn't want any Gunrunners to go hungry after all would we?

7) Realising that you've been wearing the same blazer for 14 days straight you change it for a slightly different one as you go out the front door of your cottage.

8) After endless days waking up in the Village - you suddenly wake up in the American West causing 1000s of viewers to check their tv guides to make sure 'The Prisoner' is on this week. Don't forget to resign as a sheriff this time...

9) A black cat is particularly ominous — especially when it smashes a plate then leaps quickly down to where the broken plate is before Number Six can turn round. Exactly like any cat would do.

10) Steel walls in the Green Dome should be made of a variant of aluminium foil... when this starts to bubble up - metal strats will be tried to hold it in place before a complete 'grey green wall

---

[81] Fans of the TV Show 'Mystery Science Theatre 3000' — the theme song dictates this maxim

[82] Or if you prefer to help Nadia 'swim' back to the beach while 'unconscious'

makeover' is installed overnight. Although this will be replaced by the strats and bubbled metal wall occasionally for no apparent reason.

11) The Green Dome has a 'magic door knocker' which enables it to shape shift while Nadia and Number Six have a conversation outside.

12) Nobody draws attention to the fact that when Number Six is cracking in Number Twelve's residence, the next scene is started with a stock shot of 6 private when it should be 12 private outside that residence.

13) If you feel like it — swap the private and 6 signs around so that the sign reads 'private 6' sometimes for no apparent reason.

14) If you are having a chat with a painter about his work to establish if he is a prisoner or warder beware the disembodied voice of someone in the Village from before everyone was numbered shouting 'Is it all right there Fred?'

15) Remember when teaching No.58 the phrase for 'be seeing you' to totally get the intonation of the last word wrong — but I expect when a female says the phrase it is pronounced different in that language. Which is a little harder to justify when you made the language all up yourself.

16) The telephone box must not be in the same location twice or when you find it and when you use it. In fact it should be known by Villagers as the 'teleporting telephone box'.

17) Sometimes walking into the back of the Gloriette balcony will miraculously bring you out at a different location in the Village.

18) Always leave actors names in the credits — despite the fact that all there scenes have been cut. Nobody will mind when watching the episode not the actors, not their families, not the fans 50 years later trying to explain why characters have been totally cut out of an episode...

19) Don't feel that you have to ask the extras to 'mime' cheering, when there is cheering on the soundtrack. Just say it is postmodern or avant garde. It's not like anyone's going to check whether you did it deliberately.

20) Try to avoid running about on the beach for an arty composition for the cameras, you'll probably just twist your ankle and your stunt double will have to do it.

21) Occasionally create a new shop — like a watchmakers firstly for novelty value then to labour a point about the old Number Two's 'time being up...'

22) If you are in Charge of Plan Division Q - Don't make too many bad puns on the phone to Number One - he really doesn't appreciate them.

23) Its fine to have everyone known by numbers just like Nadia, Alison and Monique aren't!

24) When making a list of this nature — get the fans to explain why at the beginning of 'the Man With the Stick's' talk with Number Six about 'discovering the prisoners and the warders' the Butler heads towards them several times!

25) In 'Fall Out' why does any of the er things that happen get used and erm did they use the resuscitation machine on Number 8/the Kid to create Number 48! (Yes that'll do. Won't it???)

20 THINGS YOU NEVER SEE IN THE PRISONER BY RICK DAVY

ORIGINALLY PUBLISHED ON THE UNMUTUAL WEBSITE AT:
http://www.theunmutual.co.uk/20things.htm

1. A maid or Village operative makes Number Six a non-drugged cup of tea which is both tasty and refreshing.

2. Number Two's male assistant is given Number Six as his latest assignment. After a tense build up, they decide not to fight at the end of the episode and have a nice beer and a game of darts instead.

3. Number Six awakens to find the Village deserted. Pleased with this sight, he decides to go back to bed and have a lie-in.

4. The Village have perfected a new experimental technique for extracting secrets. However, upon attempting it on Number Six they find it to be completely successful.

5. Number Six meets a female Villager whom he learns to trust. At the end of the episode, however, it transpires that she is completely trustworthy.

6. Number Six has his mind placed in the body of another man. Preferring it, he decides not to bother to find the Professor who devised the technology, thinking: "the wife don't seem to mind so I'll keep it".

7. Number Six decides to dupe Number Two into believing he is a spy by inventing a code which reads "pat a cake pat a cake". Little does he know, this is Village code for "Number Six to be Executed".

8. On a visit to the Green Dome, Number Six makes a "Number Twos" gag, much to the amusement of the eavesdropping Butler.

9. Number Six visits the Village shop to buy some groceries. After happily paying, he leaves the shop without spotting any items of use.

10. Number Six takes a taxi home from the Cat and Mouse, whereupon he throws up in the back, while Barbara Yu Ling comments: "You'll never guess who I had in the back of my cab the other day".

11. The female observers miss Number Six's escape attempt due to them watching the Hollyoaks omnibus.

12. Number Two answers the red phone on his desk and has a pleasant and jovial conversation with the caller.

13. Number Six finds a dead body on the beach, which he promptly reports to the proper authorities.

14. A new ex-spy is brought to The Village. After waking up in what appears to be their own home, they decide to have a spring clean and catch up with some reading — completely oblivious to the fact they are in The Village for several weeks.

15. The Supervisor video-tapes Number Six in the toilet, and precedes to make a compilation video which he sells around The Village from the back of an Ice Cream Van.

16. Number Six escapes and finds his way back to London. Upon relaying the story to his former bosses, he is taken away and placed in a secure unit for the mentally ill.

17. Number Six is brought in front of one of The Village's Committees, where he has a quiet and pleasant chat about things.

18. Number Six sabotages one of The Village cameras, at which point he electrocutes himself and is treated for 3rd degree burns at the hospital.

19. On a visit to read a bedtime story to some local children, Number Six discovers he is locally known as "old grumpy pants," and that the local kids regularly go to the sports hall to laugh at him in his Kosho gear.

20. Number Six enters a Village craft competition. With no ulterior motive whatsoever, he comes 18th out of 20 with his pathetic woodwork offering and vows to try his hand at poetry next time.

View of Village Square, Lawn Towards Hercules Statue In The Distance courtesy of Rick Davy (taken Spring/Summer between 2002-8) also found at: http://www.theunmutual.co.uk/pmgallery.htm

The Big Seven
© Leslie Glen.
Originally Published on The Unmutual Website At:
http://theunmutual.co.uk/article45.htm

From the very beginnings of Prisoner fandom, one of the most talked-about topics of conversation was the vexed question of which of the seventeen episodes of The Prisoner its creator Patrick McGoohan most admired. The debate has raged on and on and with no sign of a let-up because the late Patrick McGoohan never revealed the names of those seven episodes - The Big Seven, I call them — or in which screening order he would have placed them. Or did he? Now, for the first time on the Unmutual website, I believe I have discovered those Big Seven episodes.

On a personal level, I had always naively assumed that McGoohan's choice of his seven episodes would have been the first five partially shot on location in Portmeirion during that very warm and brilliantly sunny September of 1966. Those five episodes were, in broadcast order, "Arrival," "The Chimes of Big Ben," "Free For All," "Dance of the Dead" and "Checkmate". The two remaining episodes that Patrick McGoohan would have chosen I deduced to be "Once upon a Time" and "Fall Out," simply because of the fact that they were both written by him and that they concluded the series. How wrong I was!

Back in 1995, and during the autumn of that year, I discovered that the European premiere of Braveheart, a film Patrick McGoohan was starring in, would take place in Stirling, an appropriate choice because it was there that a famous battle had taken place in which the Scots had defeated the English. (I always considered Braveheart to be a sort of Wild West film but set in Scotland and with the Scottish and English replacing the cowboys and Indians.) Stirling, located in the central belt of Scotland, was only a 90-minute train journey for me and I reasoned that I should travel there that particular Sunday, in the slimmest hope of maybe seeing McGoohan and perhaps even get an interview off him and ask him about his Big Seven episodes. As it turned out, I did indeed fleetingly see him as he entered the Stirling University building where the premiere was being held but I never ever did get that elusive interview with him.

Metaphorically turning the clock forward to 2012, I came across an interview in David "Stimpy" Stimpson's excellent quarterly Prisoner fanzine The Tally Ho in which Patrick McGoohan had been interviewed by Tom Soter in 1984 and where four of the Big Seven episodes are mentioned. They dealt with McGoohan's favourite themes: identity ("The Schizoid Man") and trust ("Checkmate") to elections ("Free For All," written by McGoohan) and education ("The General"). To directly quote him from the interview: "I had only wanted seven. Today it would be a mini-series, ideally." Therefore, I believe that these four episodes are at the centre of the Big Seven. And what of the remaining three? Clearly, the pilot episode "Arrival" would have to be there at the beginning. As McGoohan himself said of this episode in a separate interview: "I think that is the best pilot script I have ever read."

And the two episodes to conclude McGoohan's original vision of a mini-series consisting of just seven? I believe that they would have to be the two-part finale episodes "Once upon a Time" and "Fall Out" because not only do they conclude the series but also the fact that Patrick McGoohan wrote them and that the first of these is heavily autobiographical. As to the screening order of my Big Seven, I would logically opt for their original telecast order:-

1. Arrival
2. Free For All
3. The Schizoid Man
4. The General
5. Checkmate
6. Once upon a Time
7. Fall Out

There you have it. I am not entirely one-hundred-percent certain that I am totally correct in my assumptions because, as far as I am aware, Patrick McGoohan never actually named his seven episodes, or in which screening order he would have placed them. In conclusion, therefore, perhaps it is only right that this topic should remain open to debate, just like McGoohan's marvellous creation, The Prisoner.

"Why Do We Forsake?... 'Do Not Forsake Me..?' 'Or Fetch Me An Alka-Seltzman Machine"

The Prisoner is largely the story of a character who despite his protests about being 'a free man' is known only to us as Number Six. Very little of what we see is not about his character in some way or involves him and his interactions with other characters.

It might therefore seem odd that almost an entire episode was produced with Nigel Stock stepping into the shoes of Patrick McGoohan as 'The Colonel' becomes 'Number Six' and vice versa. The real reason being that McGoohan, partly because he wanted to — partly to finance the last few episodes, was going to America to star in the movie 'Ice Station Zebra'.

Vincent Tilsley was therefore put in the unenviable position of having to write a script that allowed McGoohan to disappear and be replaced by another actor his draft script originally entitled 'Face Unknown'. Its fair to say that Vincent Tilsley was not overly enamoured with the script and expected notes on the script and then rewrites to be required. This work was not however done by Tilsley as instead the work was done in house at 'Everyman Films'.

The script which became 'Do Not Forsake Me, Oh My Darling' therefore was not seen as viable in its original form and Vincent Tilsley was paid for the work he had done on 'Face Unknown'. He was often heard stating that he felt they had created a slightly different bad script out of his own bad script. Tilsley felt strongly that the concept for the story was not strong enough and that compared to 'The Chimes of Big Ben' it was overshadowed by his previous script.

Given these factors why was 'Do Not Forsake Me, Oh My Darling' made? It would seem that at the time the remaining Production Team did not have another script to work with that in any way dealt with the issue of McGoohan's absence. Therefore we are left with an episode that doesn't seem to meet the quality control of the other episodes that surround it. 'It's Your Funeral' may have a somewhat incoherent plot but the acting of Derren Nesbitt, Annette Andre, Mark Eden and Patrick McGoohan pull it together and there is still much to admire there.

So given reasons for forsaking this episode what are the redeeming features of this episode? Well it seems we may have a possible contender for the reason for Number Six's resignation — ensuring that the secret of Professor Seltzman's reversal process remained hidden. We also have a reason why he might well have been so defensive about this; that despite everything he cared about Janet Portland as her fiancé too much to get her involved in this situation. It is quite clear that Number Six only involves Janet and Sir Charles Portland because of the fact that he has to return to his own body and prove his identity to obtain their help. Unable to convince Sir Charles fully that 'he is himself' he changes his focus to Janet in attempting to convince her that he is the man he professes to be. In a controversial move this is achieved in a way that McGoohan probably wouldn't have approved of had he been around to vet this episode, sealed with a kiss One might say.

We get to see more footage of the Lotus Seven that 'Number Six' drives as he makes his way to see Sir Charles Portland, returns home and travels via Stock Footage to Kandersfelt. We also get the chance to see the old GEC Marconi building in Borehamwood and its Paternoster lift in action. We see 'Number Six' albeit played by Nigel Stock using secret agent type skills to uncover the true location of Professor Seltzman in Kandersfeld using a combination of specially modified glasses and a selection of slides.

We even get an in-joke from the Waiter in Kandersfeld as he says 'Welcome to the Village, Sir...' Then there is the business around proving his identity through his handwriting — thanks to Seltzman's sentimental nature and an envelope addressed to Portmeirion Road.

It's clear that even with material that was not the greatest and with Plot Holes you could spend weeks trying to justify — couldn't they just use the same process to put the two minds back in place? The obvious reason being we wouldn't have had a story to watch at all and whoever said that the Prisoner has to always make sense anyway?

Given the previous episode 'A Change of Mind' perhaps we have missed something important — prior to Number Six's '—pretend' instant social conversion everyone talks to Number Six and indeed Number Two and the Supervisor talk to each other of the prospect that they may 'lose him'. Perhaps the operation actually does go ahead and goes wrong leaving Number Six in a coma, but with brain activity and the increasingly surreal events that follow throughout the rest of the series are down to this.[83]

In addition it's interesting to speculate on why Number Six might choose to marry the bosses daughter anyway. This doesn't seem to gel with our concept of him as a character - Janet doesn't at first glance seem to be the sort of person he would be attracted to. She comes across as generally quite passive — after all she only asks her father where her fiancé has been after a year's absence! It seems that the arrival of Number Six in the Colonel's body is the only reason she starts to be at all concerned about the prolonged absence of someone _**who she intended to marry.**_

However perhaps it is a case of 'opposites attract' for Janet and her husband-to-be — that their two completely different personalities compliment each other.

So what can we conclude — yes 'Do Not Forsake Me, Oh My Darling' may not be the greatest episode of the series or even most people's favourite but it has much more of merit to it than even I had previously thought. The writing of this article has enabled me to see it in a different light. What is great about this episode is it's very difference to all the other's. Nigel Stock's demand (as Number Six in the Colonel's body) to get me 'Sir Charles Portland at once' proves that he can carry some of the fire of McGoohan's Number Six.

---

[83] This theory was suggested to me by Vickie Clarke.

In addition Number Six's final line about Professor Seltzman inhabiting the Colonel's body and being free to continue his experiments peacefully means that at the end of the episode the Village has once again lost when they had seemed so close to winning. For those of you who wonder how Number Six could possibly know this remember that he, the Colonel and Seltzman all had their minds connected as part of the reversal process. If they were able to identify how the reversal process worked from Seltzman's action's it is clear that attempting it would always risk the death of one of the agents in the loop.

It's interesting that as we head towards the increasingly surreal episodes — in the standard UK viewing order[84] that this episode comes first as 'Do Not Forsake Me...' has many surreal touches itself. Some of these are clearly intentional and some caused by budget problems and some probably crop up due to reediting after the main cast of the episode left. Examples include: McGoohan helps Nigel Stock drive the Lotus 7 in some shots, The Colonel's handwriting being the same as Number Six, the Paternoster lift which is never seen before or again, the crowd at Janet's party including shots of Engadine's party in 'A, B and C', Sir Charles's meetings going on forever-as they seem to be having the same meeting as in the pre-titles halfway through the episode[85] and both the Colonel and Sir Charles' agent travelling to Kandersfeld by back projection.

So view 'Do Not Forsake Me, Oh My Darling' with an open eye next time — its musical soundtrack (with it's references to 'My Bonnie Lies Over The Ocean)[86], the interplay between the Colonel and Seltzman, the intimacy between Janet and the Colonel (her fiancé in another man's body), the meeting between Sir Charles Portland and the Colonel (ZM73, Duval, Schmidt) and everyone's attempts to get to Professor Seltzman first make for an entertaining episode. OK our favourite actor is hardly in this episode but without this we wouldn't have had 'Ice Station Zebra' with McGoohan in it and the budget to cover 'Living in Harmony,' 'The Girl Who Was Death' and 'Fall Out'. Nigel Stock and Zena Walker manage to create a frisson of romance which is lacking in other episodes — this is one explanation for Number Six's stance towards women in 'The Prisoner' he is very much in love with his fiancee.

---

[84] A great debate yet to be unleashed by a shadowy unknown figure.

[85] Perhaps they had a tea-break halfway through! (There was a lot of tea in 'A Change of Mind' after all.)

[86] An in-joke as Patrick McGoohan was filming Ice Station Zebra in America on *the other side of the Atlantic*.

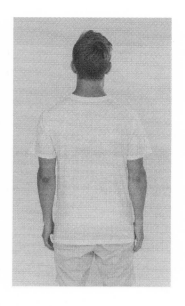

The Prisoner's Progress: Allegory and The Prisoner
by Jeff Kuykendall[87]

Go thou to Everyman,
And show him in my name
A pilgrimage he must on him take,
Which he in no wise may escape.

-God, Everyman

In an allegory, characters and places are symbols, leaving little to the imagination. In general I find allegory to be didactic, even patronising. I first think of John Bunyan's 17th century Pilgrim's Progress, in which "Christian" walks to the Celestial City and encounters temptations and obstacles along the way, all given obvious names so you needn't think too long or hard about them. I enjoyed allegories as a child – I even had a Pilgrim's Progress comic book — but as I grew older I quickly turned against them, finding more to explore and enjoy in worlds that are not just a map for this-equals-that. And yet 'The Prisoner,' my favourite television show, flirts time and again with this technique before provoking a completely allegorical interpretation in 'Fall Out.' So why do I still find this show so irresistible?

McGoohan, of course, was Catholic, so much so that he imposed his particular views on the portrayals of John Drake and No.6 (no sex, no senseless violence). McGoohan's production company for The Prisoner, formed with David Tomblin, was Everyman Films, which he named after the 15th century allegory and morality play Everyman, by an author whose name is lost to history. The story of Everyman is very similar to Pilgrim's Progress (with which McGoohan would likely have also been familiar): God sends Death to take Everyman, who is both one individual and all of mankind, to Paradise for a "reckoning." On his journey, Everyman tries to convince his friends to accompany him, including Fellowship, Kindred, Goods, etc. In the end, only "Good-Deeds" follows him into Heaven.

Everyman wouldn't make for a very compelling TV series, and let's leave it at that. But by naming his production company after the play, McGoohan was giving a nod to what he intended with 'The Prisoner.' Although his series would not be a Christian morality play, its psychological and metaphysical themes would be delivered just

---

[87] Everyman images courtesy of http://stocksnap.io

as allegorically, with the key symbols being the Everyman (the Prisoner), the Authoritarian (No.2), and Society/the Community (the Village and its mostly nameless Villagers).

If McGoohan had an affinity toward allegory, I must confront the problem of authorship, because he was not the sole writer of the series. George Markstein claimed that he invented the concept of 'The Prisoner,' but McGoohan has likewise said the whole series was his idea. Markstein stated he was inspired by Scotland's Inverlair Lodge, where "recalcitrant spies" were held. (The Unmutual website has collected some wonderful supporting details, such as the fact that the lodge, used by the Special Operations Executive during WWII, was nicknamed "No.6 Special Workshop School.") I personally tend to believe Markstein's story that he sold the idea of an Inverlair Lodge scenario to McGoohan, but it's likely that the actor then enriched the premise with ideas he had been nursing for some time, with added input from producer Tomblin and even production designer Jack Shampan. Conceiving the show was a group effort.

Markstein co-wrote 'Arrival,' one of the best entries in the series, and helped shepherd the first thirteen episodes of production before he resigned, refusing to be pushed, filed, and stamped by McGoohan. Therefore his contribution should not be diminished. The writers he brought in each had their own take on the premise, under Markstein's stamp of approval. Gerald Kelsey's 'Checkmate' is a fairly realistic prison-escape drama. Vincent Tilsley's 'The Chimes of Big Ben' has a plot which reflects and comments upon the Cold War and balances humour with human drama. Terence Feely's ingenious 'The Schizoid Man' is a psychology-themed science fiction story. None of these stories scream 'allegory.'
If you look at only one episode of the seventeen, it's like the blind men and the elephant. What is The Prisoner? Spy thriller ('Do Not Forsake Me Oh My Darling'), spy parody ('The Girl Who Was Death'), Kafkaesque surrealism ('Free for All'), Star Trek-style philosophical SF ('The General'), survivalist drama ('Many Happy Returns'), acid Western ('Living in Harmony'), a lucid trip for the counterculture ('A. B. and C.'), or avant-garde theatre ('Once Upon a Time')? It is, of course, all those things. But despite all the writers, despite the various styles the show explored, and despite the strong influence of Markstein for the bulk of the series, I believe that in the end it is McGoohan's show.

McGoohan wrote 'Free for All,' 'Once Upon a Time,' and 'Fall Out.' If the first is "only" one of the best episodes of 'The Prisoner,' the other two represent the most important. All three contain strong elements of allegory, with 'Fall Out' pressing the farthest into this realm. They're all very odd as well, perhaps the most defiantly challenging episodes of the series; again, 'Fall Out' rates the most extreme in this regard. By closing the series with a two-part finale written by its star, 'The Prisoner' guaranteed that it would forever resemble an auteur's work, even if this wasn't

Must We Be Resigned To Life Without The Jailbird? - Peek if you Dare At Page 202

technically true. But Lew Grade bought 'The Prisoner' on the basis of McGoohan's involvement, and McGoohan helped conceive it and applied a heavier and heavier hand in its production until his script editor quit and other crew members and actors were either tormented or fired (McGoohan, for example, took over direction of 'A Change of Mind'). The series may have been a group effort, but by the end McGoohan had made it his entirely, and the eccentric finale guaranteed its enduring cult status.

But I want to give Markstein a little more credit; in his cantankerous interview with Chris Rodley which would be included in the 1984 documentary Six Into One: The Prisoner File, Markstein demonstrated that he had a very nuanced understanding of the allegory which extends throughout the series, even if he doesn't approve of how McGoohan treated it in 'Fall Out':

"[The concept] was a very serious philosophical point, although I don't want to raise 'The Prisoner' to any more than it was, just a bit of television entertainment, but if it has a deeper meaning it is the fact that we are all prisoners. You know, the thin man is a prisoner because he's thin, a fat man can't go and buy the thin man's clothes, a very famous person can't go to the pub and have a drink because everyone recognises them...People are prisoners of their health, their religion, their wealth, their poverty, and that's an interesting theme to explore."

Indeed, 'Fall Out' does treat with this theme, and in a rather intelligent way. First the Prisoner discovers that he is No.1 – or, at least, some deep and dark part of himself is, beneath a Darwin-evoking monkey mask. Note that from the ending of 'Once Upon a Time' through 'Fall Out' the Prisoner is constantly descending: from the Embryo Room into the "Throne Room" where the President resides, and from there down into No.1's control room. It visualises a psychology metaphor, as if he is penetrating into his unconscious.

After staging his violent revolt, he escapes back to London. When the Butler played by Angelo Muscat walks into the Prisoner's old flat, the door automatically closes behind him with the same mechanical noise that could be heard in the Village. Then the 'Prisoner' rejoins the opening credits; the final image is of his half-smiling face as he drives right at us, just as he does in the opening of every episode. He's in a loop, a prisoner to the end. Muscat, McKern, and Alexis Kanner all get a spotlight with their names on-screen, but McGoohan only receives the credit 'Prisoner.' That's all he is and all he'll ever be.

Since 'The Prisoner' is an Everyman character (denied a real name throughout the series), he is us, too. As Markstein observed, "We are all Prisoners."

The Prisoner features many episodes in which the Villagers are recognisably human, but in the McGoohan-scripted episodes they're broadly drawn and given to a mob mentality. In 'Free for All,' they appear to be complicit in No.2's scheme against No.6, presenting "Vote for No.6" signs spontaneously when he announces he's running for office. A newspaper featuring his interview is produced seconds after he's interviewed, and the two men from the press share the same number (No.113 and No.113B), as though they're the same person split in two; put another way, they are each only half a human being. In a bizarre touch, the crowd fails to cheer when he actually wins election, adding to the climax's hangover-from-hell feeling, but also rendering them as programmed automatons obeying the will of No.2, the Village, No.1, or all three.

It's worth noting that some other writers were on McGoohan's wavelength: see Anthony Skene's haunting 'Dance of the Dead,' which culminates in a symbolism-driven trial similar to the one in "Fall Out," or the Village caricatures in Roger Parkes' 'A Change of Mind.' In these episodes it is easier to anticipate the style of the series finale, and to pay more attention to the central theme of people not just being labeled as numbers but acting like them, processed by society's great machine and now serving it, made docile by the Village.

David Tomblin's and Ian Rakoff's 'Living in Harmony,' though it uses more believable (and tragic) characters, uses tropes of the allegorical Western to restage the show's premise and delve into the issue of violence begetting violence. American Westerns, with their sense of isolation and saloon-dwelling archetypes (here we have "the Judge," the Showgirl, and "the Kid") could always represent Anyone and Anytown. The genre finds a surprisingly ideal fit within the allegorical parameters of 'The Prisoner.'

'Once Upon a Time,' for my money the best hour of The Prisoner, takes No.2 and No.6 into the Embryo Room where they reenact, as McKern explicitly puts it, Shakespeare's Seven Ages of Man. Here the Prisoner truly becomes an Everyman, dealing with authority figures from childhood through adulthood. This being the most theatrical of the series' episodes, the Embryo Room is a stage littered with symbolic props ("All the world's a stage," No.2 quotes, "and all the men and women merely players"). The various moments of his life are played out over the course of one "teenie weenie little week," but it could be anyone's life, as his roles are the Schoolboy, the Graduate, the Soldier, the Working Man, and so on. In this increasingly abstract episode, there are no logical reasons given for how "Degree Absolute" actually works or how one man's heart can stop when the timer runs out (some psychic force seems to be involved). It's staged as a play, and so we accept it on its own terms.

But 'Fall Out' plunges deepest into allegory in ways that alienated many viewers. The President (Kenneth Griffith) announces that "we are here gathered to resolve the question of revolt." With revolution established as the theme, three men are brought forward to represent three different styles of fighting back against society and authority.

Kanner's No.48 represents the type of youth who "wear[s] flowers in its hair and bells on its toes" and "rebels against any accepted norm." 'The Prisoner' calls him "Young Man," a title the President and Assembly then adopt, and indeed he represents all young people. (Never mind that we get the contemporary Flower Power version.) McKern's No.2 is the government man who "bites the hand that feeds him," and he rips off his badge before he stares into No.1's electronic eye.

Finally, the 'Prisoner' is praised as the exemplary rebel, maintaining his will against all attempts to break him, ever steadfast. But even he can't get a word in when all of society — represented here as the "Assembly" and wearing Greek tragicomedy masks, with names like Pacifists, Anarchists, Education, Reactionists, Nationalists, and so on — shout him down with "Aye, aye, aye, aye!" On the face of it, it's an allegorical representation of Everyman's inability to be understood or listened to even after he's earned the right to speak his mind; but they are triggered by the Prisoner's word "I," and we will soon learn that "I" is the No.1 who controls all.

In both Everyman and Pilgrim's Progress, the symbolic central character is on a journey to meet God, taking stock of earthly obstacles on the way. The Prisoner is on a journey toward No.1, but in McGoohan's secular and psychological morality play No.1 is himself, in a revelation that he will always be imprisoned in the cage of his own making, no matter how radical his revolt.

McGoohan further flaunts the non-literal nature of his series when the Village is revealed not to be off the coast of Morocco (as we'd learned in 'Many Happy Returns'), but just down the road from London. The Village is nowhere and anywhere.

One of the reasons 'The Prisoner' succeeds where other allegories feel flat and dull is that the mysteries remain compelling and open-ended even after watching 'Fall Out.' Some of the revelations remain open to interpretation. Chiefly, what does it mean that No.6 is a prisoner of himself? How you answer that question might be different from how I would.

But I am not sure that it is possible to completely decode 'The Prisoner,' in part because McGoohan savoured teasing audiences with his riddles. Before the series debuted he gave a press conference where reporters and photographers walked beside props and artwork from the show while the actor, dressed in his "Kosho" uniform, teased them by answering questions with more questions. That room was a microcosm for the show indeed.

'The Prisoner' contains more than just the symbols I've outlined. Take, for example, the whole "POP" mystery. "Pop Goes the Weasel" is a musical motif featured in several episodes, and we know from the surviving alternate cuts of 'Arrival' and 'The Chimes of Big Ben' that the penny-farthing bicycle, McGoohan's stated representation of "progress," turns into an image of the Earth and the universe. In the alternate "Chimes," the Earth spins at the viewer before the word "POP" fills the screen. It has an apocalyptic feel — progress leading to the destruction of the world?

In 'Once Upon a Time,' the dialogue between No.6 and No.2 suggests that "POP" might stand for "Protect Other People." Perhaps that which "protects other people" is nuclear weapons. The nuclear arms race in the name of protection also marches the world toward annihilation. Think of the Doomsday Clock managed by the Bulletin of the Atomic Scientists (which recently advanced closer to "midnight"), or like the doomsday clock in this episode, which is hidden behind a curtain and counts down the week of "Degree Absolute," with the promised ending of death. Or perhaps the Prisoner once desired to protect other people, such as he protected his schoolmate, refusing to be "a rat" (as 'Once Upon a Time' recounts). Maybe he even resigned for the same reason — when he realised that his job was no longer protecting humanity, but putting it at risk.

I'm not exactly sure. And I'm still not sure why he resigned, even though there are suggestions of answers throughout the series. 'Once Upon a Time' even offers what might be the last word on the subject — for "peace of mind," the Prisoner says, because "too many people know too much" — but I can't quite accept that, and neither does No.2. McGoohan created an allegory in which each answer leads to more questions, and each symbol could be many different things.

Everyman and Pilgrim's Progress present straightforward journeys. But the Prisoner's progress is in a circle. By the end of 'Fall Out,' he has reached not Paradise, not the Ultimate Answer, but the opening credits: he's back where he started. And we're encouraged to watch the series all over again, seeking out more clues, and puzzling on and on. 'The Prisoner' endures because it won't let us free of the Village.

SOLARIS, GERMAN EXPRESSIONIST FILM & 'THE PRISONER'
By Ed Fordham BA (Hons.)

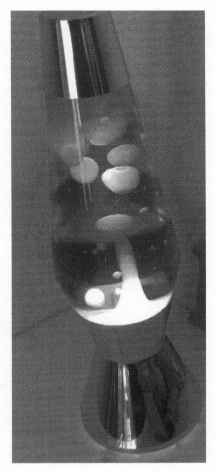

Watching the version of 'Solaris' produced by Andrei Tarkovsky in 1972 one is struck by the fact that as a film it has a lot to say about similar ideas expressed in The Prisoner and those covered much earlier in the 'German Expressionist' film period which includes films like Fritz Lang's 'Metropolis' and 'M' in the 1920s.

The earlier half of Solaris makes the real seem surrealist — a rain storm takes place in a scene where no character actually speaks and we are treated to close ups of a cup full of tea, pelted by rain. There are many scenes that rely mainly on the spoken word, attitude and inflection to convey meaning — however there are also scenes that are surreal to those used to the pacing of modern films, with silence and movement and details being treated with bizarre significance. What is actually seen by one observer is contrasted with different viewpoints — the camera tends to show us reality in surrealist detail.

It reminds me in this sense of the opening of 'Many Happy Returns' — it is the very detail of Number Six's exploration of the suddenly empty Village that sells the idea to us. From the shower not starting and the kettle not boiling to the fact that Fenella Fielding's bright and breezy voice doesn't come from the phone as the operator. Then climbing the bell-tower, discovering the abandoned mini-moke, finding the door to the Old People's Home is locked. The scenes are cleverly shot, detailed and McGoohan's reactions make the abandoned Village believable.

In Part 1 of Solaris we see Background details shot very clearly, for example a drinks trolley as the Cosmonaut Burton describes his bizarre experiences viewing the planet. When he is questioned on the validity of his experiences he becomes agitated and drinks from the drinks trolley. It is argued that his experiences are created by the atmosphere and depression (possibly pre-existing) that may have been influenced by the atmosphere's effect on his Cerebral Cortex. His descriptions are lyrical describing the oceans of Solaris becoming like:

"Collodial and Viscous Fog... after half an hour a wide open space ... yellow sludge... seethed, boiled and hardened...A garden : shrubs, trees, acacias - made of plaster... cracked and yellow sludge pours from fissures..."

However when they see no evidence of the yellow sludge or other described items on film taken of Solaris from Burton's viewpoint they believe that the planets 'bio-magnetic current' may have adversely affected his consciousness.

The clear suggestion is that this character is treating his depression with alcoholism which in turn is colouring his judgement of what he has or has not seen. The use of the drinks trolley — very clearly just behind him is used to highlight this supposition. In our minds we are supposed to link the placing of the trolley with the depression of ---- and that he is using alcohol to self-medicate never the best decision.

All this feeds into the psychological aspects of 'The Prisoner' — where Pavlov's experiments are used as a basis to influence the Rook's character in Checkmate, in Solaris they try to make a man doubt his own memories. Repeatedly asking him if he was unwell then and if he feels unwell now it is suggested his memory of Solaris is fogged or in some created within his own mind.

Which brings us to 'Fall Out', unashamed Surrealism with a whole array of people dressed in White hooded robes wearing half white/half black faces, a young hippy character who refuses to 'wear, respond or acknowledge his number' [88], a former Number Two who revels in the fact that he is no longer in the chain of command and Number Six who is lauded as a true individual although he is ignored (by repeated shouts of Aye by the crowd) when he tries to address the assembly.

What was maybe practical, if at times rather far fetched story so far, descends into chaos in this final episode with chases around a Stalactite chamber to Dem Bones by the Four Lads with Alexis Kanner sprinting around the set as Number 48, Leo McKern spitting in Number One's 'Eye'(an electronic surveillance eye that is attached to a rocket) after staring at it and then Number Six finds out he kept himself Prisoner all along when he meets a manic and hysterical McGoohan behind a mask. Greater than that Number Six assembles his motley crew of reprobates and proceeds to take down the Village – all guns blazing to the irony-drenched strains of 'All You Need Is Love'. I've stated enough for those who haven't seen it to see how odd 'Fall Out' sounds when you try and summarise it.

It's interesting that Solaristics is described as a 'mountain of disjointed, incredulous facts'. It sums up what we really know about Number Six as well...

Intriguingly the line 'You want to destroy things..." from Number Six's observer in 'Dance of The Dead' is mirrored by a comment from Burton to the psychologist Kris in 'Solaris': "You want to destroy what we are incapable of understanding..."

---

[88]   Fall Out written by Patrick McGoohan late 1967/early 1968.

But where are the roots of the interior sets created by Jack Shampan – arguably they lie in the technological, futuristic world of Fritz Lang's 'Metropolis' (1927) which later spawned the designs for the film 'Bladerunner' which is a 1980s revisualisation of elements of the design from this seminal German Expressionist film. Indeed it has only been in the last few years that an almost full version of Metropolis has been painstakingly recovered and restored from footage was excised from the print over 80 years earlier.

Watching Metropolis today — the environment where the non-workers, the rich in society live, work and play is like a cross between a futuristic New York with gardens and fountains that could easily pass in close up as Portmeirion.

The shuffling forward of the workers, in a monotone fashion without feeling, if anything a deep dread of what is ahead of them — recalls the Villagers endless parades in the square Particular in 'Free For All' and 'Dance of The Dead'[89] Indeed German Expressionism is a reflection of a dark period in the countries history between the end of World War 1 and prior to World War 2. These films hold up a mirror to the darkness of German economic, social and political issues at the time. They are melancholic in the general mood of these extraordinary pieces of cinema and tend not to feature heroic characters rather focusing on the potential of an anti-hero to capture the imagination of the audience.

Number Six is clearly an anti-hero in this mode we are aware he has secrets that he will fight compulsively to protect. He soon realises he cannot really trust other Villagers — increasingly focusing on bringing down the system from within. Ironically this trend in the latter episodes mimics closely the character traits and decisions made by Freder in 'Metropolis' (1927)

Another aspect of German Expressionism that creeps into 'The Prisoner' is the highly stylised sets used for interiors of the Control Room, Number Two's residence but particularly the strangely angled stands seen in the Town Hall during 'Dance of The Dead' which could easily be taken from the sets of 'The Cabinet of Dr. Calgari'(1920). It's clear that Jack Shampan consciously or otherwise had these sets in mind when designing the interiors of the Village.

The Second Half of 'Solaris' is really about one man being haunted by his past. Whether what Kris the psychologist and the other cosmonauts see is real, hallucinations or their minds are being altered by some force on Solaris is not clear. The important thing is that Kris who is sent to deal with the situation aboard the vessel orbiting Solaris has his own psychological problems related to the death of his wife.

Perhaps we can pause a minute: in 'Solaris' the key character of Kris does not want to confront the fact that his wife is dead. In 'The Prisoner' the key character does not want to reveal his resignation secret and other confidential information. What we can see that links

---

[89] Incidentally after the Town Criers Proclamation in 'Dance of the Dead' the Villagers parade around with blank looks on their faces.

them is they both don't want to confront the magnitude of what has happened. Is it possible that their minds are forcing them to visualise or let get of their past. Both characters are 'Prisoners' but have they created their own way of dealing with it.

In essence the Arrival at 'Solaris' is akin to the Village — some are driven to the edge of sanity :-- one of the team aboard has committed suicide. In 'Arrival' we are lead to believe that Cobb has committed suicide; In 'The Chimes of Big Ben' Nadia is questioned as to 'were you attempting Suicide....' (A ruse by Number Two?) and finally in 'Hammer Into Anvil' Number 73 is driven to suicide by Number Two's (Patrick Cargill) relentless questioning of her. 'The Lobo Man' in 'A Change of Mind' and the man watching Rover dancing on a fountain in 'Arrival' in the hospital room is motivated by insanity — are these Villagers the result of drug treatments, lobotomies and brainwashing going wrong?

'Metropolis' has points of communality due to its dystopian future — whichever way we look at The Village for all its trappings it too is ultimately dystopian in nature. Freder attempts to free the underclass from their underground slavery. This mirrors the efforts of Number Six — particularly in 'Free for All ' despite his lack of success in doing so. In addition the plot in 'Checkmate' suggests again that only 'Number Six' has the motivation to come up with an effective escape plan through his usual exuberance which is only let down because he fails to realise the Rook's understanding of the situation and by the Polotska being the Village's ship.

Many Thanks to Rick Davy of the Unmutual Website for the Green Dome Photo 1988

SECTION B
Lotus Sevens, Number Six's Identity
Meeting Peter Howell & Alexis Kanner &
Chris Gray's Epic Poem 'Villagers'...
(Strangely At Rhyme) & other stories...

David Stimpson during production of
'Village Day 'by kind permission of D. Stimpson

The History of The Lotus Seven An Evolving Story[90]

The Story of the Lotus Seven begins with Colin Chapman who became friends at University with another student called Colin Dare. Together they swept into the second hand car industry, taking cars and spacing them up to sell them profitably. Unfortunately because petrol rations were being rescinded they found themselves in a position where it was impossible to sell except by loosing money. Remaining stock was sold off and this swallowed all the money they had previously made in their cottage industry.

Colin found that he had an old-fashioned 1930 Austin Seven left unsold, he had the bright idea to remodel and alter it comprehensively. In particular he modified the chassis and body stiffness by utilising alloy-bonded ply panels along the vehicles sides. The doors were therefore quite low set very music in the manner of the later Lotus Sevens. In the first few months of 1948 Colin had 'OX9292' registered as a Lotus Mk 1 doing away with the notion of the term 'Austin Seven Special' being used.

As a small company manufacturer, working in Hornsey, just north of London, Lotus's first production car-known as the Mark VI had been extremely popular, with sales and competition results showing the company was very strong. More than one hundred had been made before 1955 ended with demand for competitive, light and economical sportscars at a high-point.

Though the Mark VII was reserved as the title for the replacement to the Mark VI other commitments during this period meant it did not go ahead for some time.

---

[90] An article in Classic Sports Car Magazine, August 2016 p130-133 helped with the writing of this item plus online articles from the Lotus Seven Register @ www.lotus7register.co.uk on the History of the Lotus and the Caterham Cars website @ http://uk.caterhamcars.com

The first Lotus Seven was effectively sold to a customer prior to the design process! Edward Lewis, the owner of "Westover Shoes," manufacturers of racing footwear, who had some fame as a Lotus racer had registered an interest in their latest design. In 1953 he had competed in a Mark VI and in 1955 he drove a works-assisted Mark IX after which he considered a Mark XI.

However he had a change of heart as he thought that his racing days should be behind him and even thought about designing his own car.

The Edward Lewis Special was based on a Mark VI chassis with Mark IX running gear, de Dion rear end, 1100cc. Coventry Climax engine and drum brakes , etc., with a Williams and Pritchard body of Lewis's own design. The West Sussex Speed Trials on 14th September 1956 saw it in competition for the very first time and it became a very successful car in motor racing circles. Between Chapman and Lewis they agreed that they would swop Lewis's Lotus based Special in exchange for the prototype Lotus Seven.

Early in 1957 the car arrived at Caterham and was left for quite a time under the ever watchful eye of Graham Hill. However, as it turned out Lewis had quite a wait before receiving his new car and so to make sure he continued to be happy he was lent a Mark XI.

According to factory records #400, the prototype which Lewis eventually received, was begun on the 31st of July and had the following specification: Coventry Climax FWA 1100cc. engine, close ratio Austin A30 gearbox, de Dion rear suspension with a 4.5:1 final drive ratio, wishbone front suspension, four-branch exhaust manifold, knock-on wire wheels, Dunlop racing tyres and spare wheel.

Photo courtesy of Rennie Chivers

Only 9 years later a Lotus 7 demonstrator was provided to Patrick McGoohan of Everyman Films registered KAR 120C (Demonstrator Cars provided by Lotus took the KAR prefix). There had been some discussion about which Lotus vehicle McGoohan's prospective character would drive but when McGoohan first cast eyes on the Seven it is said he knew it was a car for an Individual.

The Lotus Seven celebrates it's 60th Anniversary in 'The Prisoner's' 50th anniversary year so it is appropriate that the marque itself and the series are forever linked by the flash of Lotus Yellow and British Racing Green that follows those menacing thunder clouds in 'Arrival.' That both 'The Prisoner' and the Lotus Seven have survived intact so many years later is testament to the fact that they are both in their separate fields 'design classics that are always evolving'.

In 1973 Graham Nearn took control of the Lotus Seven marque forming Caterham Cars and continued to produce the Seven car amongst others. Caterham has increased the quality of the engine, ensured that it has become more powerful and has worked tirelessly in engineering better power and suspension to improve them in a way in keeping with the later moniker of 'Super Seven'.

Nearn has focused on the classic design of the Lotus Seven - the S3 of which the chassis is covered by the combination of glass-fibre and aluminium. The S3's power came from a Ford Kent power unit with a 84 bhp Crossflow Motor. The Seven S3's carburettor had twin choke which were twin side-draft from the Weber manufacturer.

Photo of Portmeirion showing Gloriette and Telfords Tower by permission of Ed Fordham

By taking an example of the 1978 Twin Cam Caterham we can see how the Lotus Marque began to evolve. At first glance it is just an extension of the design of the S3 with a pre-Caterham style Lotus Steering Wheel and if you have ever driven a later redesign of the ever-changing Caterham Seven it is clearly a blast from the past. The adjustable chassis of this iteration of the Seven gave it vintage style with the gearlever being spindly and the Lotus-style steering wheel oversized.

There were only a few bells and whistles in the cockpit — with boltheads exposed and some sharp edges which gave the whole thing a look of being not quite refined. However the steering was both light and fluid and the clamshell wings increase any body roll that you may perceive. The power delivery on this model was much the same as always with noises of displeasure if you mistreated it that could come across as spitting and banging sounds. The 'Crobby' noises remained in place and the 5000 revolutions per minute plus strong torque delivery were formidable, enabling power to peak at approximately 126 bhp at 6500 rpm.

Problems began for Caterham when the Kent power unit was discontinued by Ford in 1976 - the first alternative was the 2 litre Vauxhall for high-power cars. Rover (appropriately enough!) developed a lightweight and highly advanced twin-cam four adopted for by Caterham for Sevens from 1991 for the K-series. Andy Noble - head of Caterham's Sales and Marketing at that time spoke of this as a "brilliant engine, innovative, light... (and) powerful"

Shortly afterwards Caterham Cars made available a Limited Edition Prisoner Series 7 , on the dashboard of each car was a plaque ensuring its authenticity embossed with the signature of one Patrick McGoohan.

Anyone wishing to purchase a Caterham Seven today need only go to the Official Website at http://uk.caterhamcars.com where an array of options and variations are available for the discerning enthusiast. You can choose to construct your own or select from the Seven 160, Seven 270, Seven 310, Seven 360, Seven 420, Seven 620R and the Seven 620S and the new AeroSeven Concept with carbon-fibre body, EU6 approval, 237bhp engine and (appropriately) 6 speed manual gearbox amongst other innovations.

If you really want to drive along the same road as Number Six ensure you commit your engine number to memory!

Also there are many pages online for Lotus enthusiasts wishing to find out further information about the History of the Lotus. Unfortunately space in this publication means that much detail has been left out. Perhaps I will return to this topic if there is a Volume 2[91]

---

[91] This is 'on the cards' now as a Volume 2 has been confirmed.

David Stimpson in the Driving Seat for Fan-Film 'Village Day' -
Amusingly this photo has been published on
a website in the past as being a Photograph
of Patrick McGoohan!- photograph courtesy of David Stimpson

Location...Location...Location: Sidebar:
ARRIVAL OPENING TITLES

Poddington Raceway, Santa Pod, Northamptonshire has finally been definitely located as the Prisoner Runway where KAR 120C first appears, Assistant Director Gino Marotta had indicated that this was the case in 1993, however thanks to the Brit Movie forum and Anthony McKay of Avengerland and some Pathe Newsreel film being unearthed this is now verified.

Further details at: http://theunmutual.co.uk/podington.htm

The bizarre resignation route from 'Arrival':

Westminster Bridge, The Houses of Parliament, Right Turn off Abingdon Street, Right into Abingdon Street Car Park, Cumberland Gate Entrance to Park Lane Car Park, Double Doors in Park Lane Car Park & Corridor, Abingdon St Car Park (exit), Hearse passed in Bayswater Road, Park Lane (hearse behind Lotus), In front of Buckingham Palace, Arrives at 1 Buckingham Place.
Swaying Flats as Number Six is Gassed are in Stag Place.
Summary of info found at: http://theunmutual.co.uk/locationsguide.htm

Buckingham Palace (seen in Background in Opening Sequence) and Houses of Parliament sourced from www.publicdomainpictures.net

The Jailbird by Steve Matt

WHO IS ...NUMBER SIX?
BY STEPHEN MATTHEWS

My introduction to 'The Prisoner' occurred in the late 70's during ITV's self indulgent 'Best Of British' season which I seem to recall comprised mainly of isolated episodes representing different shows from the ITC stables. Regrettably the episode 'The Girl Who Was Death' was chosen to represent The Prisoner for reasons of copyright. Network have since released a similar video compilation this time selecting 'Checkmate' to represent 'The Prisoner' which for me makes far more sense.

Naturally I came away completely confused by what I'd just seen but I also remember feeling curious as to the nature of the series as a whole.

THANKS FOR THE TRIP DAD!

A few years later Channel 4 gave me a chance to finally view 'The Prisoner' in its proper context. Now in my teens and beginning to question authority, I had no idea that my life was about to change significantly over the following 17 weeks. 'The Girl Who Was Death' was now a vague memory as video recorders at the time (for me) were the stuff of science fiction. I remember only taking a casual interest in the Channel 4 trailer in 1983 and have my late father to thank for encouraging me to watch the series or as he put it at the time, "I think you might like this." Looking back, that was quite an understatement as no other TV show, film or medium has ever grabbed my attention and imagination in quite the same way. Perhaps if I'd viewed it any other time in my life it would be a different story — a question I'm sure many other fans have asked themselves. I later learned that the series had been repeated several times in a graveyard slot in my local region of Essex throughout the 70's — a time when I was either playing out in the street or tucked up in bed which is probably just as well.

Shortly before Channel 4's '83 screening of 'Arrival' I recall a brief documentary examining the series and I found out for the first time that the script editor George Markstein appears in the opening titles as 'the bald man behind the desk'. Fascinated by trivia even then, I was intrigued but only by the fifth episode 'The Schizoid Man' was I truly hooked.

So who was this mysterious secret agent (I never imagined the character to be anything else) driving down a London ramp and resigning every week? And why hadn't I seen this amazing actor in anything before other than 'The Girl Who Was Death'? Only after researching Patrick McGoohan did I realise our paths had crossed before when I'd viewed 'Silverstreak' and 'Escape From Alcatraz' and I scratched my head as to why he hadn't stood out at the time. Viewing the films again after 'The Prisoner' was like experiencing different movies with McGoohan added in by CGI I was no longer watching them for Gene Wilder, Richard Pryor or even Clint Eastwood. My life had changed.

I felt sure all my questions including the identity of 'No. 6' would be answered by the final episode. How naive I was...

And so the series came and went and I and millions of others were none the wiser but such was the impact it had on me I did a thesis on the programme as part of my English exam. Ironically weeks before, I overheard a boy in class discussing the series exclaiming he couldn't understand head nor tail of it. His name was Colin Gordon.

To be honest back then, the identity of No6 wasn't that important to me as it was clear the big question was the identity of No1 and for me I was satisfied by the answer provided by 'Fall Out'. But then came Danger Man.

I can still remember my initial delight when Channel 4 announced a repeat screening of the first series of 'Danger Man' particularly as by this time video recorders were no longer the stuff of science fiction. Eventually video tapes were released featuring selected episodes from series 2-4 and I could at last understand the confusion caused by Drake's contact Potter played by Christopher Benjamin. 40 years ago the actor frustrated rumour by revealing he hadn't played Potter in 'The Girl Who Was Death' as the same character but I've always interpreted this as an actor defining each part they play as 'a job'. I'm sure a popular actor like Mr Benjamin took part in many roles in-between his contracts with ITC and probably wasn't even aware that both characters had the same name. After all he played a completely different character in 'The Chimes Of Big Ben' as No2's assistant! Fortunately to support my point of view, earlier this year Christopher Benjamin reconsidered his earlier statement and confessed that the character he played in 'The Prisoner' could be the character he played in 'Danger Man.' He didn't rule it out.

Then there is the other 'evidence' to consider. One of the first reoccurring images 'The Prisoner' throws up is No. 6's resignation photo. Its common knowledge that it's a publicity pic from 'Danger Man' – a strange choice of pic by someone who doesn't wish the two characters to be confused with one another. It has also been documented (sometimes witnessed personally) that crew members were informed that 'The Prisoner' was a sequel to 'Danger Man' and that John Drake was to resign. Co-creator George Markstein had no doubt as to the identity of No. 6 and emphatically maintained that the character was John Drake. My own theory is that it was also McGoohan's conception but as the series progressed and his control on the project expanded, 'The Prisoner' became more of a personal statement and realising the series was taking on a different shape, George Markstein walked out. I'm happy to compromise and say No. 6 started out as Drake and then by 'Fall Out' became an Everyman.

Other factors to take into account is No. 6's wardrobe. Patrick McGoohan apparently wore his own clothes for both series which is one explanation for Drake wearing the 'resignation suit' in 'The Paper Chase' and other episodes. That might be true but I (conveniently) don't buy it. I'm only interested in what I see and hear on screen and as far as I'm concerned, Drake and No. 6 have the same wardrobe because they are (no pun intended) One and the same! Then there is the same nervous habit that the characters share. The clicking of their fingers. If McGoohan displays this in any other role I've yet to see it but typically I expect such damning evidence to pop up immediately after this article is published!

Putting the 'evidence' aside, doesn't it provide more dramatic impact viewing the resignation sequence believing the character to be secret agent John Drake rather than an anonymous character that nobody cares about? Originally screened shortly after the third series of Danger Man, surely that was McGoohan's, Markstein's, David Tomblin's and ultimately Lew Grade's intention! I'm sure the majority of viewers back then presumed the same and was one of the reasons they tuned in each week.

Finally allow me to indulge in something fanciful and an opinion shared with many other freethinking individuals. David Jones in the movie 'Ice Station Zebra' is also John Drake! (Did you see what I did there by the way?) But joking aside, it was so generous of author Alistair Maclean to give his character a name that can so easily be construed as a codename for agent John Drake and how fortunate it was that David Niven was not available for the role enabling Patrick McGoohan to step in at the last minute! If we can imagine No6 to be Drake then why not include the character David Jones into the mix? After all he is a British secret agent and like No. 6 in the episode 'It's Your Funeral' and Curtis masquerading as No. 6/Drake in 'The Schizoid Man,' he's a very light sleeper with sharp reflexes. Even the climax of the movie offers an explanation for Jones'/Drake's resignation and so sits nicely between 'Shinda Shima' and 'Arrival'. A Danger Man special if you will with special guest stars Rock Hudson and Ernest Borgnine.

YOU MIGHT EVEN MEET PEOPLE YOU KNOW.

Fifteen years ago I made a startling discovery and then five years later another of a more poignant nature. While viewing the episode 'It's Your Funeral' I noticed a familiar looking face amongst the extras gathered to hear No2's acceptance speech. 42 minutes into the episode, the now well known actor Roger Lloyd Pack can be seen in the bottom right holding a banner. It doesn't take Sherlock Holmes to put two and two together and ascertain that Roger's father Charles Lloyd Pack who featured more prominently in the episode obviously pulled strings in order to give his son an early break in his acting career. He most likely approached McGoohan and this fascinating detail offers an insight into the gracious generosity of Patrick. Although by this time I'd resigned from Six Of One I recall emailing Bruce Clark about this discovery but whether he passed it on or dismissed it is anyone's guess. I decided to 'sit on it' thereafter and have only recently revealed the discovery again, this time to convention organiser and on-line editor of the 'Free For All' archives Geoff Lake.

Although Roger Lloyd Pack didn't travel to Portmeirion to appear in 'The Prisoner,' 30 years later as fate would have it the actor was destined to do just that for a Prisoner spoof of the BBC sit com 'Two Point Four Children'. A strange world indeed and I'm sure the late Roger Lloyd Pack must have smiled at the irony!

- My second discovery brings us full circle as it appears in 'The Girl Who Was Death' and is something of a personal nature. Though subliminal, my late mother can be seen at the Kursaal fun park. She and my father had seen the episode at least once and neither of them had spotted it! I only noticed it a short while after she passed away and my father confirmed it when I showed it to him. Both born and raised in Southend-on-Sea (home of the Kursaal), it was still a lucky coincidence that they happened to be there while a Prisoner unit was filming. Only after seeing his late wife in the episode did my father recall further details. He and my mother had been sitting in a restaurant nearby when a couple had come in shouting about a film crew across the road 'making a promotional tourist feature'. Excited about the prospect of being included, my parents were amongst a crowd of people that went across the road and into the fun park. My father remembered a guy running around dressed as Sherlock Holmes (Frank Maher) but had forgotten the whole event up until he realised the significance. Depending on the schedule it's quite possible my mother was pregnant with me at the time as I was born in late October 1967. Sadly my mother never got to know about her 'guest appearance' as I only made the discovery after she passed away in 2006. Perhaps it was fate that introduced me to The Prisoner via 'The Girl Who Was Death'...

Thanks for the trip dad. RIP.

Frame Grab From YouTube video of Prisoner Convention 1996 with apologies to the owner of the material — this is your erstwhile (idiot)editor in John Lennon sunglasses and Prisoner T- Shirt, festooned with badges. Long hair and beard and moustache
are no longer included.

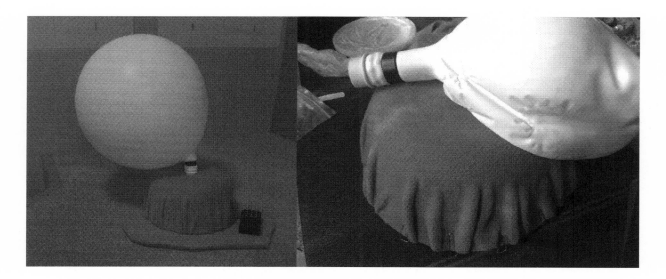

Chris Gray : CG Systems RC Rover

This second attempt at a radio-controlled Rover - lest we forget the schoolboy cap on top of Michelin Man Tubing on top of a go-kart - has several advantages over its predecessor. One it comes with preinstalled Rover sound-effects and can say 'Be Seeing You' or even outdo Number Six in 'The Girl Who Was Death' and tell Children a Bedtime story.

Also 'in these days of horror, fictional or otherwise' can we really do without an RC Rover to protect us, rather than carrying out its original role from 'The Prisoner'. Certainly the average intruder is more likely to be scared away by the terrifying sound produced by the RC Rover than a barking dog. Make up your own minds by visiting the YouTube link below. By the Way: the Radio Controlled Rover is Not For Sale - It's Just For Fun!
https://www.youtube.com/watch?v=ikAHxAbZONM
Updates on Mark II RC Rover: http://cgsng.com/page71.htm

Some Notes on 'The Prisoner'
or The Continuity Announcer

Fifty years later, we have the opportunity to see an episode of 'The Prisoner' in detail that was not apparent in VHS or DVD through BLU RAY copies of the series which enable us to notice and see things that were unclear before.

One problem with this is that we are able to see the fight between continuity and editing at close range. To take an example in 'Free For All' as Number Six is convincing the Villagers that if 'you place your trust in the old regime' — you will be stuck with the old Number Two there is a sudden edit and the plants and foliage no longer look as they would in September and we see a shot of Villager's smiling and waving.

In terms of continuity—you would probably rip your hair out seeing this, however no doubt somebody higher in production (possibly McGoohan) vetoed this stating that they needed a shot of the Villagers behaving this way even if the continuity of the sequence was broken.

As it happens BLU RAY didn't bring us this continuity vs. Editing conundrum which was spotted by Max Hora many years previously, however it is fair to say that we can now see this clearer than ever before.

Sometimes we can put these down to the dreamlike nature of the Village but other times a sudden alteration between shots or the sight of chess squares burnt into a lawn in the opening sequence after shooting 'Checkmate' create problems.

In other episodes the bottom of the pool in the Village Square changes from a beautiful rich blue to a muddy green colour within a few minutes or across an episode. Guy Doleman might be replaced by a double with a loudhailer due to personal problems of an urgent nature that meant he had to leave Portmeirion.[92]

However production also lead to some interesting and agreeable effects occurring by chance, or at least unplanned, the Allouette II helicopter shots on Thursday 15th September 1966 were proof of this. Number Six attempts an escape by speedboat but Rover is summoned to retrieve him. To gain aerial shots of this scene for Free For All the helicopter was used and the downdraft that was created by its rotor blades gave the weather balloon the appearance of being alive[93]

A major production problem was that of the Mechanical Rover originally intended for use in the programme, while stories abounded of its demise in the Portmeirion estuary the truth was much simpler. The design of the machine meant that visibility was poor — as it had to be driven as a go-kart and the fumes and noise of its engine meant that it was naturally un-

---

[92] 'The Prisoner Investigated Part 1' - Steven Ricks-TR7 Productions - 1990

[93] The Prisoner - A Complete Production Guide by Andrew Pixley - Network - 2007

usable for a film shoot of this nature. How fortunate that the replacement — a weather balloon made no external sound and created no fumes to potentially harm its operator, apparently they just had a habit of bursting instead. The fact that the Rover balloons were difficult to keep in one piece probably explains why they were phased out of the series. They are seen prominently in 'Arrival,' 'The Chimes of Big Ben,' 'Free For All,' 'The Schizoid Man,' 'Checkmate,' 'Dance of The Dead,' 'Once Upon A Time' & briefly in 'Fall Out.' All other Rover appearances are stock footage or in the closing credits. In production order it seems that Rover is actually decommissioned after it kills Curtis in 'The Schizoid Man' - Rover may not have killed Number Six but the Village clearly saw Curtis as a valuable asset.

Dr. Peter Harrison from Emergency Ward 10

Peter Howell in 'The General' means a lot to me as more years ago than I can remember I met him in Portmeirion and he even signed a photograph with my name on it. I knew that there were probably hundreds of people that day who had a similar experience with Peter Howell signing autographs. However this was the first time I had met someone from the series and I was admittedly a bit star struck. Secretly 'The General' remains one of my favourite episodes — partly because that night I saw it at the Coliseum Cinema in Porthmadog[94] where the original rushes had been screened during the September 1966 Portmeirion shoot.

Sadly however Peter Howell passed away on April 21st 2015 at the age of 95. My impression of Peter on the one occasion that I met him was that he was a pure gentleman. I think he was particularly happy to be invited to a Convention as his scenes for 'The General' had all been filmed at MGM Borehamwood.

The other reason was about education and I have to admit it's the theme of 'The General' coupled with the superb acting of Patrick McGoohan, Peter Howell, Betty McDowall, Colin Gordon & John Castle that I find so enduring. The idea that in a few minutes you could have impressed on your mind a 3 Year University Course intrigued me because at that stage I was just about to start a 3 Year University Course.

The concept of making the Villager's Knowledgeable Cabbage's - only able to repeat parrot fashion what they had learnt — the tedious, wasteful schooling swept aside was simultaneously a frightening idea and at the time a tiny part of me wished something similar was possible.

'The General' had me caught between wanting a process similar to it to be readily available while at the same time being fearful of the possibilities of being hypnotically taught whatever the Village (or the state, government or status-quo) wanted me to be taught. In other words as a timesaving device it seemed alluring but as a means of preventing individual thought a major concern.

---

[94] Sadly the Coliseum Cinema has now been demolished despite a campaign for its preservation.

Peter Howell and Betty McDowall's performances are key to making this work — they act largely separately but you believe that they are husband and wife something that is very rare in the Village. However Peter's authoritative voice when he describes Speedlearn and it's beneficial nature is breathtaking because he makes a 'fantastic concept' sound believable. Howell has the rare quality in an actor of enabling us to suspend our disbelief when something sounds part of a fantasy.

Betty McDowall's scenes with McGoohan as she explains the concept of Modern Art to him and that "Construction Arises Out Of The Ashes of Destruction" is another intriguing few minutes of television. McDowall sell's the ideas and concepts of Modern Art to us but she is forced to act alongside McGoohan who treats her ideas with dry witty adjoiners in the dialogue that they perform alongside each other splendidly.

I find the last few moments of the episode when Number Six 'silently' tells the Professor's wife that her husband has passed away incredibly touching. It's a rare moment where Number Six shoulder's his 'responsibility' for what has happened. It also makes me think what if the Professor and his wife had children or grandchildren in the Village - is the Children's Story in 'The Girl Who Was Death'-Number Six looking after the half-orphaned children of a Villager whose demise is partially his fault. We could include Curtis or Number 73 in this equation as well — perhaps the bereaved children need a father figure and 'Number Six' temporarily agrees to provide one.[95]

BOXED KLEVER

I also had the honour of meeting and sharing a few brief words with 'the one and only' Alexis Kanner. He also signed a photograph for me personally although sadly through moving house several times since the photo has gone astray. However those few moments are seared onto my memory as only a few years earlier I had seen 'Living In Harmony,' 'The Girl Who Was Death' & 'Fall Out' for the first time. These 3 episodes undoubtedly affect our impression of the whole series. The book 'Inside The Prisoner' by Ian Rakoff details the trials and tribulations of getting 'Living In Harmony' to screen and documents his other work and influences.

Alexis Kanner brings the role of the Kid and his alter ego 'in the Village' alive; as the Kid he never speaks but his performance is writ large because of it. Every movement and gesture is important within his acting in this episode and tells us more about him than words can. Has anyone noted that his silence has him fulfilling the role of Angelo Muscat's Butler albeit transposed in a Western setting. No wonder he was the only member of the cast to receive a special boxed credit.

In 'Fall Out' as 'Number 48' he is the spirit of chaos, he sings a spiritual song in 'Dem Bones' — and I wonder now if this actually on some level is McGoohan's signpost to the 'Destruction of the Village'. When 'Evacuation' of the Village occurs it happens, in a mass

---

[95] I'd like to thank Steve Matt who helped me to extend this theory based on his views and to also credit him for his ideas and input into this discussion.

panic — the same chaotic movement as seen in the stalactite ridden chamber beneath the Village during Number 48's act.

So this leaves me and I know I've not scratched the surface of Number 48's motivation but some points have too be left to others. I would like to say a little about the character that 'Alexis' plays in 'The Girl Who Was Death'.

The clearly dubbed lines beginning 'Hey, what's your game Sherlock Holmes...' as Kanner's character promises to beat up 'Number Six's ' alter ego trailing the 'titular Girl' are deliberately overplayed. Unfortunately there is no let up for our hero here as he has discovered a look alike. Later on in the Fairground he thinks he has made the same mistake and the appearance of Kanner's character appears to confirm this ; however the 'Girl' - Doctor Schnipp's Daughter is this time being protected by Kanner. For this short part Alexis Kanner goes uncredited — presumably he was asked to participate between 'Living In Harmony' and the 'Final Episode' going into production.

<u>Photograph of Plaque outside reopened Prisoner Shop</u>
<u>Unveiled in 1999 by Fenella Fielding (The Village Voice)</u>
<u>- Courtesy of Ed Fordham/Ian Orchard 2016</u>

Rick Davy - Webchat with Jon Blum and Rupert Booth - Authors of 'The Prisoner's Dilemma'

On Friday February 11th 2005, Rick Davy of The Unmutual Website conducted an exclusive 2-hour web-chat with the authors. An edited transcript follows.
Please note that the following interview includes some "spoilers" regarding the book.
Article Can Also Be Found On The Unmutual Website At:
http://theunmutual.co.uk/webchat.htm

Rick began by asking how the authors got involved in writing:

JB: As a fan, I started writing back in the '80s, for my local 'Doctor Who' club. As a pro, I got my break because of my then-wife-to-be Kate Orman, who agreed to co-write a 'Doctor Who' book with me.

RB: For me, it's just something I've always done. I think that the only way to be vaguely good at anything is lots of practice. The trick was then going pro with it all. I'd had one or two short stories published before this, had screened films (amateur) and so on.

JB: The thing is, I already knew Rupert by then.

RD: Did you meet through 'Dr Who'?

RB: I'm an ex 'Who' fan ;-)

JB: Yeah, because I'd seen him doing a 'Doctor Who' fan video!

RD: That sounds interesting — what was the video like?

RB: I thought it was protey! Please say it was protey!

JB: The Who video came first, then you showed me one of your Protoverse films and then I was hooked.
Basically, our secret shame is that we each did some fan-video work in the mid-'90s. There's still video evidence of each of us playing the Doctor!

RD: So how did you get involved in writing your 'Dr Who' novel?

JB: Again, my wife's to blame! She knew I was a writer from the video I'd done, I wrote some short stories which she liked, and then we worked out a novel plot together.

RD: I believe it won an award?

JB: Our latest book did — we've done four 'Who' books together. One won the DWM annual poll, one won the Aurealis Award for Best Australian SF Novel. Another was nominated for the Aurealis but was deservedly beaten.

RD: Have you been tempted, Rupert, to write a full 'Who' novel?

JB: I'd love him to!

RB: Hmmmm......not really! Unless the money was good!

JB: The money's better than the 'Prisoner books... so far, at least! (It all depends on sales. And with the new series, sales will go through the roof.)

RD: So who came up with the idea of doing a 'Prisoner' novel?

JB: Me!

RB: Over to you, Jon!

JB: It was because of Mateo Latosa, our editor. He took my wife and me to dinner to see if we wanted to write something original for Powys. He mentioned that they'd been offered the 'Prisoner' franchise....I jumped at the chance.

RB: Next thing I know, Jon approaches me in a hotel room with a big grin on his face and says "Do you want to write a Prisoner book with me?" Whereupon I ponder for a millisecond and say "Yeah".

JB: Just luck that Mateo mentioned it — lots of hard work after that! We had to do an outline, which he approved. Then they had to get the rights sorted out. Basically, Mateo hadn't been sure whether it was possible to do a good 'Prisoner' novel, after the sixties efforts, but we came up with something which convinced him, so we got the gig!

RD: Can we talk about the show? When did you each first see it?

RB: I first saw half of it in about 1989, when a mate bought some of the channel 5 vids whereupon I had to go out and buy 'Fall Out' because I HAD to know how it ended.

RD: When did you first see The Prisoner, Jon?

JB: I first saw Priz in the mid '80s, probably about '84. I'd read about it in John Peel's articles in Fantasy Empire magazine in the States. It sounded amazing, and it was! It blew my thirteen-year-old head wide open.

RD: Better than 'Doctor Who?' ;-)

JB: Different from Who, and so intense!

RB: Same sort of reaction here especially after seeing 'Fall Out' without 'Once upon A Time' preceding it. I assumed it would make more sense once I saw 'Once Upon....'.WRONG!!!

JB: No 'OUAT'? You poor soul. Me, I missed 'Arrival' the first time around, but knew what was happening from the articles.

RD: Do either of you have a favourite episode?

JB: Hmmm... Probably 'Dance of the Dead,' this week. But I love them all. Even 'Do Not Forsake Me' has something about it.

RB: I like all the weird ones. 'Dance', 'OUAT', 'Fall Out'.

RD: What other shows were you into at that time, apart from 'Doctor Who?'

JB: God, all sorts of British stuff. 'Blake's 7', 'Sapphire and Steel'..... We had a great PBS station which got all the 'cult' shows and aired them late at night.

RB: Oh the whole telefantasy genre ....'Blakes 7', 'Sapphire', 'Ace of Wands'...... lots of comedy shows also.

JB: Oh yeah, 'The Goodies'!

RB: 'The Goodies' rock.

JB: Ran for about thirteen weeks on Channel 26 in DC, and scarred me for life.

RD: So. You got the gig for 'The Prisoner' — what made you decide to write the book together?

JB: Once I got the offer, I knew Rupe was a mad fan as well, and he was attending the same convention in LA as us.

RB: Well, I didn't so much decide as accept, delightedly!

JB: So I immediately came up to him with an evil grin......

RB: It was evil, yeah.

JB: . ...And we had half the story worked out that night!

RD: Had you written "in tandem" on anything before?

RB: No, but we had talked about it

JB: Well, we sort of had. We'd done one film script which was very, very silly. Actually, "Script" is a bit of an overstatement!

RD: What was it about?

RB: Oh, don't ask!

JB: Oh God. Rupe, do you want to explain "Mrs. Krill" to him?

RB: I don't know if I can!

JB: Let's say it was.....surreal. It involved toast.

RB: It's a simple love story. Boy exists, is destroyed by God, girl misses boy, girl gets boy back by reconstituting him from pieces of crumpled up paper, everyone dances, boy and girl both happen to be oversized anthropomorphic jumpers. It's all very poignant.

JB: We basically just did this film in a few days when I was visiting Rupert up in Newcastle. It was just for fun, it's never seen the light of day, but it was a joy just to be creative with nothing at stake! Kind of like 'Fall Out' in a way. Like 'Fall Out' because of the sheer sense of glee and anything-goes to it.

RB: I really must edit what there is of it someday....

RD: Sounds great!

RB: Bless you for saying that ;-)

RD: So as soon as you got the 'Prisoner' gig, did you have a storyline already?

JB: We started work on the storyline that night.

RB: With beer.

JB: I think the first thought we had was "face the Prisoner with the Prisoner's Dilemma" — the whole logic-puzzle thing about cooperation or defection.

RB: I remember fairly early on coming up with the reality TV stuff, in a vague sort of way. Seemed to make sense with the constant surveillance aspect.

JB: Another early point was the idea of having Number 6's "opposite number" be a woman — someone who could be a lot like him, and that's what he can't stand about her!

RD: How did you decide who would actually write what? How does dual-writing work?

RB: Both of us had certain bits we wanted to do, themes to explore and so on.

JB: The co-writing thing was a juggling act.

RB: Lots of phone calls.

JB: We'd each write scenes we'd picked out of the outline, and rewrite each others work.

RB: Lots of emails back and forth sorting out the skeleton of the story.

JB: Mostly me getting my grubby hands on Rupert's prose, I'm afraid! In the end I think I did the biggest share of the prose, because Rupert was also working on a TV pilot for a sketch comedy at the time.

RB: I always say that what would happen was that I would fret for a month and come up with three paragraphs, whereupon Jon would then send three finished chapters to me.

JB: Which is unusual for me, because I'm usually the slow one! That's why the book took more than a year to write.

RB: That's slow??? Jeezzz.....

JB: I'm terribly slow compared to Kate. She can do thousands of words a day, I can manage maybe 400-500.

RB: Kate is therefore evil.

RD: Who came up with "The Irrationals"?

JB: The Irrationals were... God, I don't remember!

RB: No, I don't either!

JB: I do remember that at one point we thought about calling them the Unmutuals, but changed our mind because we thought the characters were turning into complete twits! No reflection intended on anyone real. :-)

RD: I believe some are based on real people?

RB: Heh. Yeah. there's a description of them the first time we meet them and all of them are mates of mine in that bit.

JB: Hang on — who *were* you basing them on?

RD: Are any characters based on either of you two?

JB: On me? No.

RB: Just the physical descriptions! Equinox is me.

JB: I think you could say the whole book was based on Rupert's impression of Patrick McGoohan!

RB: (Laughs).

JB: Just giving him the fear. Equinox is Rupert at about 18, I think.

RD: So, the Number Two character.

JB: We went through a bunch of possible Number 2 images.

RB: He started out in my mind as being John Le Mesurier. Terribly diffident, you know.

JB: My first thought was to make him Yaphet Kotto! (Played very much against type.) Later on the idea was to make the general at the end Mr. Kotto, but that went by the wayside when we decided he should be Russian rather than a UN representative. (That's probably a spoiler, BTW!)

RB: We had pretty much the whole thing cast at various points, just in case anyone wants to turn it into a film ;-)

JB: We never did decide on who Number 18 was though! Who decided to put in Alan Turing? Was that me?

RB: Turing was definitely you.

RD: Were there any moments where you thought "bloody hell, how are we supposed to write a Prisoner story?"

JB: The "bloody hell" moments came early on, and never really stopped!

RB: Absolutely!

JB: I ended up rewatching the whole series, and in that time I noticed just how many different bits of ground there were to cover, to try to get *everything* we thought was cool about 'The Prisoner' into one hopefully neat package.

RB: One thing I was very keen on was the gameshow in the middle and having nasty twists — 'Many Happy Returns-esque' kicks in the teeth.

RD: Had you read other Prisoner fiction?

JB: I've read the three Sixties books, and the graphic novel, but that's about it.

RB: I'd read some. The only one that sticks in the mind was "A Day in the Life" — the message of which appeared to be "Cannabis is nice".

JB: I can sympathise tremendously with those authors — they've each got their own distinctive styles, but you miss out on the feel of the whole of the show.

RD: Did you think "we've bitten off more than we can chew here"?

RB: Oh I frequently thought that

JB: Bitten off too much? Repeatedly!

RB: Ha!

JB: The biggest challenge was Number 6.

RB: ABSOLUTELY!

JB: There were bits where every line was a struggle to try to get across the feel of each line.

RD: So why go through with it? Seems like you're on a hiding to nothing.

JB: Why go through with it? Because I love the series.

RB: Well, at the end of the day......damn, he just said it. It was nice to be able to look at the contemporary world through the medium of 'The Prisoner'.

JB: And I couldn't resist the chance to do something that *hadn't* been seen before with it. In some ways the whole 'Prisoner' thing is infinitely more relevant now than it was then. A lot of my other writing has been in a similar vein of social satire — if 'The Prisoner' hadn't been done already, I'd have been struggling to come up with something like that!

RD: Did you think about setting it post-escape? i.e.: have a non-McGoohan lead character?

RB: Never, I think 6 IS 'The Prisoner'.

JB: I think the ending of the show is perfect as it stands.

RB: Agreed. It's not something that should be followed up on.

RD: So setting it mid-series — what problems did this create for you?

JB: The thing about 6 is, he was a hell of a challenge, but when we got him *right* — and I think we did, in some moments at least — it's just a joy. I think the secret to writing him is not to let him talk too much! If I ever got the chance to go back and revise the book, there are bits I'd try to shorten what he's saying.

RB: I think I said in this very chatroom a while back that one of the things you realise when trying to write 6 is how much of the character comes from the performance. Something that's very difficult to replicate in prose, simply because it's a completely different medium to TV.

RD: In a 300+ page book, he's going to have to talk, though. Was this the hardest thing?

JB: Probably.

RB: Well, we did consider him using mime throughout. But heroes don't mime.

RD: (Laughter)

JB: He has to talk, and more importantly — because it's a novel, the form demands that he have a bit more complexity as a character. The challenge there is dealing with someone who doesn't give anything away, and trying to suggest what it is he's not giving away! There are some bits where we deliberately went beyond what you'd expect from 6 - because part of the story demands that he realise that he's getting predictable. So he's going outside of his own comfort zone a bit.

RB: Also, he's a very closed down character. He gives very little away. So it was difficult to decide just how much to go inside his head.

RD: Did you think at times — "he's Number 6 - its impossible to write him in prose!"

RB: Yep!

JB: I never thought impossible. I thought "really, BLOODY hard".

RB: I thought impossible several times. ;-)

JB: We really didn't want him to be a caricature.

RB: No, absolutely.

JB: In fact the book is about 6 fighting against his own caricature-ness, in a way — the whole stereotype of him which the Village has developed.

RD: How about the other characters? Were these easier to write because they didn't exist up until that point?

RB: Oh, the other characters were a doddle compared to 6.

JB: Some of the others were easy.

RB: We could do pretty much what we liked with them.

JB: Number 18 was difficult in a similar way.

RB: Yeah, she was hard work sometimes. I think we discussed her more than anyone else bar 6.

JB: Like him, she's hard to get ahold of.

RD: Any particular favourites?

JB: Favourites? Number 101 was great for me. There are some bits with 2 I'm really happy with — you quoted a couple of them, in fact!

RD: :-)

RB: The Irrationals. I had a lot of fun with them.

JB: Rupert's "salad sequence" is fab.

RB: Was that mine?

JB: And the confrontation in the square where 6 nearly kills him. 6 was much easier to write when he was really really angry. He becomes this towering icon.

RB: I remember we both chuckled at how 6 would react to a character that seemed completely uninterested in pushing him.

JB: The irresistible force meets the comfy chair!

RB: Yeah!

RD: Did you draw anything from the series itself to inspire your characters?

JB: Hmm... I actually resisted drawing on the series itself too much — the frustrating bit was that our stuff kept looking like it was based on the series! EG, Number 101 seeming so much like the Professor.

RB: Not so much the characters, no, but the general....'Prisonerishness'

JB: With 101, the idea was "what if Alan Turing's suicide was faked," and he's been in the Village for twenty years pioneering new computer technology. But it sort of crept in the direction of looking like we were just doing 'The General'.

RD: I saw a bit of Nadia in Number 18, and Colin Gordon in Number Two.
RB: I saw a lot more of Annette Andre's character in 18 than Nadia.
JB: Interesting - I kept thinking of 18 as Bernice Summerfield! ('Doctor Who' books companion.)
RB: Oh you 'Who' fan you ;-)
JB: Someone who would react to 6's intense seriousness by being frivolous, but could be intensely serious when it suited her.
RB: Whereupon he uses the same trick back at her!
RD: Did you find yourself at times writing for 'Dr Who'?
JB: Not really.
RB: Never.
JB: The closest I got to a similarity is that 6 and the Doctor are each characters who you never see what they're actually thinking. We almost always get other characters' perceptions of the Doctor but no internal monologues. That's sort of the approach we took with 6 - it's either other characters' POV like 18, or just the narrator's POV. :-)

RD: You mentioned the gameshow, Rupert - without giving too many spoilers, did you get inspiration from 'The Truman Show' for this?
RB: Mostly from 'Big Brother' actually!
JB: 'Big Brother' was the biggie.
RB: And the raft of reality gameshows that have swept the airwaves.
JB: In a way 'Big Brother' was the sign that our civilisation had become a self-parody.
RB: I was always interested in the fact that these shows are touted as "reality". I mean, how can they be? This is an artificial environment we're looking at.

RD: Did you feel it was tricky to get that Reality TV idea into The Village?
JB: It seemed right up their alley!
RB: No, it seemed to fit perfectly. Just the sort of thing they would do, especially to someone like 6 who is so intensely private.
JB: The only thing that's odd about the Village is that we never see what they run on TV. I wanted to have them showing 'Gilligan's Island'!
RB: But I didn't know what 'Gilligan's Island' was!
JB: I feel like such the ugly American.
RB: There were times when Jon would put in an Americanism that I would simply have no frame of reference for, but i'd just flag that up to him and it was usually

replaced.

RD: Where did some of the other ideas come from? The war, for instance?

JB: The war was me in post-9/11 curmudgeon mode, I think.

RB: Where did the idea for the war come from? Hmmmm, let me think... ;-)

JB: It was Rupert's idea that the war would actually be part of the gameshow in some way.

RD: Did you think it was a bit of an outlandish idea, even for 'The Prisoner'?

RB: Outlandish? Have you SEEN 'Fall Out'?

RD: (Laughter)

RB: I think we both felt that we needed to up the ante a bit in the third part of the book.

JB: If we're playing with the idea of manufactured heroes then there's a sort of parallel between the reality TV and Fox News.

RB: Plus, it was nice to be able to do something that would have cost millions to do on screen — really open things out.

JB: At one point Mateo thought the war stuff could make a whole separate book — maybe

The front cover of 'The Prisoner's Dilemma' courtesy of Ed Fordham

we should have done that and gotten more money!

RD: Were you writing it as an "episode" of 'The Prisoner'?

JB: I saw it as about four episodes!

RB: A feature length one.

JB: One of the things about the books is, you can have consequences from one bit into the next — it doesn't have to fit within 45 minutes, or even within one volume. There's a bit at the end which sets up Lance's book, and another which is hinting at book #3. By the way, the Minister will be coming back! The idea is that he's sort of a dark reflection of Number 6 - someone who's a self-motivated individual, but with no conscience or concern for others at all.

RD: Although relevant to 'The Prisoner', a lot of the themes are for a "modern audience" — did you feel you might lose some of that 'Prisonerishness'?

RB: We talked a lot about this. Eventually, we pretty much settled on trying to make the setting as timeless as possible. Of course, nowadays, everyone is a number and doesn't really care. That whole 60's psychosis wasn't really relevant anymore.

JB: About the themes....I don't know, because I think these themes are actually common to the Sixties experience. I mean, we're talking about social control, propaganda, manipulating the masses... the technology has shifted but the battle is the same. Even in the show, they were trying to make it timeless, most of the time. Look at the design of The Village - the Sixties bits are downplayed on the surface.

RB: See what I mean? Three chapters to three paragraphs ;-)

RD: (Laughter)

JB: The number thing was tricky to sell — part of what I wanted with "The Irrationals" was to show the dangers of accepting this stuff ironically, and not actually doing anything about it!

RD: Were you tempted to reference characters from the series more than you did?

JB: Hmm... I think most of the things we were tempted to include, we shoved in!

RB: I wasn't really tempted to ref existing characters much, no!

JB: The cat, the old Number 2 cameo, the mysterious twin technicians.

RB: Number 48....but they're all throwaways.

JB: Little things like that.

RB: We wanted to avoid fanw**k.

JB: But we hoped to keep them to the margins, and let the new stuff carry the story. The 48 gag was me! I loved the idea that he was too genuinely weird for the pseudo-weirdos.

RB: Rover, of course.

JB: Oh God, Rover was *fun* to write! I wanted to remind people of just how freakish and insane this thing is.

RB: You did all the best stuff with Rover.

JB: I also wanted to send up the "pointed stick" jokes, and have that come back to haunt them. Kind of like having a Dalek suddenly go up the stairs!

RB: Yeah, I loved the pointed stick bit.

RD: Without sounding arrogant, do you expect people to like the book?

JB: Do I expect people to like it? I *hope* they will. I don't think the book is perfect; give me a bit more hindsight and I'll find things I wish I could fix, but on the whole I think there's a lot of good stuff in there.

RB: I'm expecting to be mobbed in the street by angry fans screaming "unworthy of the Albertus typeface!!"

RD: Did you get any feedback from Patrick McGoohan?

JB: Not a sausage!

RB: Nope

JB: We sent him the manuscript with a somewhat crawly letter, saying we wanted to make him proud - I suspect maybe we should have said "here we are, this is our individual take on the Prisoner, what do you think?" Then at least he would have had to respect our guts!

RD: Rupert, your writing background is in comedy. Were you tempted to make the book a comedy romp?

RB: No, but you have to have some humour in it otherwise you have this unremitting grimness going on.

JB: His comedy can get really dark at times — that's what I like about it! At its best 'The Prisoner' is absurdism in the classic sense.

RD: Were there times when you thought "it's getting too silly "?

RB: There was one very silly sequence I rewrote which didn't make it. Where 6 needs to capture some ducks, for reasons that escape me, and eventually sets Rover on them.

JB: *Just* one very silly sequence??

RB: Well..one or two ;-)

JB: Oh wait, I remember the ducks. There was a reason for it, I'm sure. Oh yeah, it was an early draft of the "getting stuff for everyone" sequence. The bit with Number 35 the receptionist.

RB: But yes, as Jon says, the series is absurdism. It's one of the things I love about it. Throwaway bits of insanity — that's what the stenographer's about, for example.

JB: The show is a modern 'Alice In Wonderland,' in a way. "Pop Kafka," as Lloyd Rose said.

RD: Any other ideas which didn't make it into the final draft?

RB: Oh, there was tons of stuff that didn't make it.

JB: Other bits that didn't make it? Hmm.

RD: Enough for another book? ;-)

JB: If we do another book, it'll be seriously different and probably a lot shorter!

RB: I'd be up for writing another!

RD: Is it an option?

JB: It might be, but not for a while yet. They've commissioned the first four books, which takes it up till early 2007, and they've got plenty of candidates for 5 and 6. If there's a second batch of books, though. I'd also love to see a short story collection.

RB: Yes, me too. We need to relax first ;-)

JB: You can get far weirder in 5,000 words than 120,000! With that much story, people expect it to be more coherent on some levels!

RB: Do they? Oh hell!

RD/JB: (Laughter)

JB: If I ever do a short story, I want to do one with the Mary Morris Number 2. She just blows my mind.

RB: Mine would probably be about training Rover.

RD: Was Mary Morris your favourite Number Two?

JB: Probably. I always wondered how *she'd* approach Degree Absolute. Imagine if we got to explore 6's mother issues.

RB: Heroes don't have mother issues.

JB: Heroes don't have mothers.

RB: Good point!

JB: Heroes certainly don't have mothers-in-law.

RD: I wanted to ask you about Number 18. Being that Number 6 had already been betrayed by Nadia, Alison - lots of women in the series, did you wonder if another female ally would work?

JB: That was part of what we were playing with.

RB: Yeah, he's out to distrust right from the start.

JB: They've paired him up with female betrayers, and you have to wonder if it suits their purposes to have him completely mistrusting of everyone, so that if someone *does* come along, he won't trust them.

RB: Or rather HE has to wonder.

JB: Like the Watchmaker's daughter, at least at first. I didn't want him to be an easy mark, though. He does suspect a set-up from the word go, like he says in the interrogation. I think it's only when she actually gets her mind wiped that he really believes her.

RD: There seemed to be some sexual tension at times.

RB: I was keen on sexual tension. Did I just say that?

JB: I wanted to evoke the tension without actually showing anything physical - like with the maid in 'Arrival' or the Observer in 'Dance,' where there's a sense of implied tension without even any contact.

RB: Well, apart from in the snake sequence.

JB: The snake sequence was you, wasn't it? Very phallic. I remember we had to get the right balance in that scene, so that it didn't seem too crass.

RB: Yes...I've actually only just realised the biblical implications of that bit! The final scene with them was a hell of a lot of hard work to get right. That one went back and forth between us for a long time.

JB: I worried about whether McGoohan would object to that bit, actually!

RB: Well at least it would make him notice it!

JB: But then I remembered Kathy bulging out of her Western outfit, and decided he can't have been *that* conservative. I think 6 is in many ways a perfect gentleman.

RB: Absolutely. He's terribly old fashioned and upright.

JB: I worried about putting him in an ungentlemanly situation, but I wanted to show him maintaining as much propriety as possible. There was never any question of 6 kissing her, or any actual advances on either side. I did want to get the sense that she was a potential kindred spirit, but they just couldn't connect.

RB: Plus of course, any attraction would be offset by the lack of trust.

JB: If I remember, I think we talked about how that sort of tension would have been carefully created for the reality show!

RB: Yeah, that's right. Just as in 'Big Brother,' the situation is engineered — which is why you have the edited highlights that he sees afterwards completely distorting their "relationship".

JB: Or the bit on the boat where she tells him her name. I wanted to show her reaching out in an emotional rather than a sexual way. And 6's response had to be deeply oblique. He's trying to communicate without actually giving anything away!

RD: Was it tricky, as 21st century guys, to write sixties-Prisoner-type dialogue?

RB: Tricky? Hey, get with it! I didn't find it tricky. We had the series there as a template.

JB: Nah, it was fab. The main tricky bit was like I said, stopping 6 from gassing on too much! If you can keep it terse, you can get a rhythm going.

RD: I must ask about "Roadrunner".....

JB: Ah, the roadrunner bit! That's one of the things I mentioned earlier — where 6 is going a bit outside his comfort zone. It seems to be a love-or-hate-it thing.

RD: But would Number 6 ever talk about "Roadrunner"? Sorry if I sound harsh.

JB: Lloyd Rose (Doctor Who author) loved it, other people think it's a step too far. It was a deliberate attempt to show him being humanised — whether that was him

actually being humanised or just putting on a human act to fool her is another matter! (I think we pointed that out in the prose somewhere.) At the very least he's creating the *appearance* of relaxing around her. Maybe he really is relaxing and showing a new side, maybe it's a John Drake undercover act. Even I'm not quite sure. If you look at the "Roadrunner" line, we even put in the ellipses and italics to suggest a particular sort of McGoohan inflection. If you actually look at 6's lines in the scripts, you can't see McGoohan in them — they're surprisingly flat. So much of it is the performance finding nuances that aren't obvious in the words!

RD: Does that make it even harder for you as a writer? Being that you don't have McGoohan to give you the performance?
JB: Yeah, it does make it harder — the scriptwriters also didn't need to worry about replicating a pre-existing feel, they were creating something new, and that something new changed incredibly as the show went along. There's no way you can predict something that feels like 'Fall Out' when you're doing 'Arrival'.

RD: Is this your main worry for people buying the book? That they won't see "your" Number 6 as McGoohan enough for them?
JB: We had to try to add in enough McGoohan-isms into the descriptions and phrasings to suggest his performance, without taking it over the line into caricature. It's definitely a worry that either 6 or the Village won't measure up to peoples' personal standards but at the end of the day, there's only so much you can do and peoples' individual standards are so idiosyncratic in many ways......like "Heroes don't birdwatch!" (That moment is in the book because 6 actually *does* birdwatch, briefly, in "A Change Of Mind")

RD: However good your book is, it's still going to be compared to the best TV series ever made. Is this unfair?
JB: I don't mind being *compared* — as long as the comparisons are reasonable ones. By reasonable, I mean that they recognise the whole range of what 'The Prisoner' is like. We may not be as good as the best, but we're better than the worst, I think!

RD: Should people view your book as part of the Prisoner "opus" or as something different?
JB: I don't think we have a prayer of being better than McGoohan/Markstein/etc when they were on peak form. But we can bring some things to the table which they couldn't (if only because we've got nearly 40 years of hindsight)......
RB: I wouldn't view it as "canon," no more than anything else produced outside the series.
JB: .....and hopefully that'll be enough to make the book worthy in its own right.

RB: I just hope it goes over okay and that people enjoy it.

JB: I don't really care about whether its "canon" or not — what matters is the *idea* of 'The Prisoner,' which is astonishingly universal for such an individual work.

There then followed a brief conversation concerning the authors forthcoming projects, and their experiences of Portmeirion. Unfortunately, due to technical difficulties, this part of the webchat has been lost in the mists of time.

RD: Having spent so much time on it, do you feel its all been worth it?
JB: The book is very much worth it.
RB: Oh, it's definitely been worth it!
JB: The only hard bit has been....
RB: The writing?
JB: ....the aftermath of writing it — trying to get the line launched successfully! The book has been a hell of a lot of work, but I wouldn't have missed it for the world. Oh, one footnote to the earlier story about starting work with Rupert - I did ask Kate first if she wanted to co-write a Prisoner book with me, but she said she didn't think she could pull it off!
RB: (Laughter)
JB: It was really flattering that she thought I could, though.
RB: Bless you, Kate!

JB: It's deeply weird to think about how all these things are resurfacing at once — new 'Who', new 'BSG', new 'Sapphire and Steel' audios, and even new 'Prisoner'. All we'll need is new 'Blake's 7' and we'll have the whole set of our childhood again!
RB: I tell you, the time is ripe for an 'Ace Of Wands' revival!
RD: Thank-you both very much.

27 MILES FROM HOME?[96]

What actually happened after the violent shoot-out of 'Fall Out,' that extraordinary final episode of something we call a TV series, and the launching of a rocket, the evacuation and the final destruction of the Village? Could that be? The cyclical nature of 'THE PRISONER' would tell us: no. But we cannot be sure.

Well, easy enough, isn't it. Number Six, Number 48 and the former Number Two are on the run and end up in that mobile home, the same cell used in the previous episode 'Once Upon A Time,' which is mounted on a mobile truck. The truck is set in motion and makes its way through a disused railway tunnel. All of a sudden we see it driving on a dual carriageway which appears to be in Great Britain. And then there's the signpost telling us: A20 London 27. Which, of course, does nothing less than make us think the Village of Number Six's captivity would be located right next to the British capital!

But is it? Mind you, in other episodes the Village was said to be either at the Baltic Sea, near the Polish border ('The Chimes Of Big Ben')[97], or southwest of Portugal and Spain, near the Moroccan coast ('Many Happy Returns'). The latter hint at its geographical position being especially intriguing because Number Six himself had gone on a search mission in which he actually found the place. But the very moment he recognised his find he was subsequently ejected from the aircraft and returned to where he had come from. It can be

---

[96] Photo of Campanile and surrounding buildings courtesy of Ed Fordham/Ian Orchard

[97] Maybe but was this a ruse on the part of 'Nadia' — after all the watch didn't show Polish time...

surmised that the aircraft pilot was actually working for the Village and that Number Six, although in charge of the search route and equipped with a compass, was in fact deluded: Be seeing you! It is a clear conception, the location of the Village isn't meant to be rationalised.

A20 London 27.

The geographical features, however, of both the Village and London or south England do not support the insinuation of the Village being located in that very area. The Village, after all, is a seaside resort, surrounded by high alpine mountains while the south of England is primarily flat (aside from the chalk rocks) and the coastline still a considerable distance away.

JUMP CUT FROM THE TWILIGHT ZONE

It's a mind game, for sure. One can try to explore and bring into accordance how it could happen that the truck all of a sudden is only a few miles away from London, and — as it may seem — the Village, too, is just around the corner! The editing of the scenes is very fast, even volatile and could be said elliptical. But nothing here urges us to believe that there's a real continuity of the action from the moment of the cavern shootings until the truck exits the tunnel and reaches British soil. So, let's take that jump-cut...

NUMBER SIX NEURALISED INTO OBLIVION?

Imagine the three escapees were "conditioned" — nothing uncommon in the series — and their memories of the recent past wiped out or "neuralised" as the process was called in the MEN IN BLACK films. We cannot honestly say how the process of making them forget their journey and the events before it was achieved. But thinking of how Number Six - when he was interrogated by the Council Chamber of 'Free For All' — was so quickly subjected to that hypnotising blue light may be a hint towards how they managed to do it and how quickly it was done. Also, in 'Once Upon A Time,' in the Embryo Room, a very similar, potentially hypnotising blue light emanates somewhere from the ceiling and both Number Two and the Butler wear special glasses whereas Number Six doesn't. The ideal moment for the erasing treatment would seem to be when the truck enters the tunnel. In fact, the truck had been provided, hadn't it.

The three would've been put to sleep, the container/cell covered, possibly sealed and most likely shipped on board whichever port of departure. The truck would be driven under a diplomatic label, so no customs officer would be allowed to inspect it. Later, before we see them on the A20, they would be reanimated or woken up. Thus, we still don't know where the Village really is, do we?

Why the dancing to the rhythm of the song "Dry Bones"? They wouldn't remember that hours, perhaps days had passed, only experience their successful escape. Certainly, there would be joy but their state of mind would be the result of the hypnotising effects on them,

Another exciting instalment of 'The Jailbird' by Steve Matt in 'Out of Order'

Look's like he's Incarcer...In...incer...held Prisoner again See Page 305 if you dare...

the feeling of lightheadedness and serenity about their escape from the prison without walls. The scenes from 'Fall Out' would seem to underline that.

CALCULATED RETURN

And the Butler? The Butler is the fourth person of the group to escape from the Village. But can he be called an escapee? He drives the truck out of the Village and through the tunnel implying that the accelerator, the clutch and the brake pedals must have been adjusted beforehand to his stunted physical growth. Arguably, he has a good deal of insight into the structures that constitute the Village system. And he always seems to follow some plan. But the Butler role still remains an enigmatic one, the same way it was before in the series. He is a (literal) key figure. No real clue is given until the end as to whether he joins Number Six out of his free will or whether perhaps it's his assignment.

All this leaves us with the question, or the fact rather, that this prison break must have been foreseen and arranged by the Village powers or the government behind it, especially as on their route state borders and customs barriers had to be bypassed. Even more so as the Village had already granted Number Six his return home, also money, the key to his house as well as his car. Could it be they'd let him leave the Village on a helicopter, simply and without any "credible" complications? There can be doubt about it. They corrected their mistake, it would seem.

MENTAL MANIFESTATION?

At the beginning and repeatedly in most of the credit sequences the individual we're about to know as 'Number Six' strides down a long and dark corridor. Could it be, the tunnel apparently leading to the A20 is actually that corridor, either literally or metaphorically, a 'wormhole' at the opposite end of which resurrection from the Twilight Zone that the Village is, back to London and back to reality which, however, isn't the same as it was before?

Looking at 'THE PRISONER' as a whole it can be taken for granted that the Village is actually a solid, physical reality. The main character is abducted to that place, that's where he lives and breathes. And also there's an infrastructure of some sort etc However, as soon as we enter the final episode 'Fall Out,' as viewers we enter a different level because now this episode is completely different from the previous ones. 'Fall Out' as we see it does nothing in terms of "explaining" — who, where, why — or resolution. It can be guessed that Patrick McGoohan didn't care about plot holes, he deliberately wanted to leave it unresolved, all the more as his approach is both allegorical and symbolic with the elliptical narrative mode of dropping rationalisations supporting his intentions.

NAMES AND NUMBERS: NUMBER SIX - PRISONER? THE VILLAGE - WHERE IS IT?

Certain elements about 'Fall Out' as well as of the 'Dance Of The Dead' episode, the scene on the beach in the twilight, appear to support the thesis that the Village is a mental manifestation, perhaps part of our unconscious self. Thus, it could have hardly been destroyed or left by escape. wherever one went the Village would be with you. And this, it seems, is what McGoohan himself and the final images of 'THE PRISONER' are telling us. Every man has a Village of his own, his own prison.

Written by : ARNO BAUMGÄRTEL IN COLLABORATION WITH DAVID STIMPSON & JANA MÜLLER

'The Mini Moke & The Prisoner'-
Or "Local Service Only!"

The Mini Moke is a key part of the appeal of 'The Prisoner' — the little taxis that will only allow you to be driven around the Village with their canopies and penny-farthing emblems which were clearly specially adapted just for the series. Over and beyond that is the story of what happened to each of the 4 original Mini Moke's and how they turned up again and were restored.

Then there is the various ways in which the Moke is used across the series ranging from Taxis to Electioneering to Ambulances. In 'The Schizoid Man' - Number Six even uses a Moke to decoy Rover away from himself so that he can make his way back to his old cottage 6 private and confront his double Curtis.

The Moke was designed by Alec Issigonis in response to a request from the British Army in the late 1950s for a new lightweight vehicle.The Army decided ultimately that Issigonis's design wasn't quite right for use in the military. Alec would never have guessed that the car

would end up being such an icon and that one of its initial fans would be the actress Brigitte Bardot.[98]

The BMC made amendments to the vehicle's initial design, increasing tyre sizes, upgrading the suspension and changes to the 848 cc engine to ensure the Moke could run as a 4x4 and improve as an off-road vehicle in 1962. In February 1962 the car now officially a 'Mini Moke' was shown at a commercial vehicle show in [99]Amsterdam. Before this event changes were made to the engine size so that it reached 948cc in an attempt to overcome the underpowered problems of the initial model.[100]

Two years later a commercial version of the Moke was launched in order for the company to make back the costs of developing the Moke over the past few years.

In August 1964 the cost of a Morris or Austin Mini Moke (incidentally the only difference

---

[98] http://mokeinternational.com/about/

[99] Photo of Prisoner style Mini Moke at Lincoln Drayford Pool Mini Event 2016 - courtesy Carl Draper

[100] Hora M 'Village World' 1987, p24, NUMBER SIX publication

was the name badge) was a little more than £400, for this you got just one seat — for the driver. Passenger seating for these vehicles was therefore only available as an extra.

In September 1966 some specially designed and amended Mini Mokes arrived in Portmeirion, with wood veneer in much of the inside of the car in addition to the 'exterior side panels'. The windscreens were not the standard angled version with a vertical makeover and taxi plates had been adopted to ensure car registrations did not help locate the Village. Finally in pride of place on the bonnet of all 4 Mokes was the Village emblem of a penny-farthing.[101]

Sadly the Austin Mini Moke despite it's distinct advantages over similar vehicles of the time (marketing it as both VAT exempt and expressing it's usefulness for the 'civilian population') and its exposure as the vehicle of the moment in 'The Prisoner' the Moke failed commercially. The Longbridge plant had produced 14,518 vehicles of which around only 10% were sold and as a result the production of the Austin Mini Moke ended in 1968.

Australia was introduced to a variation of the Austin Moke named the Morris Mini Moke in 1966 - it was fitted with larger wheels than the British version 13 inches as opposed to 10 inches. In addition it's engine at 998cc (40 Horse Power) gave it considerably more poke and it could reach a top speed of around 130 km/h.

Meanwhile a few years later in 1973 the Morris Mini Moke was revived as the Leyland Moke eventually being fitted with an even more powerful engine than Australia's Morris Mini Moke. 1976 saw the advent of this 1098 cc motor and the following year a 1275 cc engine was rolled out. This variation was known as the Moke Californian of which 26,142 vehicles were produced it was kept in production until 1981 but by that time the model and the Mini Moke had gained considerable cult appeal.

The BMC's Portuguese subsidiary started production of the Moke in 1980 leading to the construction of 10,000 vehicles over the following 13 years.

However the story of the Moke doesn't end here as in 2016 Moke International made an announcement that the Mini Moke was being revived for the 21st Century. According to their website the "new, much anticipated model remains faithful to its origins and classic look..." however the design has also incorporated the important elements of current automotive technology into Michael Young's vision of the Moke for today's driver.[102]

---

[101] Hora M 'Village World' 1987 p25, A NUMBER SIX Publication

[102] http://mokeinternational.com/about/

"Villagers (Strangely at Rhyme)"
By Chris Gray[103]

#72 Well, what do you all think so far?

[104]

#73 Delightful. It's beautiful and bizarre.
#74 The place itself... is gonna be a star.

#77 It's heaven, our real world's gone bye
bye.
      I don't think we'll need any more
high...
    We'd be going higher than the sky.

#76 I'll be counting and dreaming multi-coloured sheep
    I'll wake, pull back the curtain for a peep,
    Think of funny farms and hurry back to sleep!

#78 Every bit of the place's been thought about,
    Every stone, like it's indoors, not out. A shrine.
    Made by the artistically devout.

#75 Yeah, and I didn't see one bit of litter.
    The hero's like James Bond - loads of glitter,
    But can't bear the place! They're always bitter.

#72 Bitter - at the end of a rainbow...!
    But when you see the mock-ups at the studio...
    Some hellish stuff in the story. We'll see tomorrow.

#72 If you aren't, wake up Numbers 73 to 78!
    The funny farm's outside and on with the day's fête.
    Rainbow clothes on, time to get into ornate state.

#77 In my dream... I was a multi-coloured ape
    In a multi-coloured tree of the strangest shape...
    I'm starting to feel why he wants to escape!

[103] https://www.youtube.com/watch?v=2bql7-Sal1o - link to Section 1 of 7 on YouTube of 'Villagers - (Strangely at Rhyme)

[104] Courtesy of Rick Davy from the Unmutual Website - 2007

#78 In the story, the highest price...
        Is for freedom. And even this paradise,
        - We see is something he'd always sacrifice.

#74 I don't think I'd ride that Penny Farthing bike...
        High enough to attract a lightning strike.
        What was the inventor's mind like?

#72 No talking or thinking now... wash that brain!
        Out here remember... no wonder, no complain.
        Be seeing you all later! Meet at the ship again.

#77 Does #6 get to pop that 'Rover' balloon?
                          105

#72 It's indestructible. Not even with that harpoon.
        But I didn't know it was in action this soon...

        They're building in mystery and fear from the start.
        And total control. Showing Villagers without heart.
        6 needs out. It's shown he feels a world apart.

#74 Introducing robots or clones, so it looks.
#75 Yes undermining all hope, by all hooks and crooks.
        All new and unreal. Rewriting all the books...

#72 The chess player's in every other episode.
#77 Is this ship... by any chance torpedoed?
        - Nah.. it's not Yank drama, it won't all explode!

#78 Imaginations are going. We should note it all.
#76 Infectious, a sort of wake-up call...
        If we're ever hypnotised... What a ball!

#75 Anyone said their name yet?
        Don't! And let's begin now... a cash pool or bet...
        It'll reveal more, something, the further we get.

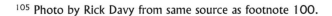

105 Photo by Rick Davy from same source as footnote 100.

#77 What do you mean, like a mental test?
#75 Open minded ramble, not a goal or quest.
      Might even show... if names or numbers are best!
#78 Stereotypes, impressions, for 'East and West'?
      A name is deep, identifying, what we suggest.
      It ties or deflects us, and shapes what we digest.

#77 The politics... can't peace have one chance?
      We're in this place, and where's the romance?
#72 Don't lose the plot, the dance... fall into a trance!

#74 What happened to #75? There, and then not...
#72 I popped a Rover! Telescope mirrors, got it red hot!
      Didn't roar or anything! Ha! A bit too hot to trot!

      Very undramatic. It didn't go with a bang.
#73 Yes where is 75? Gone to another gang?
#72 Rover's revenge... he fell prey to another one's fang.

#77 The women so far... today's wasn't so gleaming.
#72 An 'Iron Curtain' one... politics are a-scheming!
      Heat shields... maybe. Rover's gently steaming.

#74 Sometimes a balloon just doesn't float my boat!
      It can do pretty well, up to space it can float,
      Back to heat shields. Pick up again on that note.

#78 All extremes are in this business, really every sort
      Get a good act and they're easy sport.
      Get your act right and they're always in your court.

#76 The industry attracts them. They try their luck.
      And some just like us, can only get firmly stuck.
      Some get to make that quick million-buck.

#72 There's one that follows him, smiling, everywhere.
      And when he's dropped all his guard, to his despair...
      She slaps him crazy and kills the promising affair.

#77 You shouldn't spoil it, we know what to expect...
      Take away the surprise and take away the effect...
#72 This isn't normally though, it will deaden... disaffect.

#73 Mmmm. We're not so much zombies, a bit in between...
  - Safe zombies... without the flesh-eating gene
#74 - Fairground figures staring out at the unseen.

#78 Is it all safe here? We might need a de-brief...
  Or counselling, or distracting from the mischief.
  We might want to turn over, or break off this leaf!

#73 They've brought in mind control, using science and drugs
  Surveillance scrutiny from video cameras and bugs.
  And hints of terrible punishment... from approved thugs.

#76 Even the ones in charge all seem broken,
  Controlling their staff with threats, barely spoken...
  Maybe Rover, or something worse will be woken...

#77 It killed in the first one, and then saved a life...
  The swimmer, with another so maybe it has a wife...
#72 Escape! Rover grounded by his Trouble and Strife...

#74 Yes... in that one he did get a hell of a shock.
  Suddenly king, straight from the dock...
#73 I felt silliest yet... in that campaigning flock.

#72 And he gave away his soul in the process
  - Every time, in the words of his public address,
  He lost himself and donated to their success.

#74 He should have seen through it — a simple trick...
  But he's vulnerable like us all, and a bit thick.
  So it's good, he's made his character realistic.

#73 Done for the day, so I'm off for a nice stroll.
  I'll miss out on the night's levitation, and Rock 'n'
Roll.
#76 Watch the tides and sandbank or you'll be a lost soul.

#77 What about the castle... is that off our limits?
#76 Not tackled yet by... he's not yet made it the Ritz.
#72 Clough, the architect. Magician. No the castle's in bits.[106]
  He owns the place as well. And he's not on coke!

106 Castell Deudraeth/The Hospital from 'The Prisoner' courtesy Ian Orchard/Ed Fordham

All who could have got it without going broke...
#78 I'm more convinced... money does nowt for folk.
        It waited to be rekindled, rebuilt, given a stoke...
        Just someone who'd awoke. Good on the bloke!
#74 Hey... I think they've decided to make us a joke...
        #73 went out, but he's taken all his stuff...
#76 Gone home as well? They can't go off in a huff...
A scheme I reckon, psychology. He hadn't had enough...

#78 What else is there... anything else look suspicious?
#74 Uhh... well apart from the unreality, and the vicious...
        Yes - we're background. It's suspiciously over-ambitious!
#76 Keeping up the spirit... making us superstitious?
#77 Maybe something's coming up, extra-malicious...
        Gotta be. No harm is there? That they'd wish us?

#78 Hey hey hey hey hey! No telepathy please!
        The hero accepts... but with science he disagrees!
        Come on hero, don't kick us in the teeth.... Jeez...!

#76 Have to agree, with him on this!
        When you've seen results that you can't dismiss...
#78 Results? Are you taking the piss?

#72 No he's not. But what he says is as good as bent!
        'Cos if you keep on testing, without relent...
        Random makes great patters and... a hundred percent.

        Contact 75 and 73 if you believe that crap!
        Close you eyes... and don't take a nap...
        Speak to their minds, open that mental tap....

#76 We can't all do it, and not at a command!
        It is a natural event, has to be unplanned!
#78 And you phone them 72. Until then, all keep it canned.

        A hot topic all round! And the overnight moustache?
#74 Good episode it looks, one to pass round the hash.
#77 All are I think. All gonna be a bash.

#78 So they forced him to comply again, with his place
        Had to loudly and proudly swear the disgrace...
        Anyone would end up a complete nutcase.

#77 I'd stay here, with my number and no name,
      Like I'm in a beautiful picture in a posh frame.
      If we'd reject this, we should feel shame...

#78 Is it... promotion of the usual politics?
      - If this place isn't good enough for Number Six...
      So the real world... is OK? Are we missing tricks?

      Because our politicians usher in a real hustle...
      'Freedom', and that Commies are hustle, bustle, tussle.
      But they waste us - Commies have got the muscle.

#74 Has this put freedom right here, on the table...?
      - A frivolous concept, dangerous, an unrealistic fable?
      We don't give it either, not much when we're able.

#72 It's nothing without resources, opportunity, a plan.
      Adam Smith economics is bad for the barbarian.
#78 Right. Pun also! - right wing brings on the clergyman.

#76 This setup does show off good morals
      - There's been no staged rampant quarrels,
      Except from 6. And those roaring, inflatable corals...

#72 The title suggests he, out of all the rest - is alone.
      Is he deluded, so different like a king overthrown?
      Or is it mockery, implied, that everyone is a clone?

#74 Speed learning - does anyone think that's tosh?
      But a three minute degree... no... a bit of a squash!
      Gotta have some use. Even if it is just brainwash.

#78 They said it was slavery, sort of. It's dictated.
      Unthought, unfelt. When lies are deeply penetrated...
      - With trust and... what monsters could be created?

#72 75 and 73 left. Short contract they were on.
      I couldn't phone, but they said they and others had gone.
#76 The flippin... creepy gets! Didn't tell anyone!

#72 Last stints at the studios. Still a bad sign.
#77 In character I suppose, I didn't think they'd resign.
#76 And my dreams have mimicked this storyline!

#77 I reckon you're next #72, to disappear!
#72 Maybe... You could get another overseer.

That would be telling. Though the next is in here!

Sunny it looks, for our longest break hitherto...

But we'll miss... Gypsy Girl - in our red and blue.

Take care and... won't be seeing all of you!

#74 Oh, do gypsies help him escape?
#72 No, just a few moments to put him in shape.

That bit's England, rural. A lot is seascape.

Photo of Beachy Head Lighthouse

Courtesy of :
www.pubicdomainpictures.net

_____

#72 The Gypsy Girl... for no one. Let's not blaspheme..!
Countach! She came to the world from a dream.
The heat shields fellas, wouldn't stop a laser beam!

They contrasted the setting and what she wore...
And a village skirt, so viewers come back for more?
Or to make clear, an actress is what to take her for?

Anyway, she isn't back... Medication for heartache...
Though we should die inside fellas... or it'll look fake!
So, keep up the spirit. We did get a nice break.

#76 72 I'm sure you're a paid masochist.
Or maybe our secret sadist hypnotist...
Did they net you in a full moon sea mist...?

#77 Yeah... this is like horror, but you thrive!
Did you really... dispose of 73 and 75?
#72 Yes pals! They were skinned and boiled alive!

#74 But we're all back, except the skinned and boiled.
    Were you joking, or was some sordid plot foiled?
#72 Yep - Lighthouse stairs with a giant serpent, coiled.

#78 As long as it isn't waiting on our stairs.
    Anyway, a couple of scenes today for spares,
    - And after, how about The Grotto and beach chairs?

#77 Is this the famous Grotto then?
    This to me is natural, not a sculpted den
#74 Cool and a perfect view. Ten out of ten!
    If I was Buddhist, I'd call it Zen...
    If a Christian, I'd be saying... Amen.
#77 Hold those thoughts while I get a pen..!

#72 Yes write them down, they're about to shatter...
    - Photo taken during a boating regatta...
    And each time witnessed... it's got fatter!

#74 Well... definitely too big for an eel,
    And not the shape of an upturned boat keel...
    No one's looking at it! This photo's not real.

#72 Too fast, and last photo. They were nearly crying!
#78 And of course, there was no denying...
    'They wouldn't lie'. Yes #72, we're all buying!

#72 I've noticed you've all started looking!
    One photo... but is the possibility, hooking?
    You're not sure! We're definitely cooking...

#74 Tail end of that land, that peninsula.
    Sand, contours... like those exposed, etcetera
#72 Rotated against the flow? Strange phenomena...
    - See the photos and don't try to join Mensa!
#74 One X plus zero X equals... Don't compete in algebra!
#72 Oh did I say there were no other photos... Voilà.

#74 Jump off a cliff. Jump out that opening, fraud!

But we have to give you that, have to applaud
And yes, we'll have to find you a suitable award.

#78 Did we all enjoy the carnival and the prep?
#77 I think the best part was the ten-minute... pep!
    More than the merry-go-round-the-pond in step.

#76 Nice day for it though, but felt like a dip
    - Would have gone well with the pleasure trip.
        Or to break the mould... if we'd all decided to
strip!

#74 Good idea for when we next soberly assemble...
        Neatly, more petrified than the buildings we
resemble.
#78 Anywhere else, the thought would make me tremble.

    Back to strange... some of this is wacky baccy inspired
    2nd half, or after us lot were retired.
#76 If this was smoked everyone would have expired.

#77 A new, flirty maid. Threw herself at his feet!
    I'd fall for her. With her. Don't care how indiscrete...
    - Even if there was a camera under the sheet.

#78 They used this place today for a shoot.
#72 Yeah, he was up on here in an evening suit.
    And they put on ancient garb... to prosecute.

#74 Wacky baccy... sure. And sentenced him to death!
    Could easily have been scenes from Macbeth.
    Either that or the whole crew is guzzling meth.

#77 Is the death sentence to do with that black cat?
#76 Dunno, is it supposed to be good or bad luck that?
#72 Sea snakes... no. But happy with this sort of chat?

#78 Can't fathom this... how he escapes execution...
#74 I can't, ongoing blackmail or persecution,
    And I think the jury goes to a mental institution!

#76 There's no one from another gang gone missing,
        So the possibility, that we shouldn't be dismissing,
        Is that 72's sea serpent is very much alive and hissing...

#72 They're just keeping quiet about it. Just a bit paranoid.
     Like us, embarrassed and annoyed.
     And as prescribed also - they're turning schizoid!

#74 Busiest yet? Got through... how many drinks?
#76 I saw eyes trying to close for a hundred and forty winks.
#74 I bet everyone in the whole place stinks.

#77 Busy yes. A fun one also, or it's becoming.
#78 I reckon so, in between spells of twiddle-thumbing.
#72 No not one bit. I'm finding it mind-numbing.

     And I don't like chess. It's over-rated, for the mind.
#77 Chess is the greatest game invented by mankind!
#72 Poe said that Whist, was it? That leaves it miles behind.
     Poe led writers to fortune and fame, who were blind...
     Verne, Doyle, loads of them became enshrined.
     Chess is for the memory, and I bet - keeps it entwined.

#76 Well Number 72, that's quite a revelation...
     Top players would sentence you to an amputation...
     With a meat cleaver if you're lucky... for the castration!

#74 #6 isn't castrated is he? He's almost celibate...
     - She's almost branded with "you + me = smut!"
     Totally open, available, nice... and him? Totally shut!

#78 He doesn't trust her for his latest escape attempt.
     He's looking for a technical brain, to tempt.
     - And her love, seems hypnotised or vividly dreamt.

#74 I'm sure I saw that creature near the lighthouse...
#76 You what, the serpent? Oh... in joins the Scouse...
     Another one who's watched too much Mickey Mouse.

#74 Says... a Yorkshireman. With his 'Don't be a Friend!'
     With the all-take and no-give condescend...
     - Be a crook or baby... where Yorkshirethink must end.
#76 The saying? No, it only declares... 'Hey... don't depend'
#74 Crook or baby. Your great thinkers need to amend...
     - Deep down secret decisions, it gets used to defend.

     Can't see it now. Looked like one of them snakes.
     Totally unexpected, out there where the tide breaks.
#72 Calm the county-hate or we'll all have headaches

#74 Quiet day for us now, 'seems it's all eyes to the waves!
#76 Beyond the lighthouse you know, there are caves...
     And the tide's out... so... he who braves...

#77 From the lighthouse the water will be clearer.
#78 For the cave lairs 77, we need to be a bit nearer.
#74 Worried you'll be the next disappear-er?

#78 They're filming the beach around eleven,
     And the ship also, so when it feeds on #77...
     In episode 10... his ghost going up to heaven!

#72 We'll have to watch we're not in the way,
     Scenes everywhere, from the woods to the bay.
     New faces involved, no more for us again today.
     They've devised, a duelling game the aggrieved play.
     And he gets Number 2 to sack himself, total disarray!
     Vendetta for killing someone, and makes him pay.

#74 Are any of us going to be doing any speaking?
#72 The last one I think, has lots of laughter and shrieking!
     Otherwise, only be more parading, walking or sneaking.

#76 What is this creature going to leave as clues?
#78 Could be some eggs, or old skin coloured like tattoos.
     Tattered clothes, especially snakeskin jackets and shoes.

#76 Has there ever been a recorded or possible kill?
#72 Don't think so. But if it gets bigger it probably will...
#74 Look at us prats wading about, we'll get a proper chill.

#78 A proper chill... that's how The Famous Five sound!
#74 In Five go off with a Sea Monster they were found...
Wasn't published like... found trapped and drowned.

#77 Weed's kicking in now - the seaweed's looking good!
#72 Let's head back. Forget the seaweed and mushy wood.
#76 They're getting ready for filming now so we should.

#77 I've met a few today who know of the beast!
   Some joke it's being farmed, bred to feast...
   On flesh. To be a weapon in the Far East.

#78 Oh, America's vision... achingly persists.
   Politically cleansing, wiping out Communists.
   Cambodia... currently top of their stomping lists.

#74 Will they finish, and stop Russia's moon landing?
   Or will Russia cop out, backhanders for disbanding?
   Otherwise no one'll see Capitalism as upstanding!

#76 NASA might get there first... Reputation un-tarred!
#74 As the U.S. holds competitors in the highest dis-regard,
   - Once again... Capitalism's trying to work less hard.

#76 Still our #6 does nothing for a job...
   If he wasn't so confident I'd think him a slob.
   A charisma that... is he the ladies perfect heart throb?

#77 That guy is I bet, the latest #2 successor.
   He's in Where Eagles Dare... very smooth... oppressor!
   Formidable. If anyone can make #6 a confessor...

#72 Not seen her about, this lady friend, the blonde...
   Sizzler. She's the fifth brought by magic wand.
   No sign of her now. Gone back to... beyond.

#74 Switching off that lamp... has he done his first dish?
#77 Plenty of others flaunt at him... all available fish,
   I couldn't act dead... having everything I wish!

#78 At the top in real life? Is it how he really feels?
   Few see life as a game, the rest pick from what it deals.
   This TV series could be his latest set of wheels.

   I don't mean literally. In a philosophical sense...
   The venture's something to help him dispense,
   'The Prisoner'. Is his part really not pretence?

#72 That's a possibility. And that we just see as style.
   Genuine guy. Even with only a sly or hidden smile...
   - More human than Bond by a mile.

#74 Bond's Britain's biggest brat... partly masquerading.
   We let him hold the light that he's shading.

The insult, mockery he's internationally parading...
Seduction, the whole show is persuading,
Bloats us. And while our reality is fading,
He trashes us, brands us. Tabloid-like degrading.

#72 #76's out at the cave as bait. As a self-appointee!
     He thinks he can reel in our... absentee...
#78 He must be on LSD. If he is, this'll be RIP...
     He'll be either trapped or washed out to sea!
     Drugs bring out the idiot. Seriously, has he?
#72 Course not! But he's the latest... to leave the marquee.

     Cleared his locker, cupboard and berth.
     It's something... for what it's worth,
     - At least two of us are still fully on planet Earth!

#78 Could think of it... as a sort of decanting!
     And less of us coughing tonight, from that chanting.
#72 First speaking parts, like lunatics ranting!

#78 Lot of lunacy in this one, in every neck of the woods.
     Some hypnosis... and they've dredged their childhoods
     - It seems, for all their lost, damaged goods!

#72 That court of clowns will be back again later.
     And of course, we've a new Number 2 dictator...
#78 Why did Nesbitt go? Would things be straighter?

#72 Yes. And the umbrellas-beating of #6... a few excited girls!
     - Is that how the Summer of Love unfurls..?
#78 Some of them found themselves doing twirls...

#72 Did you hear about Che Guevara... executed?
#78 I did. More and more of the good, diluted.
     Thirteenth this decade - great voice muted.

#72 The West won't like China getting the H-bomb...
#78 Nope. Another long-lasting, trouble-making sitcom.
     Every opportunity for an international programme.

#72 On the plus side, we got the World Cup!
     Getting a role in this, in colour... and cool lineup
#78 Everywhere's in colour. Lot of things waking up...

#72 Yeah... the football world cup, got there at last!
      Among the champions, up from the downcast.
      We'll make the small-league a thing of the past.

#78 But the gloomier side is easier to master!
      - Example... When's Japan's next aircraft disaster?
      Safety... does it make good times go faster?

#78 Hi guys. I gather 76 did the disappearing act...
#74 Made a pact, carried out with the prescribed tact...
      Or our unseen friend has once again attacked.

#72 How are we all feeling about the er... numbering?
      Is your name bursting out or peacefully slumbering?
  #74 When we're done, I'm recording my... disencumbering!

#77 Feels awkward still, claustrophobic. But still going.
#72 Some dropped out who did it, said it was mind-blowing.
      And, others agree there's something for the knowing...

#78 Still then, we haven't had any definite synopsis.
      At worst - a name, a memory, could trigger neurosis...
      At best - make easy cheating. But purity is in the basis...

      - Of freedom. Freedom is declared essential to maturity,
      Freedom may have a place on a pedestal, but for surety,
      Names don't, if for good or bad - they mess up purity.

#77 Yes, freedom essentially includes being unaffected.
      But a number instead of a name, feels a bit injected
      Unless used to it, it feels... coldly disconnected.
#74 And numbers would have to be carefully selected,
      Otherwise ones like '...666...' might be disrespected...
      Not very free. They'd end up being very misdirected!

#77 I'm going to remember mine forever.

107

---

[107] One of Clough-William Ellis's Whimsical Follies — A Statue between the Piazza and Number Six's house — Courtesy of Ian Orchard

The indelible impression will never go, never,
So I'll sue #72 for damages for his endeavour!

#72 We're done for this episode. I'm off into town.
#78 I signed my number on a cheque, like a clown!
    - I'll try again this time, and no multi-coloured gown.

#78 His employer... couldn't have had more evil ways... '
    You'll be suitably rewarded' that big-wig says...
    After a mind transplant! Who wouldn't leave in a blaze?

#72 Dictation in the real world... carried out by ourselves
    But the seeds are planted as if by elves.
    Production lines and then back onto our shelves...

    The nuclear family... set of unlike peas in pod
    God's really a muscle... gotta be the cheekiest sod.
    Politics are in with that, all part of the same squad.

#78 Things are rougher than that rocky outcrop.
    How about going to the chip shop,
    And grabbing a nice feast to eat at the top?

#72 Spot on. Fabulous day for sight-seeing
    - The mountains and woods. For the mind's freeing!
    A person needs to look, at least. It's part of our being.

#78 Which buildings do we look like the most?
#72 Salutation I reckon, where 77 reckons there's a ghost.
#78 I don't know their names, not been that engrossed...

#72 Gatehouse, or Lady's Lodge next to Patrick M.
    Fountain, where Noël Coward wrote a gem...
#78 No, I don't know the names of them!

    Dressed for colour TV though, we'll look spectacular.
    Just like the Village, anything but vernacular.
    We've got as much red as a film about Dracula!

#72 Luxury in our hands, and then it damn well rains...
    Clouds darkening fast, we can't see those plains.

#78 Better go back down, with what daylight remains.

#74 I've begun thinking of nature as a sandy beach...
      And wildlife, as a crow's call or gull's screech.
      These sprawling brambles... have me in reach.

      Advancing, everything is, until meet one another,
      And a bargain is made - one, or the other,
      Or both. Or we make our mark - uproot or smother.

#72 Taking observations to the more man-made...
      This Wild West scene, here... seems a downgrade.
      Almost like there needs to be a brutal serenade!
#74 You've been got there, by Hollywood's crusade.
      Sat yourself in front of the TV and overstayed!
      The world around you, seems in the shade.

#72 This episode mimics the main prison events
      - Plight of #6, the main roles and their intents.
      Like with Shakespeare plays, transplantable contents.

#77 I don't know who the dude is, like a statue or toy.
      Reminds me of 'Harpo Marx,' mute naughty boy.
#74 Acts the automaton, controlled. And loves to destroy.

      6 sounds very different, not often heard him speak.
#77 In this film setting the educated normally look weak.
      And he seems to have his usual mystique.

#78 Last scenes this time, another easy stint.
      Merry-go-round mainly, while he has a squint.
      - How much support is there for a naturist sprint?

#72 Not enough... ha! Not for that sort of chaff.
#78 It's a serious statement, or act. It is not for a laugh.
      It is by positive, intelligent people. Not by riff-raff.

#72 Do it soon 78, I think you've only a few more scenes.
#77 I think the place suits flesh more than tee-shirts and jeans.
      Or than village uniforms as if we're clothed figurines.

#74 What's the story for this one, anyone had a look?
#78 In this he's as daft as Bond. Too comic-book...
    Assassin-ess and a Napoleon-dressed master crook.

    Napoleon, once again made to look a fool.
    He made Brunel's father's.... type of school...
    More than once, have the French made us cool.

    Most of it's a female villain. A total psychopath.
    Who spends her life dealing out high-tech wrath,
    In view of everyone... who can't do any math.

#72 Assassin-ess... one of the cleverest killers,
    Was a woman, one of that trade's pillars.
    Wrote a textbook. Is amongst the most banned... thrillers.

#77 That's right, for fifty years very hard to acquire.
#72 Say 'evil woman' fifty from now, you'll be called a liar,
    Yet assassin women... will be available for hire.

#74 The squeeze is on, deeper trenches are being dug.
    In-the-know and corrupt versus blind and smug,
    Hypocritically trapped. We'll all get the mind of a thug.

#78 Anyway, next episode's when it gets real crazy.
    Nursery rhymes, domination, hypnosis. Very hazy.
#77 How about we go pack some stuff, go and get lazy?

#72 These last scenes will go quick... nearly all studio work,
    We may still be needed there, it's all complex and berserk.
    So have your party but not too much, don't shirk.

#72 You and me 78, are the last fully alert.
    It might still be of use at this stage, to disconcert,
    - I think they're not expecting you to desert.
    So until later... time for you to divert!
#78 Yep... time for Number 78 to bite the dirt...
#72 Take that jacket with you, and that underskirt.

#78 I've got someone in the final parade and racket,
    When the helicopter films... waving this jacket!
    - Sentimental, I know it won't be worth any packet.

#77 All about done. I'm going to get such a stoning!
#74 Nowt left important, 72 can do his moaning,
      Watchtower unlocked... Let's think about rezoning!

#77 Yes, on this final studio stuff I'll have to pass...
      I'd forget my lines, many thanks to this grass!
      And, the script looks... we've got the rest of the ass!

      He trashes a secret base, becomes a total vandal.
      Oooh... some of this is too heavy to handle.
#74 Don't use the light later, just light a candle...

      Don't want to be called up now, before the home run.
      Got everything. Torches in reach, and we're done.
      Let's get bombed to bits and wake in the afternoon sun.

#77 That Dem Bones and a Beatles hit are in the ending.
      From the secret base, deep, a catastrophe begins ascending,
      Finally back to the real world. It all starts blending.

      Rover scurries off into a geyser, is that back to hell?
      The automaton, dwarf, #6 and 2 say their farewell,
      In a living room, on a trailer. Couldn't be an easier sell!

#74 In fashion. I reckon they have to use the studio spaces,
      - To isolate the finale. Where they play the darkest aces.
#77 I think The Beatles boss stays in one of these places...

#74 They tell 6 in the court, he's qualified to be re-named.
      And, 'the only individual', 'to lead them' he's claimed.
      But once again it's an illusion, instead he's defamed.

      They escape Hollywood style, don't know if anyone dies.
      The Villagers escape, and then there's Rover's demise.
      Plenty of detail. The whole of this last script is surprise.

      I think this Harpo bloke is a role model in the making.
      Patrick illuminates him, as someone who's just waking,
      Addresses him as if the ground under him is quaking.

      If that's a version of masculinity,
      With corresponding versions of femininity...

Bad trips. Conflict... on into infinity?

This is good weed. I've read all the pages in clarity.
I have my head round all the intended... angularity.
And where it is, I perfectly interpret the jocularity.

#77 Jocularity? Well I've taken root. I'm in three dimensions,
But my mind's in various other extensions.
And body has no detectable further intentions.

#74 Not the best idea, falling asleep on tiles.
With pillows of... rags on top of... document files!
#72's going to rant we're juveniles.

#77 I find that sometimes, 72 badly hurts.
Like this floor. One of them 'progress' converts.
He thinks we're nothing but squirts.

#74 Three hours before the final scene starts.
Go out to play... our last partying parts,
Strolling about like visual pop-arts.

#77 Sounds like they're doing some sound testing.
#74 Or rehearsal... everyone seems to be congesting...
Look... anywhere else... police would be arresting.

#77 What was that? Stone thrown at the rail?
...Guess who... and he hasn't brought any ginger ale.
Has he been shot? Looks dead pale...

Seen us. Why's he standing there signing?
#74 Keep the window closed, don't wanna hear him whining.
#77 Come to join us, showing us some water divining?

Errrhh! It's got in...!
That thing is here, it's genuine!
#74 Keep quiet, don't even drop a pin...
We won't hear its skin...
Listen... can you hear it in the kitchen?
#77 No. If we try to race it... not gonna win...
Maybe we can set fire to gin...
#74 Not a blaze. Is the warning lamp paraffin?
#77 Electric. And no bulb. Is this our coffin...?

Sharpen this for a javelin?
#74 The files are empty, so is the bin.
#77 Where's the screechy Psycho violin?

#74 Who's that, someone yelling?
#77 72 we don't need our fortune telling...
He's stood down there like someone selling...

#72 I'm off for help! It's trapped, this door's closed!
#77 You mean... see if the army's indisposed?
Builders... we'll jump, you get it bulldozed!

We won't smash this. Got to keep calm...
#74 Even if they could hear - no fire alarm!
Don't suppose there's any napalm?

Sound in the kitchen... I heard it...
#77 Yes. Want to go down the stairs, a bit?
#74 OK... I'll go in socks in case of grit...

Back in! Back! Back or we're dead!
It's on the stairs! I saw it's head!
Get it closed! Wedged! We've got a fight ahead...
Tail in kitchen... It must be dinosaur-bred!
#77 Surprised it maybe, or it's already fed...
#74 Wow... My legs were as heavy as lead!

#77 Tip this under the door... get it drunk...
Give it the rest of the skunk...
Yes give it the whole chunk!

No! You watch out! You take heed!
No place here for your foul breed!
#74 Won't light. May as well have peed...
#77 Do that then! Both of us... feel the need!
Or we're gonna bleed...
#74 Hey we're not much, not worth this for a feed...

That snake's deep enough for all our gang. Deeper.
- The Grim Swallower. Ours is no Reaper.
#72 Don't make it harder! Give in, I am The Keeper!

I am collecting you. I am the sacred ward.
Your numbers are up. Come to The Lord
You will suffer more if she is ignored
You will submit yourselves as reward...

Each surrender, fall on your sword.
The Lord is served. Your lives are abhorred.

#77 But who the... Why don't you let us live?
#72 You are proving uncooperative.
This The Lord will not forgive
The Lord has no mercy on the fugitive
And relishes a kill most destructive!
You may kneel to drink up your sedative.

#72 Not joining the party boys?
Or are you lot the hardcore... playboys?
Still alive in there? Come on, make some noise!

What happened, have you been assailed?
#74 72... Trying to... well you failed!
But you're going to... your head's gonna be impaled.

#72 'Owt can 'appen I suppose, but you passed!
Sort of! Maybe... lower first classed.
I apologise, you were pretty well harassed!

#77 You made us pee - which you should have sniffed.
So you're cleaning up. While we watch. Shift!
And what's the serpent? Is that your parting gift?

#72 It's on loan from a mate. It's not yet served...
Made this summer. Hasn't properly unnerved!
#77 Hasn't stayed clean! I think that's deserved.

#72 Controller, and a head, tail and a middle section.
Still a few niggles but almost got it to perfection.
Convincing in photos, and ably showed you affection!

#78 The door didn't give us away, I'm not surprised...
Claw hammer, and chopping board perfectly sized.
#77 You got us, 78 and 72. But look at you! Urine-baptised!

#74 And really, I know one bloke you'd have flipped,
Who's lived 'here' for real, by the fully equipped.

House of horrors. Closed doors, body bag zipped.

Ceaseless display of knowledge and power,
Of scrutiny, every day hour after hour.
Like child-battery. Twice sent to that Tower.

No script for him, shocks 'til he complied.
Senseless unpredictability liberally applied.
Aimless lunacy, unaccountable joyride.
And one day found washed up with the tide,
No explanation. Like how Joseph K. was tried.
Wake yourself. This stuff... you'll never be qualified.

#72 I'm sorry. And you'd have found it easier to cope,
With a little less LSD and a little less dope...
Switched yourselves off - you could only hope.
This sealed you, in an envelope,
And really strung you up with a rope.
Couldn't get a grip, and so you could only grope.

#74 Britain's secret drug enforcement copper...
#72 Anti-drug enforcement, is more proper -
Stopping a fashion! For drugs, yes I'd be a show-stopper.

Did you see #78's tattered remains...
Here look... clothing tangled in those chains?
#77 Luckily no! You went for the kill... When it rains...

#72 The stones at the window were also a distraction.
And I looked deathly, that was a reaction!
If you'd looked there, we'd have been out of action.

#74 Seen these before... I am the Serpent Master...
I will make your heart beat faster and faster...
I am Number 72! I am your heart's... disaster!

#77 You even used the voice-modulating Rolls Royce.
This could voice-over a whole cast. What a choice...
One last punishment... let's see your invoice!

#72 Borrowed it also. I manage to get good stature.
I'm a techy but I could be a plot-hatcher...
#74 I bet you volunteered, to a Body Snatcher.

#72 No one else did disappear, it was a hoax.
You know when you asked about other folks?

Simple. It was real, I didn't have to coax.

#77 Is that spoon-bending for real or a scam?
#72 Boil some alloys in water, they spread like jam.
    They say 'this is real...' so, that's where I am.

#77 Are they solid at room temperature, or a mush?
#74 I've seen that trick, keys passed round in a rush!
#72 Cool, they feel right. Definitely wouldn't crush.

#77 So you could rub spoons 'til soft as petals...
#72 Yes. And solder melts way below either of it's metals.
#74 The techy... Wow, how the techy fatally fettles!

    As we've seen today already. Anyway, as for the hero...
    Number Six. We've read he defeats 'Emperor Nero',
    And he's named again, and the Villagers, are zero...

#77 Hang on, you told us the wrong time. It hadn't started early.
#72 You didn't find out! If you'd have asked Shirley...
    We'd have been thwarted, you'd have seen your girlie!

#78 Let's go now. Leave the wind to dry the room...
    Don't want any trace of the err... exotic perfume!
    And happily, we can all go. No one met their doom.

#72 Clothing in the chains, nothing else is remaining.
#78 Leave it for souvenir hunters. It'll be entertaining!
#74 Errr!... does anyone feel like explaining..?
    The last episode. My vision has been draining,
    And puzzling it out myself... I'm straining.
#77 Lets read the viewers - praising and complaining.

    Slow walk back. Take in the... painting...
    I'll come back here sometime, for a re-acquainting.
    I'll never believe, in there... I was nearly fainting.

#72 Think of those extra... shear terror acting skills!
    That's what's needed to pay the bills.
#74 It's true. More and more in demand, those thrills.

#72 Chilling forecast... we'll have to take any,
    Any part we can to get every penny.
#77 Parts? Parts? 72 divides into... how many?

#78 A lot #77! His number is purest gold!
#77 No, silence is that. #72 is too hot to hold.
#72 No, silence is pure. And purity is undersold.
#74 But this quiet, no... is starting to feel cold!
    Before we sign out, a few minutes to behold...
    Here. #6. Carnivals. Penny Farthing. Rover.
    Magical Women. Us.
                Now ceased or uncontrolled.

Villagers (Strangely at Rhyme) was written shortly before the UK EU Referendum.[108]

[108]Photo of the Editor upon the Gloriette balcony courtesy of Ian Orchard 2014

Parlez-vous 'Le Prisonnier'
Bienvenue au Village : 'L'Arrivée'

SORTIE = WAY OUT
Demissions = RESIGNED

As an experiment I have decided to watch 'Arrival' or 'L'Arrivee' in French to see what if anything this reveals — to achieve this (as I am not a fluent French speaker) I am actually watching it in English with French subtitles to see what I can gather from this aspect.

We will call this:
EXPERIMENT FRANGLAIS:

For the first few minutes there are no spoken words and 'Arrival' proceeds as usual - we move on to the Cafe...

Having established that there is no police station or name other than au Village — our Numero Six enquires after telephone facilities.

-D'ou puis-je telephoner? : Where can I make a phone call
-Il y a une cabine la : Well there's a phone box around the corner

When Numero Six arrives at the phone box (which shifts location depending on long shots or close ups) He lifts and presses the button on the strangely cordless phone (Remember kids Mobile Phones would not come into usage at all until the 1980s and this was 1966)

The operator asks - Quel numero? : Number please?
Vous êtes le central?: What exchange is this?
Numero, sil vous plait: Number please? (A more literal translation this time)
Je veux: I want to make a call to...
Dans le Village uniquement: Local calls only.

109

Already the translation is straying from the original words spoken in the English version. The operator for example asks 'Quel Numero' meaning 'What Number' in the first line rather than Number please. Also instead of a literal translation of local calls only we have 'Dans le Village Uniquement' meaning 'In The Village Only'. This quantifies what is meant more — 'Local Calls Only' could mean that outside lines are down or inaccessible whereas 'In The Village Only' suggests that no outside calls are ever possible more strongly. Also Numero Six is hearing 'the Village' or 'le Village' to be accurate again — does it make things clearer or more mysterious?
Let's now look at the first meeting with Numero Deux in Le Dôme Vert:
- Enfin ! Ravi de vous voir. : At last delighted to see you

---

109 Photo of Triumphal Arch Portmeirion : 2014 Courtesy of Ian Orchard

> - This is translated as 'Finally! Nice to see you' when run through my translation matrix 'The Admiral'

Significantly when Number Two/Numero Deux provides an automatically rising chair through a hatch in the floor for our hero/antihero the meaning of the phrase is changed again somewhat.

In English : 'I'm sorry I can never resist that?' Becomes 'Ça m'a tourjours amuse' which when translated into English is more like 'It always amuses me'

———————————————————————————————————————

"Je ne passe pas de marche avec vous. J'ai démissionné Je ne veux pas me faire, ficher, enregistrer, classer déclasser ou numéroter.Ma vie m'appartient."

This is harder to translate back into English. Obviously it is the phrase "I will not make any deals with you… ". However the translation suggests the French version begins "I do not (will not?) walk with you." This seems metaphorical rather than literal. It's alike to the English phrase "I will not follow in your footsteps."

The conundrum continues after 'I have resigned' which translates well. However "I will not be pushed, filed, stamped, indexed or numbered" as a complete phrase comes out of my limited translation matrix as 'I do want to make myself, filed, record, file downgrade or numbered' I am not sure this really helps justify this article as a key phrase has come back as a gobbledegook travesty of itself. It feels like the spirit of Professor Stanley Unwin is looking over my shoulder.

Breaking the phrase down into it's component parts works better as other meanings of individual words are revealed and we gain "I do want to make me, to file, checked/record/booked/tallied/logged; pigeonholded/listed/filed/classified/sorted; downgraded, or numbered"

From this we gain a meaning akin to "I do not want to be forced to be(make myself), filed, checked, sorted, downgraded or numbered'

Finally 'My Life Is My Own' comes back in slightly softer form 'My life belongs to me…'. This at least conveys the meaning of the phrase but, in my humble opinion, loses some of bite of the original.

In the Hospital the Old Women knitting speaks softly to Numero Six after an encounter with L'Rodeur
- Ca va bien : 'How are you feeling, son?' (Things are going well/You're okay)
- Que d'emotions : 'You've had a nasty experience' (What emotions… Or You've had a emotional experience which seems to be what this is hinting at.)

-Restez tranquille : 'You mustn't exert yourself' - (Stay calm - not really the same meaning at all here)
-Je vais dire au docteur que vous êtes reveille : 'I'll just tell the Doctor, you're awake'
(I will tell the Doctor that you are awake — this is interesting as it's very nearly a literal translation of the English yet omits the key word 'just' which suggests 'now' or 'right away' — perhaps in scripting the dub they wanted to allow time for Numero Six and Cobb's talk.)

Unfortunately time and space permit no more than a few examples of the changes to see what makes 'Arrival' - 'L'Arrivee' - So for now its 'Bonjour Chez Vous' ☝ (Good-Day To You) rather than 'Be Seeing You'. ☝

Abersoch, North Wales : The Gunrunners Boat in 'Many Happy Returns'
& MS Polotska in Checkmate filmed here
aka the 'Breda' owned by Mr and Mrs Beer

Thanks to Rick Davy for the photograph and Information
http://theunmutual.co.uk/abersoch.htm

Jan Davis
Some Thoughts...on 'The Prisoner'

We all follow No.6 as he is captured, imprisoned in The Village, and watch how he attempts to escape every week. We focus on him and him alone and hope against hope every week that he will eventually escape.

But what about the fate of the other Village residents? What sort of life do they have to lead as they, just like No. 6, have been imprisoned too. I have thought a bit about these other inmates, and wonder how they survive the daily routine of life inside.

Firstly, how come all the residents seem to have accepted their lot and are happy, smiling and without a care in the world? Could this be because of the use of forced drugs and hypnotics.   However, if this is so; how does No.6 avoid this?

How do the residents spend their days? There are no [110]shops, cinema and community centres that we ever glimpse. At night we see a nightclub in one episode which sells non alcoholic drinks but this is all that there seems to be. Did every resident have a television in their dwelling?   If so, the programmes were certainly monitored. Was it constant propaganda or genuine television listings of the time?

We see the Villagers in the summer sunshine, but what do they do in the depths of winter with snow on the ground?   How do they pass the time of day?   There doesn't seem to be any work-related activity except from the control room, and that is almost certainly brought in from outside.

Where do they get their shopping from?   The Village Stores is ok for basics like bread and milk but the choice is very limited.   Do they have a balance diet? Are they healthy?   Do they actually cook for themselves, or go to a communal dining hall for their meals?

---

[110] Image of Villagers in Portmeirion courtesy VJ Clarke

Talking of healthy...with many young people living so close together, surely relationships must have formed and the inevitable would have happened....where would any possible babies be born, and what would become of them? Or, was birth control fed to the under 50's through the drinking water?

Did they have cleaners to keep their dwellings clean, like No. 6 had? Maybe the cleaners were sent every day to spy on the Prisoners.

We see how unmutual Villagers are treated with lobotomy, deprivation techniques etc. How did they fare once back in society? Friends and family would surely notice such a change in their loved ones?

Were the Village doctors and hospital staff also Prisoners but possibly, like No. 6, enjoyed a higher standard of consideration because of their importance ?

When these people originally disappeared, did their families start to query their whereabouts? Was there a blackout to all who started asking questions about their missing loved one?

The programme did focus on No. 6 of course, but I still can't help wondering that if this were a real situation, what did become of No. 6's neighbours, and what a dreadful place this would have been to have been 'imprisoned' in.

Lastly, we see a new No.2 each week. Did they have a separate accommodation unit inside, or outside of the Village? Could they come and go as they pleased, or did they have restrictions whilst they were in charge for that period of time?

Questions, questions questions..."a still tongue — keeps a quiet mind"......not here.....it's 'Free For All' ...

Jan Davis

Leo's Trio by Vaughan Brunt

Originally published on the Unmutual Website at:
http://theunmutual.co.uk/article19.htm

In 'Chimes', McKern shows his mastery of the role of Number Two in the opening dialogue. He displays a variety of apparently conflicting impressions, deliberately off-putting to the Prisoner's desire for straight answers. For example:

"In The Village" - Unconcerned, non-imposing, in a matter-of-fact way.

"Information" - Sterner, more directly aimed at the Prisoner.

"That would be telling" - Reproachful, as if an unwritten law was being violated.

"We want information, information, information!" - Becoming more sinister, secretive and dangerous.

"By hook or by crook we will" - Both certain and determined. His smile denotes an easy confidence.

"The new Number Two" - Matter-of-fact again, non-threatening and explanatory as if it is a perfectly logical thing for him to be.

"You are Number Six!" - Dominant, giving the implication that there is no option, no room for argument.

The laugh - No sudden burst of sound like Colin Gordon's response. McKern starts with a Santa-like upward roll of sound then finishes as if the Prisoner was an old friend with whom he was sharing a familiar joke. They would seem to be playing pre-determined roles with an inevitable outcome which they may just as well sit back and accept.

McKern's is certainly the most subtly intelligent reading of those lines in the series. One which more than any other makes Number Six's angry delivery feel like pointless posturing. The implication is obvious, "You are here and this is where you are going to stay!"

McKern's first appearance proper in 'Chimes' features Number Two rising imperially from his round chair. His lines show him to feel Number Six is an adversary to be admired. Someone who will be an important challenge to Number Two personally. He is clearly very determined to win. He is quick to anger at Christopher Benjamin's over-confidence concerning Number Six. His arrival at the chess game shows him in an extrovertly amiable mood. All friends together and all's right with the world. He is happy to laugh at the irony of Number Six's comments and avoids the 'Hammer Into Anvil' approach of Patrick Cargill's character. His confidence is genuine and needs no role-playing subservience from others to boost his ego. The 'we don't need to be enemies' stance continues as they have tea in the Green Dome. His dismissal of the Butler however shows an obvious dislike of the silent servant. He begins to lose patience with the Prisoner when Number Six tells him to use his file for information on how many sugars he takes. It is as if he is saying how much more pleasant things are for them both when everyone co-operates. It could almost be a scene from 'Wind In The Willows'. All jolly nice chaps together so long as no-one makes any waves.

In fact, when Number Six says he is going to escape, come back and obliterate the place, Number Two's reaction is the same as Badger's when he hears that the weasels have taken over Toad Hall. How dare Number Six think he is important enough to ruin the 'amicable' ambience of the Village. For an Aussie, McKern captures that Edwardian Englishness perfectly. It is no surprise to me that one of his favourite parts in the theatre was when he played Mr. Toad.

When viewing the revival of Nadia he asks the Prisoner if he remembers his first day as if it were a treasured nostalgic event! On seeing her reaction to the new view from the window he laughs like Jeremy Beadle on the success of another of his sadistic schoolboy pranks. He bids Number Eight "Good morning" and like an amiable family doctor asks how she feels. He then becomes serious for a moment as he delivers his suggestion that all they need is for Number Six to say why he resigned. He makes the Village sound like a golf club which Number Six can easily join if only he will answer that simple question. But when Number Six leaves still smiling, Number Two shows an almost violent determination to get what he wants from the Prisoner.

Later, Number Two is back to his affable old self when he and Number Six meet by the beach. Now he has the air of a politician on "Question Time" as he orates his opinions to a potential convert. Resignation in this instances would more likely refer to his acknowledgement that he too is a prisoner. In view of what is to happen later in the series, this scene has an added significance when watched after seeing 'Fall Out'.

He seemed surprised to see the information in Number Eight's file that she was a good swimmer so perhaps he was not informed in advance that she would fake an escape attempt that way.

Once again, his amiability is in stark contracts to Swanwick's robotic Supervisor. Number Two's "Oh well, Orange Alert" also contrasts strongly against the abstract horror of the launch of Rover. His demand of Number Six to meet him in the hospital may seem a little out of character but that may have more to do with the line actually being said by Robert Rietty in post-production. The scene where Number Two and Number Six watch Number Eight's treatment in the hospital is underplayed by McKern as he talks to Number Six almost as if they were both doctors diagnosing a puzzling patient. The menace of the electronic floor is handled in a matter-of-fact manner.

Number Two mocks Number Six's suggestion that he is prepared to collaborate and seems greatly amused by it. He is however optimistic and slightly paternal as he checks how the relationship between Number Six and Number Eight develops. But, is he pleased because he thinks Number Six is settling in or because he has anticipated the Prisoner's escape attempt? McKern has to fool the audience as well as Number Six at this point. During the exhibition scene he could not be happier with Number Six, even feigning mock alarm at the Admiral's reproach over Number Six's exhibit. The `village fete' atmosphere is utilised to delineate the irony in the fact that all the entries show the real mind control the wardens have over the others.

Number Two is unconcerned at the radar sighting of the raft but again, the viewer is not tipped off by this as to the Village's hidden agenda. When all is revealed and departs from the Village for real this time, Number Two seems fatalistic about the failure to beat Number Six, as if he expected no other conclusion. This shows that as far as he was concerned, a very different method would be needed to make the Prisoner crack.

At the start of 'Once Upon A Time', McKern rises into the control room of the Green Dome in a stern, angry bad temper. He is the only Number Two willing to argue with Number One on the phone as he reiterates that they were using the wrong methods. He stares at Number Six on the giant screen. His obsession makes him talk to the screen image even though he cannot hear him. There is almost fear in McKem's voice as he knows what must be done. His question is now "Why do you care?" It has become Number Six's motivations which intrigue McKern.

Both men are clearly close to breaking point. Number Two's call for `Degree Absolute' is spoken in the knowledge that it is to be 'all or nothing' in their battle of wills. He is willing to risk himself and has to demand Number One implements his decision no matter what the consequences. Impatient and fuming, Number Two shouts and rants his orders to the Supervisor as they go into `Double night time!' He is a man summoning up the courage to meet the ultimate challenge head on as the Prisoner's treatment begins. He is weary and unhappy as he screams the nursery rhymes at the sleeping Prisoner. He then returns to the school-masterly ways of 'Chimes' as he heads Number Six into the Embryo Room contrasting with McGoohan's child-like performance. His lecture on the seven ages of man plus his strident ordering of the Butler also show this.

He sounds soothing as they rock on the see-saw until the word `master' is rejected by McGoohan. Then the unfriendly facade of `Authority' (the school master) takes over using violence to ensure the citizens conform. That same figure declares pride in the Prisoner's total obedience as he graduates from school, but when Number Six refuses to say why he resigned Number Two quickly loses his temper and this acts as a catalyst for Number Six's own violent rejection of childhood authority. The Prisoner thus strikes the master and tries to kill him.

So far the duel seems to have taken more out of McKern than McGoohan and when Number Two says, "I'm beginning to like him" for the first time we can probably believe him. The dominating parental figure is utilised as Number Two challenges Number Six at boxing and fencing. In both instances, when the crunch comes, violence erupts.

McKern returns to his ebullient mask next for the interview in a manner identical to the `world as the Village' sequence in 'Chimes'. He then creates an impatient, shouting personality to bully Number Six into rushing to meet the managing director. At this point, McKern's performance is still dominating McGoohan's because the prisoner is only allowed to react to Number Two's scenarios. Number Two is now furtive and secretive as he cajoles Number Six into `secret work'.

McGoohan becomes desperate and nervous as he tries to defend himself in the courtroom scene. McKern turns the judgement into a test before asserting the Prisoner's obligatory position as a `unit' in the Village via intense anger and force. Nor surprisingly, Number Two is close to complete exhaustion as the `Degree Absolute' goes inexorably on. His is almost in a daze as he asks `Why?' through the cell bars. He begins to panic as he aims the knife at McGoohan's neck and finds that he is now being tested by the Prisoner. After the bombing raid and McKern's astonishing `German' interrogator, he seems to lose the dominance he had previously maintained. He is no longer in total control of events and fear returns as his questioning becomes more [111]desperate, while Number Six, walking out of his cell simply smiles and asks for supper.

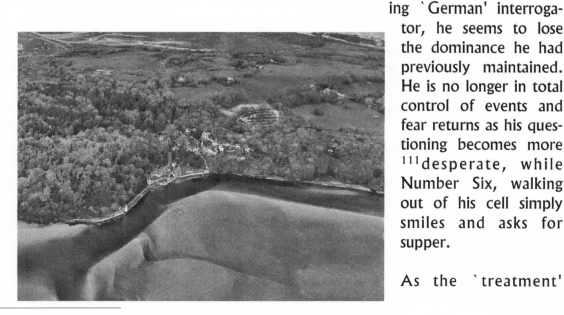

As the `treatment'

[111] Aerial Photograph of Portmeirion courtesy of Phillip John Wickwar

seems to have worn off Number Six, it is Number Two who be-comes manipulated. As equals they lookaround their `home from home'. McKern dances through the Embryo Room as if intoxicated (or perhaps in the first stages of a nervous break-down?) They then calm down as Number Two admits they have `mutual problems'. There is a childish glee in Number Two's voice as he explains the me-chanics of the room but this turns to screaming panic as he sees he has only five minutes left!

McKem's delivery by now has become almost delirious as the Prisoner becomes `the boss'. Number Two rejects Number Six's offer of freedom even though Mc-Goohan states that he did not resign, he rejected! McKern begs for another answer to why he resigned and crawling in dejected defeat, he attacked the Prisoner. He is totally confused and rambling by the time the drink does its work and no amount of pleading can stop the apparently tragic outcome. The fact that Leo McKern did not even get nominated for a best supporting actor award for this literally staggering performance must go down as one of the great mysteries of British television.

After the condensed pre-credit version of 'Once Upon A Time' which opens 'Fall Out', our first view of McKern in the final episode is as a corpse lying on the floor of the cell. The butler opens the cell door and the `resuscitation' begins. Number Two's inert body is carried in by the green-garbed `doctors' to the flashing `hair dryer' and after a quick shave and heart jolt his next appearance is not for another ten minutes or so.

As the unbearded, grey-haired McKern awakens, the sound of his mighty laugh fills the cavern. He is puzzled and feels his heart. He slowly staggers towards the presi-dential dais. He shouts to the assembly `I feel a new man!' and invites them with a gesture to laugh with him. His initial reaction to seeing Number Six throned is to shake his hand and ask how he is keeping. He knew it was inevitable all along that this was to be Number Six's destiny.

Number Two is reflective and saddened to see that the butler no longer considered himself to be his servant (Muscat turns to Number Six in distaste at this). He sees that he is not the man in charge any more. McKern's speech to the masked collec-tive has all the overblown rhetoric of a false politician. There is great irony in his voice as he accepts and thanks them for recognizing his former power. Number Two's sudden realisation that he had been `killed' by his masters for failing releases an angry outburst and his hatred for the Village system is finally established as they would not even let him `rest in peace'.

He laughs at the Prisoner's idea that he could have actually met Number One. "Meet him?" implying that there is some reason why this had to be impossible. maybe Number Two had already guessed the true nature of Number One. His final act of revolt, spitting in the eye of authority, gives him pleasure by displaying his contempt for "whatever" it is. Number One's control over him has ended. Number Two mocks the guards who lead him off to his fate. The `late' Number Two's laughter as he says a final "Be seeing you" shows a man who will no longer play his master's game.

Later, encased in the `Orbit 2' tube, he guffaws like

Photo of Moke in Village Livery courtesy of Andy Worsfold

the mechanical clown in 'The Girl Who Was Death'. The Village has reduced their best man to a human puppet. The laughter stops as the fight with the guards begins. Number Two, now disguised as a white-cloaked figure, joins Number Six, Number 48 and the butler against the Village. They sneak up to the cavern and the tumultuously violent gun battle shows the rebels making their way to the cell. This time, turning it into their eventual getaway vehicle. McKern makes an unlikely all-action figure but the whole sequence is meant to be symbolic rather than literal so that does not matter.

The journey down the motorway shows them acting like characters from the mid-60s movie 'The Knack' or even 'Help!'. They dance and sing in a way totally alien to virtually anything in the series prior to 'Fall Out'. He does not bid farewell to the Prisoner or the Butler as he leaves the truck but he may have acknowledged McGoohan's quick handwave as he enters the parliamentary building. Maybe he is to be the insider within the establishment but this time without the control normally inherent in such a position. Finally he has his bowler hat and brolly as well as the policeman's recognition as he returns to the halls of power a happy man. So perhaps his prison has gone into orbit - but for how long?

Unlike the other two episodes, there is no confrontation between McKern and McGoohan, however the traces of earlier portrayals are still apparent. if the revolution of strong-minded individuals like McKern's Number Two could occur then logically their attempt to convert Number Six must have been doomed from the start.

'The Prisoner' and Brainwashing and the use of Mind Control

The use of Mind Controlling or Brainwashing techniques is a recurrent theme in 'The Prisoner' most obvious in episodes like 'Free For All' (where Number Six becomes a mouth-piece for Village Rhetoric under the guise of offering the Villagers 'freedom'), 'The Schizoid Man' (where Number Six is brainwashed into believing that he is left handed and weirdly that flapjacks are his favourite dish amongst other things) and 'A Change of Mind' (where other Villagers apparently undergo Instant Social Conversion to persuade Number Six that the process exists — notably the Lobo Man)

However it is fair to say that the theme is common to other episodes in 'Arrival' (the aversion therapy room in the Hospital), 'Checkmate' (the Rook being made 'cooperative' by inducing him to use the Blue Water Dispenser & the White Queen being convinced by Mind Control methods that she is in love with Number Six) and 'Do Not Forsake Me, Oh My Darling' (where as part of the process Number Six is initially unaware that he is the Colonel by having his memories of the Village suppressed).

However it is also fair to say that Brainwashing and Mind Control are significant in the fact of the use of these techniques in real world organisations and governments.

The Moscow Show Trials (1936-38) are a significant example - Stalin had a number of his inner circle arrested and tried under inexplicable and hugely improbable charges. The State Prosecutor Andrei Vyshinsky howled claiming those being tried were 'mad dogs' who had gone insane and due their crimes should be taken out and shot. The accused began agreeing with such statements and concurred that as such they had no right to any form of defence.

One by one those accused came forward assenting that they were responsible for reprehensible crimes - Sergei Mrachovsky (who was known to have been a committed revolutionary) bizarrely stated that he had plotted to murder Stalin. Lev Kamenev put forward the supposed fact that he was an enemy of the state who had been so 'blood thirsty' that he had attempted to assassinate Kirov. Richard Pickel also claimed he had been involved in the plot to assassinate Kirov. Yuri Piatakov put forward the idea that the other defendants crimes were of such a nature that they deserved to be shot and that he wanted the right to shoot them. The defendants included Yuri Piatakov's ex-wife.

The fact is there was no tangible evidence that any of the defendants in the Soviet Show Trials had actually been involved in any of the crimes they were accused of. At first it was suggested that hypnosis or drugs were used as a means to an end[112] of extracting unlikely confessions, however at the time no-one was clear why or how this was accomplished.

It later transpired that the techniques used to create these confessions was more down to earth than might be supposed. Psychological techniques were the major component of the Soviet method of mind control rather than drugs or hypnosis. Prisoners were placed in solitary confinement to ensure that they felt alone, uncared for and abandoned and this continued for between 4-6 weeks. While in this state they were forced to remain standing for extremely long periods, to sleep in uncomfortable positions and received both physical and verbal abuse if they didn't adhere to what they were told to do. There was no way of contacting the outside world during this and also a complete lack of natural light ensuring that those imprisoned had no sense of time passing.

In order to create additional confusion the routines and mealtimes were randomly varied and prisoners were kept in the cold and often underfed in order to weaken them mentally, emotionally and physically. Sleep was disrupted in order to make prisoners more uncomfortable and to create a feeling of unreality - prisoners were either deprived of sleep or forced to sleep facing an extremely bright light.

Ultimately these techniques when combined would lead to an isolated and confused person filled with feelings of dread and frightened and in general a nervous wreck. In their cells they would weep, mutter prayers and often begin to hallucinate. Only at this point would the interrogation begin-the victim would first be asked repeatedly to name their crimes without receiving any information as to what if anything they were accused of.

The next step would be to insist that 'the accused' write down a full and accurate record of the crimes that they had supposedly been involved in. The paper would then be torn up and subjected by the interrogator to derision. Abuse would follow if the story of the apparent crimes had discrepancies or the prisoner did not follow instructions to the letter. As a result of all this the prisoner would lose an awareness of just what they had supposed confessed or what they should be confessing to. As a means to obtaining the required confession humiliation techniques were often utilised such as denying access to toilets and forcing the 'accused' to remain standing until they could no longer do so.

Rewards of cigarettes, toilet breaks and coffee were given for 'good behaviour', alternatively the prisoner would be abused or rewarded for no adequate reason. Instead of a reward for good behaviour a prisoner would be threatened with being

---

[112] See 'The Chimes of Big Ben',* 'A, B & C', 'Free for All', 'The Schizoid Man', 'Dance of The Dead', 'Checkmate', 'Hammer Into Anvil', 'A Change of Mind', 'It's Your Funeral', 'Do Not Forsake Me, Oh My Darling', 'Living In Harmony' &'Once Upon A Time' for evidence of the Village using these and similar techniques on Number Six or other Villagers.

* Allegedly only - Nadia is tortured by the on/off Electric floor but as we become aware *SPOILER ALERT*

Nadia is a Village agent, Her reactions in this scene are very likely pre-rehearsed by the Village to motivate Number Six to assist her as 'a damsel in distress'.

shot imminently. All of this would mean that the prisoner would move towards confessing to anything regardless of whether death would be the response. The Soviet way was to use these methods of 'brutal psychological manipulation' to achieve their own ends.[113]

No doubt there are many examples of this kind of thing littered throughout recent history that would be instructive in understanding the way this theme is used and developed in 'The Prisoner'. We can see parallels between this and 'The Schizoid Man' where Number Two, Curtis & Alison work together to convince Number Six that he is not the man he claims to be. Subtle changes to the way he looks, his left handed nature and the use of the Zenner cards amongst other things are used to convince

Number Six that he is in fact Curtis his doppleganger. Hypnotic lights, a Truth Test in which Number Six is rewarded only if he thinks the truth and the persuasive voice of an 'ex-Civil-Servant' are used to Brainwash Number Six into creating an election campaign where he behaves very much like any other Number Two. The 'freedom' he promises remains very much within Village boundaries and is largely a reward for opening up to the Village Authorities and telling them your secrets.

In 'Do Not Forsake Me, Oh My Darling' Number Six's memory is wiped in the Amnesia Room to make him think it is Janet's Birthday over a year ago, effectively until he sees the image of the Colonel in the mirror he is unaware that anything is amiss - note 'his thoughts' are depicted in McGoohan's voice to emphasise this.

The Pantheon/Dome @Portmeirion - courtesy Ed Fordham

---

[113] Information used here adapted from Brainwashing - The Secret History of Mind Control, p4-12 Dominic Streatfield

Not two, not One. The non-duality of Fall Out
by Paul Weston

Some say 'Fall Out' was either the product of an over exhausted mind, psychedelic drugs, or just chaotic rubbish selling a great series short.
Others call it a work of art.

I call it a signpost to Man-kinds true identity...

A big claim but I'll explain.

Even if you are in the 'chaotic rubbish' camp you cannot fail to glimpse that something other than the end of a Spy-Fi series was going on in the final episode.

I propose that we were being invited to share in the esoteric knowledge of the series' driving force, Patrick McGoohan (PMcG).

My qualification for making this statement comes from my own insights initially sparked by watching 'The Prisoner' back in '83/84' and a subsequent life enquiring into the esoteric.

After originally watching 'Fall Out' back in January 1984 I literally walked around for the next day in a daze with the dull realisation that some kind of profound message had been beamed into my living room on that holy night. The realisation (spoiler alert!) that this whole thing was a tool to get each viewer to see the philosophical truth behind the unveiling of Number 1 as the machinations of Number 6's own mind hit me hard and a crack in my own psyche gradually widened and deepened from that day onwards.

I became my own Prisoner trying to figure out my own true identity. And like Sir I finally found my way home, but it took another 30 years...

Non-duality - the perennial philosophy

Before I go on to analyse the episode (which has been done many many times over the last 50 years) I would like first to share an understanding of 'the perennial philosophy' which some believe permeates all religions and philosophies and has been handed down by Sages and Mystics through the ages — hopefully as a way of explaining PMcGs (conscious or unconscious) influences in creating 'Fall Out' - remember the graphic of the marble statues of long dead philosophers disappearing into the hazy distance on the end credits?!

In doing so I aim to demonstrate the evidence for PMcG writing 'Fall Out' as a veiled guide to his own insight into this 'perennial philosophy' — in the unlikely form of the summation of a prime time 'entertainment' TV series!

Various Eastern philosophies and Christian Mystics have stressed the importance of letting go of egoic identity as the only route to escape the prison of suffering.

The primary route being meditation whereby an alert but passive state of observation of your own thought processes allows full consciousness to be witnessed — the end of suffering.

Buddhism states that all suffering is caused by our own delusional belief in a separate individual identity and that to end suffering we merely have to 'see' this identity at work as the cause of our imprisonment for that imprisonment to cease instantly.

Advaita Vedanta, a sect of Hinduism shows a person how to ask the question 'Who am I' and to use this as a tool to strip away the psychological masks we don't even realise that we wear in every life situation we find ourselves — the loving spouse with our partner, the competent boss with our employees, the fun guy with our mates , etc.

Non-duality – not two

Non-duality is what Advaita points towards — "the only thing that exists is the Self, or pure consciousness". That all apparent separation is an illusion, that the cause of all suffering is not being able to realise this and clinging to the ego, which IS suffering.

Not one

Advaita states 'not two,' meaning that when the monkey like mind is quietened by meditation our natural state of consciousness begins to reassert itself. But even calling the ensuing state 'One-ness' is misleading as this still implies 'form' whereas non-duality (true freedom) is neither form nor formless...

'The Prisoner' – the quest for freedom

From the word go 'The Prisoner' concept has the duality between 'the other' and 'the individual' at its heart but it took 'Fall Out' to express this esoterically.

With this in mind let's review Number Six's journey to 'Fall Out'.

A person who deliberately strives to shed himself of identity nevertheless identifies himself as 'the person who isn't Number Six'. This is typical of the delusion that by changing a label a person can change themselves. Six spends 16 episodes proving that 'I am not a number' is just another form of identity.

However his motives are good and eventually he twigs that instead of trying to escape externally that he needs to 'enquire within'.

In the penultimate episode 'Once Upon A Time' we see a classic battle, which can be interpreted, esoterically as the egoic self trying to crush Six's growing self-awareness. At one point we even hear '6' (PMcG) exhort the Number 2 character (McKern) to "Die Six, Die!"

This represents PMcG himself realising that he must shed that part of his egoic identity that Number Two represents and that he himself has been obsessing with.

Interestingly it is at the point of the 'death' of Six who 'Sir' finally divests himself of, transferring this illusion back to its source (ego / Number Two) that The Supervisor appears with the question "What do you desire?'"This I believe to be another trick of the egoic mind, and within the 'human condition' represents another strategy of the ego to evade destruction, as 'desire' is a fundamental building block of the ego.

Of course after all that he has gone through Sir answers with "Number One," following his growing self-awareness that the truth lies within but also gambling that it's not just another trick of his egoic identity (which it is, more shortly).

The next sequence is a visual representation of the process of going deeper within the mind — descending through what seem to be seven levels.

Out – of the Fall

We hear the Supervisor say "we thought you would feel happier, as yourself?" as Six is presented with his black suit, last seen in 'Arrival.' Why this suit, why black? It is devoid of symbol or colour and represents the formless 'Universal Consciousness' that is each person's true identity.

Esoterically 'Arrival' can be seen as PMcG characters fall from this union with Universal Consciousness (Christians refer to this as Adam and Eves 'Fall') he appears wearing black, no signs or symbols attached but quickly becomes uniformed, numbered. Here in 'Fall Out' when we see Number 6 donning the black suit we are witnessing the beginning of his return to 'Universal Consciousness' / spiritual self awakening, call it what you will (it is without labels).

The three men travel down the corridor lined with Juke boxes, it's no coincidence that these are playing The Beatles 'All You Need Is Love' — containing the key phrase "you can learn how to be you in time". This is the Prisoner's goal — self-awareness of his condition.

On entry to the subterranean cavern the Supervisor dons his cape and mask, and takes his place with all of the other masked and labeled characters. This esoterically represents Six or should we now say 'Sir' finally perceiving the egoic masks that the different players in our mind have been wearing all along.

What does Sir nonchalantly sitting on the throne symbolise? The passive alert present moment awareness described during meditation. This passivity of Sir always puzzled me on initial viewings but now I understand this is PMcG demonstrating his growing self-awareness, with the introductions of Numbers 2 and 48 an example of the meditation process.

Ten thousand, not Two

The resurrection of Number 2 may strike viewers as a simple plot device to reintroduce a well liked character but esoterically represents Sir contemplating this aspect of his own persona rather than being swept along in its games / stories.

Why is Number Two being represented by just this Number Two out of the many changing faces of Two? Buddhists call this 'the ten thousand things' — there may appear to be a multiplicity of problems / enemies 'out there' but they are really only one enemy — our inability to perceive them purely as facets or thought forms in our minds, and as such part of us...

The scene where 2 dares to spit in the mechanical eye labeled '1' is symbolic of the changes that Sir's self-awareness is making to his 2 persona.

The whole scene is presided over by The Judge - a potent symbol of the duality that 'Sir' is beginning to finally understand. What is judgment but identification with one position over another, subtle imprisonment that leaves the judger believing there is something needing to be escaped from?

Then we revisit Number 48 - representing all forms of rebellion — The Judge himself refers to the character as if a cardboard cut out caricature as he actually is in PMcGs allegory.
But for all of the so-called rebellion it's just another uniform (in fact the 'young man' is wearing a form of old fashioned military uniform), it may as well be a cloak and mask. Interestingly this style of military uniform is more commonly seen in more vibrant colours and I would suggest that the black version was chosen to enforce this idea that Number 48 is an aspect of Sir's own psyche, as Sir's black suit has been reinstated.

'Sir' is actually acknowledging this rebellious side of his own egoic identity with his outburst "YOUNG MAN, Don't Knock Yourself Out," which has another implication for our species as a whole — this fake rebellion could lead to global disaster. A none too veiled pointer that 48 is a facet of PMcG own mind is given when 48 says "these bones is yours Dad"..

The Judge finally addresses 'Sir' but this really represents the judging faculties of the ego trying to flatter 'Sir' into 'joining them' — i.e. keeping egoic mind at the controls.
'Sir's growing passive detachment from the egoic minds tricks is wonderfully demonstrated by his series of "Why?" Questions to the Judges gushing adulation.

The Judges' address ends with "keep us in mind, Sir, we are all yours", another none too veiled hint that the whole thing is playing out in 'The Prisoner's own mind. Esoterically this represents the last machinations of egoic identity, using flattery to appeal to the dying ego in 'Sir', throwing worldly gifts to trick him into becoming the new Number 1 (for Christians very reminiscent of Satan tempting Jesus with the World).

'Sir' is offered and takes the stand; the final ego delusion remaining in him is that as a separate identity he still has a voice that will be heard.

'Sir's none speech

Many religions and philosophies state that suffering is the surest route to redemption, and we witness 'Sir's own breakdown when he realises that the egoic identity (in the form of the faceless masked delegates) can never be beaten on its own terms. My own personal highlight of the whole series is the anguish turning to realisation on 'Sir's face.

This surrender (another kind of death) initiates his meeting with Number 1, which in esoteric terms is the only way to understand the source of our suffering.

'Sir' is led past the 'orbit tubes' containing Number 2 and 48, representing Sir's new awareness of them as parts of his own egoic identity, no longer able to pull his strings, contained by this new insight into himself.

The pivotal scene - One, not two

I'd like to pay special attention now to the scene where Number 1 is revealed as this is the most direct indication that PMcG was sharing esoteric wisdom with his viewers and the first clue to me back in 1984 that there is more to the World than meets the eye.

'Sir' ascends the spiral stairs to a totally man-made scene, not even human flesh is on view. Man-made in more ways than one...
World globes crowd the view, these represent the control human ego craves over the divine.

We see the cloaked huddled figure seemingly gazing into the screen showing 6 on a loop while holding a crystal ball. Why? This one scene encapsulates the Prisoners dilemma — humanities predicament. Sir's self-reflection in the form of the 17 episodes to this point represents his final realisation into the source of his (our) imprisonment. We create a false version of our world by perpetually living in the past (represented in this scene by the "I will not be pushed, filed..." loop on the screen) or living in the future (represented by the crystal ball).

This creates a false mental version of the world — 'the Village' of the series, it separates us from each other — 'the Numbered population' and it tricks us into believing that we are imprisoned and need to 'escape' (Six from episode one onwards).

Sir then does what very few people in each generation do — confronts this false identity (esoterically represented by Number 1 chanting 'I I I I') — no clearer example could have been used to show the death throes of his own egoic identity than its most basic expression 'I' — 'I' and '1' were always one and the same...

Sir does this by deliberately dropping and smashing the crystal ball, (the ego/Number 1's obsessive futures) In actuality a person must intently keep inquiring "who am I" but drop the instinctive urge to answer from first a base animal urge — 'I am my urges / desires' (represented by the ape mask of Number 1) then drop the urge to answer the "who am I" question from the egoic identity itself — it can only ever answer from self preservation — giving you a false answer to who you are esoterically.

<u>'The Prisoner' no more</u>

The final unveiling reveals the embodiment of tortured evil — that it is seen finally as 'false self' and not blamed on 'other' is the dawning of a free man. For what then remains is 'the Prisoner' no longer but the witness of the end of Number 1 / delusional egoic self.

'The Prisoner' has shed his labels, no longer Number 6, no longer a prisoner no longer even not a number. This is true freedom. It sets in motion the metaphorical destruction of the Village caused by Love. For true freedom in esoteric terms is Love, the spiritual kind, represented by the reprise of The Beatles as the bullets fly.

Many viewers are puzzled as to why '6/Sir' resisted using weapons throughout the series but did in 'Fall Out'. They are allegorical bullets of love which is the death of fear / delusion.

Fitting also that the escape scene utilises the cage, which represents our bodily form, able to move us about but imprisoning. It's a vehicle for getting us where we need to go and here shows 'Sir' dispatching those personas back into the 'real' world but this time enlightened by awareness of the trap of egoic identity.

'Sir' himself returns 'home' attended to by the dwarf Butler, a symbol of blind human intellect, formerly serving every whim of the egoic mind (Number 2's), now serving the needs of its master, the awakened person.

When we see the electronic door to his house automatically open it is a symbol of his new found awareness into the traps of duality, that never go away, but of which he was formerly unaware.

He drives purposefully toward us, the viewer, daring us to become 'a free man'...

In my introduction I called 'The Prisoner' a sign-post to Man-kinds true identity...

Some have interpreted the end sequence of 'Fall Out' to represent some kind of global catastrophe bought on by man's egoic shadow self (represented by Number 1) bringing about Nuclear destruction.

Me? It's the opposite. It's called 'Fall Out' and it can be viewed another way — we can evolve from this state of being 'fallen' – Out...   Paul Weston, May 2017

END OF SECTION B

SECTION C
NEW PARAGRAPH 4
CODENAME : RAFFERTY

RAFFERTY
Articles by Tom Mayer

Illustration - McGoohan as Rafferty with IV Drip by Ed Fordham

NO YESTERDAY AND NO TOMORROW:
A LOOK BACK AT 'RAFFERTY'
By Tom Mayer
Also Available on The Unmutual Website At:
http://theunmutual.co.uk/rafferty1.htm

When admirers of Patrick McGoohan have completed viewing 'The Prisoner' or 'Danger Man' ('Secret Agent' in the US), they may be inspired to delve further into his filmography. His appearances in 'Columbo,' as well as in such notable films as 'Ice Station Zebra,' 'Escape From Alcatraz' and 'Braveheart,' would inevitably be watched next. For those who dig deeper, additional surprises await, including 'Hell Drivers,' 'All Night Long' and 'Dr. Syn: The Scarecrow of Romney Marsh'. Yet, for the truly dedicated, one of the most intriguing curiosities of McGoohan's career eventually presents itself -- his third television series, the short-lived 1977 CBS medical drama 'Rafferty.'

This program, like so many other TV obscurities from the past, has been impossible to see over the last few decades. It has never been rerun, nor has it ever been commercially released on VHS or DVD. Among McGoohan fans, much curiosity surrounds this show. It wasn't a success when it first aired, while its reputation in the years that followed has been largely negative. Summaries in books and websites are almost always critical, while the comments from McGoohan himself in later interviews are full of outright hatred. As a result, later generations of McGoohan fans who were curious about the program had little information to consult; and, most importantly, they were unable to view it. How was a discerning viewer able to get access to the show, 1) to watch it for entertainment, and 2) to analyse and evaluate it?

Today, thanks to DVDs and internet streaming, footage of just about everything from pop culture's shadowy past eventually surfaces online or on disc. 'Rafferty' has been no exception. Copies of the series' thirteen episodes began circulating on the DVD collector's market a few years ago. This has provided McGoohan fans (and connoisseurs of obscure TV) with a long-awaited opportunity to finally see the program, as well as to make their own judgments about its quality. While many books, websites and years of study have been dedicated to 'The Prisoner' and 'Secret Agent,' comparatively little has been written about 'Rafferty.' Apart from cast lists and episode summaries, detailed information on the show is still scarce. With September 2012 having marked the 35th anniversary of its US. premiere, perhaps the time is due for an in-depth look at the series, analysing just what 'Rafferty' was, and was not.

HISTORY AND PRODUCTION

In the spring of 1977, writer/producer James Lee came up with the idea for a medical series featuring a gruff, individualistic doctor. He pitched the idea to executive producer Jerry

Thorpe who liked the premise enough to give Lee the go-ahead to put the series in production. By this time, the two men had a proven track record in television. Lee had been a producer and writer for the anthology series 'Omnibus' in the fifties, the law drama 'The Defenders' in the sixties, and the groundbreaking miniseries 'Roots' which (along with 'Rafferty') aired in 1977. He later produced the successful miniseries 'Napoleon & Josephine: A Love Story' in 1987. Thorpe (also an occasional director) had executive-produced many notable series over the years including 'The Untouchables,' 'Kung Fu,' and later, 'Falcon Crest.' With solid TV experience between them, 'Rafferty' looked as though it might be a hit.

Lee teamed up with Norman S. Powell and Robert Van Scoyk to produce the series. They sent out scripts and one found its way to McGoohan. "I don't like to read pilot scripts," he told TV Guide in 1977. "Too many pilots never sell. But my agent sent me this script. I liked this doctor guy." He added, "Doctors are important. But plumbers and garbage collectors are even more important. If [they] go on strike, that's when we need doctors." The Boston Globe quoted him around the same time: "The philosophy of the series is that doctors are angels of mercy, hospitals are sanctuaries, they're there to help us when we need." With a lead of McGoohan's stature signed on, and medical series still popular in primetime, all the pieces were in place for success. By the summer, filming was underway on an initial order of thirteen episodes. Thorpe was happy with his choice for the series' lead, telling TV Guide that McGoohan "is a consummate performer. There's an enormous amount of spontaneity in his acting. He finds fresh ways of doing clichés." Yet, he acknowledged McGoohan's personality and the distance he kept from those around him: "If there's anything people find abrasive, it probably grows out of his shyness ... I like him personally, but we have not socialised. I don't think we will." Co-producer Norman Powell said positive things as well to the Ventura County Press Courier: "McGoohan is involved in every aspect of the creative process. He's a workaholic. He is very strongly involved in making this the best possible series."

Thorpe had every reason to be optimistic. He had recently produced the detective series 'Harry O,' starring David Janssen, which ran from 1974-76. Janssen played sarcastic, world-weary private eye Harry Orwell, who lived in a beachside bungalow, rode the bus everywhere (due to his perennially broken-down car), and was quick with smart-aleck remarks to cops and crooks alike.

Here, the parallels between McGoohan and Janssen are worth noting. Both actors were born within three years of each other, in 1928 and 1931 respectively; and both achieved their greatest fame in the mid-1960s while in their mid-thirties: Janssen with 'The Fugitive' (running 120 episodes from 1963-67); and McGoohan with 'Secret Agent' and 'The Prisoner' (64 episodes combined, running 1964-68). By the mid-1970s, after a slight fall-off in their careers, they both ended up in the title roles on shows produced by Jerry Thorpe, portraying gruff loners who did things their own way. Thorpe even directed the pilot episodes for both series. Yet, while 'Harry O' had a successful run of two seasons, Rafferty (as we shall see) barely lasted a fraction of that time.

'Rafferty' was one of the first programs of the new season to debut (two weeks earlier than usual), airing on Monday, September 5th on CBS. Interestingly, it was the only medical drama on the air during the 1977-78 season. As a result, it garnered much attention from critics and those within the TV industry. However, the show had its work cut out for it ratings-wise: it aired at 10pm opposite 'ABC's Monday Night Football' and the 'NBC Movie of the Week.' McGoohan himself acknowledged this in TV Guide: "When O. J. [Simpson] is on, I'll be watchin' him. I'm not denigratin' my show. I never watch my show, except when I have directed it."

PREMISE

Dr. Sidney Rafferty, a widower, is an army doctor with 23 years of military service who has since retired. He is now on staff at City General Hospital in Los Angeles, where he diagnoses patients and performs surgery when needed. The rest of the time he runs a private practice, assisted by his receptionist, Nurse Vera Wales (Millie Slavin), and his young protégé, Dr. Daniel Gentry (John Getz). 'Rafferty' is gruff, sarcastic and cantankerous with an individual streak. In an article by Don Freeman, McGoohan elaborated on the character: "We've got a real doctor here in Sid Rafferty. He is a doctor, one of the few, I must say, with a heart and a soul and a mind, and he is not just interested in sending out bills. Furthermore, he doesn't carry malpractice insurance and for a good reason -- he doesn't intend to malpractice. He won't be driving about in a fine car, either. It will be serviceable, although not as dilapidated as Columbo's."

Each episode sees him dealing with a medical crisis that usually brings him into conflict with patients, members of their family or any number of hospital staff. He does things his own way, and doesn't like bureaucratic red tape. In extreme situations, he takes matters into his own hands, such as performing emergency surgery (without permission) on a stabbing victim; to racing around town trying to find the cause of a botulism outbreak; to traveling to the scene of a wildfire to confirm the symptoms of a suspected plague. Being a product of 1970s television, there is no serialisation or continuing plots between instalments. Each story is self-contained, and the episodes can be watched in any order.

'Rafferty's wardrobe is simple. He sports a light or dark blue dress shirt while in the hospital, and wears a grey blazer when going out. Occasionally, he wears a short-brimmed fedora. Whether this image was McGoohan's idea or the costume designer's is unknown, but Rafferty projects a unique appearance from the rest of the hospital staff. In one episode, a policewoman remarks, "He doesn't look like a doctor." A fellow physician replies, "And he is a disreputable character." Rafferty, within earshot, quietly responds, "Thank you."

With his puffy, 1970s hair and thick-rimmed glasses, McGoohan barely resembles the John Drake of 1965. Gone is the smooth, charming mid-Atlantic accent he spoke with in 'Secret Agent' and 'The Prisoner'. Instead, Rafferty's delivery is abrupt, clipped and sometimes high-pitched. He is often indifferent to (or sometimes annoyed with) everyone around him. He occasionally shows absent-mindedness, from losing notes and phone numbers in his office, to asking people to repeat themselves during conversations. These touches add to a true quirky character. Yet, Rafferty has a sensitive side as well. In scenes with sick children, or with co-workers during personal moments, it's obvious that he's a good guy with the requisite heart of gold. Regardless, McGoohan commands viewers' attention whenever he's onscreen.

SUPPORTING CAST

Millie Slavin does a good job as Vera. She has a world-weary tone and a droll sense of humour -- apparently she's seen it all during her career as a nurse and receptionist. She's also one of the few who isn't rattled by Rafferty's gruffness. She knows he has a sensitive side, and he respects her as well. As a result, their onscreen rapport is one of the series' highlights. Slavin has appeared many films and TV shows including 'St. Elsewhere,' 'Forever Young,' 'The Truman Show' and 'Collateral Damage.'

The nature of Rafferty and Vera's relationship is hard to figure out. Most summaries of the show state that she is madly in unrequited love with him, yet several episodes hint that they're in a relationship. They're seen eating dinner in his apartment in 'The Narrow Thread'; attending a symphony in 'The Cutting Edge'; and even leaving for a vacation together at the beginning of 'No Yesterday and No Tomorrow.' However, other episodes contradict this. In 'The Price of Pain,' Vera asks Rafferty out for a Mexican dinner, and he replies, "You never give up, do you?" And in 'Will To Live,' when Rafferty brings Vera home to treat her while she is sick, he remarks that it's the first time he's ever been in her apartment. Perhaps the writers wanted to keep the couple's relationship vague, allowing it to go either way in viewers' minds.

John Getz adequately fills the role of Dan Gentry that of the young, handsome sidekick to the older, leading man. He appears in most of the episodes, even taking the lead in one story when Rafferty is out of town. Getz performs with an easygoing, friendly air that makes him a good counterpoint to Rafferty's crustiness. The series came early in Getz's career, and he later carved out an impressive resume as a character actor. He's appeared in such diverse films as 'The Fly,' 'Zodiac' and 'The Social Network'; and has guest-starred in many TV shows including 'Three's Company,' 'Murphy Brown,' 'The West Wing' and 'Mad Men.' In 1984, he played the lead role in the Coen Brothers' excellent directorial debut, 'Blood Simple.'

The rest of the cast is filled out with recurring characters that appear throughout the series. They include Joan Pringle as Nurse Beryl Keynes, David Clennon as Dr. Calvin (Rafferty's main foil at City General), Michael C. Gwynne as Dr. Prud'homme, and Craig Wasson as the young resident, Dr. Furey. Also, in a clever casting touch, McGoohan's wife, Joan, 'plays' Rafferty's wife. In a panning shot around his office in the pilot, the photos that we see on the wall of the late Mrs. Rafferty are really those of Joan McGoohan.

REVIEWS AND CANCELLATION

Two major entertainment magazines started things off well. The editors of TV Guide had positive words about the series the week it premiered, calling McGoohan "excellent in the title role." Yet their optimism for the program was misplaced, when they stated that while

"Rafferty is one of the first new series to arrive this season, it's not likely to be the first to leave..." A review in Variety was upbeat as well: "McGoohan's medic is as brilliant as any of his film and TV predecessors," and "the show was aided by first-rate production values and crisp direction, which did a good deal to gloss over the weakness of the script and characterisations."

The major national newspapers included ads for the new CBS shows. The promo for 'Rafferty' used a pensive close-up of McGoohan with the following over-the-top slogan: "Come hell or hospital foul-ups -- no one steps between 'Rafferty' and his patients!" In smaller type below, the hype continued: "Disease and red tape are his enemies. Guts and dedication are his ammo. Patrick McGoohan is the rugged, outspoken doctor you want on (and at!) your side!"

Reviews in the national papers were mixed. If a writer was critical about the show however, they almost always praised McGoohan. In the New York Times, John J. O'Connor stated that 'Rafferty' was "the same old medical-show song in a different key, [but] McGoohan's hard-edged performance may make this one worth listening to occasionally." In the Los Angeles Times, Cecil Smith observed that the show was "routine stuff made watchable primarily because of McGoohan. He is, as always, one of the most gifted actors in this wind-blown diversion and is a pleasure to watch. Though this is not 'The Prisoner,' not by miles." After a summary of the pilot, he finished his review with a sigh, ironically stating, "It looks like a long season."

Carole Ashkinaze of the Atlanta Journal-Constitution listed 'Rafferty' as a "best bet" in a preview of the new season. She admitted that the paper's writing staff "were Patrick McGoohan fans to begin with, and he's won us over with his portrayal of perhaps the first TV doctor with human failings." In the same paper two days later, critic Paul Jones dedicated several paragraphs of his column to the show, calling McGoohan "just right for the part ... a hard-nosed Irishman [who's] ... a fine actor, a good writer and a top director." He added, "[McGoohan's] own personality suggests that he is a man not far different from 'Rafferty' -- a man who might confound, upset and overturn the world of medicine now and then."

Apparently these reviews were based just on the pilot, which was a good effort, and probably the only episode available for critics to sample. Yet not every review was positive this early. Charles Witbeck, in a syndicated article lamented, "the new medical hour [brings] yawns because it's so predictable. Kids could ad-lib the dialogue, and tell what was coming next since we've seen it all before." Jay Sharbutt of the Youngstown Vindicator prophetically stated, "McGoohan has a cult following from his fine 'Secret Agent' and 'The Prisoner' series, but even this and his superior acting need a real miracle -- better writing -- to keep 'Rafferty' alive past December."

As the weeks wore on, the few later reviews that appeared were hardly positive once the weaknesses of the series became apparent. By far, the most negative (yet funniest) comments came from an article by Jim Tripodi of the Beaver County (Pennsylvania) Times. Here are some highlights:

"Rafferty is the greatest doctor in the world. If you don't believe it, just ask him. The guy can diagnose disease faster than a speeding bullet and can perform medical miracles in 60 minutes or less."

"The series is a drama, or attempts to be a drama. The continual crisis that plagues the good doctor in just one hour makes the show laughable."

"His bedside manners are that of a two-car accident."

"It would seem 'Rafferty' is ... a one-man crusader against everything from acne to cancer. If it were up to [him], he would be the hospital administrator, chief surgeon, consultant, scrub nurse, dietician and chief of security."

"Once a smooth operator on 'Secret Agent' and 'The Prisoner', McGoohan has taken on a different method of delivery; like a guy trying to squeeze out words between bouts with heartburn. His slow, choppy speaking urges the viewer to switch [to 'Monday Night Football'] to the soothing voice of Howard Cosell."

Indeed, 'Rafferty' ended up being a huge step down from the high quality of McGoohan's previous two series. The show was best summed up years later by McGoohan biographer Rupert Booth in 2011: "[The] storylines were predictable and the format largely uninspired, saved only from mediocrity by the lead performance."

It was obvious that the series was stuck in a tired formula, with lacklustre writing and direction. The conflict for most episodes involved 'Rafferty' trying to convince a stubborn patient that they needed a certain medical treatment, which they, in turn, refused for any number of reasons. On cue, this would bring 'Rafferty' into a series of arguments with everyone from the patient's family to fellow hospital staff to judges, the police, and anyone else in range of the good doctor's crusty demeanour. The disease-of-the-week was usually explained in a scene of expositional dialog, acting as 'painless' medical education for the viewer (or maybe just to prove that the writers did actual medical research).

Looking at what Rafferty dealt with over the course of the series, the episodes could have been titled with the name of that week's ailment, and no one would have been the wiser:
'Pilot' (Paralysis)
'Brothers and Sons' (Kidney Transplant)
'A Point Of View' (Hysterical Blindness)
'The Cutting Edge' (Brain Tumour)
'The Narrow Thread' (Deafness)
'The Epidemic' (Botulism)
'The Wild Child' (Tourette's Syndrome)
'Will To Live' (Viral Infection)
'Walking Wounded' (Anorexia Nervosa)
'No Yesterday and No Tomorrow' (Brain Aneurysm)
'The Price of Pain' (Drug Addiction/Coma)

'The Burning Man' (Pneumonic Plague)
'Death Out Of a Blue Sky' (Medical Cause of a Plane Crash)
At this rate, if the show hadn't been cancelled, the writers probably would have run out of diseases to focus on.

In the end, death came, not out of a blue sky, but rather from the office of the network president. Having run just under three months, with soft ratings, mixed reviews, and an unhappy star (as we shall see), there was little protest when the show was quietly cancelled -- one of the first to go from the new season. Three episodes remained unaired, due to the series having been preempted on October 10th, 24th and November 21st. Little was said in the papers at the time (unlike today, when the slightest change to every show makes news online and in print). TV Guide included the phrase "Last show of the series" after the summary of the November 28th episode. It also announced that the Robert Wagner detective show 'Switch' would take over 'Rafferty's time-slot the following week (ironically 'Switch' would be cancelled by the end of the season anyway).

By the end of the year, McGoohan was in Canada filming 'Kings and Desperate Men' written and directed by his 'Prisoner' co-star, Alexis Kanner. By 1978 and '79, he secured high-profile roles in 'Brass Target' and 'Escape from Alcatraz,' so his career was not hurting in any way after the cancellation of 'Rafferty'. Without a doubt, he was glad to put it behind him and move on.

CRITIQUE OF SERIES

Of all the words said about 'Rafferty,' both positive and negative, the most damning comments came from the star himself. During a resurgence in his career in 1985, while he was appearing in 'Pack of Lies' on Broadway, McGoohan was the subject of two major interviews in which he discussed his career. Talking to Bill King for Anglofile magazine, McGoohan said flat-out that 'Rafferty' was "a disaster ... the most miserable job I've ever done in my life ... a total frustration from start to finish." To Ed Siegel of The Boston Globe, he called 'Rafferty' a "horrendous experience ... the antithesis of having the artistic freedom of 'The Prisoner'." With seven years of hindsight, McGoohan was probably happy to finally explain what happened back in 1977.

How did this show that seemed to have the ingredients of a hit, that had a star and producers with vast TV experience, fail in such a short time? Upon analysis, several reasons present themselves (supported by McGoohan's comments from the King and Siegel interviews).

The first problem was weak scripts. Apparently, a stable of writers churned out stories that could have played unchanged on any other medical drama. "The scripts [were] monstrous pieces of garbage, [with] no time to rewrite them," McGoohan recalled. "I couldn't get any decent scripts, and I remember saying to one gentleman who was supposedly in charge -- this is when I had a script delivered and couldn't believe what I had read -- "I will give half my salary to anyone who can find a writer. But that would be setting a precedent you know, this sort of attitude. So we were all delighted to part company." At the very least,

McGoohan recognised the importance of good stories, without which, makes it difficult to keep an audience or to ensure a program's survival.

Second, was tension behind the scenes. Trouble apparently hit right from the start, as Mc-Goohan's plans for the character differed from what the producers wanted. "... I had been promised all sorts of things that were going to happen to make it an original series. And they didn't transpire," he explained. "I wanted him to be a roving doctor. And they promised me this would happen. And instead of that, I was spending all my time walking up and down fucking hospital corridors! I said, 'Get me out of this fucking hospital!' Because it's been done to death. There's nothing new to say about that."

Interestingly, the producers themselves alluded to this conflict at the time. Jerry Thorpe said in TV Guide, "[McGoohan's] difficult on a script. He is very critical. If something doesn't appear to be in character, he lets you know ... His standards are inordinately high." Norman Powell said to the Press Courier, "[McGoohan] doesn't like to think he is in TV. He sees it as making a lot of little features which creates some conflict, since Warner Brothers thinks it is making a TV series." With Lee in charge of stories and scripts, and Powell in charge of casting and production details, there was little left for McGoohan to oversee.
He explained this Hollywood mindset: "[Producers will] say, 'We'll let you do what you want,' but then they realise the individual wants to do something individualistic, as opposed to en masse and according to an ordinary pattern that they're conditioned to ... well that's when, you see, the individual goes out the window. Because it's done on a conveyor belt, and you're making sausages of a certain shape and size." Authority on the show wasn't delegated well, either. "There were too many people in charge and all passing the buck," McGoohan recalled. "I counted them. There were 11 people who thought that they were the 'creators' of this load of garbage. But you couldn't find one to take responsibility [when it failed]."

McGoohan was a perfectionist who thrived on having major input in the productions he starred in. Although he began as "just" the lead role in 'Secret Agent,' he soon increased his input in the program, from having say in the development of his character, to eventually directing episodes. This experience, of course, led to 'The Prisoner' where he had total control as executive producer, as well as the help of a seasoned and talented crew to back him up. 'Rafferty' was none of these things. Thorpe, Lee, Powell, etc., called the shots by hiring writers, directors and crew. Scripts were churned out with little time to analyse or rewrite them. With McGoohan stuck in the middle, something was bound to suffer -- namely, the quality of the show. Once caught in this situation, it was no wonder he was "miserable." Factor in his dislike of the series, along with a tough time-slot, and it became a poisonous combination. There was no way the series could have lasted longer than it did.

During this frustrating experience, one wonders what McGoohan was like on the set, and how he treated the cast and crew. A clue comes in a 1981 interview with actress Morgan Fairchild who guest-starred in the episode 'A Point Of View.' She told the Philadelphia Inquirer, "Two weeks after I got [to Hollywood], I was working in a 'Rafferty.' Patrick Mc-Goohan was a doll, very encouraging. I was playing a blind Peace Corps worker, and finding it difficult. I'd never played anyone blind." Although McGoohan might have been unhappy, he apparently kept a professional, friendly demeanour toward his colleagues.

A third point to consider for the series' failure is the character of 'Rafferty' himself. With his gruff crustiness and McGoohan's idiosyncratic performance, 'Rafferty' was, at times, a hard person to warm up to. Sure, he had his friendly, sympathetic moments, but his clipped, high-pitched delivery, and frequent conflicts with other characters might have been a turn-off for casual viewers. In 1977, the viewing public probably wasn't ready for such a quirky, sarcastic character for a series lead. Viewers were still getting used to acerbic personalities such as Archie Bunker from 'All in the Family' and the title character from its spin-off 'Maude' (which aired just before 'Rafferty' on Monday nights). Also, it would have been doubly difficult to accept a character like 'Rafferty' in a medical drama, while the soothing, nostalgic memories of 'Dr. Kildare' and 'Marcus Welby, MD' were still fresh in viewers' minds.

Yet things would change within the next few years, beginning with J. R. Ewing and Alexis Carrington -- the over-the-top villains of 'Dallas' and 'Dynasty.' While they were larger-than-life characters meant to be disliked, little by little, ambiguity, realism and human failings began to define mainstream television characters more and more. By the 1980s, 'Hill Street Blues' and 'St. Elsewhere' broke down the last barriers for gritty realism in characters. Today, we expect these characteristics in our series' leads. Consider the incredible success of the most popular programs of the past decade -- 'The Sopranos', 'The Wire,' 'Lost,' 'Deadwood' and 'Breaking Bad' to name a few. All feature flawed antiheroes in lead roles that were unthinkable twenty or thirty years ago. Next to them, Sid Rafferty looks tame by comparison. In his own quirky and obscure way, he was ahead of his time.

Finally, one can bluntly state that it was low ratings that killed the show. 'Rafferty' couldn't stand up against the 'Movie of the Week' and 'Monday Night Football.' If the series' star himself was watching the game with everyone else, then what chance did the show have? However, upon viewing 'Rafferty' decades later, one can see that it wasn't a complete disaster -- it's actually not as bad as its reputation has led people to believe. While McGoohan was justified in hating the worst episodes, he may have been unfairly harsh toward the better stories. 'The Pilot,' 'The Cutting Edge' and 'Walking Wounded' are all acceptable, entertaining hours of television. Interestingly, the better episodes always seemed to contain McGoohan's best performances -- coincidence? Plus, several stories actually got Rafferty out of the hospital, with varying degrees of success ('The Wild Child,' 'Death Out Of a Blue Sky'). Obviously, some attention was paid to his requests for a "roving doctor" premise.

As for the bad episodes, many had decent premises that could have been salvaged with better writing and directing. Probably the biggest mistake on the part of the writers, was not taking advantage more of the unique character of 'Rafferty.' His past as an army doctor, along with his vast medical experience and non-conformist demeanour should have been enough to provide several good storylines (or to at least accent any mediocre scripts). One wonders how (or if) the series could have improved if McGoohan had more control over the production.

Regardless, 'Rafferty' was simply ordinary, middle-of-the-road, network television -- everything Patrick McGoohan (and his career) was not.

LEGACY AND HOUSE

In an effort to make more money out of the failed show, Warner Brothers sold the program to other countries. It aired in Sydney, Australia in the summer of 1978; while Thames Television in the UK broadcast the series later that year into early 1979. Apparently, these screenings were the only times the series was ever rerun.

As the years went on, 'Rafferty' still garnered the occasional negative comment, when it wasn't the answer to a trivia question or listed as a footnote to McGoohan's career. In a 1987 article, columnist Ron Miller of the San Jose Mercury News, was looking back on his first decade as a television critic. He recalled that 'Rafferty' was the first show he reviewed in his first column from September 1977. He repeated the amusing comments he made at the time, saying that the program "insulted the intelligence of anybody who'd ever been to a doctor," and that, "accident victims in Rafferty's town should carry cards advising ambulance attendants to leave them lying in the street rather than take them to 'Rafferty'."

In 1989, Harry Castleman and Walter J. Podrazik included an entry on 'Rafferty' in their excellent reference book, Harry & Wally's Favourite TV Shows. They observed the character of Rafferty as "a tight-lipped enigma" who "might explode at any moment in an argument (usually over some matter of principle)." They called the stories "equally puzzling, reflecting an obvious desire to break from the boundaries of the hospital corridors, but not all certain where to go." They concluded their write-up with McGoohan's 1985 "miserable job" comment, adding that, "afterward, he kept his distance from US television productions."

The series lay forgotten for another decade or so, until a new medical show inspired viewers to reconsider the premise of 'Rafferty' in an updated context. In November 2004, a U.K.-based actor speaking with an American accent, who had relocated to Los Angeles, premiered in the title role of a sarcastic, gruff, individualistic doctor at odds with his patients and staff in a new medical series. Sound familiar? No, McGoohan didn't revive 'Rafferty' after 27 years. Instead, the show was 'House, MD,' starring Oxford-born Hugh Laurie as the cantankerous title character, Dr. Gregory House. Each episode saw him and his staff racing to treat that week's patient who was suffering from mysterious life-threatening symptoms. Along the way, 'House' would come into conflict with everyone from his hospital administrator to his diagnostic team to the patients themselves. Everything was served with a healthy dose of insults and rule-breaking, just before a cure was found in time for the closing credits.

The similarities between the shows are notable, to the point where most online descriptions of 'Rafferty' have since been reduced to the simple phrase of "a precursor to House." Both programs even had episodes directed by their star actors! Yet, there are marked differences as well. While 'Rafferty' lasted barely half a season, House would go on for an astounding eight years and 177 episodes. At one point (after it was in syndication), it was the most-watched TV series in the world. How was it able to hang on for so long? Evidently, 'House' got right several points that 'Rafferty' got wrong.

First, 'House' had a diagnostic team to explain his motivations to (as well as to insult). They were a "cushion" between him and everyone else, so at least he wasn't insulting patients directly. 'Rafferty' was a lone-wolf who had only Vera and Dan to explain his reasoning to (if at all). Apart from them, he dealt directly with patients and staff who saw his gruffness up-close. Also, the motivation for 'Rafferty's behaviour was never fully explained. His regimented military background, or residual grief over his late wife, could be possible reasons. 'House,' on the other hand, was the victim of a failed leg operation that left him with a painful limp and an addiction to Vicodin. His bitterness over this handicap at least explained his gruffness, and made his meanness a bit more "acceptable."

'House' also succeeded by properly focusing on its title character. The stories were based around him and how he fit in to that week's crisis. Viewers didn't tune in for diseases and cures, they watched for House's opinions, expertise and sarcasm that was unique to him. 'Rafferty' merely filled a token doctor role, simply reacting to what was happening around him, with little in the way of character development. Again, the 'Rafferty' writers didn't know how much potential they had in their lead character.

Finally, 'Rafferty' had uninspired, self-contained episodes in a more conservative time. The show was poised on a crucial cusp in the evolution of the medical drama. Gone were the years of 'Dr. Kildare' and 'Marcus Welby,' idealistic doctors who worked in conditions with hardly a trace of blood. Ahead lay the era of 'St. Elsewhere' and 'ER' -- gritty medical shows that focused on everything that was wrong with the doctors as well as the patients. It was in this period of transition that 'Rafferty' found itself, with an undeveloped, idiosyncratic lead, reacting his way through not-quite-yet unconventional storylines.

By the mid-2000s, 'House' was able to succeed in a more accepting time -- that of the post-'Sopranos' era, with gritty, serialised stories and characters sporting ironic, sarcastic attitudes. It was perfectly acceptable for 'House' to be an outright jerk, whereas 'Rafferty' required the stereotypical heart of gold. House, popping his Vicodin, was a drug addict as well -- something McGoohan wouldn't have allowed on his show (or 'Rafferty' in his hospital, for that matter). Even if 'Rafferty' had been perfect on all counts, it still took another three decades until the viewing public was ready for such a doctor.

Another interesting link between the two shows deserves a mention. 'The Laughing Prisoner' was a 1987 UK special written by and starring Stephen Fry and Jools Holland. It's mainly an extended comedy skit, involving Holland being abducted to the Village with Fry as the No.2 character. There are song interludes from bands of the time (including XTC and Siouxsie & The Banshees) performing on location in the Village. McGoohan, as No.6, appears via archive footage from the original series. Interestingly, in a small role, is Stephen Fry's long-time friend and comedy partner, Hugh Laurie.

DVD AVAILABILITY

Apart from the Australia and UK screenings, 'Rafferty' has not been seen since its original US airing. In the years that followed, new generations of McGoohan fans would inevitably learn about the series' existence, but were unable to see it. Today, comments regarding the show online always include questions about its availability. As of this writing (September 2012), it has yet to be officially released on DVD. However, it is available if one is curious enough to search it out. An early VCR owner in the UK recorded all thirteen episodes from the Thames screening. It is from this source that the show has been burned to DVD, and sold through collectors' websites over the past few years. We are fortunate that this has happened, since the show would be impossible to see otherwise.

However, if any readers are interested in acquiring these DVDs, a word of warning: the picture quality is extremely poor, bordering on unwatchable. At times, it seems the original VHS tape was getting chewed in the machine as it was being transferred to DVD. In many places, the image is completely scrambled, making for a difficult viewing experience. The rest of the time, the quality is acceptable (suffering only from faded colour), but it's still a chore to get through. All copies currently for sale online appear to be from this source. There is always the slim chance of better VHS copies resurfacing, but until that happens (or if there is an official release), this is the only way to view the show.

Yet, we should be grateful that even these copies exist. This isn't the case for many other forgotten failures, such as 'Hot L. Baltimore,' Norman Lear's short-lived 1975 sitcom. Another thirteen-episode obscurity, this program hasn't turned up anywhere in recent years, apart from a 30-second promo online. Unofficial copies have not surfaced, apparently because no one taped the original broadcast in 1975. Internet searches for this series also bring up the inevitable questions about its availability. Thankfully, 'Rafferty' is around in some form for us to view today!

Potential viewers should also keep in mind that 'Rafferty' is not some forgotten gem awaiting rediscovery. It is not a treasure trove of brilliant stories or famous guest stars. It is simply an average TV show that died a quick death, and nothing more. Once someone sees it for themselves, they can finally agree, "Yes, it not that good. I understand now why it didn't last." As a result, it will be a tough sell for the home video market. The obvious selling points are McGoohan's presence and the similarities to 'House', but that might not be enough to reel in potential buyers today.

Still, if several thousand McGoohan fans showed an interest somehow, it might cause the studio to consider a release. A small hope is that the show is owned by Warner Brothers who specialise in the Warner Archive Collection. This consists of MOD (Manufacture-On-Demand) DVDs that are pressed in small quantities according to how many orders are placed. The previously mentioned David Janssen series, 'Harry O' (which is also owned by Warner), was finally released on DVD through the Archive in July 2012. Viewing this set, it's apparent that the series has not undergone any significant remastering. Occasional dirt or graininess is present throughout the episodes, but overall, the picture quality is very good. At least an effort was made to get the best prints from the vaults, and transfer them to DVD to finally make the show available.

'Rafferty' would be an excellent candidate for this program. A prospective release wouldn't need to be very elaborate with extras or deluxe packaging. Most fans would simply be happy with good-quality copies of the thirteen episodes in a three or four-disc set. Anything would be an improvement over the unofficial copies that are floating around. Most importantly, an official release would provide McGoohan fans with a nice opportunity to see him in something "new."

So with 'Rafferty' virtually forgotten by the general public, and the episodes sitting in the vaults with little chance of a future release, the current state of the show's existence can truly be described as one of "no yesterday and no tomorrow." However, that scenario might change with news of an official release (it would be fantastic to update this article one day with such an announcement). In the meantime, the unofficial copies are out there for the truly dedicated to find their way to. Many facets of pop culture are rediscovered and reevaluated through the tenacity of fans, and this obscure footnote to a great actor's career is no exception. For audiences and critics of the time, 'Rafferty' was forgettable; but for admirers of Patrick McGoohan today, it remains essential viewing.

Many thanks to Rick Davy, Lara Dent and Bill King for their assistance during the writing of this article.

SOURCES

PERIODICALS:

Ashkinaze, Carole. "The Best and the Worst." Atlanta Journal-Constitution (September 3, 1977).

Crosby, Joan. "'Rafferty' In Skilful Hands." [Ventura Co.] Press Courier (October 30, 1977).

Freeman, Don. "Patrick McGoohan Explains His Accent." Kingsport [Tennessee] Post (September 1, 1977).

Hano, Arnold. "I'm Always Scared." TV Guide (September 17, 1977).

Harris, Harry. "Morgan Fairchild: Bad and Beautiful." Philadelphia Inquirer (January 4, 1981).

Henry, William A. "Guess Who's Practicing Medicine?" Boston Globe (September 4, 1977).

Jones, Paul. "You Can Get 1st Look At Some New Shows." Atlanta Journal-Constitution (September 5, 1977).

King, Bill. "Patrick McGoohan: An Interview with the Man Behind 'The Prisoner.'" Anglofile Magazine, 1988.

_____. "Return To Stage Is First Step In Reemergence Of Patrick McGoohan." Atlanta Journal-Constitution (April 7, 1985).

Miller, Ron. "Confessions of a TV Editor In 10 Years On the Job..." San Jose Mercury News (September 20, 1987).

O'Connor, John J. "TV: The New Season Is Upon Us." New York Times (September 5, 1977).

Sharbutt, Jay. "Zany Laugh-In Returns Monday." Youngstown [Ohio] Vindicator (September 2, 1977).

Siegel, Ed. "Patrick McGoohan: The Prisoner Has Escaped; Now What?" Boston Globe (January 13, 1985).

Smith, Cecil. "New TV Season Out Of Starting Gate." Los Angeles Times (September 5, 1977).

Tripodi, Jim. "Pink Slip Prescription." Beaver County [Pennsylvania] Times (October 1, 1977).

TV Guide editors. "The Screening Room." TV Guide (September 3, 1977).

Variety editors. "Rafferty" review. Variety (September 7, 1977).

Witbeck, Charles. "McGoohan Is TV's Newest Doctor." Boca Raton News. (September 16, 1977).

BOOKS:

Booth, Rupert. Not a Number: Patrick McGoohan -- A Life. Supernova Books, 2011.

Brooks, Tim and Earle Marsh. The Complete Directory to Prime Time Network and Cable TV Shows (Eighth Ed.). Ballantine Books, 2003.

Castleman, Harry and Walter J. Podrazik. Harry and Wally's Favourite TV Shows. Prentice Hall Press, 1989.

WEBSITES:

www.imdb.com/title/tt0075562 (Internet Movie Database entry on 'Rafferty')

http://ctva.biz/US/Medical/Rafferty.htm (Classic TV Archive entry on 'Rafferty')

www.tvrage.com/shows/id-12678 (TV Rage entry on 'Rafferty')

http://en.wikipedia.org/wiki/House_MD (Wikipedia entry on 'House')

'Rafferty' - An Episode Guide
By Tom Mayer
© 2012

Also Available on the Unmutual Website At: http://theunmutual.co.uk/rafferty2.htm

A Warner Brothers Television Production

Created by James Lee

Executive Producer
Jerry Thorpe

Produced by James Lee, Norman S. Powell and Robert Van Scoyk

Starring:
Patrick McGoohan as Dr. Sidney Rafferty
Millie Slavin as Nurse Vera Wales
and John Getz as Dr. Daniel Gentry

Also starring Joan Pringle as Nurse Beryl Keynes, David Clennon as Dr. Calvin, Craig Wasson as Dr. Furey and Michael C. Gwynne as Dr. Prud'homme.

Each episode is rated according to the following scale:

**** -- Excellent
*** -- Good
** -- Fair
* -- Poor

The episodes are listed in the order of their original US airdates, with the exception of the unaired instalments. I have slotted them in before the final episode, since they were filmed 10th, 11th and 12th respectively. Any memorable scenes involving the series' star have been singled out as a Best McGoohan Moment. Notable appearances by guest stars in other films and TV series have been mentioned as well.
This article is the second of a two-part look at 'Rafferty'.[114]

---

[114] 'For more Information please reread' pages 256-269 (With apologies to Scarfolk Council and it's creator Richard Littler for borrowing their Prisoneresque slogan — scarfolk.blogspot.co.uk)

EPISODE 01:
PILOT (A.K.A. 'RAFFERTY')
Written By James Lee
Directed By Jerry Thorpe
Original US Airdate: September 05, 1977
Production Number: Unknown (most likely the first episode filmed).
Rating: * * *

In the premiere episode of the series, Dr. Sid Rafferty deals with two complicated medical cases over a 24-hour period. After saving the life of a man who was stabbed on a bus during a robbery attempt, Rafferty is threatened with legal action for having performed major surgery on the victim without his (or his wife's) permission. Second, Rafferty tries to convince both a fellow surgeon and a concerned father that a paralysed teenage girl might not need surgery -- she may recover on her own if given time.

This is a good opening episode (written and directed by the program's creators, no less) that sets the tone for the series and illustrates how Rafferty's unconventional style of doctoring sometimes pays off. When Rafferty advises that the girl's operation be postponed, he must contend with protests from the girl's father and his fellow staff, resulting in a solitary stand against what is expected. Eventually, he is proven right when the girl regains movement in her legs the next morning -- just when she was to be operated on. This individualistic streak in Rafferty's character is obviously what appealed to McGoohan when he took on the role.

His performance is solid and confident, yet he seems a bit clipped and quirkier than usual. Perhaps he was still trying to get a handle on the character, or maybe he was already getting uncomfortable with the role this early in the show's production. As a result, casual viewers not accustomed to McGoohan's acting style may have had difficulty warming to the character. However, the writers were smart to give Rafferty several moments where he shows a sympathetic side. First, in several scenes with his secretary, Vera, he slyly acknowledges her obvious attraction to him. Later, he offers to sleep on a chair in the paralysed girl's hospital room to comfort her throughout the night before her surgery.

Being the pilot episode, this instalment doesn't begin with the standard title sequence. Instead, the credits and an alternate version of the theme music are played over a sequence of Rafferty sitting on a bench feeding birds while waiting for the bus. Once Rafferty boards the bus, the man he eventually saves is attacked and stabbed. In an unusual twist, the mugger escapes, and is never referred to again for the rest of the episode. This is a strange oversight to forget a major subplot, as well as to let an obvious criminal go free. Perhaps the writers wanted to establish that the series would not be about solving crimes, but would instead deal with the treatment of Rafferty's patients -- no matter how they end up in his care.

Based on this episode, the series appears to be off to a decent start. The writing is solid with good drama, and genuine respect for the characters. However, the predictable recovery of the paralysed girl shows that the series was not above clichéd melodrama, even this early in its run.

Best McGoohan Moment: when Rafferty is threatened with a $3.8 million lawsuit from an attorney representing the wounded man, McGoohan launches into the following monologue in his inimitable style:

"First of all, there is no insurance company, and second, my bedrock financial worth is the $11,500 a year pension I get as a field grade officer, United States Army. Also, I'm not gettin' rich on my practice, believe it or not. Now, I probably have more faith in the jury system than you, and if ... IF! ... a jury would award you the WHOLE enchilada, it would have to come out of MY hide. Now, an educated guess, I would say that'd be ... let's see ... a hundred dollars a month, until the year 4,000, by which time it wouldn't be one of my pressing problems, now would it?"

Notable guest stars include familiar character actor Richard Herd ('V: The Original Miniseries') as the attorney who gets an earful from Rafferty, and Sam Wanamaker as the girl's father. Wanamaker had guest-starred with McGoohan 17 years earlier in the excellent 1960 Danger Man episode 'The Lonely Chair.'

EPISODE 02: 'BROTHERS AND SONS'
Written by Arthur Heinmann & James Lee
Story by Jerry De Bono
Directed by Barry Crane
Original US Airdate: September 12, 1977
Production No. 166734 (5th filmed)
Rating: **

Rafferty helps an African American family of young siblings who are living alone after the disappearance of their mother. He also attempts to find a donor for a teenage girl needing a kidney transplant. A candidate ends up being her half-brother who was given up for adoption 21 years earlier. He's now a college track star, and a transplant procedure may ruin his chances for a successful sports career.

A forgettable episode, again utilising two separate plot-lines that never come together (many shows of the 1970s and 80s used this device). The story of the missing mother comes to a hurried conclusion in a scene with a group-hug set to some melodramatic music. Rafferty looks rather unmoved.

This is the first episode to feature the standard title sequence. It consists of a single shot of Rafferty walking through a sunny park, intercut with split-second freeze-frames of him taken from the pilot episode. The instrumental theme, by Leonard Rosenman, is heavy on the syrupy strings, reminiscent of "The Theme From A Summer Place" by Percy Faith. Since the premise of the show plays up Rafferty's acerbic, individualistic nature, it's odd that the producers chose such a soft, saccharine piece of music for the theme.

We also see Rafferty's car for the first time -- a 1965 Ford Mustang convertible. At first I thought it was white, but was surprised to hear a character in a later episode describe it as yellow! Apparently, the horrendous picture quality of the DVDs has bleached much colour out of the exterior scenes. Regardless, after John Drake's Mini Cooper and No.6's Lotus Seven, McGoohan thankfully has another decent vehicle to tool around in!

EPISODE 03: 'A POINT OF VIEW'
Written by James Lee
Directed by Alexander Singer
Original US Airdate: September 19, 1977
Production No. 166731 (2nd filmed)
Rating: **

A psychiatrist at Rafferty's hospital is attacked and raped one night in the parking garage. She refuses to report the incident to the police, causing Rafferty to question her motives. Rafferty also befriends a young blind woman who refuses his help in an attempt to restore her eyesight.

An average episode that comes close to being good, but never quite makes it. The major drawback is the predicable conclusions to both storylines. The blind girl (surprise!) gets her sight back, while the psychiatrist's attacker is revealed to be (wait for it!) one of her patients. These are disappointing endings to an otherwise intriguing premise -- that of Rafferty determining why both women will not seek help for their respective misfortunes.

There are memorable moments though. The scene where Rafferty meets Lisa, the blind woman, is amusing. His Mustang stalls at a red light, where she is waiting for a bus. While Rafferty is waving angry motorists around his stalled vehicle, she helps him restart the car by directing him to the loose engine hoses that are causing the trouble. She explains that she learned about engines in the Peace Corps.

It was there that she lost her sight in a bus accident that took the lives of several children. Rafferty surmises that her blindness is hysterical -- a way of punishing herself for the accident. In a dramatic scene on the beach, Rafferty forces Lisa to face that her condition is psychological. She refuses to accept the idea, until the sound of a young girl calling for help in the nearby surf, causes her to have a breakdown. This sequence illustrates how forceful Rafferty can be when trying to help someone in need.

Morgan Fairchild guest stars as Lisa. She's appeared in many films and TV series including 'North and South,' 'Flamingo Road,' 'Falcon Crest' and 'Friends.'

Prisoner fans will get a kick out of the following scenes. First, while at Lisa's oceanfront house, Rafferty asks her if she ever goes swimming:

"I never go in unless I've got someone with me," she says. "Someone, or good old Rover."

"Rover?" says Rafferty surprised.

"My dog." She explains.

"Oh, Rover," Rafferty says, "that's my idea of a name for a dog!"

Later, when Rafferty visits Lisa at her office, he sees the dog sleeping under her desk. "This must be Rover," Rafferty deadpans, while petting him. "A really ferocious-lookin' beast!"

EPISODE 04: 'THE CUTTING EDGE'
Written by John Meredyth Lucas
Directed by Barry Crane
Original US Airdate: September 26, 1977
Production No. 166732 (3rd filmed)
Rating: ***

This instalment features three parallel plot lines, each given equal time. First, Rafferty zeros in on a possible neurological disorder in Victor Ehren, a concert violinist; second, Dan Gentry's girlfriend, Ellen, is diagnosed with a terminal disease; and third, a young singer's manager/husband gives her cocaine after an operation, causing Rafferty to throw him out of the hospital -- resulting in the husband slapping Rafferty with a lawsuit.

A very good episode featuring one of McGoohan's best outings as 'Rafferty'. Much of the cantankerous, quirky demeanour of past episodes is gone, replaced with a relaxed, enjoyable performance. For once, Rafferty seems happy to be at the hospital, and McGoohan seems happy to be on the set. Still, the occasional weak melodrama creeps in. The scenes of Dan breaking the news to his girlfriend about her disease (as well as a visit to the zoo to cheer her up) are somewhat mawkish; while Rafferty's advice to Janis, the singer, seems forced, as he tells her to live life on her own terms. Regardless, the episode overall, is a fine effort, and would have benefitted the series if it had been broadcast second. Coming directly after the Pilot, it would have made a stronger introduction to the show, rather than 'Brothers And Sons' or 'A Point Of View.'

The opening sequence at the symphony (where Rafferty picks up on Ehren's condition) is well directed, and is a nice departure from beginning a story with another medical emergency. Likewise, the end of the episode contains a charming scene with McGoohan, Slavin and Getz. The three characters are standing in an empty hospital hallway at the end of the day. They share a few words and Rafferty offers to take them out for coffee. He puts his arms around them and, in a long shot, they slowly walk down the hall. It's a nice sequence that quietly reflects their friendship and respect. It's rare that we get to see the three of them together like this.

Best McGoohan Moments: while scrubbing up for an operation, a fellow doctor asks, "You assaulted your patient's husband? Threw him in an elevator!?" Not missing a beat, Rafferty replies, "Couldn't find an open window." (This line is doubly amusing decades later, in light of McGoohan's most memorable scene in 'Braveheart.') Later, Janis is impressed with Rafferty's personality. "I love the way you talk. You went to college, didn't ya?" she asks. "Yeah, I'm still goin,'" Rafferty deadpans.

McGoohan also manages to quote a phrase from his past when he visits an old lawyer friend. She claims he didn't say goodbye after their last meeting. Rafferty replies, "No I didn't -- I remember the exact words. I said, 'Be seeing you.' And here I am, seeing you!"

Peter Donat guest stars as Victor Ehren. A familiar character actor, he appeared in The 'Godfather Part 2', 'Rich Man, Poor Man', and 'The X-Files' (as Fox Mulder's father). Writer John Meredyth Lucas had a successful career behind the scenes in US television from the 1950s through the 70s. He produced, wrote and directed for many shows including 'Star Trek,' 'The Fugitive,' 'The Six Million Dollar Man,' 'Logan's Run' and 'Harry O.'

During the scene where Rafferty throws out Janis's husband, a cover version of Van Morrison's 'Wild Night' is blasting from a radio. Due to many instances of pop songs being replaced when programs come out on home video, one wonders if this music will be intact if Rafferty is ever officially released on DVD.

EPISODE 05:
'THE NARROW THREAD'
Teleplay by Robert C. Dennis
Story by Anthony Lawrence
Directed by Barry Crane
Original U.S. Airdate: October 03, 1977
Production No. 166735 (6th filmed)
Rating: *

A pregnant flight attendant fears she may have received radiation poisoning from secret cargo stored on a recent flight she was on. Rafferty offers to help, by calling on a government contact from his army days to investigate. Meanwhile a grumpy, handicapped cartoonist and a deaf orphan form an unlikely bond while sharing a room at City General Hospital.

This episode is 'Rafferty' at its worst -- one of the "monstrous pieces of garbage" McGoohan mentioned. It's tedious viewing from start to finish. The scenes with Byron Murray, the cartoonist, interacting with Dewey, the orphan, seem like they're from another show entirely -- an insipid sitcom at that. Murray's exasperation over learning that Dewey will be his roommate is cringe-inducing. Later, they become fast friends while a syrupy score plays in the background. Eventually, they end up racing wheelchairs down the hospital hallways. Murray crashes into a food cart and tumbles to the floor -- just in time to have Rafferty and Dewey's case worker arrive, and stand there exchanging looks on a long fade out to a merciful commercial break. For once, we can understand exactly why McGoohan hated this show so much.

His clipped, high-pitched voice is back in force during several awkward scenes where he yells at Dewey to get the boy to understand him. As a result, Rafferty is the only one who communicates with Dewey throughout the episode -- apparently, no other character knows how to raise their voice. The poor guy's gotta do everything around here...

The subplot of Rafferty contacting his government agent friend is an interesting angle, with shades of 'Secret Agent'. Rafferty saved the man's injured leg in combat, so to cash in on the debt, he's asking for information on the radioactive cargo. Several mysterious phone calls, and an unofficial meeting in a park add to the "spy" atmosphere. However, the storyline barely registers any screen time and is thus undeveloped. This is unfortunate, because it shows how characters and events from Rafferty's past could have been utilised for a number of storylines.

On the unofficial DVDs that are in circulation, this episode contains some of the worst picture quality of the entire series. The image loses colour, gets scrambled and freezes for several seconds at a time, making viewing difficult for an already weak episode.

EPISODE 06: 'THE EPIDEMIC'
Written by David P. Lewis
Directed by Barry Crane
Original U.S. Airdate: October 17, 1977
Production No. 166736 (7th filmed)
Rating: ***

City General Hospital ends up with several cases of what is initially assumed to be a polio epidemic. Rafferty finds out that it is really botulism (food poisoning), and he sets out to discover the source before more people end up sick. He interviews the victims' families to find out where (and what) they have eaten the past few days, but comes up empty. He eventually surmises that perhaps they didn't go to the food, but rather the food came to them. A local catering van is found to be responsible.

A well-paced episode that features Rafferty as both doctor and detective. Like 'The Pilot' and 'The Cutting Edge,' this is another example of how the producers could come up with a decent story when they tried. While hardly a groundbreaking hour of television, it is nonetheless well written and suspenseful enough to keep the viewer engaged. Most importantly, it contains a good combination of scenes with 'Rafferty' both in and out of the hospital. It's too bad more episodes couldn't have maintained this quality and balance.

McGoohan turns in another good performance -- nicely understated, yet forceful enough to convey Rafferty's awareness of the severity of the situation. With all the investigating and legwork he and Vera undertake in this episode, they could open a detective agency as well! In an amusing scene, Rafferty (who needs a court order to administer an anti-toxin) barges into the office of a judge who owes him a favour. When the judge tells him he has to wait, Rafferty shoots back, "You didn't have to wait when you came to me that night with a broken finger. You needed a doctor, now I need a judge!"

The final scene is one of the most memorable of the series, as Rafferty races to a practice field to prevent members of a marching band from eating the contaminated food. As the band breaks for lunch, the kids run toward the van and Rafferty's Mustang speeds into the parking lot. He screeches to a stop, jumps out, and runs to the van a second before the kids arrive. As he blocks their way, the scene freezes, the picture fades out, and the story is over just like that. I've never seen an episode of television end so abruptly.

Guest stars include Bonnie Bartlett ('V: The Original Miniseries,' 'St. Elsewhere,' 'Firefly') as a nurse at City General; and familiar character actor James Karen ('Wall Street', 'Mulholland Drive') as a smarmy real estate agent giving Vera a hard time. Edward James Olmos ('Miami Vice,' 'Battlestar Galactica') has a small role as either a doctor or an ambulance driver. He's somewhere in a group of hospital staff wheeling the first victim into the emergency room, but it's difficult to identify him due to the poor picture quality.

EPISODE 07: 'THE WILD CHILD'
Written by Sue Milburn
Directed by Patrick McGoohan
Original U.S. Airdate: October 31, 1977
Production No. 166733 (4th filmed)
Rating: ***

On a bus ride home from an out-of-town trip, Rafferty ends up staying overnight in the small town of Indigo to help an injured girl. He eventually discovers a screaming teenage boy, Bobby Dane, locked in a shack behind his parents' house. The town's residents believe the boy is possessed, and have asked a local minister to perform an exorcism. After receiving information from Dr. Gentry back in LA, Rafferty learns that Bobby is suffering from Tourette's Syndrome (involuntary screaming and twitching). With the mother's permission, Rafferty attempts to take the boy back to the hospital for tests -- but the father has strong objections about his son leaving.

This is Rafferty's most unique and memorable episode. First, it is successful in getting 'Rafferty' out of the hospital for almost the entire hour -- something that McGoohan was no doubt pleased with. This story most likely fit in perfectly with his "roving doctor" image of the character. Second, the fact that McGoohan directed this episode is the big draw here. For someone who always preferred to have as much input in the productions he worked on, he no doubt jumped at the chance to direct when possible.

Of the many episodes of television he directed, from his first 'Danger Man' in 1960 to his final 'Columbo' in 2000, his style could change from surreal (The Prisoner's 'Fall Out'), to quirky (Columbo's 'Last Salute To The Commodore'), to traditional and direct (Secret Agent's 'To Our Best Friend,' The Prisoner's 'Many Happy Returns'). 'The Wild Child,' definitely falls into the latter category. Any viewer expecting a heady mix of surrealism and allegory will be disappointed.

Instead, McGoohan tells the story in the most straightforward way possible. His direction is smooth and doesn't call attention to itself. He succeeds in establishing a mood of alienation, first as Rafferty explores the town and encounters resistance from the residents who won't discuss Bobby's condition; and later, as he tries to convince everyone that the boy's symptoms are purely medical.

Yet, several notable moments stand out. The first being when Rafferty initially hears the boy's far-off screams coming from the shack -- there is a definite moment of unease. Later, when Rafferty introduces himself to Bobby in an attempt to calm him down, the boy begins screaming again. Rafferty repeats in monotone over the yelling, "Let it out ... let it out. You can stop it, Bobby!", all while trying to diagnose his condition. Both scenes create an eerie, uncomfortable mood that is enhanced by a unique piano and synthesiser score.

Another good sequence is when Rafferty makes his way to the town's empty church, and twice debates with the local minister; first about Bobby's condition, and later, over whether the minister is qualified to carry out an exorcism.

The only misstep is toward the end, once Rafferty tries to convince Bobby's father that the boy should go to the hospital. The story falls into the clichéd, predictable conflict of Rafferty's "modern" medical diagnosis clashing with the "old fashioned" religious views of the father.

Best McGoohan Moment: the woman who runs the local general store tells Rafferty he won't have any more food or a place to stay, and must leave town. Rafferty slowly walks behind the store counter commenting, "Is that the way ya usually treat people in Indigo? Ya starve 'em out, or uh ... exorcise them!" he exclaims, hitting the cash register, causing the bell to ring and the drawer to slam open.

Rafferty's outfit is also memorable. He sports a blue and white striped dress shirt, with a grey fedora. It's a unique appearance that further sets him apart from the town that sees him as an outsider.

Guest stars include K Callen (Martha Kent from 'Lois And Clark: The New Adventures Of Superman') as Bobby's mother, and Richard Sanders (Les Nessman from 'WKRP' In Cincinnati) as the town minister.

EPISODE 08: 'WILL TO LIVE'
Teleplay by Sue Milburn
Story by Arthur Joel Katz and Sue Milburn
Directed by Edward H. Feldman
Original U.S. Airdate: November 07, 1977
Production No. 166737 (8th filmed)
Rating: **

Rafferty's secretary, Vera, ends up in the hospital with a viral infection that causes her protein levels to spike. When a fellow doctor prescribes too many painkillers instead of searching for a cure, Rafferty objects. He elects to take Vera home and care for her himself. He eventually realises that she is hiding behind her illness to avoid her life. Meanwhile, Dr. Furey wants to perform an appendectomy on a young woman, but runs into resistance from Dr. Calvin who believes it may be an ovarian disease.

This episode is a mixed bag. While it's an interesting premise to have Vera sick and vulnerable, she acts too out of character. For such a strong person, she gives up too easily, wanting to die by the end of the story. Also puzzling is Rafferty's complete rejection of all hospital care, in favour of taking Vera home. While it's a credit to the writers for presenting a "natural" health treatment (as opposed to pumping a patient full of drugs), you'd think 'Rafferty' would at least exhaust all hospital options before taking Vera home.

McGoohan gives a capable performance, showing enough concern for Vera's condition, yet still keeping Rafferty's aloof distance. Most of his scenes are with Millie Slavin, and it's apparent that the two enjoy each other's company. Slavin's performance works in the frustration she shows of someone in the medical profession being confined to bed as a patient (along with trying to out-guess Rafferty at what he's thinking while treating her). As Rafferty comments, "Nurses make the worst cases. Uncooperative, embarrassed by any sign of weakness -- and fearful."

There's a nice moment during the night when Vera is anxious and can't fall asleep. She asks Rafferty if he knows any songs. After some hesitance, he proceeds to circle the room talking/singing, "I Belong to Glasgow" in a Scottish brogue. McGoohan's "singing" in this scene is reminiscent of his similar duet with Alexis Kanner on "God Rest Ye Merry Gentleman" in Kings And Desperate Men, filmed the same year.

The subplot of Dr. Calvin and Dr. Furey's debate over the latter's patient is forgettable, but it leads to a memorable line by Dr. Calvin. When Furey is performing the appendectomy (with Rafferty's blessing), Calvin quips to McGoohan, "Your disciple is doing his 'Rafferty' imitation -- damn the torpedoes and full speed ahead!"

EPISODE 09: 'WALKING WOUNDED'
Written by James Lee
Directed by Arnold Laven
Original U.S. Airdate: November 14, 1977
Production No. 166738 (9th filmed)
Rating: ***

Mike Bakersmith, a young doctor Rafferty knows, quits his position at the hospital and soon injures himself in a hang-gliding accident. After hearing him lament about his perceived failure in becoming a world-renowned surgeon (along with plans for more risky hobbies), Rafferty surmises that Bakersmith might be suicidal. Meanwhile, a policeman with a bullet lodged near his spine is informed by Rafferty that, after seven years, the area is now infected and an operation must be performed to remove the bullet. Finally, Rafferty discovers that a teenaged gymnast is suffering from anorexia nervosa, which is threatening both her physical and emotional well-being.

A good episode -- nothing brilliant, but no cringe-inducing scenes either. The three storylines are equally balanced throughout the hour, while McGoohan turns in another nice performance. If the series had maintained this quality, McGoohan might've been happier and the series could've lasted longer. Again, it's too bad this episode didn't air earlier in the run. For casual viewers, it would have made a better introduction to the series.

The subplot of a policeman in pain due a bullet in his back is yet another striking similarity to the David Janssen series 'Harry O,' also produced by Jerry Thorpe. The premise of the show was that Harry made his living as a private eye, and often lived in pain due to a bullet lodged near his spine -- the result of a shootout that caused him to retire from the police force. James Lee must have written this story as a nod to his executive producer's previous series.

Ron Rifkin ('Husbands And Wives,' 'LA Confidential,' 'Alias') guest-stars as Dr. Bakersmith. And, believe it or not, there's a direct connection between 'The Prisoner' and the 1986 hit song 'Take My Breath Away.' The young gymnast in this episode is played by 16-year-old Terri Nunn, later the lead singer of the pop group Berlin. She began her career as an actress, appearing in other late-seventies/early eighties programmes such as 'Lou Grant,' 'Vega$' and 'TJ Hooker.'

EPISODE 10:
'NO YESTERDAY AND NO TOMORROW'
Teleplay by James Menzies
Story by Rift Fournier
Directed by Arnold Laven
Original U.S. Airdate: Never aired.
Production No. 166739 (10th filmed)
Rating: ***

After blacking out while driving, a man (Paul Bennett) is reluctant to submit to hospital tests or to divulge any medical history to Dr. Gentry. It turns out that Bennett and his wife are in the Witness Protection Program after having testified against a mobster wanted for embezzlement. The government agents guarding Bennett believe that any investigation into his medical past by Dr. Gentry will endanger Bennett's cover. However, Bennett is in need of brain surgery due to an aneurysm, and any time spent postponing the operation brings him closer to death.

This is a very good episode that belongs to John Getz, taking over the lead as Dr. Dan Gentry (as a special title at the beginning informs us). He does an excellent job, carrying the story with a relaxed and likeable air. He does his best to help his patient, while dealing with the federal agents who are overprotective of their star witness. Getz is so good, in fact, that the series could have continued with him as the star after McGoohan moved on. We get an intriguing hint that the show (with some retooling) could have come back as Gentry -- and might have worked.

In an amusing lack of continuity between stories, this episode finds Dan happily flirting with a new lady in his life. He bounced back awfully fast from his last girlfriend, who was diagnosed with a terminal disease just six episodes ago!

McGoohan is gone for most of the hour, thus making this episode the 'Rafferty' equivalent of 'Do Not Forsake Me, Oh My Darling.' He has a brief scene in the beginning however, when Rafferty breaks the news to a nervous patient that his excruciating foot pain is being caused by a "classic case" of ... gout.

James B. Sikking ('Hill Street Blues;' 'Star Trek III') guest-stars as one of the government agents.

EPISODE 11: 'THE PRICE OF PAIN'
Written by John Meredyth Lucas
Directed by Arnold Laven
Original U.S. Airdate: Never aired.
Production No. 166740 (11th filmed)
Rating: *

'Rafferty' saves the life of an actress after her car overturns. During her hospital stay, the police become suspicious about the source of her past pain medication, causing Rafferty to think she may be a drug addict. Meanwhile, a nurse's aide from the hospital finds a young woman badly beaten in the park. Once under Rafferty's care, the victim remains in a coma with her identity still unknown.

Another "monstrous piece of garbage." Just when the series looked like it was improving, it stumbles with another weak outing. The premises of both stories are acceptable, but the entire production suffers from dull writing and direction in another hospital-bound episode. McGoohan seems uninterested in the proceedings. He plays 'Rafferty' at his most clipped and cantankerous. His performance must be seen to be believed. The rhythm of many scenes is off-kilter, as he takes his time with several strange pauses and inflections in his delivery, while the rest of the cast appear to hurry through their lines. The awkward pacing and seriousness with which the actors treat such weak material, seems tailor-made for comedy treatment by the likes of 'Mystery Science Theater 3000.'

In a nice bit of continuity, the nurse's aide (Melissa) who finds the woman in the park, was first seen in 'The Epidemic,' impressing a nurse with how knowledgeable she was about the hospital disaster manual.

Best McGoohan Moment: when a police sergeant accuses Rafferty of interfering with the law, Rafferty shoots back, "Me, interfering with the law? With a name like Rafferty!? I grew up with half the police force having Sunday lunch in our kitchen! You were interfering with a patient!"

Bruce Kirby plays the sergeant. He appeared in many episodes of 'Columbo,' including two of McGoohan's best as guest-murderer and director: 'Identity Crisis' (1975) and 'Agenda For Murder' (1990).

EPISODE 12: 'THE BURNING MAN'
Written by Sue Milburn
Directed by Barry Crane
Original U.S. Airdate: Never aired.
Production No. 166741 (12th filmed)
Rating: **

While fighting a raging wildfire, several Native American firemen fall ill. Rafferty travels to the firefighter's camp where he discovers they are suffering from pneumonic plague. He attempts to treat them, but meets resistance from both the Indians and the other firefighters.

Another average, yet forgettable episode. Like 'A Point Of View,' the story has a good premise, but misses the mark by not knowing in which direction to go. The Indians helping the firefighters seem to want to rebel against them several times; there are references made to the Indians having been forced off their land in the recent past; and the head firefighter angrily tries to do things his way in fighting the blaze. This includes leaving Rafferty stranded overnight at the Indians' house -- right in the path of the fire! All of this results in a muddled episode. It's a shame too, since the subplots logically grow out of the main story of the wildfire. This is a nice departure from the usual two-to-three unrelated subplots per episode.

'Rafferty' (and by extension, McGoohan) again seems bored. At this point in the show's production, he was probably fed up and ready to move on. A plus, however, is that Rafferty gets out of the hospital again. Writer Sue Milburn (who also penned 'The Wild Child') must have known about McGoohan's "roving doctor" idea, so she made an effort to craft such episodes accordingly.

There are a few notable moments. After confirming that the ill victims are suffering from the plague, a firefighter says, "The plague went out with the Dark Ages." Rafferty snaps back, "We're still in the Dark Ages!"
Later, an elderly Indian woman lets Rafferty treat a sick man after her natural medicine has failed:
"Does your medicine always work?" he asks.
"No," she replies. "Does yours?"
"No." Rafferty admits. "We haven't come far, have we?"

And when a young Indian man continually refuses Rafferty's help in treating his illness, Rafferty remarks, "You're one of the most stubborn men I've ever met. You sure you're not half-Irish?"

EPISODE 13:
'DEATH OUT OF A BLUE SKY'
Written by Robert Van Scoyk
Directed by Barry Crane
Original US Airdate: November 28, 1977 (Final episode aired)
Production No. 166742 (13th and final episode filmed)
Rating: * * *

After the husband of one of his patients dies in a single-engine plane crash, Rafferty begins an investigation into the cause of the accident. Was it health-related or suicide? All clues point to the latter, since the man's business was failing and he seemed despondent. Meanwhile, a pushy insurance agent threatens to withhold paying the widow if the reason turns out to be suicide. Rafferty, however, persists in believing the cause was medical.

Things take a bit of an upward swing for the final episode. The only story written by co-producer Robert Van Scoyk, it is a confident, capable instalment, that shows the amount of unused potential the series had. While hardly brilliant, the hour is full of decent drama, with an intriguing mystery to boot. As in 'The Epidemic,' Rafferty takes on the role of detective, thus getting him out of the hospital again. Except for two brief scenes at City General, Rafferty spends the episode either outdoors, or visiting several fine houses (much like Lt. Columbo, who you keep expecting 'Rafferty' to bump into at any moment). As a result, this is one of the more visually unique episodes of the series. It makes one realise how claustrophobic the hospital corridors become after a while.

Another plus is the presence of only one story, without other subplots to distract from it. In real life, a doctor probably wouldn't concern himself with such an investigation (the man has already died, after all), but for the purpose of this episode, it works. This is another candidate for the "roving doctor" premise -- McGoohan was definitely on to a good idea. It's too bad the series couldn't have continued in this vein.

McGoohan goes out on a good note acting-wise. He plays Rafferty quiet and determined, only resorting to his high-pitched, clipped delivery a few times -- usually when annoyed or trying to prove a point. Next to 'The Cutting Edge' and 'Walking Wounded' this is one of his better performances. It makes for a fitting end to the series.

SECTION D
FILED UNDER: INTO THE UNKNOWABLE:

Free Form
What to make of 'Fall Out.'
Absurd Conclusions,
The Jailbird -
'Out of Order' Part 1
Concludes, Final Part of 'Looking
Out For Number One', A New
Vision of 'The Prisoner' &
Conclusions : Can We
'Understand' — 'The Prisoner'?

Free Form
What to make of 'Fall Out.' By Jez Winship.
Absurd Conclusions

Its radical abandonment of traditional narrative structure and refusal to offer neat conclusions or some overarching explicatory rationale to round things off annoyed the hell out of many viewers. It resembled some of the science fiction being published in 'New Worlds magazine' at the time under the tutelage of Michael Moorcock and his merry band of rebels, taking generic conventions and inverting them, cutting them up and rearranging them in new and kaleidoscopic configurations. Inner space was the new destination, the controls set for the heart of the collective unconscious, cruising above the media landscape and confronting the spectres of modernist alienation rather than the aliens of outer space fiction. There's something of the playfully revolutionary jouissance of the Jerry Cornelius stories, written by Moorcock and other hands and featuring the Harlequinesque anti-hero who was something of a New Worlds house character, to the seemingly chaotic free for all of

this grand folly of a finale. Entirely apposite, then, that the novelisation of 'The Prisoner,' published in 1969, was written by a stalwart of the New Worlds scene, Thomas Disch. His own highly cerebral, witty, absurdist novel 'Camp Concentration,' serialised in New Worlds in 1967 and published in 1968,

Photo courtesy of Rick Davy

had a definite air of 'The Prisoner' about it.

The title itself could be interpreted in any number of ways, and hints at the way language itself is toyed with, dissected and punningly reassembled to probe new meanings, in the last two episodes. It could indicate the radioactive devastation of nuclear fallout; or it could be a falling out of love, something which the general public certainly experienced in the wake of the final episode; a falling out of favour; the tumbling out of some environment or vehicle; or the outcome or after effect of some momentous event. So the very choice of title breathes ambiguity and a multiple set of possible meanings. Nothing is fixed, everything is open and fluid, inviting a personal response, a direct and active engagement. It's really the perfect form with which to finish the series. The viewer is not directed, there is no imposed message; Merely a succession of suggestive pointers, symbols, archetypes and associative triggers which invite the viewer to make their own connections, to unspool their own thread through the labyrinth. It's a free improvisation, written in a burst of intense and fevered creativity by Patrick McGoohan, the structure forming in its own arc of burning creation; A Pink Floyd 'UFO Club' freak out or 'Coltrane Ayler' blast, communing with the divine fire or with some inner core of self-immolating spirit. In keeping with this spirit, I will follow the freeform line wheresoever it might lead me, allowing it to spark whatever connections and flaring associations light up my brain. Tune in, turn on, fall out.

A funereal organ plays as we are guided through a recap of the previous episode, this singular 'previously on...' convention introduced to make the continuity between Once Upon A Time and Fall Out apparent. The 'till death do us part' zero sum game is condensed into a couple of highly charged minutes, the seven ages of man played out briefly on the notional stage, stripped of all but significant or emotionally resonant props. A spare setting for the psychodramatic duel played out in the arena of inner space. Such staging would be taken to its ultimate filmic conclusion in Lars Von Trier's 'Dogville,' houses and streets delineated by lines drawn on bare boards.   The influence of the theatre of the absurd seems apparent here, of playwrights like Eugene Ionesco, Harold Pinter and Samuel Beckett. Minimal props (two dustbins, a single bare tree) paring external reality to its essence; circular, sparring dialogue used as power play, actual meaningful communication frequently devolving into fragmented and nonsensical anti-language; a similar breakdown in logic and the accepted moral order; and a general air of universality, unanchored to specific time or place. These are internal stages upon which the eternal dramas of the human condition are played out, often with a nod and a wink, an antic aspect and dark, gallows humour which sticks two fingers up at whoever is in charge of the whole mess, whoever is Number One.

Absurdism was a popular artistic mode in countries oppressed by authoritarian regimes. The existential condition could easily be translated into the political. Vaclav Havel's plays from the 1960 were filled with absurdism and one of the finest films of the Czech 'New Wave cinema', which flourished in the brief Prague Spring before the Soviet tanks rolled in during 1968, Jan Nemec's 'The Party and the Guests, 'is distinctly 'Prisoner'-like in its mood. Protagonists of absurdist dramas, generally of lowly state and lacking appreciable power or agency, struggle to find meaning in a world which seems almost comically arbitrary and full of cruel irony. They seldom succeed in their quest. Some come to accept that this is the fundamental nature of the universe and adjust their perspective and expectations accordingly. Or not. A paradigmatic scene occurs at the end of Samuel Beckett's 'Waiting for Godot.' The two Chaplinesque (or Keatonesque?) clowns debate the practicalities of hanging themselves on the single bleak tree which has been the central focus of the spartan theatrical landscape throughout. One of them removes his belt for the purpose. His trousers fall down. Ya gotta laugh.

So, Number 2 lies dead in the shipping container bedsit prison, the steel shutter slamming shut with conclusive finality. A book loudly closed. In this Seven Ages of Man scenario, he was tricked into taking on the final role, a transference with fatal consequence. A deadly fall out. The smooth-headed surveillance 'eye' from the control room asks Number 6 "what do you desire?" A highly suggestive question with hints of fairy tale wizardry. Be careful what you wish for. No.6 wishes to meet No.1. "I'll take you," he is told, and they walk out of the room, past the red 'doomsday' countdown clock, it's hands set in the midnight position.

The titles are a variant on the repetitive norm, the reiterated words of defiance followed by the mocking laughter of authority. A circling aerial shot celebrates the eccentric architectural hodge-podge of Portmeirion, and its equally eccentric architect, Clough Williams-Ellis, is thanked (with a free advertisement for The Hotel Portmeirion – you too can come and stay in The Village). A different, looser take on Ron Grainer's theme emphasises heavy bass brass, creating an atmosphere of ominous anticipation. Alexis Kanner's credit is boxed, making it look like a calling card. Look out for him, Patrick McGoohan is saying. As the circling gyre narrows, we home in on the dome of Number 2's residence, at which point Patrick McGoohan's writing and directing credit is superimposed on the screen. We are spiralling in to the heart of the maze, to the secret chamber within which the mystery of power, of the ultimate authority will be revealed. Or so we might innocently assume.

In the lift to the underworld. Close ups of the faces of the scrutiniser and the butler are like masks of fixed solemnity. Number 6, in contrast, has a mildly sardonic turn to his lips, a refusal to take this funereal parade with the same level of gravity. He has become aware of the essential absurdity of the environment in which he has found himself. To accept it on its own terms, to accede to the hierarchical structure it has created, would be to become a part of it, to cease questioning and seeking to uncover and ultimately destroy the power which underlies it. His shadow is cast on steel doors as they slide apart; the divided self, 'the schizoid man'. Beyond are two portable clothes racks hung with shivering, clacking coat hangers. They are like surrealist objets trouvées, the kind of suggestive sculptures made from everyday artefacts that are lent a sinister or uncanny air by a focus on their form or likeness to other forms, their utility de-emphasised; Duchamp's bicycle wheel or Max Ernst's vacuum cleaner (later appropriated by Frank Zappa). At the end of the corridor they form, a pallid plaster-cast dummy wearing Number 6's civvies. "We thought you'd be happier as yourself," the scrutiniser says in a hollow, machine-like voice. It's the first hint at an instability, a hollowness at the heart of Number 6. The costumes of the Village pageant, the guises he has put on in the course of his enforced role on its artificially bright stage, have all been put away. He is left with the rather austere clothing of the self. No hint of holiday camp jollity, adventure story regalia or Western cowboy gear here. What is the self we are left with when the dressing-up box is put away?

The white-faced dummy looks tense, hunched, with a lurching gait. Together with its broad forehead and dangling, apelike arms, it has the bearing of Frankenstein's pitiful creature, sundered from its contemptuous father-creator at its unnatural birth and stumbling blindly through a hostile world, prone to exploitation by manipulative forces offering the semblance of friendship. The camera zooms in on this mocking dummy, the kind of effigy carried in procession before being burned in a ritual blaze. Number 6's shadow stands beside it for a brief instant before it merges with this pale self. The black and the white, the shadow and the light. We shall see this motif repeated shortly. A close-up of the dummy's head, and we see Number 6's hand reach for the neck as if to throttle it. A hint of self-negation, of an aspect of the hidden self which needs to be eliminated? Shadows of revelations to come. This implicit gesture of violence, momentary though it is (the hand, after a brief hesitation, moves down to unbutton the 'casual' shirt) heralds the fanfare of the French national anthem, leading in to the Beatles 'All You Need Is Love.' From the very outset its use is highly ironic.

More doors slide open (this is an underground lair with a proliferation of sliding doors) revealing Number 6 in his grey everyman suit, the institutional grey of the steely corridors. We process through a rocky corridor whose geological nooks are filled with an installation of jukeboxes, all seemingly playing the Beatles anthem, beamed to the world via communication satellite on 25th June 1967. The jukeboxes make for an incongruously sleek chrome and glass, neon-illuminated presence in these chthonic corridors; the natural and artificial set in uneasy juxtaposition. The shaky, hand-held camera, which gives an air of 'cinema verité' immediacy, zooms in on the jukeboxes, isolating them as pop art objects, signifiers of primary coloured space-age consumerism. The culture of the future NOW. Oddly enough, none of the songs glimpsed remotely conjures the spirit of the psychedelic age, the summer of love now 50 years distant as I am writing. One which particularly catches the eye is Al Jolson, the embodiment of minstrelsy, the black-face entertainments whose grotesque stereotyping of African-American performers were being torn to shreds by the fierce rhetoric of black power revolutionaries.

At the end of the rocky corridor, an imposing wooden door with massive, rust-aged lock. A door heavy with the weight and mass of immemorial power and authority, only to be opened by those entrusted with the impressively sized key. This in close proximity to the array of juke boxes, surface modernity co-existing with a super-structure of unchanging tradition. Britain was never very good at 'going modern', as the artist Paul Nash put it. There was always likely to be a foundation of romantic, pre-modern antiquity beneath the sleek, silvery façade. The old guard remained in control, despite surface appearances. And the Butler, of course, is ready with the key, opening the way into the underworld.

On the other side of the door, an illuminated sign reading Well Come. Words cracked apart, new meaning created, as in classic proto-absurdist writings such as 'Alice in Wonderland' and the nonsense poetry of Edward Lear (whose 'Incidents in the Life of My Uncle Arly' had been filmed to memorably haunting effect by Peter Cook and Dudley Moore in the company of John Lennon; Cook also making a daffily distracted and hyperactive white rabbit in Jonathan Miller's 1966 BBC play of 'Alice'). Here, the open greeting becomes a testy command as well as another reference to 'wellness', mental stability. The large cavern we enter is like a parody of a James Bond villain's lair. All bustling activity amongst clearly distinguished groups of functionaries. The disposable minions. Clusters of stalactites hang down like swords of Damocles in racked arrays, or inverted rows of rockets ready for launching. The whole idea of a subterranean rocket base draws on the experimental laboratories set up by the Nazis in the hollowed out caverns of the Mittelwerk complex under Kohnstein Mountain in central Germany, near Nordhausen. It was here that V2 rockets were built and tested, technology co-opted by the Americans after the war, leading to intercontinental ballistic missile capability (and the Apollo missions leading to the first Moon landing which led to the modernist, techno-utopian space age dreaming of the 60s). The NORAD (North American Air Defense Command) base was installed in a complex beneath Cheyenne Mountain in the 1960s, becoming fully functional in 1967 (the year that McGoohan wrote 'Fall Out') and housing aerial surveillance and space defence facilities.

The cavern is full of bustling activity, but there seem to be distinct areas, zones of designated purpose. Medics in green gowns attend to clusters of clinical equipment, scientists in lab coat robes fine tune the dials of imposing banks of electronic control units; 60s computers the size of cathedral organs whose executive capacity could now be condensed onto a hand held device. And mobile cadres of military police, their uniforms having a distinctly American cut. National guardsmen on call to protect the people against themselves. All the stratified elements of a technocratic society.

The echoing 4:4 tympani of marching military manoeuvres segues seamlessly into the rippling applause of a robed and masked gathering, figures ranked in raked seating. The camera's panning glide combined with this sonic splicing makes a clear connection between armed force and this occult, masonic judiciary; the secret cult of the elite, those born to power. The masks worn by this select order are split into black and white divisions, happy/sad turns of the smiling or downcast mouth. The theatrical masks of comedy and tragedy combined, the one containing the other. This is the theatre of the absurd, after all, where we laugh at the tragic madness inherent in the human condition, at the tautological justifications of power, control and oppression in the name of freedom, happiness and peace. The black and white divisions betoken a simple-minded dualism, an us and them worldview which creates the conditions for conflict and authoritarian 'mutuality'.

The masks give the robed individuals a universalised lack of identity, freedom from the burden of the self. They are reduced to singular types, the fixed and unresponsive face of authority. Approval or opprobrium — the masks offer both. The raised or downturned thumb, according to whim or expediency. Desktop name blocks assign particular areas of control or scrutiny, ranging from specific groups of people to more notional social and philosophical concepts or movements. Direct control and mind control, the baton and the gun combined with the treatise, headline-courting speech and propaganda broadcast. The first three we see are 'welfare,' 'pacifists' and 'activists'. Elements of the liberal agenda and world view which must be allowed a certain degree of expression and purchase, but not permitted to take root too firmly and thus grow beyond the compass of control. There's a vagueness about these blanket terms too, which makes them useful tools. When language loses its definition, its precision of meaning, it can be used to evade responsibility and accountability. Amorphous and malleable language can be formed into a weapon, broad terminology honed and sharpened into an insulting dart aimed at an opponent. 'Pacifist' and 'activist' as reductive, dismissive shorthand for 'troublemaker,' 'malcontent,' 'enemy'; 'welfare' as 'dependency,' 'weakness,' 'burden'. The echoes of 'All You Need Is Love' fade away, dying into the rocky crevasses of the age-old chamber. Power is deep rooted, geologically embedded. Its tinny strains in this environment make the ideals of pacifism and activism seem hollow, without any substantial grounding. Flowers in gun barrels are unlikely to make any impact here.

The overseeing eye, the central, orange alerting scrutiniser, puts on his own robe with an economical, flapping crispness of gesture and affixes his concealing mask. His identity, such as it is, is willingly subsumed. He will be identified as 'identification' itself, taking his place next to 'therapy,' 'reactionists' and 'nationalists'. The latter qualities forms of madness requiring therapeutic 'readjustment,' in the manner of Soviet dissidents silenced with treatments in mental hospitals.

A wide-angled camera follows No.6 around the stage-set scene. As with 'Once Upon A Time,' the sense of stage-set design is deliberate, its artificiality foregrounded. And here is our master of ceremonies, looking down from an elevated speaker's podium, dressed in judge's drag, red ermine-trimmed robes and 18th century wig. It is none other than the No.2 subjected to mocking caricature as a petty, tantrum-throwing Napoleon in the bedtime story told by No.6 in 'The Girl Who Was Death.' "Well, come" he invites, leading the guest of honour on. Alexis Kanner, now in the guise of No.48, briefly pops up from a hissing silo which belches clouds of vaporous steam, bound with metallic bands to a sturdy steel rod. A latterday heretic at a technocratic stake, babbling nonsense rhymes to himself as he awaits his fate. An inconvenient reminder that, despite the rapturous applause greeting No.6, the embodiment of resistance and individual integrity, this is not the land of the free.

The judge is a comic, gavel-thumping buffoon. The red robes and long-outmoded wigs of the judiciary make them a natural target for caricature. They make for a readily available symbol of the establishment's distance from the realities of the modern world, its rootedness in arcane ritual and tradition. The judge looks as if he belongs in the parochial world of Anthony Trollope novels rather than in this hi-tech bunker. This incongruous blend of tradition and modernity, conservative nostalgia existing side by side with technocratic sleekness, was exploited to quirkily amusing effect in 'The Avengers,' filmed in colour for the first time in 1966 and using its potential to full pop art effect. In Lindsay Anderson's 'If...,' released in 1968 (the year of Fall Out's first broadcast) Peter Jeffrey's headmaster declares that "Britain today is a powerhouse of ideas, experiments, imagination, everything from pop music to pig breeding, from atom power stations to mini skirts. That's the challenge we've got to meet". He says this with his schoolmaster's robes flapping out behind him whilst standing in front of the neo-gothic arches of a public school steeped in ritual and tradition valorising the continuity of inherited power, addressing boys dressed in a uniform which appears to have remained unchanged since the mid-Victorian period. There is little hint of modernity here.

Order is called, the applause instantly silenced and "a matter of democratic crisis" announced. Is this to be a trial? If so, then of whom, or what? The intention seems to be "to resolve the question of revolt," an abstruse matter more suited to the sociology classes newly emergent in the 60s. A sanctimonious appeal for civilised conduct is swiftly followed by the observation that "errant children must sometimes be brought to book with a smack on their backside," a remark made with a significant glance at Alexis Kanner's distractedly humming No.48 and accompanied with a clap of the hands and a manic look of unrestrained glee. I'm reminded of Lindsay Anderson once again (he and Patrick McGoohan seem very much fellow spirits) and the scene in his modern 1970s picaresque 'O Lucky Man!' in which a judge, having pronounced firm and punitive sentence on Malcolm McDowell's hapless everyman Travis, retreats to the private chambers to undress and receive a damn good thrashing. The judge's gestures towards corporal punishment gain immediate, reflexive applause. The crowd-pleasing prospect of the Roman circus, give 'em a bit of blood, a good hanging. As a 'deterrent,' of course. The ultimate extension of such thinking onto a global scale would be the "regrettable bullet," the bomb which hisses and steams in the corner of the cavern. It is the devouring, fire breathing dragon, the focus of fear from countless mythologies, and this is its lair. And as in the tales of old, it is imperative not to waken it from its torpid slumber.

The assembly is declared "in security"; more dissected words, meanings prised apart and realigned. Fuse them and create insecurity, a more accurate reason for convening, perhaps. No.6 is presented and the judge reaches for heights of elevated, over the top rhetoric. The tone is fawning, obsequious, and leads to the approbatory order "this assembly rises to you — sir'" He has been ennobled, given a new title. From Six to 'Sir'. A new kind of depersonalisation? Conducted applause is quelled at a gesture. There is a sense that the whole ceremony is carefully scripted, orchestrated by some unknown author. "The transfer of ultimate power requires some tedious ceremony," the judge apologises with unctuous, hand-wringing deference. The mode of address is modified according to the position of the addressee within the hierarchy of power. No.6, 'Sir,' is invited to ascend a dais atop which sits "the chair of honour," a gilded throne with ornate, rococo putti poutingly looking down from its carved frame. It's an ego seat, the sort of vanity throne millionaire footballers or property magnates like to be photographed in. The furnishings of self-importance and inflated self-regard. Sir takes the seat, a comic rendition of 'For He's A Jolly Good Fellow," in the manner of the "Pop Goes The Weasel" variants which have sent mocking echoes through the Village in previous episodes, accompanying his enthronement, undermining any air of grandiose ceremony which might otherwise attend it. Does it suit him? He looks quietly pleased at this point, poised and relaxed. But we have come to learn that he is very good at biding his time.

A crane shot looks down over the back of the throne to the guards below. He really is in an elevated position now. A position of power. The throne facing the judge's podium (or, given his predilection for priestly pronouncement, pulpit). From 'Sir's perspective, we switch to a bomb's-eye view, the baleful green-eyed gaze looking down over all. The symbol of ultimate power, the high-pressure exhalations of steam suggestive of huge latent energies on the verge of destructive release. The switch between elevated throne and bomb perspectives is already hinting at a link between 'Sir' and whatever power fuels the terrible missile.

The shipping crate descends with clunking metallic gracelessness, its loud and effortful docking giving an impression of great bulk and mass. The barred room is revealed with No.2 still lying dead within. A rising alarm is combined with the closing of steel eyelids over the green eye, and we notice the emphatic red stripe of a number 1 above it for the first time. The all-seeing surveillance eye, the eye of God, or some gnostic demi-urge ruling over its delusory sub-creation. Some kind of command is conveyed to the judge, who complies by issuing the order to "resuscitate". It is all too apparent who (or what) is truly in charge here. The judge's rhetoric will increasingly appear as empty bombast from hereon in. The bomb itself is the soul of concision. Its message is very clear, and brooks no disobedience. Erect and monumental, it is its own towering, modernist statue testifying to totalitarian power.

No.2's final collapse into breathlessness and death is reversed on the oversized monitor projection screen, accompanied by a sped up and backward masked soundtrack; the self-consuming concrète signature of the psychedelic summer of love, as rehearsed on The Beatles' 'Tomorrow Never Knows' and further explored by the likes of 'Traffic,' 'The Pretty Things,' 'The Jimi Hendrix Experience' and many others. The sound of heady dislocation, of senses being deranged. "Revolution," the judge smilingly observes, as if acknowledging the cultural upheavals such sounds evoke. The revolution in the head. It's an odd word to hear from his lips. But this is not the sloganeering word which would accrue such hip cachet in 1968 amongst the rock, dope and Ché set. This is evolution with an 'r' added; refashioned evolution, enabled by advanced medical technology and occult science. Control over the body, over the state of life and death. Godlike power! A celluloid resurrection. The image is all, as our idea of the self becomes increasingly mediated.

The corporeal remains of No.2 are wheeled out by medics, masks perpetuating the general state of anonymous depersonalisation amongst the various cadres which pervades the cavern. The Butler climbs the dais to stand by No.6 (for let us maintain his old identification for the time being, to avoid confusion), giving him the slightest of deferent nods. As the prospect of resurrection is mooted, realigned allegiances are subtly acknowledged. No.2 is subjected to an undignified makeover, accompanied by inappropriate romantic music; part extreme day at the hairdressers, part invasive surgical procedure. With head positioned beneath a conical, 50s robot hairstyling 'pod,' face entirely covered with shaving foam, he is menaced by a mask extending on a telescoping arm to smother him. It is vaguely reminiscent of a Dalek's sink plunger appendage. No.2 appears to be turning into a cybernetic hybrid, a techno-medical miracle man. But what will remain of his essential, true self? Is our humanity somehow diminished by our reliance on technology? On the screen, we see the spinning mobile familiar from 'The General's' speedlearn broadcasts, the camera zooming in and out on its flashing, gyroscopic form. It's our cue to go into the ads, a little bit of metafictional commentary. 'Consume,' 'Obey,' 'Conform,' 'Do Not Question Authority' as the hidden subliminal messages in John Carpenter's satirical science fiction movie 'They Live' direct us.

We come back from our interlude of subliminal suggestion, mnemonic jingles firmly lodged in the filing systems of the subconscious, to hear an instructive lecture from the judge. "Revolt can take many forms", he explains with tedious pedantry. We are about to witness the first of three examples. No.48 emerges from his silo. "Thanks for the trip, dad," he says, with more than a little sardonicism (censor alert! Drug reference!) He will continue speaking in this strange, archaic beatnik argot throughout. Perhaps Patrick McGoohan was thinking back to his role as the jazz drummer Johnny Cousin in the 1961 Othello adaptation All Night Long. This mode of speech, staccato in delivery and pared down to the simplest of syllabic utterances, feels strangely removed from any particular time period. It has more in common with the invented Nadsat lingo of Alex and his droogs in 'A Clockwork Orange,' or of the abbreviated, simplified vocabulary of the media-saturated future portrayed in Nigel Kneale's TV play 'The Year of the Sex Olympics' (1968), a key referent when thinking of 'The Prisoner.'

His theme tune is 'Dem Bones', a piece of minstrelsy which harks back to our glimpse of Al Jolson on the jukebox (the version here is by the white Canadian vocal quartet The Four Lads, recorded in 1961). It's a resurrection song, drawing on the biblical story of Ezekiel in the Valley of Dry Bones. He prophesies that the bones will rise again at the word of the Lord, an allegory for the rebirth of nation. Harlem Renaissance writer James Weldon Johnson imagines them drawing together and reconnecting, conjuring up a vision of dancing Harryhausen skeletons in a barren wilderness (a post-apocalyptic landscape?) It's a song with an implicit sense of mortality, but not a morbid one. These are the kind of skeletons who might be seen, bedecked with roses and sporting Uncle Sam hats, on the covers of Grateful Dead albums.

No.48 is set free from his 'stake' and cautiously creeps out. With his top hat, roguishly ruffled shirt, black jacket and trousers rounded off with white sneakers, he is like a mocking parody of the sinister funereal aspect adopted by the Village 'collectors'. An aspect which would also be adopted by the apple 'bonkers' in the animated Beatles fantasia 'Yellow Submarine' the following year. A red flower affixed to the hat offsets the dolorous black and a cowbell pendant from a long chain gives the appearance either of a pilgrim or a leper; the bell one of the hippy accoutrements co-opted from the Indian subcontinent. Gold-braided epaulettes also dandify military dress, 'Sgt Pepper', I Was Lord Kitchener's Valet Edwardian finery from the London Summer of Love. Hippie uniforms. No.48 is alert and wary, like an animal emerging from cover, from the rabbit hole. He looks like an artful dodger urchin, sweaty and besmirched from his confinement in the underworld, the purgatorial holding tube. His look is part London hippy, part LA freak. There's a certain resemblance to the San Francisco 'Digger' Emmett Grogan, particularly in a well-known photo in which he is adopting a wide-legged pose (as if afflicted by poverty-induced Dickensian rickets) and sticking two fingers up with cheeky ragamuffin defiance. No.48 is definitely more merry prankster than passive flower child, more yippie than hippie.

Judge and jury are driven wild by the strains of 'Dem Bones' unleashed along with No.48. The infectious rhythm throws them into a state of chaotic outrage, this flaunting of due solemnity stirring up a flapping, flustered commotion. The eye of No.1 cracks open and the alarm sounds, adding an extra level of tension to the general panic. Music as revolutionary force, the intoxicating power of Pan's flute driving celebrants and unwitting auditors alike in to a state of wild, frenzied ecstasy. The music is silenced and order restored. The judge launches into a pontificating speech, puffed up with the dramatic pomp of his own oratory. "Youth with its enthusiasm, which rebels against any accepted norm because it must, and we sympathise," he declaims, turning No.48 into the embodiment of an entire generation. He himself is momentarily like an archetypal progressive 60s judge, one of the 'Lady Chatterley' trial liberalisers inching their confused, class bound and morally earnest way towards greater tolerance and openness. Turning again to 'If...,' he is once more like Peter Jeffrey's headmaster. He stands in the college quadrangle on founder's day as Mick Travis and his crusaders launch their armed revolution against the hated establishment figures in this public-school as microcosm of Britain allegory: the church, the army, the teachers as political and judicial legislators and the prefects as brutal police enforcers. "Boys! Boys! I understand you! Listen to reason and trust me. Trust me!" he complacently pleads, arms outstretched in earnest entreaty. The outsider in their group, the woman in their male bande à part, puts a bullet in his head. Again, no peace and love here.

The judge's tone soon turns from exaggerated sympathy, the affected understanding of the patronising patriarch, to spittle-flecked vehemence, the rhetoric becoming violent and punitive. 'When the function of society is endangered, such revolts must cease. They are non-productive and must be ABOLISHED". Crushed, quashed, eliminated, ranks of militarised police sent in with shields and batons. There is a close-up on No.48's still face, frozen in a look of crestfallen dejection, like a melancholy mime. He raises his bell and gives it a sad little tinkle. "Hear the word of the Lord," he says in conclusion. 'Lord' here takes on a satirical cast; M'Lord, your honour, honourable member of the upper chamber, the House of Lords. Sir!

The tinkle of the bell is like a call to revolt, a meditative cue leading to violent action. Kill for peace. No.6 was repeatedly goaded in the Degree Absolute duel of 'Once Upon A Time' to relinquish his pacifism and go for the kill. He is reminded that "in the war, you killed," an assertion to which he accedes, with the qualification that he killed "for peace". With Dem Bones echoing around the cavern once more, No.48 leads everybody on a merry dance. It's like a revolutionary Gene Kelly number, a choreographed ballet of evasion and pursuit covering all the spaces of this underground microcosm. Leaping up onto the science embankment, waltzing around the mobile medical camp, ascending the judicial dais before finally falling to the ground, surrounded by a thicket of pointing gun barrels. The moment where Gene Kelly ('Gene' Kanner) slides to his knees and raises his arms to the skies, the camera craning up and drawing the routine to a conclusion.

Into this tense moment of frozen suspension, No.6 throws in the words "young man". Not so much a means of address as a formal naming. A granting of identity. "Give it to me again," No.48 says with a look of eager anticipation. Someone is listening, he has got through. The routine has found its audience. No.6 gives a tight, controlled smile. Sincere for its lack of phoney beam, its cool. "Don't knock yourself out," he replies in his characteristically terse manner. No.48 springs up, standing rigidly, as if to attention. The camera glides swiftly over to a close-up on his smiling face, turned sideways to look at No.6. "I'm borne all over," he declares, with evident satisfaction. A connection has been made, bo(r)ne on bone. A new body of outsiders is forming.

A high crane shot looks down from on high at No.48, corralled by the prodding guns of the military police. It is the judge's elevated perspective. "We must maintain the status quo," he proclaims, the word of the Lord. Familiarity is discouraged, divisions and social ranks are to be maintained, given numbers observed. Contact across class or professional borders is frowned upon and made note of. Number 1 communicates once more in its alarm siren language, a dialect which commands attention, its green, glowing eye fixing on the judge. He understands the dialect, although he obviously can't respond in kind. The military police retreat and the new form of address is accepted. No.6's will is being done. "We are obliged, sir," the judge genuflects. "Don't mention it, dad" comes the response, followed by a wry exchange of glances between No.6 and No.48.

There follows a farcical trial which takes the form of a rapid-fire exchange of dialogue between No.48 and the judge in a hip pidgin argot. The judge may not be able to speak like an armed warhead, but he makes the attempting at adopting youth speak ("give it to me baby"). Sense is less important than the interplay between the two figures in what amounts to a fast rally, short phrases racketed back and forth, rapid camera cutting creating a kinetic momentum. Some kind of transference take place through the adoption of this condensed lingo, new sense winkled out from nonsense. An Edward Lear or Alfred Jarry Ubu Roi dialogue, advanced pataphysics in action. No.48 instigates a table thumping "take, take" chant, spreading from judge to jury, the elevated crane shot showing the judge joining in the percussive beat with a look of frenzied greed upon his face. No.48 has conducted the dialogue on his own terms and revealed the true nature of authority, the simple, base motivation beneath its platitudinous posturing, the puffed up pontifications of the judge. He kneels down, as if carrying the weight of this knowledge, and holds his arms out in a cruciform pose, head bowed. Youth as sacrificial victim, Isaac offered before the Lord. The camera glides past the 'Rehabilitation, Education, Youngsters' name blocks on the jury desks, more aspects of society requiring scrutiny and control.

A ring of the bell brings the judge and jury out of their trance state, the conductor bringing the performance to a close. The tiny tinkle of the peace bell, held delicately between thumb and forefinger, is the converse sound to the aggressive thumping of the gavel. But it proves just as effective in bringing the gathering to order.

The judge, completely misreading (mistranslating) the situation, failing to perceive the act of self-revelation into which he has been conducted, says "now you're high!" "I'm low," No.48 corrects him. An offer of inter-generational connection is made, an attempt to reach across the generation gap, to create a universality out of ancestral descent, of common humanity; "The bones is yours, dad. They came from you my daddy". But the judge is only interested in using his perceived communication breakthrough to exert power and authority. "Confess, confess", he chants, like come Counter-reformation inquisitor. The chant is taken up by the jury, who fall easily into mass sloganeering chorus. And we are back to the St Vitus Dance of Dem Bones, this time soaked with reverb, as if to emphasise its artificiality, the sense that this time it is a recording being cued up once more. No.48, still in Christlike pose, looks back to No.6 and the Butler, who calmly watch the proceedings whilst the judge and jury are once more possessed with the frenzied spirit of reactionary revelry. Filled with intoxication of power. A small tip of the topper acknowledges their co-fraternity. They stand (or sit) outside this mass hysteria, individuals observing the mob mentality of the conformist mind. As the music plays on, cued by an invisible hand, we see the 'Entertainments' and 'Recreation' name blocks, further elements of social control (thinking once more of those hidden 'They Live' commands). These blocks are becoming like chapter headings, or markers of the end of episodes.

The judge seems possessed by a spirit of demented hatred as he twitches and jerks to the music. "Hip, hip, hooray," rounds off the chanting, and once more we "hear the word of the Lord". That word is "Guilty!", spat out with venomous vituperation. The charge, only now read out, after the verdict has been arrived at, is elucidated by one of the anonymous jury members whose board identifies him as being in charge of 'Anarchists' (nestled in between 'Identification' and 'Recreation'). We can see a grey beard projecting beneath the chin of his mask, however, trembling with anger and indignation. This is the judgement of age upon youth, the father upon the son. The accusations of "total defiance," the questioning of authority, "unhealthy aspects of speech and dress" and, perhaps most seriously, "the refusal to observe, wear or respond to his number". To know his place. No.48 looks on with amusement, little surprised at the foreordained outcome and punctuating the grave oratory with the occasional tinkle of his bell. The judge looks to No.6 to seek his approval, an acknowledgement of new authority, even if it is only nominal. A regal nod of assent from the throne. "I...note them," Sir remarks of the proceedings, maintaining a cool neutrality. "I take it you have no comment at this stage," the judge prompts. "....Not at this stage," No.6 replies after a dramatic pause. Not at this stage and not on this stage. But he will have comment, at the right time. He awaits his moment. He has learned patience.

No.48 is carried back to his silo, cross-legged and folded-armed, offering no resistance but no assistance. He is like a peaceful protestor being removed from a sit-in demonstration by the police. He descends, still singing in a babbling undertone, the rebel song of defiant nonsense which conveys another new sense (to some, just a nuisance). 'I think you'll find our next revolutionary a different kettle of fish altogether,' the judge announces before collapsing into uproarious, semi-hysterical laughter. The flashing 'General' gyroscope appears on the screen again. Its time for more subliminal conditioning, the advent of the ad break. Be seeing you on the other side.

The Dalek suction cup is removed to reveal No.2 freshly shaved and shorn with a neatly clipped moustache. He awakens bemused and shaken and reaches for his heart, as if to check that he really is alive. Or perhaps he reaches for his number badge to affirm his identity, his current position. On the large screen there is a reminder of his former self, the hale and hearty fellow bellowing with laughter. It sounds as if the screen self is mocking this new, bewildered incarnation, staggering from his seat of medical resurrection. All present point to the stilled image of No.2 on the screen and join in with the guffaws which still reverberate around the cavern. He has become a figure of fun. But he maintains a vestige of authority and stills the hollow hilarity with a raised hand. Into the ensuing, anticipatory silence he roars "I feel a new man," and laughs in a direct echo of the recorded example we've just heard. But no-one joins in with the present laughter.

Turning to see No.6 on the throne, he greets him with the same jocular familiarity with which he addressed him in his first stint as No.2. "My dear chap," he says with real warmth. "Enthroned at last, eh". He has understood No.6's underlying psychology, the compulsions and principles which drive him, better than anyone. Turning to the Butler, "my little friend, ever faithful," he beckons him down as if he were a dog. But he remains in his new place, stoically impassive as ever. "New allegiances", No.2 observes with weary resignation. "Such is the price of fame". He turns to address the gathering in a grandiloquent and theatrical manner. "My Lords, Ladies and Gentlemen". Are there any ladies present? This is a notably male affair, with not one single female member of the cast. Then again, 60s counterculture and politics, revolutionary or otherwise, and were notable male. It wouldn't be until the 70s that feminism (a genuine, continuing and lasting revolution) would begin fully to assert itself. "A most extraordinary thing happened on my way…here," he continues.

Now the laughter comes, the jury transformed into a quaking mass of mirth. He seems in absolute command of proceedings, a seasoned orator in his element. Not waiting for an invitation, he ascends the judge's podium and delivers a speech as if he were at the despatch box. Noting the political power he once wielded, and the 'use' the 'community' found for him, abducted into the Village just as No.6 had been, he comes out as a born-again rebel, repudiating the weakness of his old self. "What is deplorable is that I resisted for so short a time. A fine tribute to your methods". He really is a new man. Or the old man back again.

His demise is replayed on the big screen; a terrible thing for anyone to witness, their own death. "You couldn't even let me rest in peace," he observes with considerable bitterness. "How was it done?" But if he expects explication here, then he has learned nothing (and perhaps the same could be said of the TV audience). "Did you ever meet Him?", No.6 asks, having to further clarify 'meet Number One'. "Face to face?", No.2 responds, but it comes out sounding like 'faith to faith'. When No.6 affirms, he roars "Meet Him?" (the capital H implied) with a tone of utter incredulity. The very idea is regarded with contemptuous dismissiveness. And if this No.2 never came near to such an encounter, it's highly unlikely that any other did. Number One remains the great unknown, the enduring mystery. The Great I Am who has departed the stage set which he constructed.

Now is the time for such an encounter, however. He approaches the Number One bomb with sidling steps, as if edging towards the brink of a deep chasm, and stares at its closed metal lids. The eye lazily opens like that of a sluggish lizard and he averts his gaze, his sober face lit a sickly green. A naughty, impish look overtakes his features, and he suddenly resembles a mischievous schoolboy plotting some puckish prank. One of the 'If...' gang, grown up but recalling rebellious days. "Shall I?", he wonders aloud. "Give him a stare?" Then, with self-responsive determination, "I shall give him a stare!" He walks proudly up to the eye. Distantly, a voice cries "you'll die,' all but drowned out by the rising outrage of the keening siren. "Then I'll die with my own mind," he declares, the honourable code of an intellectual hero. He tears his number badge off and flips it aside, discarding it with contemptuous disregard. Throwing the idea away with its physical emblem. "You'll hypnotise me no longer,'"he promises. There is a billowing exhalation and the eye slides fully open. He spits on it and lets forth a laugh of unbridled glee, as if he can't quite believe the bold recklessness of his own actions. He turns around with a 'whatcha gonna do now' look, a 'come and get me' readiness.

No.6 now gives the order, his authority seemingly intensifying. "Hold him...until my inauguration". No.2 is led away in a dignified processional, arms outstretched in cruciform acquiescence between two military policemen. Another rebel martyr. Returned to his restrictive silo, he goes down laughing; loud and extended laughter at the establishment, at its manifold absurdities. A refusal to take it as seriously as it takes itself, one form of resistance. This was the decade of the satire boom, after all, with the 'Cambridge Footlights', 'That Was The Week That Was,' the birth of 'Private Eye' and Peter Cook's 'Establishment club.' The old No.2 (now, like No. 48, numberless) has one last word before descending. Looking up into the camera with a fourth wall breaking aside to the audience, he utters that signature Village farewell, "Be Seeing You". The last time we will hear those words, in The Prisoner at any rate. Exit, laughing uproariously.

We now look up at a sober and reflective judge, the camera angles of power adjusted. Having played very little part in No.2's 'trial', he embarks on his next explicatory exegesis. At this point it feels like a summary speech before proceedings move onto the next stage. No.6's 'inauguration' perhaps. "We have just witnessed two forms of revolt," he explains, as if to a hall full of slightly dim students. The first was "uncoordinated youth,' the words spat out with undisguised venom. The second "an established, successful, secure member of the establishment turning upon and biting the hand that feeds him". "These attitudes are dangerous", he concludes, the camera pulling back to reveal the military police standing at attention beneath the podium. "They contribute nothing to our culture and are to be stamped out". And the means to achieve that erasure are readily displayed before our eyes. The fascistic nature of authority wielded through armed strength is laid bare. This kind of brutish, firmly stated philosophy is popular amongst certain sections of the populace, however. Give 'em a dose of national service. The judge's words are greeted with a round of applause. The camera retreats until No.6 is drawn into the frame, raised throne facing judge's podium.

The Number One bomb beeps into life, as if prompting the puppet judge to utter his following encomium. No.6 is subjected to a glowing paean of praise, a valorisation which places him at the other end of the scale. The fawning rhetoric is accompanied by footage of his house being purchased for him, the KAR 120C racer being polished and prepared. All is to be restored, the pre-Village status quo reinstated. He is the heroic rebel, the exemplar, the moral compass. He has prevailed "despite materialistic efforts". Is the judge making some allusion to the soul here, introducing the idea of some spiritual dimension to man's being? "All that remains is recognition of a man," he concludes, the kind of pompous puffery which you might find on the sleevenotes of another tedious 1960s Frank Sinatra LP. 'Lead us or go,' he offers, holding out the possibility of power (the same offer once proffered to No. 2?) We are witnessing the Temptation of No.6.

A treasure box wheeled in on a hostess trolley offers the material means for freedom. Money, shelter (the key to his house) and unimpeded mobility (passport and traveller's cheques). A small purse with 'petty cash' looks suspiciously like a pouch filled with 30 pieces of silver. 'Blood money.' Hearing that he is free to go, No.6 uses his old interrogatory method. The Occam's razored question which can be repeated ad infinitum, the five year old's neverending inquisition. In 'The General,' it destroyed the all-knowing computer with the one simple yet unanswerable question, fed into it by No.6: 'W.H.Y. Question mark'. Now he uses it to press the judge Into clarifying his position. Each response amplifies his standing until he is effectively granted the holy status of sainthood. "You are pure, you know the way, show us... your revolt is good and honest. You are the only individual, we need you.[115]" By

---

[115] All quotes are taken from 'Fall Out' by Patrick McGoohan — late 1967, Everyman Films

this point, the judge's speech has taken on the cadence and language of liturgical incantation. "I see," No.6 finally concedes, although perhaps he is only responding to those final words, "we need you." "I'm an individual?" He asks tentatively, as if this assertion weren't at the centre of his crusade throughout his Village sojourn. The response, "you are on your own," puzzles him, however. "I fail to see," he replies. Is individuality an aspect of egotism? Does it involve a rejection of the idea of community, of communal identity (the Village sacrilege of 'unmutuality')? There is no such thing as society, as another leader once declared.

"All of this is...yours," the judge indicates with an expansive sweep of the arm whose import seems to extend well beyond the confines of the cavern. "We plead for you to lead us". He descends from the podium, inviting No. 6 to "take the stand —address us." To take to the podium and turn it into a pulpit, a barricade from which to preach revolution, the downfall of all he surveys. He appears hesit-ant, however. Unsure of himself, the "why?' Still echoing around his mind. Can it all really be this easy? Such a sudden and wholesale reversal of the around his mind. Can it all really be this easy? Such a sudden and wholesale reversal of the former power dynamic, a ceding of authority which amounts to complete surrender. The Temptation of No.6 continues with a direct appeal to his ego, the 'I' of pride and self-belief, the core of the unbending pillar of individuality. "You are the greatest, make a statement, Sir, we are all yours."

No.6 is won over, the ego rises and 'Sir' descends from his throne, taking the key, cash and passport as he passes. Preparing for a quick getaway. But he must make his proclamation first, his firebrand speech which will, of course, be a masterclass in impassioned oratory, transforming hearts and minds and destined to be quoted by succeeding generations. A ripple of applause urges him onward, celebratory proces-sional music adding to the sense of momentous occasion. This will be the climax, No.6 speaks, excoriates the evils of political coercion, mind control and enforced conformity.

A gentle tap of the gavel to still the applause, and indrawn breath and... "I". The following words are drowned out by loud, raptors affirmation, applause and bovine yeasaying. A House of Commons cacophony. A bang of the gavel and a glance at the convocation gathered behind him brings silence, but another "I' immediately triggers further censorious approbation. This too is the price of fame. You never get beyond that towering "I." Once you become (or are made into) an icon, an objec-tified embodiment of a set of beliefs or ideals, your actual opinion is of little in-terest. You are the vessel for the opinions and provocations of others. No. 6's ego, his 'I,' has proved his downfall, the 'fall out' of his heroic struggle and the renown it has brought him. He has been co-opted and thus lost his voice. His passionate speech, so long in the mental composition, is reduced to a series of hollow and in creasingly desperate physical gestures. A look of awful horror distorts his face. The judge stills the humiliating hubbub with one casually upraised finger. He is the conductor now. A lesson learned. Things cannot be changed from within.

No.6's look of horror relaxes into a dawning of resigned awareness; A painful but necessary enlightenment. "Sir, on behalf of us all, we thank you," the judge says, the fawning language now coloured with a distinctly sardonic shade. His ego has been shattered, but this is a necessary prelude. A ritual humbling before the meeting with Number One. He takes one last look at the gathering before allowing himself to be led to the silo, an accompanying fanfare now mocking and undermining rather than ceremonial, in true Village style. One final rendezvous, a descent into the underworld, a conclusive unveiling. After these commercial messages, beamed directly at your id.

We view No.6's descent into the underworld from below. He has gone down the rabbit hole. What further episodes of Carrollian absurdity await him below, what homicidal monarchs will he encounter? The waning elliptical moon of light from the world above crowns No.6's noble brow as it looms above us. He truly looks like an icon, complete with glowing halo. Having been ennobled, is he now to be sanctified? From 'Sir' to 'Saint.' Will such elevation to the ranks of the holy prove equally hollow? He takes a slightly sardonic but at the same time bewildered look back at the world above. Will he ever return, see the light again (even if it is artificial). Sweat beads his brow, just had besmirched the faces of Nos.2 and 48 after they had been risen. It's the heat of the Inferno, the first circle of Hell. In the grey corridors below, Nos.2 and 48 are locked into their 'orbits', just as the sinners in Dante's Inferno are trapped in their own circles within Hell's poetically judicial structure. These transparent tubes are like museum specimen jars, designed to display informative exemplars of particular 'types'. Their unceasing jive song and volcanic laughter continue within the narrow confines, waiting to burst out and infect the world once more.

Another, unnumbered 'orbit' tube opens up to give No.6/Sir (Sir Six?) access. An orbit especially prepared for him, awaiting this climactic moment? The Village announcement jingle heralds the arrival of the Butler, striding purposefully down the corridor. Robed scientists are absorbed in adjusting dials on the walls, looking like acolytes in some technocratic temple. Occult technology, demonic science. The Butler arrives at his side and with the merest of gestures (he is the most economical of fellows) gives him permission to ascend the spiral stair. We began the episode with a helicoptered point of view spiralling into towards No.2's house. Now we spiral up a coiling staircase into the final chamber of power, the heart of the nautilus shell. Power with Power. It's the endpoint of the spiralling path we've been taking with No.6 from the very beginning, with numerous illuminating diversions and wrong turns along the way.

No.6 ascends, a look of tense anticipation on his face. Does he secretly know what he will discover? The camera circles up and into the room, its wayward hand-held navigation and wide-angled distortions adding to a sense of perceptual dislocation, of a sensorium on the brink of some disastrous implosion. We are crossing an event horizon beyond which some immense mental gravitation force compresses and stretches consensual reality to the point of complete breakdown. We are in the heart of Rocket Number One, the volatile bomb and it is Revelation time.

Control centre is spartan and functional. The steady drip of electronic sound is suggestive of a heart monitor registering life signs. A collection of planetary globes of varying sizes is clustered on a tabletop like so many pale blue bowling balls. One is clearly not enough. Here is a multitude of worlds, hinting at megalomania. If the planet is many things to many people, then total control can only be exerted by claiming all possible worlds, all dreamed of worldviews. The vision of Charlie Chaplin's Hitlerian caricature 'Adenoid Hinckel' dancing about his command room with a giant inflatable globe comes to mind. Of course, the routine ends when the balloon bursts with a resounding bang.

The curved pop art bones of plastic phones stand out with brightly coloured red and yellow contrast against the grey metal walls. These are the phones through which so many commands have been issued, gaily coloured, childlike objects which have inspired so much fear. Modern pop art design as a symbol of doom. The tyrannical terror lying beneath the plastic surface of cheerful commercialism. The authoritarianism which makes children of all of us. A TV screen broadcasts No.6's cautious approach. A McLuhanesque mirror reflecting the true self, the mediated self. As Professor Brian O'Blivion would suggest some 20 years later in David Cronenberg's 'Videodrome,' 'the TV screen is the retina of the mind's eye'. And this the retina of the baleful green eye of the Number One bomb which has been watching proceedings beyond. We are in the confined space delineated by the walls of the braincase, the bone cave of the mind, a skull reinforced by metallic shielding. This is the source of all power, the human mind and the myriad possibilities it is able to imagine, the potentialities it can unleash. No.6's defiant declaration of independence appears on the screen. "I will not be pushed, filed, indexed, stamped, briefed, debriefed or numbered. My life is my own". A positive negation repeated three times, like Peter's denial after the crucifixion. Three is the magic number.

A cowled figure slowly proffers a glass globe to No.6, holding it with the reverence and care due to something of both immense value and brittle fragility. It's like the crystal snowglobe which Charles Foster Kane holds at the start of Orson Welles' dissection of power and public reputation 'Citizen Kane,' and which he drops as he utters his dying words. A globe which somehow contains the condensed singularity of his life. The delicate container of the hidden self. The globe held out here is a scrying glass offering true insight. Its inverted fish-eye lens perspective encompasses the control panels and phones, the instrumentation of power. And the circuitry of the mind? The globe is ceremoniously transferred just as the mediated No.6 on the screen says "my life is my own". Well, here it is then. This is your life. The recording stutters, reductively distilling the heroic statement of individualism into a shrill, chittering "I,I,I". The bars crash on No.6's head as it rushes forward with a look of intense determination. It's a symbolic scene we've seen over and over again at the end of every episode. The prisoner failing to escape, either physically or, increasingly as time unfolds, in some metaphysical sense. The rushing head is reminiscent of the bizarre and disturbing scene in Hitchcock's 'Vertigo' in which James Stewart's Scotty's abstracted head is propelled down a vertiginous corridor somewhere in the depths of his inner landscape as his outer form sits with catatonic blankness in a hospital room. The bars crash three times, a ringing percussion. Here is the ultimate prison, the cells of the self, Piranesian catacombs of the mind. The globe falls to the ground, shattering into a thousand scintillant fragments.

The time of revelation is now upon us. The robed figure draws his arms wide, like a cult leader offering some unholy sacrament (or like Christopher Lee's Lord Summerisle telling poor old Inspector Howie "it is time for your appointment with the Wicker Man"). It is the cult of the self, of the ego fascinated by its own reflection, studiously posing in front of the mirror. A cult which has only magnified over the ensuing decades. The circled Number One is ironed onto the front of the robes like the identifying number on a goalkeeper's jersey (the most existential position on the pitch, as Camus, Nabokov and Wim Wenders would attest). The "I" is repeated, accelerating and rising to a pitch of hysteria which is the herald of madness. No.6's hair has lost its usual brylcreemed sheen and sculpted lacquer and flops in uncombed disarray (another echo of Scotty). Hairstyles as indicators of mental states. Although the look of wild edginess on his face is indicator enough that No.6 is on the borders of sanity. It is the rictus grin familiar from the films and TV shows of David Lynch.

He rips off the black and white theatrical mask, the stage persona, to reveal an ape mask below, gibbering its repeated "I" chant. No.1 is I, the base self, the babbling, grasping, unreasoning creature of the id. Unfiltered desire, greed and acquisitiveness. The "I want" part of the mind (the "take, take, take' which No.48 exposed) concerned only with the instant gratification of its own instincts and impulses. It contains unconscious wells of destructive as well as creative force, the death drive as well as the life impulse, Eros and Thanatos both. Here, in the heart of the bomb, the Thanatopic principle has become dominant. Just as it had in 'Forbidden Planet,' the forces of the Professor's id disastrously magnified by the alien Krell machinery to create and indestructible monster, let loose in a seeming Arcadian idyll. The monkey mask of the id is torn off to reveal the ego below. And as he must have known, the face revealed is his own. No.6, or perhaps Patrick McGoohan himself. The character in search of an author successful in his quest. The insane laughter which is loosened by his unmasking is partly the madness courted by the artist who delves deeply within themselves to unearth some fundamental truth, some core of the self which pushes the creative impulse to its limits. "Humankind cannot bear very much reality," as TS Eliot suggested, but it is the duty of the serious artist to bare as much of it as they are able, no matter the cost.

No.6 chases his insane ego around the globe table. The camera movements are now wholly uncoordinated, catching a black and white blur of robes and suit, with a brief flash of warning red from the fire extinguisher and a defining tone of sick green light (again hearkening back to 'Vertigo' and the scene in which the refashioned Madeleine walks into the room). Number One Ego is chased babbling from the no-secone, No.6 locking the hatch after him. Get out of my head! It is done, the over-inflated ego, the amplified "I"has been expelled. It's akin to an exorcism, banishing the ghost inside. Outside, the steel lids of the bomb eye are shuttered. For good? The judge, now seated in the throne (his throne all along, perhaps) looks pensively on. Has this all been anticipated? Is No.6 still being manipulated like a puppet?

Back down below, the camera focuses on the red of the fire extinguisher, the bright primary colour of revolution, danger, passion, anger, blood. No.6 picks it up and descends. Revolution starts in the head before spreading out into the world. Battle commences, the Butler joining in as a loyal foot soldier. The fire extinguisher, intended for the damping down of flames, is used as a weapon to fan them. Guns are requisitioned and the songs and laughter of Nos.2 and 48 set free from their silos to join in the insurgency. The bomb is primed and a doom organ accompanies the chaos erupting in the cavern above. The rebels ascend in robed disguise and open fire with machine guns. This is like the armed revolution with which 'If... 'climaxes. A full on surrealist assault on the establishment order which can be taken on an allegorical level. Even if no blood is actually shed, if the revolution is in the head rather than on the streets (The Stones' 'Street Fighting Man' would set the modish tone for revolutionary '68) violence on some level seems unavoidable. Power, or dominant ideologies, are not relinquished without a struggle. The strains of 'All You Need Is Love,' echoing down the jukebox tunnel, are drowned out by the percussive rattle of gunfire. It's a symbolically ironic sound collage, anticipated by the song's fading into the parade ground stomp of military boots at the start of the episode.

Driven on by bullets and the urgent alarm of the countdown warning, the cavern assembly flees in a bizarre panicked parade of red robed judges, soldiers and a column of frogmen on fold-up bikes. Again, 'If...' springs to mind, with its emblematic founders day gathering of armoured knights, mitred bishops, floral-hatted ladies, uniformed generals, gowned masters and embroidered-waistcoated prefect police falling under fire. The frogmen add a surreal touch. After all, surrealism was initially a revolutionary movement (the revolution in the head) before it was watered down into shorthand for freaky weirdness for weirdness' sake. A similar fate which befell psychedelia and the whole idea of 60s experimentalism, the urge to discover new forms and once more set about deranging the senses to uncover new perspectives and hidden truths. Yeah, far out. It's a trip, man. Like, what were they on when they made that? 'Fall Out' has suffered from this syndrome. From the idea that it was a modish, throwaway indulgence, more weirdness for weirdness' sake. It's all too easy to dismiss vividly imaginative or challenging work on this basis (and if it's not drugs, it must be madness) particularly when it emerges from this period. But a 'revolution in the head', a conceptual breakthrough, a shift in consciousness requires new forms. New waves, new worlds.

The fold-up bikes, a 60s innovation and symbol of mobile urban modernity, are a diminished form of the penny farthing, which had been such a central, enigmatic symbol throughout the series. Constructed piece by piece during the end credits of each episode. These little versions are now pedalled out in a hurried and far from dignified fashion. The baroque and elevated perspective of power reduced to the hunched-up fluster of these comical clown bikes. Frogmen pedallers are as near to fish on bicycles as we are likely to get. The frogmen costumes may also be a sly pastiche of the underwater scenes in 'Thunderball,' and by extension of the studied cool of the Bond series as a whole. Elegant in their element, absurd out of it.

Fast cut scenes show us the panicked evacuation of the Village, fleets of helicopters rising above the children's storybook domes and minarets. Saigon was a few years in the future, but the helicopter as the emblematic vessel of the Viet Nam war was already fixed in people's minds via regular news footage. The mad dash of the colourfully caped villagers, scattering blindly in all directions, contrasts with the opening aerial shots in which all were calmly going about their daily business.

The rebels exit in the prison room, No.2's container coffin, which turns out to be attached to the back of an articulated lorry. A poetically ironic means of escape. Escape from incarceration by taking your prison cell with you. What once confined now protects. The Butler's smashing through the gates at the end of the tunnel coincides with the launching of the rocket, which rises between the old residences of No.2 and No.6, the gulf between individual and institutional power filled with fire. Stock footage of one of the Apollo launches (yet to land a man on the Moon, of course), notionally arising from the hollowed out caverns below, tacitly acknowledges the origins of the American space programme with Werner von Braun and those terrible workshops beneath the Kohnstein mountains.

And it's goodbye to Rover, who rises briefly only to dissolve in a bubbling Venusian soup, a primordial broth. A speeded up version of "I Love You Very Much" accompanies its return to undivided matter, protozoan gloop. An "I,I,I" song in an absurd register, another ego bubble burst. This odd, childlike Pinky and Perky ditty blends with electronic Village concrète sound to unsettling effect. We never see the fall out from the rocket. There is never any explosive conclusion, the concrete answers or fiery destruction which people were expecting. The rocket rises in the sky and we can imagine it continuing to rise beyond the Earth's atmosphere, the destructive impulse expelled into the outer reaches of space (or perhaps transformed into that race to reach the Moon). Like the orbiting craft in '2001: A Space Odyssey' which is the ultimate product of early man's discovery of the weapon, the bludgeoning bone tossed triumphantly up into the starry heavens.

The final scenes, in which our 'bande à part' enjoy their newly won freedom, are filled with a spirit of lightness and joy which remains infectiously uplifting on every viewing. They breathe the heady optimism of their times. The room on the road, the rebels hastily divesting themselves of their robes and throwing the guns out. They were a means of overthrowing power, not of maintaining it. An archetypal city gent in his Roller (a type long since consigned to cultural history), bowler-hatted and with red rosebud in his buttonhole (the rose rhyming with that pinned to No.48's topper) tunes in his radio with an elegantly grey-gloved hand. 'Dem Bones' has infected his airwaves, and he is soon passing the articulated human zoo cage in which the rebels are dancing to the music in their heads. No.6 sashays with a silver tea tray (he's the butler now in this democratic band) while No.2 and No.48 link arms and dosey-doe. Wild youth and reflective establishment dancing together, the songs of innocence and experience combining to the tune of this foolishly wise nonsense refrain of connection and resurrection. The gent in his status car does a comedy double-take before accelerating past towards the City and more sensible affairs.

No.48 jumps off and says his farewells, hitching along the A20. Shots of London are accompanied by romantic music. No.6 is on home territory again. The lorry pulls up on the Embankment, immediately attracting the attention of a passing bobby (remember them?). No.2 walks proudly towards the Houses of Parliament and strikes an iconic pose, looking up at Big Ben as the chimes strike. A little nod to his former self, the incumbent No.2 in the first 'escape' episode, 'The Chimes of Big Ben'. We can assume that these chimes are authentic, however, witnessed and heard in situ. No.6 watches him enter the House of Commons, waving goodbye from across the road, a safely neutral distance. We can imagine him becoming a rebellious backbencher, a principled thorn in the side of whatever government holds power. Turning around, he sees a policeman (the same one who greeted their arrival?). We switch to the perspective of the Butler, who impassively watches him doing the hip bone dance as the music makes once last appearance. In the real, extra-fictional world, passersby throw curious glances at Patrick McGoohan's antic behaviour. But with characteristic Englishness, they pretend that nothing unusual is occurring and pass hurriedly on. And then we get that glorious final image, No.6 hand in hand with the Butler as they run to catch the departing no.59 bus (numbers useful in this context), leaping up onto the Routemaster's platform. Be seeing you!

Alexis Kanner is privileged in the credits once more. And here he is, happily striding along in the middle of the road. Taking a step outside the fiction, here are actors utterly committed to the singular vision of Patrick McGoohan, ready to follow him to the edge of madness. Willing to risk life, limb and sanity. To dodge traffic on a busy (for the time) A road. Having tried one direction, he skips through the passing cars and gives the other way a go. Life lies ahead of him, he can try out all routes. Let fate play its part. Who knows where the wind will blow him. His optimism and openness to the play of chance are the tokens of bright-eyed youth, carefree and yet to accumulate the experiential burden of caution and suspicion.

No.6 arrives back at No.1, his home, with KAR120C parked outside, and the door glides open for Angelo Muscat's Butler, now credited. He gives a hint of a departing bow, to us as much as to his new boss and liberator (although where does the real power lie? If anywhere now). And for Patrick McGoohan? The credit simply reads 'Prisoner.' The prisoner of his own creation, which has driven him to the edge of sanity? The credit suggests and intense level of identification between actor (and in the end writer and director) and character. This is a part and an artistic endeavour in to which he has put everything. The credit suggests that he knows that it will to a large part be his greatest legacy, the work with which he will forever by most closely identified. It's an intuition which would prove entire accurate. Leo McKern is now dressed in standard bowler hat with white carnation in his buttonhole, formally attired for his credit. He poses by the statue of Richard the Lionheart in front of the Houses of Parliament. A visual pun, perhaps. Leo the Lion.

And we're back to the start, looping to the opening shot of the credits. The KAR on the runway, No.6 smiling as he races into the future. This time he really is going somewhere unimaginable though. No longer to stride furiously down that underground corridor and burst through those institutional doors like a gunfighter entering a saloon. Now the road is open. The choices are his and they are manifold. Freedom!

The penny farthing assembles itself one last time. We are still not sure as to why, or what it might signify. We never will be. "Goodnight children. Everywhere!"

Photo Courtesy of Andy Worsfold - Mini Moke in 'The Village' Livery

Portmeirion Photo showing Bristol Colonnade
& Green Dome (1982) - Courtesy of Mike Grant

Find out how Part 1 of 'Out of Order' concludes...Now!!!

TO BE CONTINUED...**WANT TO BE A VILLAGER IN PARTS 2 AND 3 OF STEVE MATT'S 'OUT OF ORDER'?** —-Well you can! Simply send a clear pic of yourself to Steve's email address below and he'll include your caricature amongst the Villagers somewhere between Arrival and Fall Out! —Be SEEING YOU!!: stevemattpr1soner@gmail.com

Please Send Your Contributions to:

itmeanswhatitsays50@gmail.com

In addition to Theories on Episode Order please send any
Portmeirion Convention Photos, Photos of Yourself, Family and Friends in costumes
inspired by characters from 'The Prisoner'.

Also theories or personal pieces about any aspect of the series such as is 'The General' the same one mentioned in 'The Schizoid Man', The Production of The Prisoner, the work of Vincent Tilsley, McGoohan and Anthony Skene as writers on the series — their influences and importance in creating their vision of where 'The Prisoner' was going, is Number One — a 'damaged' Curtis who has been resuscitated or an aspect of Number Six's Psyche, also please "feel free" to cover any aspect in Volume One in your own way.

We are also looking for any articles/essays/personal writing on 'Danger Man' (a.k.a. Secret Agent), McGoohan's input as Director/Actor in 'Columbo' with Peter Falk, McGoohan's interpretation of 'Brand', McGoohan's role in 'Mary Queen of Scots', 'The Phantom', 'Silver Streak', 'The Simpsons', 'Thomisina' 'Braveheart', 'Kings and Desperate Men', 'Scanners', 'The Man In The Iron Mask', 'The Hard Way', 'Jamaica Inn' — Armchair Theatre 'The Man Out There' & 'The Greatest Man In The World', 'Dr Syn — The Scarecrow of Romney Marsh', 'Hysteria','Escape From Alcatraz', 'A Time To Kill', 'Treasure Planet' and any other work on Film or Television featuring Patrick McGoohan.

If you feel there are other films and television programmes, or books that bear comparison with 'The Prisoner' please send us something on these topics as well.

BCNU! ☝: Closing Date June 30th 2018

(Please try to avoid profanity [swearing], negative comments for the sake of it, critical analysis is fine though, 3000 word limit for shorter pieces, however if you have more to say please 'feel free' to do so. We cannot accept Prose or Scripted Fiction based directly on 'The Prisoner' for legal reasons involving the current Copyright Holders of 'The Prisoner'. However Poetry is an acceptable form)

Kafkaesque

One of the descriptions of The Prisoner that keeps popping up is "Kafkaesque"[116]. At first, I had trouble understanding this simile, as the only Kafka I had been introduced to was his ramblings on the mundanities of everyday life, and his bizarre short story, Metamorphosis, in which an indolent middle aged man in transformed into a giant cockroach. Kafka was born in Prague, and lived between 1883 and 1924. He died young from tuberculosis, but in his short life created a huge body of work ranging from short stories and vignettes to novellas, few of which were actually published during his lifetime.

The two stories which relate directly to The Prisoner are The Trial and The Castle, neither of which would have been published at all, as Kafka wanted the manuscripts destroyed, but his friend and literacy agent Max Brod had them published after his untimely death. The Trial tells the story of Joseph K, a banker, who is arrested on his thirtieth birthday for an unspecified crime. After a short tribunal, K is left free and told to await further instruction from the Committee of Affairs. K is summoned to court, but finds the shabby courtroom overcrowded and chaotic, and during his address a couple are even having sex on the floor. K goes through a number of weird situations, still completely unaware of his crime, whereby he is seduced by a woman with webbed fingers, witnesses the two agents who arrested him being flogged, and has to deal with red tape and awkward bureaucrats at every level. After being pushed from pillar to post, and made to jump through hoops by the powers that be, K eventually gets to see a courtroom artist who had dealings with the court bureaucracy, who says he can help him to get a professional verdict of innocence from the lower court, which would be overturned by the higher court allowing the process to continue ad infinitum, or to slow down the process by seeking favour with the lower court judges. Either way, his fate is unavoidable. K is then sexually harassed by a number of

---

[116] Kafkaesque: (citation from dictionary.com) — Pronounciation: [kahf-kuh-esk]
adjective:- 1.of, pertaining to, characteristic of, or resembling the literary work of Franz Kafka:
the Kafkaesque terror of the endless interrogations.
2.marked by a senseless, disorienting, often menacing complexity:
Kafkaesque bureaucracies. (Origin 1945-50)

teenage girls, before escaping through a hatch which leads him back to the dusty, shabby courtroom. K goes to see a lawyer, but meets one of the lawyer's clients, Block, another man being pursued by the powers that be for an unknown crime, and has gone from being a successful businessman to a down and out, and now entirely dependent on the lawyer, who mocks Block for his subservience. The back asks K to meet a client at the cathedral, who does not turn up, so K explores the empty cathedral, eventually seeing a priest preparing to give a sermon. The Priest though, calls K's name and, from the pulpit berates K for his attitude towards the trial, and his weakness in pursuing women for help, eventually telling K a fable intended to explain his unfortunate situation. The fable tells of a man who wishes to seek entry to the Law through an open doorway, but the doorkeeper tells him he cannot pass at the present time. The man asks the doorkeeper when he can pass, but is told that it is possible, but not yet. The man waits at the door for years, trying to bribe the doorkeeper, but is still not allowed passage. The man continues to wait until the doorman is close to death. Before his death, the man asks the doorman why nobody else came to the doorway to seek the Law, and the doorman replies, that nobody else could be admitted here, since this doorway was made only for you, and now I am going to shut it. The Priest tells K that the parable is an ancient court text, and every generation has interpreted it differently. On the eve of K's 31st birthday, K doors nothing to resist as two officials come to his apartment and drag him away to his execution. The story expresses all the frustration of a man living in a country with a totalitarian government, his only escape from oppression being his death. A man who has no choice but to accept the inevitable. There are several movie versions of The Trial, the most celebrated being Orson Welles 1962 version, but Twin Peaks fans might enjoy the 1993 BBC version based on Harold Pinter stage adaptation starring Kyle McLaughlin as Joseph K and Anthony Hopkins as the Priest.

The other story by Franz Kafka, and the one I feel parallels Number 6's quest to find the identity of Number 1 is The Castle. Kafka began writing this story in the first person before contacting his protagonist's name to simply a letter, K. This seems in itself another way to reduce somebody to anonymity and dehumanize them, much like the numbers in The Prisoner. In another coincidence, the Critical Editions imprint of the book named the opening chapter "Arrival". K arrives in a village which appears to be governed by bureaucrats based in a mysterious nearby Castle. Wishing to figure out what's going on, K claims to be a chartered surveyor working for the castle authorities. He is assigned a contact with an official called Klamm, who arranges to introduce K to the mayor. The Mayor doesn't require K as a surveyor, presuming he was summoned by mistake, but instead gives him a job as a school caretaker, so K tries to get to grips with the strange customs and bureaucracy of the village. He tries to reach Klamm again to find out what is going on, but this is considered taboo. K believes Klamm to be the one person who holds all the secrets, but he is elusive and K never gets to find out. Nobody in the village knows what goes on in the castle, or what the officials actually do, other than that it is a bureaucracy which maintains flawless paperwork. K knows this is not true when he witnesses a bureaucrat destroying paperwork because he couldn't work out who the recipient should be. The Castle officials seem to want to preserve an illusion of being efficient and omnipotent, even though this is a lie. K manages to live in the village, forging relationships, and even marrying and settling down, but the true purpose of the Castle still eludes him. The officials are regarded as god like and attractive, despite being grotesquely ugly, rude and brutal, even sending for women from the village to sleep with them, which is seen as an honor, rather than a shameful act. Despite their unprofessional and incompetent behaviour, the officials are pretty much worshipped by the villagers and held in awe. Everybody has their own subjective theories and interpretations of what the officials actually do, and to what purpose, but these theories are conflicting and only cause more confusion. Few villagers have been to the Castle, except K's twin assistants and a messenger called Barnabus, but they have only seen the outer rooms. K, as an outsider, is the only person who dares to question the authority of the Castle, and seeks to understand it, although he never finds his answers. On his death bed, the Castle notifies him that "his legal claim to live in the village was not valid, yet, taking certain auxiliary circumstances into account, he was permitted to live and work there."

The 1991 cult movie Kafka, directed by Steven Sonderberg and starring Jeremy Irons looking pale and cadaverous as the eponymous author, is one part biopic one part surrealist mystery, all weird, mixing elements of The Castle with scenes from Kafka's own life. It wasn't a big box office hit, but has achieved cult status, and is often compared with Terry Gilliam's Brazil. The movie is stylistically beautiful, and switches from black and white to colour for the bizarre science fiction scenes. Kafka works as an insurance clerk by day, and a writer of short stories by night. By chance he becomes embroiled in a conspiracy after one of his colleagues is found murdered, joining a revolutionary terrorist group who plan to overthrow the secret organisation controlling society from the castle on the hill. Unlike in Kafka's book, The Castle, Kafka actually manages to gain access, finding a scene which wouldn't be out of place in the Prisoner, where captured revolutionaries are undergoing horrific brain surgery to rehabilitate them into society. His showdown with Ian Holm's villainous Dr. Murnau is the most Prisoneresque scene of all, and is reminiscent of many of the interchanges between Number 6 and Number 2.

Kafka.   What will you say when the great faceless mass come calling?

Dr M: Well, a crowd is easier to control than an individual. A crowd has a common purpose. The purpose of the individual is always in question.

Kafka.   That's what you're trying to eliminate, isn't it? Everything that makes one human being different from another. But you'll never, never, never, reach a man's soul through a lens.

Dr M.   That rather depends on which end of the microscope you're on doesn't it?

Isn't this scene strikingly similar to the exchange between Brand and the Provost we discussed earlier?

In a twist on the term "Kafkaesque", I would suggest we now use "Prisoneresque" to describe the new media which pays homage to the surreal postmodernism of the Prisoner, and McGoohan's individual vision. It can be used to describe movies such as the Wachowski sister's Matrix trilogy dating from 1999, 1997 Canadian sci fi movie Cube, Park Chanwook's 2003 Old Boy and it's 2013 Spike Lee remake, the previously discussed Divergent series, The Congress, A Clockwork Orange, Inception, Shutter Island, Suckerpunch and Kafka (of course), TV shows such as Lost and Wayward Pines, through to more recent mind benders such as The Cure For Wellness, a 2013 psychological thriller directed by Gore Verbinski. All share the same paranoia, clinical elitism and explore what it is to be an individual, and celebrate the individuals standing up against an oppressive or disingenuous regime, exactly as Kafka did in his celebrated novellas, and Number 6 did in The Village.

If we choose, we can live in a world of comforting illusion - Noam Chomsky

Clough Williams Ellis's grand design, the Portmeirion village is the perfect setting for the Prisoner in more ways than one. On the surface, it provides a Wonderland for Number 6's Alice, a candy coloured Ponyville which would not be out of place in a nursery rhyme, or Pee Wee Herman fantasy. Portmeirion was built in Gwynedd, North Wales by Sir Clough, between 1925 and 1975, and resembles an Italianate village, like Portofino on the Italian Riviera. It was built of fragments of demolished buildings, elaborate facades, relics and pieces of set dressing, never the work of one architect, but curated, collected in bits like a magpie's nest of trinkets. It's been the setting for music videos, Doctor Who and even

CBeebies shows for toddlers, and has enthralled visitors for decades. It is very much like the Potemkin villages I described earlier, because nothing is quite what it seems to be on the surface.

On a deeper level, the structural design of Portmeirion village is a whimsical example of postmodernism, where architectural edifices and statues from diverse cultures and historical periods are crammed into one gaudy and ostentatious whole. The Gloriette is modeled after the Schonbraunn palace in Vienna. The famous Green Dome (Which is now grey) is fabricated ad hoc from plywood and lead sheeting. Portions of Hindu temples, Buddha figures and Greek gods jostle for space amongst Edwardian and Victorian facades, with no concern for their symbolic or religious meaning. The meanings have been long lost, and the images are retained purely for their aesthetic value. It is fitting that The Prisoner, as a TV show is a grand example of postmodernism too. The definition of postmodern media can be described thus: as embodying scepticism towards ideas and ideals of the modern era, especially the idea of progress, reason, objectivity, certainty and personal identity. It takes great delight in deconstructing conventions and traditions, and considers everything, including the grand ideas of science and religion to be nothing but social constructions. McGoohan's comments in the 1977 Prisoner Puzzle interview make it clear that he understood postmodern concepts very well. Maybe it's wrong to say this, but McGoohan did seem to aspire to a form of intellectual elitism, the intellectual liberals of the 1960's who'd grown up versed in Marxism and Sartre had now turned to the "avant garde" and high culture, completely disregarding public taste, and trying to be all the more controversial and "way out". Indeed, The Prisoner did frustrate and anger those "lowest common denominator" viewers who expected the TV to do their thinking for them, but it excited the Mensa class of high IQ free-thinkers who'd grown bored with Coronation Street and The Saint, and the "one size fits all" approach to televisual entertainment. The Prisoner itself is a deconstruction, firstly of the spy drama popular during the Cold War era, but also of the western and science fiction. It comments on psychiatry, conformity and human nature. Both the monkey mask and the ubiquitous penny farthing bicycle are intended by McGoohan to ironically represent the concept of progress. The penny farthing bike brings to mind Mahatma Gandhi's spinning wheel, in itself also a powerful representation of anti industrialization, and a route to economic independence for India's poor. Unlike the spinning wheel tho, the penny farthing produces nothing, it is not even adequate as a viable form of transport. (Which is why we never see one being actually ridden in the Village) It could almost be considered Zen in its uselessness, much like a Japanese "chindogu" or "unuseless" creation.

In the world of "hypernormalisation", the world of Solaris, our current "information age", we are constantly bombarded with multiple narratives, all with multiple agendas, it's being increasingly hard to tell the programs from the adverts, the news from propaganda, the "truth" from the fictions created with the sole purpose of parting us from our money and our morals. We are all at once being deceived, and choosing to device ourselves, clinging to and then discarding ideologies like old clothes, one they get worn out, or are no longer relevant. We pick and choose from a pot pourri of different, very often conflicting narratives, instead of the former absolutes of politics, religion and culture that people before us fought and died to defend. It is the very nature of postmodernism reject the idea of a single, objective truth, instead viewing truth to be subjective and mutable. If there is no objective truth, why should your your truth also be my truth? Jean Francois Lyotard, in his book The Postmodern Condition, A Report on Knowledge, defines postmodernism thus: a matter of incredulity towards meta-narratives, the overarching single stories which attempt to sum up the whole of human history, or that attempt to put all of our knowledge into a single framework, such as the idea that humanity's story is one of progress towards greater social justice and understanding through science. We have become sceptical of these ideas, no where more obviously than in the blossoming of the alternative media. Flat Earthers, UFOlogists, white supremacists, transhumanists, and televangelists all offer alternative meta-narratives, each to their own advantage, and if indeed there is no objective truth, their ideas are just as valid as science, the Big Bang, Darwinism, the Bible and any other effort to prove the unprovable. As Yann Martell concludes in his great postmodern novel, The Life of Pi, it doesn't actually matter which story is true, but which story you like.

British conspiracy theory writer (or conspiracy fact) David Icke, in his books and seminars describes the physical world we live in as "The Matrix", after the Wachowski's seminal films, but this concept goes back much further, to the early Christian Gnostics. To the Gnostics, there was a very clear delineation between the spiritual and physical world, between the sacred and profane. We are, to quote The Police, "Spirits in the Material World", beings of infinite consciousness trapped in a cage created for us, what we perceive as the "real world" nothing but a cheap carbon copy of the divine. This "Matrix" was created by the Archons, or the Masters, who Icke describes as reptilian aliens. The Gnostics believed it to have been created by Yaldabaoth, the despotic creator god who resembled a serpent with a lion's head, who some identify as the ancient god of the Hebrews who demanded sacrificial blood offerings and punished his worshippers, others consider him and

Satan to be one and the same. Kafka played with the idea of Gnostic demons, or deceiving spirits, in his Klamm character, and the grotesque officials in The Castle. K's search for enlightenment drives him to understand who it is deceiving and controlling them, just like Number 6's search for Number 1 in The Prisoner. Can we really trust anything we see and hear, or take at "face value"? Either way, the world around us is not what we think it is, it is a Star Trek holodeck projection we have become conditioned to see as reality. This projection is personal, our Village, our reality. One wishes it was as simple as taking a red pill to see beyond the veil, and leave the "world of comforting illusion". Plato illustrated this with his cave analogy. Imagine we are in a cave, chained so unable to turn our heads. Behind is a fire is burning, and a walkway over which puppeteers can hold up puppets, casting shadows on the wall before us. We prisoners are unable to see the puppets, just the shadows they cast on the wall. Would we take what we see as real? Do we not do this every time we open our eyes? Do we feel imprisoned, our are we happy to be misled, and live indolent lives, unquestioning the powers that be as "good citizens"? Do we prefer to watch the shadows on the wall, without wishing to find out who or what is making them? As The priest tells Joseph K in The Trial, "You don't need to accept everything as true, you only have to accept it as necessary", to which K replies, "depressing view, the lie made into the rule of the world".

Who is Number One?

Does Number 6 ever escape? Can anyone ever escape the prisons they make for themselves? The prisons of their own minds and their own bodies? Conscious as we are, we must be aware of our own limitations, we are practically blind and deaf creatures which live for our short four score years and ten on an isolated rock spinning through infinite space. (Or do we?) No-one can escape their own situation, time and the aging process. We are prisoners of our own biology, our hormones, our chromosomes going back to Adam and Eve, going back to the monkey people. One of the biggest existential mysteries of life is the big question of whether or not we even have free will, or are we simply automatons, living or our pre determined lives as part of the cosmic computer program. Are we even responsible for our actions, be they good or bad? Can anyone break free of their programming? As Number 6 faces Number 1, he is shown his future in the crystal ball, traditionally a mystical scrying tool for clairvoyance. But what does he see? Prison bars slamming in his face, again and again, ad infinitum. We know at this moment there is no escape for Number 6. Can anybody cheat fate? In the immortal words of Patrick McGoohan, "Your village may be different from other people's villages, but we are all prisoners." So this brings us the the second big McGuffin in that series. Who is Number 1? Well, I think by now that is glaringly obvious that Number 1 is none other than PATRICK MCGOOHAN HIMSELF! He, the auteur, the writer of the show bible, the embodiment of Brand, of Drake and the rebellious Dr Syn, is the Great Architect himself. He, just like anyone of us is confronted with his shadow self, his bestiality and his mortality, and shown that he cannot run away from himself, and the snarling, insane face behind the mask is his own. There is no escape for any of us, we are all Number 1 in our own, personal, village. As he returns to his home at 1 Buckingham Place, we are acutely aware of the big number 1 on the door, the door opens automatically, and he enters. The next thing we we see is him screaming up the airstrip again, in his tiny green and yellow Lotus, icy blue eyes blazing, wind in his hair, and just as the crystal ball showed him, it begins again.

But what does it mean? The philosopher Albert Camus (1913 - 1960) saw it this way. Because we have consciousness, we feel that life is meaningful. However, as the universe has no meaning, we are conflicted. We need to embrace this meaninglessness to overcome this contradiction. Therefore, life will be lived all the better if it has no meaning. Indeed, it really does mean what it says. And it says nothing.

BCNU
V.J Clarke, July 2017

A New Vision of 'The Prisoner'

It seems appropriate somehow that I write a piece as this book draws to an end looking at the various threads of the series and that have formed a part of this book.

However first I will make clear that a second volume has been proposed and will be produced in due course simply as the amount of material available and submitted has been overwhelming. There has simply not been enough time to incorporate all the material in this single volume and in addition some material has not been available by the deadline and is being held over for Volume 2.

There are so many elements to 'The Prisoner' and its' relationship to the rest of McGoohan's work — with the greatest respect to Patrick and his family he remained in certain ways a 'Prisoner' of the series (its influence never leaving him) until he finally sadly left this mortal coil in early 2009. I can only hope that he is finally a free man as he had so memorably strived to be all his life.

Moke with Prisoner-esque Seven in background in Portmeirion courtesy of VJ Clarke

We have examined everything from the History of the Lotus Seven and the Mini Moke to Psychology and Psychiatry, Christianity thanks to Peter Dunn, Who Number Six Really Is – thanks to Vickie Clarke, the Controversy of the Episode Order – which will be continued in Volume 2; to the quirks of the dubbing of 'Arrival' into French. The Role of Number Two as the Village Administrator has occupied some discussion but this is an aspect for greater discussion in the next volume of 'It Means What It Says...'

It would be fair to say that I never would have expected this book to have been quite so extensive and to cover so much in the course of it's pages.

I would like to conclude by offering some thoughts on one more topic before I acknowledge everyone who has helped make this book the fine tome that it is by contributing their work or their time towards making this a worthwhile endeavour.

A DANCE INTO THE UNDERWORLD

I have admired 'Dance of the Dead' as a key episode of 'The Prisoner' since I first saw it — the opening scenes in which the Doctor pushes Number Six for classified information with the assistance of Roland Walter Dutton seem exactly what the series needs. Here there is conflict between Number Two and the Doctor — who feels he can actually break Number Six and Mary Morris' is slightly stern but clear that 'he must be won over...'

What we get is a sense that this unauthorised interrogation of Number Six has been duly noted and although later on she claims she will overlook this when making a report — we don't know that she is being entirely truthful. There is a great deal of subtext and subterfuge in this episode, much of what we see and hear is misdirection.

We are led to believe many different things — that somehow Number Six's floating of the body washed up on the Village shore will act as a gruesome message in a bottle. It also seems that Number Two is behaving in a very hands-off way to the whole issue of Number Six's resignation — as mentioned above she actually halts an interrogation that might have shed light on this. Roland Walter Dutton becomes an unwilling pawn in the plans of the Village — possibly he is used to spy on Number Six against his will then interrogated about his activities and whereabouts.

However over and beyond this are the influences of Dance of the Dead such as the Jean Cocteau movie 'Orphee' and by connection the tale of Orpheus and the Underworld. Anthony Skene takes the opportunity to reference the tale in particular by placing the second half of the episode in the Underworld of the Village. This is represented by the Town Hall which only allows Number Six to gain entry because it is carnival, following his attendance at the dancehall Number Six explores the Underworld on his own. The corridors, secret and locked doors only accessible by a key found by chance and luck form part of this Underworld. It is significant that on the two occasions Number Six tries to follow them he is effectively led to locations despite having seemingly chosen his own path. Indeed the layout is suitably labyrinth-like particularly in the scene where the Villagers give chase with there maddening howl-seemingly a scream of the already dead.

Also some of the phrases in the English translation of 'Orphee' have a familiar feel for example the Princess and Orpheus have this exchange early in the film:

Princess: "Sleeping or dreaming. The Dreamer must accept his dreams."
Orpheus: "I have a right to an explanation"
Princess: "You have every right, my dear and so do I...so we're even"

The words and phrasing have a similar feel to the lyrical (and beautifully shot) scene on Portmeirion's beach with Number Two (Mary Morris) dressed as Peter Pan and Number Six in his own suit (specially delivered for the occasion).

Number Two: What were you looking at?
Number Six: A light.
Number Two: A star.
Number Six: A boat.
Number Two: An insect.
Number Six: A plane.
Number Two: A flying fish.
Number Six: Somebody who belongs to my world.
Number Two: This is your world. I am your world. If you insist on living a dream you may be taken for mad.
Number Six: I like my dream.
Number Two: Then you are mad.[117]

Jean Cocteau's 'Orphee' (1950) may have more influence on the writing of the series than the writing of 'Dance of the Dead' — the English subtitled version includes a radio message with the words 'Your Attention Please...' as regularly used in Fenella Fielding's announcements as the 'Village Voice' in 'The Prisoner'. Of course as with many things related to 'The Prisoner' this may be a coincidence — the phrase would have been common usage during the Second World War when significant announcements or developments took place. In addition it would probably have been used in British Holiday Camps to make a Public Announcement to Holidaymakers.

As Dave Barrie attests there are 'dark haunting undercurrents' [118] in Dance of the Dead and this is perhaps more true of this than any other episode of 'The Prisoner' — as it has a many layered plot. Just when you feel you are following a linear narrative — a conventional action-adventure series albeit with other deeper aspects — 'Dance of The Dead' throws a curveball at us. We are no longer sure of the reality of events, which progress as if in a dream — at times it's as if Number Six is asleep dreaming a disjointed [119]surreal story of life in the Village.

A concern has been raised that 'Dance of The Dead' doesn't belong halfway through the series because he protests

---

[117] Taken from Dance of the Dead, Anthony Skene, 1966, Everyman Films.

[118] 'In The Land of Dark Dreams And Long Shadows' - Dave Barrie

[119] Photograph of Lady's Lodge and The Prisoner Shop, Battery Square 2016 courtesy of Ian Orchard.

"I'm New Here"[120] but by way of explanation perhaps he is in the midst of a nightmare brought on by the attempts in the opening scene to get him to talk. He hears Dutton's voice on the telephone during this experiment and the rest of the episode is his nightmarish vision of his time in the Village, not necessarily in any chronological order, creating an imaginary Village Carnival and Number Six inwardly punishing himself mentally. Indeed perhaps the Village actually have gone too far and have broken Number Six and the remainder of the series is him in a Waking Coma - mental activity taking place but his mind gradually deteriorating as we head towards 'Fall Out'. There are many layers here and we can never be sure that we have imbibed it all.

There are those that suggest the whole series has been a nightmare and that the gas administered by the 'Undertaker' was either fatal or has left him permanently unconsciousness and the Village is the world he creates either to destroy himself or to retain his mental faculties.

Indeed in this episode the Villagers act at their most fully conditioned, they move as one in the Carnival Parade and Dance together in a single room. When Number Six is sentenced to death they become like a pack of animals and the implication is that if they caught him they would actually kill him. The concept of altering the body from the beach to resemble Number Six also means that in theory Number Six would be dead to the outside world after this episode. This throws another spanner in the works for the running order of the episodes of the series. Of course that assumes we take these events as having literally happened.

Obviously this episode is about death both literally and 'figuratively' — Number Two (Mary Morris) is trying to destroy (create the 'death' of) Number Six's hope of ever escaping and returning to the outside world and was to have originally have included the Doctor involved in burying a corpse. Presumably Patrick McGoohan decided this aspect was to have been too gruesome for family viewing.

Returning for the moment to Cocteau's 'Orphee' we can see how its influence may be far wider ranging than we first thought on Anthony Skene's work on the series. One of many obscure, surreal radio messages in a similar vein to that heard in 'Dance of the Dead' states:

"The mirrors would do well to reflect further..."[121]

This suggests all manner of interpretations — 'reflect' being a term related to thinking about as well as its literal reflection in the mirror. Of course both Curtis in 'The Schizoid Man' and Number One in 'Fall Out' are to some extent reflections of Number Six. More relevant to Anthony Skene's work is the lop sided mirror in 'A, B. And C' which Number Six struggles to straighten to regain control of the 'Dreamy Party'.

---

[120] Or if this really follows 'Many Happy Returns' his long 'absence' makes him feel his residence in the Village is in some way: 'residence'.

[121] Jean Cocteau, 'Orphee' (1950)

Photograph of Piazza/Village Square courtesy Ed Fordham

Its also interesting that the Princess in Orphee insists on telling Orpheus that

"You try too hard to understand what's going on young man and that's a serious mistake."[122]

On one level we have Orpheus being told to avoid looking for explanations even being warned not too. On another more-meta level the line is aimed at the audience of the film — by analysing too much the ideas, influences and meanings of a film or a television series we become lost. Instead of understanding something more we can end up hopelessly tangled in different, contradictory interpretations.

The Villagers' not cheering visibly after the Town Crier's announcement of Carnival although the sound effect is heard on the soundtrack mysteriously adds to the feel of them being 'dead to the world' and 'somewhat unreal'. The faces of the Villagers look more haunted than ever during this episode — by virtue of liberties taken with the soundtrack — on several occasions there is the sound of cheering, murmuring and so on but the shots chosen show that the Villagers themselves are silent.

As a society we can often feel our voice is not heeded, that those in power are not concerned with our potential or our concerns and needs. Our superiors seem not to notice our abilities or to run roughshod over them, our local councillors may be more concerned with internal policy and political manoeuvring than how policies affect the people and our candidates to become MPs, Political Parties, Government and Party Leaders are more concerned at Election time with point scoring against one another and setting out a raft of contradictory, even inflammatory policies rather than listening to the public at grassroots level and their concerns.

That's just a snapshot of a democracy at work, so imagine how it must feel in a country run by Dictatorship where only one viewpoint is allowed — the ruling Party and in particular its leader — all minorities are crushed and any possibility of rights for women, foreigners due to xenophobia, or LGBT people negated.

It seems odd that this topic should come up, even as an aside, when discussing 'Dance of

---

[122] Ibid

the Dead' as this is very much the area covered in greater depth by 'Free For All'. This just goes to show that 'The Prisoner' is never really a single issue in each episode series and that the major themes of lack of freedom, loss of identity, misuse and abuse of science, society and by extension the world progressing too fast and so on are part and parcel of the series as a whole.

So what can we say in summary about 'Dance Of The Dead' — we are watching a very deep episode with layers like that of an onion, which can be peeled away to reveal different ideas, concepts and aspects of itself. The carnival with its jolly atmosphere and the opportunity for the Villagers' to take on other roles is opposed by the darkness at the heart of the Village. Number Six is victimised for being himself having self-will while the other Villagers obey the herd and at the episodes end threaten to kill him after he is tried for contravening 'the rules'. Mary Morris' Number Two is also ultimately ruthless enough to allow the mob to chase down Number Six — stating sinisterly "It's the rules, my dear".
Her final words to Number Six when he insists the Village won't ever win "Then how very uncomfortable for you, dear chap..." say it all. Number Six will suffer trying desperately to ensure the Village doesn't overwhelm and overcome him.

Conclusions : Can We 'Understand' — 'The Prisoner'?

This is not an anthology show where each week a different topic or slant is looked at — the whole series across all its episodes retains its identity : although it is sometimes stretched to breaking point — 'The Girl Who Was Death' for example seems to have little to do with the other episodes. However by looking closely we can see that the character McGoohan plays in the Village Story Book is trapped into a sequence of events by narrative causality. He has to take over from Colonel Hawk English to investigate his Death as requested by his 'Boss' in the Record Booth and then because of the message intended for him has to go to his local pub to drink the poison and enough alcoholic shots to expel it. Each step in 'Deaths' plan has to be followed by McGoohan because the plot cannot conclude with him winning over against the Girl and her mad Scientist father without him following her rules and resolving them to advance the plot. If at any point the McGoohan character resigned from his job and chose not to stop London's destruction the narratives wheels fall off. It would also be very underwhelming to end a children's story with — so I kept out of her way from then on so I wasn't killed and the mad scientist succeeded in his plans to attack London.[123] In other words as this is a story in a book he can only follow the route laid out in the story itself, as a character between pages he is just as trapped 'by events' as he is in the Village itself. Even in a children's story book Number Six is a Prisoner.

The fact is that 'The Prisoner' is part action-adventure, part spy-fi, part allegory, part 'unconventional' drama, part a map for people's personal growth & part a heady brew of Cocteau, Orwell, Kafka but more importantly McGoohan, Markstein, Tomblin, Tilsley, Shampan, Mival, Dearberg, S. Smith, Skene and so on... (ironically too many names to

---

[123] It's hard to talk about this without reference to terrorist attacks in Manchester and London over the month during which I wrote of this piece. Suffice it to say that my thoughts are with those who lost loved ones or who were injured in these attacks.

number). [124]

One thing we can be sure of 'The Prisoner' is about social conflict — this is particularly in evidence between Number Six and Number Two as he clashes with successive leaders desperate for him to reveal his secrets. This type of conflict according to D. Lockwood is 'interpersonal and occurs only within social interactions' [125] What the Village hopes to gain from Number Six is in point of fact 'internalisation' where Number Six as an individual both learns to follow and accepts the social reality and norms of Village society [126] — this is something encouraged by Number Two (Leo McKern) in 'The Chimes of Big Ben when he convinces Number Six to settle down and carve for the Arts and Crafts Exhibition.

Weber's theory of rationalisation — splits itself into 7 emphases the last of which focuses on society and how a combination of state control, administration and bureaucracy formed part of his vision of capitalist societies. He saw such societies as creating a 'iron cage' where individuals would become more subject to bureaucratic regulation and government surveillance. This can be perceived as one of the general tenets of the series where paranoia in the knowledge that you could be constantly watched and the Village bureaucracy — in Arrival we see an extensive file on Number Six and the corridor lined with filing cabinets in the opening titles emphasise this aspect. Further to this Weber believed that all human action in a capitalist society must involve control, measurement and calculation. [127]

In fact Max Weber's position became 'the founder of modern sociology' who managed through a series of empirical studies to discover and create the various areas of sociological debate within the discipline and help establish what we now consider to be the boundaries of 'Sociology'. His analysis of society comes painfully close to Marxism in that the two theories of alienation and rationalisation are closely related. [128] However there are other ways in which the two theories differentiated in particular Weber did not regard as imminent the potential collapse of Capitalism as Marx and many Marxist theorists do so. [129]

Given this, is 'Fall Out' about the collapse of a capitalist society, a commentary on the Vietnam War as sometimes supposed, or indeed a subtle commentary on racism (through the Ku Klux Clan Outfits compromised by the half black-half white masks?) Is 'Fall Out' instead depicting a society allowing an individual to choose to lead or to leave the Village or his need for authority behind? By extension is this final decision really about Number Six

---

[124] What I'm trying to say is it takes its form and meaning from the personal preference of the person following it at that particular time. The fact is that each individual's view of what the series represents can and will change over time. In other words we chip away at 'the meaning of The Prisoner' but we can never truly understand it — because of these shifts in meaning.

[125] (Abercrombie N, Hill S & Turner B.S.,1988, Dictionary of Sociology, p49)

[126] Ibid, p 127

[127] Ibid, p202

[128] Ibid, p267-9

[129] Ibid p268

choosing to resign once again — he refuses the offer of Village leadership 'metaphorically he resigns the post before taking it up'. Then just a few minutes later we see him in his Lotus 7 speeding towards us — on his way to resign from his top secret position creating an ouroboros situation — Number Six ends up chasing his own tail.[130] Conversely does the rocket launch really mean the Village needs to be evacuated — is its destruction imminent — or is the chaos that takes place merely due to the time-limited pressure under which the script was written?[131]

Our desire to understand 'The Prisoner' can at times make us like the subjects in Pavlov's experiments with Dogs or the treatment of the Rook in this mode in 'Checkmate'. Each piece of information, each insight we gather into the series, each interpretation may actually take us further away from 'Understanding' what we feel we need to Understand. As we read other people's interpretations we gain new insight as we take on board their thoughts and feelings on a particular topic. Essentially we create a 'metaphysical' buffet for ourselves taking what we want and leaving the rest behind. We may begin to understand one area of the series better but we quickly find that each new insight contradicts something we have either long believed or opens up a discussion.

I hope that rather than explaining 'The Prisoner' once and for all in this book we have instead revitalised discussion about what it really all means. While we may all be essentially aware that this is something that can never be fully resolved the 'fun' or 'intellectual exercise' is in the effort. There are some things that a variety of us may agree on — however its almost certain that someone has a contrasting view and that is the beauty of 'The Prisoner' — the discussion will continue. It has stood the test of 50 years and shown itself to be relevant in the present maybe even more so than when it was first shown. It has often been banded about that 'The Prisoner' was ahead of its time and we are just now catching up with some of its warnings.

Jean-Francois Lyotard, to take another avenue for a moment, saw the student revolt which took place in the wake of 'Fall Out' in 1968 as anarchist and libertarian.[132] The posters and graffiti of the time carried this message forward stating in bold terms 'it is forbidden to forbid'. Lyotard saw this as being a protest against bureaucracy, depersonalisation, repression and routininization the very themes that are central to our reading of 'The Prisoner'. Lyotard also suggests that if we are always thinking and theorising we cannot 'let go' or enjoy things for what they are.[133]

Postmodernism is about the changes often huge, sweeping ones that take place in our

---

[130] This actually occurred to me when watching YouTube videos of Cats & Dogs chasing their own tails. I knew that it would come in useful one day!

[131] This is the most probable explanation for the manner in which 'Fall Out' proceeds but it is much more fun to create theories around what happens. After all without that attitude you wouldn't be reading this book.

[132] Sarup M 'An Introductory Guide to Post-Structualism & Postmodernism' p99

[133] Ibid p100

contemporary culture and society.As such it covers many strands of thought from drama and film to architecture and philosophy, anthropology, sociology, geography and many more.[134]It is certainly about ambivalence maybe even a state of mind an attack on as Lyotard says in 'The Postmodern Condition' "the grand narratives" — postmodernism criticises the idea of universal knowledge. In a sense therefore the Village's striving for 'Information' from Number Six reflects on this — they can never attain the knowledge or information they seek. In effect we can never grasp the meanings of society and by extension those of 'The Prisoner'[135]In addition the ability to pause video/dvd/bluray means we can escape the 'auteur' and replay parts we adore or have missed or search for meaning particularly when the visual text has an 'allegorical element'. The 'immediacy' of 'The Prisoner' draws us into its web but we discover it is actually 'artifice'. At the end of the day we each see something different or 'subjective'.[136]

Video, DVD, Blu-Ray and Downloadable versions of the series have enabled us to get inside scenes or episodes, pausing the action, backing up to check on whether we actually saw what we think we saw — in essence we have the opportunity 'in increasing quality' to provide fuel for new ideas and theories or to correct misunderstandings or spot continuity or production errors. For example the 6 private sign outside Number Six's cottage is sometimes reversed to read private 6 and we can rings around ourselves trying to explain why — especially if the correct version was seen in the same episode or moments earlier.

Fandom can thus become a rewriting of the manual of itself — certain aspects of fandom search for deeper meaning and analysis of the series they celebrate — while other aspects of fandom want information from the actors, the crew, the extras and so on about the making of the series. Still others are primarily interested in McGoohan as an individual his very tenacity, his strengths and his weaknesses — his ability to play loners well for example impacts on his ability to play relationships. Certainly that was true at this stage of his career when the majority of his roles were loners in some way, even when a character was familial there was a distance between him and his wife and children on screen. I speak in particular of his performance in Brand where his religious fervour for want of a better term leads to his downfall. Brand is flawed in that he cannot see that his 'fundamentalist doctrine' does not fit well with the people who become his flock including his family.

This 'all or nothing' concept can be relayed in to 'The Prisoner' — McGoohan has the option of telling the Village authorities 'nothing' about his resignation and by extension his secret work. Or he can assume that now he has resigned it is safe to 'breach security' and cough up his secrets — as we established the Village are not just interested in the 'McGuffin' of his resignation but other extensive details regarding his secret work. This leaves 'P' as he is known in the scripts or Number Six as we often refer to him as we have no other 'real name' to give him with a quandary. If he tells them nothing — the Village tries again using a different method to systemically break him until he tells them his secrets.

---

[134] Ibid p129

[135] Ibid p147

[136] Ibid p175-6

Perhaps he has done so — perhaps what we see at the end of 'A Change of Mind' as suggested earlier by Vickie Clarke is a distortion of the reality of 'Instant Social Conversion'. How do we know the wool was not pulled over our eyes — they finally carried out an 'invasive method' and were able to extract the information they required? The fact is we were fed false information as early as 'The Chimes of Big Ben' — the trip tallied and the various expected forms of transport were shown but Nadia and Number Six were on a round trip back to the Village not London.

At this stage Number Six questions whether he has risked his own and Nadia's lives to return to a place that is 'different' from the Village. Indeed actions in fairly recent history prove that Britain was not always that 'different' from the way the Village was run. The Defence of the Realm Act passed through the Houses of Parliament in August of 1914. It lead to the declaration of martial law and when all DORA laws were consolidated a few months later in November 1914 it passed certain powers to officer above that of captain. In effect they were given the legal justification to put on trial or 'sentence to death' any citizen who was deemed to be breaking 'wartime regulations'. [137] Lord Halsbury considered that this was the "most unconstitutional thing that has ever happened in this country."[138] In fact we can reflect upon how the power of the individual's free-will has been increasingly eroded since 1967. Many of the things depicted in 'The Prisoner' have come to pass — more often than not we are known by numbers or alpha-numeric codes : mobile phone numbers, library card numbers, bank account numbers, credit card numbers, account numbers of all types, National Insurance numbers and so on. Although we still have names the majority of the time people are interested in these codes or cards rather than our names.

Our ability to change the way society is run even in so-called 'liberal democracies' is reduced, once a leader and political party have their feet under the table they will do whatever they can to stay there. In the past Mrs Thatcher started a war with the Falkland Islands to create jingoistic support for herself and the Conservative Party. In the USA despite fighting a campaign in which he insulted everyone Donald Trump won through because the Electoral Colleges enabled him to do so. Ever since it could be said that President Trump has attempted to insult the intelligence not just of American's but people across the world. Meanwhile Theresa May scrabbles around with her attempts to hold on to power at all costs, trying to gain the support and any ideas from the opposition. No wonder Jeremy Corbyn offered to send her a copy of the Labour Manifesto from the recent Election.

How therefore can we be 'free' as Number Six so memorably protested, we strive to be individuals — yet it is really only when we work together that we can change society for the better. Do we compromise our 'freedom' in this way by becoming part of the herd — doesn't this just mean we are absorbed into a group's way of thinking. Or does it give the opportunity for our voice to be heard? What if we are shouted down or ignored in the

---

[137] Wilson B, 'What Price Liberty? — How Freedom Was Won And Is Being Lost' pp191-192, Faber and Faber

[138] Ibid p192

same way Number Six or Sir is during 'Fall Out'?

This discussion shows us why I subtitled this book 'Trying To Understand 'The Prisoner'' —
We will never completely understand this in the way that any piece of art cannot be
understood. Whatever the initial intentions were in creating the series by the final episode
'Fall Out' we have strayed a long way from the 'almost' conventional action-adventure of
'Arrival'. We are left with more questions than answers and we loop back from the closing
shot of 'Fall Out' to the beginning of 'Arrival'. Of course while we remain 'individuals' we
can never fully agree if "It Means What It Says..."

All unattributed photographs from the collection of Ian Orchard &
Ed Fordham taken in Portmeirion 2014 or 2016...

Bibliography & Further Reading

Brainwashing - The Secret History of Mind Control — Dominic Streatfield
The Prisoner - The Original Scripts - Vol 1 & 2 - Edited and Annotated by Robert Fairclough
The Prisoner and Danger Man - Dave Rogers
The Prisoner, Alaine Carraze & Helene Oswald, 1990, Virgin Publications
The Cooler - George Markstein
Village World, Max Hora, A NUMBER SIX PUBLICATION
Fall Out - The Unofficial and Unauthorised Guide To The Prisoner - Alan Stevens & Fiona Moore
The Dictionary of Espionage-Christopher Dobson & Ronald Payne
Nineteen Eighty-Four - George Orwell
The Trial - Franz Kafka
Brave New World - Aldous Huxley
The Handmaid's Tale - Margaret Atwood
Fahrenheit 451 - Ray Bradbury
A Clockwork Orange - Anthony Burgess
Animal Farm - George Orwell
The Prisoner Handbook - Steven Paul Davis (Foreword by Alex Cox)
MI6 Fifty Years of Special Operations - Stephen Dorril
An Introduction to Film Analysis - Technique and meaning in Narrative Film - Michael Ryan and Melissa Lenos
Exploring Your Dreams - How to use dreams for personal growth and creative inspiration - Ruth Snowden
An Introductory Guide to Post-Structialism and Postmodernism - Madan Sarup
George Markstein & The Prisoner - edited by Roger Goodman
The Prisoner - A Complete Production Guide by Andrew Pixley
The Official Prisoner Companion - Matthew White & Jaffer Ali
Be Seeing You... Decoding The Prisoner - Chris Gregory
Cutting Edge - My Life in Film and Television - Eric Mival
'What Price Liberty? — How Freedom Was Won And Is Being Lost' Ben Wilson, Faber and Faber

On VHS/DVD/BLURAY

Danger Man Complete Series One - Carlton
Danger Man - Complete Series 2-4 - Network
The Prisoner - The Complete Series - Network
Nummer 6 -Koch Media
Patrick McGoohan est le Prisonnier-TFI VIDEO
Patrick McGoohan il Prigioniero -episodi 1-9 - CULT MEDIA/ITV GLOBAL ENTERTAINMENT
Patrick McGoohan il Prigioniero -episodi 10-17-CULT MEDIA/ITV GLOBAL ENTERTAINMENT

The Prisoner Investigated - Hosted by Peter Howell and Rachel Herbert —Steven Ricks — TR 7 PRODUCTIONS 1990

The Prisoner In Depth 1 - Complete Interviews with Katherine Kath, David Tomblin & Robert Monks - Steven Ricks - TR7 PRODUCTIONS 1991

The Prisoner In Depth 2 - Complete interviews with George Baker, Doris Martin & Jack Lowin - Steven Ricks - TR7 PRODUCTIONS

The Prisoner In Depth 3 - Complete Interviews With Derren Nesbitt, Noreen Ackland, John Connor, Len Harris - Steven Ricks - TR7 PRODUCTIONS

The Prisoner In Depth 4 - Complete Interviews With Shiela Allen, Sidney Palmer, David Arlen & David Garfield - Steven Ricks - TR7 PRODUCTIONS

The Prisoner In Depth 6 - Complete Interviews With Kenneth Griffith, Terence Feely & Earl Cameron - Steven Ricks - TR7 PRODUCTIONS

The Prisoner Inspired - Hosted by Peter Howell and James Bree - Steven Ricks - TR7 PRODUCTIONS 1992

The Prisoner In Conclusion - Hosted By Norma West with Norman Mitchell, David Arlen & James Bree - Steven Ricks - TR7 PRODUCTIONS 1994

The Prisoner On Location — Hosted by Kenneth Griffiths — Steven Ricks & Max Hora — TR7 PRODUCTIONS 1996

Fauvist Village by Warren Green
http://www.warrengreenartist.co.uk

The obligatory episode guide

'Arrival' - Number Six resigns, arrives in the Village and tries to escape.

'The Chimes of Big Ben' — Nadia arrives, says she resigned, tries to escape and then escapes with Number Six. She's a Village Agent and they don't escape.

'A, B and C' —Number Two wants to know if Number Six sold out. He and Number Fourteen use a dangerous drug, Number Six foils their plans and he was going on holiday like he said.

'Free for All' — Number Six stands for Election, the Villagers' lap it up, He's brainwashed but later tries to escape, then a bit more brainwashing, he talks like politicians do,. He wins. The maid was Number Two.

'The Schizoid Man' — 6=12 then 6=12=6 then 12=6 for a bit Then things get complicated and Alison can't wash her hair because the 3D Photocopier went wrong. 6 goes over the edge and then some more stuff happens. 12's wife is dead.

'The General' - 3 year courses in 3 minutes. Never worried about 'suspension of disbelief' Number Two keeps an eye on the Professor. Don't ask me WHY? Though

'Many Happy Returns' — The Village is Empty. So Number Six is off (taking supplies and food - although the silly bugger hardly eats anything) He finds an attractive woman lives in his house and drives his car. So he buggers off in the car after eating all her food. Ends up going back to the Village. Daft if you ask me.

'Dance of The Dead' — A Carnival, A Cat, A Radio , A Dead Body, An Old Friend, The Cabaret isn't as good as last year...

'Checkmate' — Chess with Human Beings as Pieces. Loads of stuff about chess. Escape plan based on 'Can you do this for me?' — 'O.K.' — Prisoner and so on. Escape plan fails dismally

'Hammer Into Anvil' — Number Two is sadistic *******. Causing a woman to commit suicide, Six exacts revenge — Destroys Number Two's confidence in himself to lead.

'It's Your Funeral '— 2 Number Two's. Young one uses an aide plus watchmaker to plot assignation of Old Number Two. Plan Division Q Fails Dismally.

'A Change of Mind' — Fed up with Number Six and generally fed with biscuits stashed in Number Six's kitchen Number Two's new plan 'takes the biscuit'. He gets Number Six branded Unmutual and has someone drug his tea after a supposed lobotomy, But Number Six gets Number Two posted Unmutual to keep his bikkies safe.

'Do Not Forsake Me, Oh My Darling' — Tired of cleverly written episodes this carbuncle lets Nigel Stock be 'Number Six'. I am losing hope.

'Living In Harmony' — 'The Prisoner' if it had been a Western. But here a Western is just part of The Prisoner

'The Girl Who Was Death' — A Female character tries to kill 'Number Six' in a weird story which turns up in the Village Story Book.

'Once Upon A Time': — 3 characters in one room reenact the Seven Ages of Man then Number Two Drops Dead

'Fall Out' :— "All You Need Is Love" "Dem bones...dem bones"... "Aye,aye,aye..."

👌 Be Seeing You

Made in the USA
Middletown, DE
05 August 2021